Science Fiction and the Dismal Science

Science Fiction and the Dismal Science

Essays on Economics in and of the Genre

Edited by GARY WESTFAHL,
GREGORY BENFORD, HOWARD V. HENDRIX
and JONATHAN ALEXANDER

McFarland & Company, Inc., Publishers
Jefferson, North Carolina

LIBRARY OF CONGRESS CATALOGUING-IN-PUBLICATION DATA

Names: Westfahl, Gary, editor. | Benford, Gregory, 1941– editor. |
  Hendrix, Howard V., 1959– editor. | Alexander, Jonathan, 1967– editor.
Title: Science fiction and the dismal science : essays on economics
  in and of the genre / edited by Gary Westfahl, Gregory Benford,
  Howard V. Hendrix, and Jonathan Alexander.
Description: Jefferson : McFarland & Company, Inc., Publishers, 2020. |
  Includes bibliographical references and index.
Identifiers: LCCN 2019047446 | ISBN 9781476677385 (paperback : acid free paper) ∞
  ISBN 9781476637563 (ebook)
Subjects: LCSH: Science fiction, American—History and criticism. |
  Economics in literature. | Economics and literature. | Publishers and publishing—
  United States—History. | Books and reading—United States—History. |
  Book and reading—United States—History.
Classification: LCC PS374.S35 S3323 2020 | DDC 813/.08762093553—dc23
LC record available at https://lccn.loc.gov/2019047446

BRITISH LIBRARY CATALOGUING DATA ARE AVAILABLE

ISBN (print) 978-1-4766-7738-5
ISBN (ebook) 978-1-4766-3756-3

Front cover image © 2020 Shutterstock

Printed in the United States of America

McFarland & Company, Inc., Publishers
  Box 611, Jefferson, North Carolina 28640
    www.mcfarlandpub.com

Table of Contents

Introduction

Gary Westfahl, Gregory Benford,
Howard V. Hendrix *and*
Jonathan Alexander

According to old, stereotypical views, scholars reside both physically and mentally in the isolated "Ivory Tower" of academia, oblivious to all worldly concerns as they carry on researching and writing about their arcane areas of specialization. In some respects, clearly, this is no longer the case. For today, it is increasingly difficult for qualified scholars to obtain the full-time, tenure-track positions that represent the only way they can achieve financial security; professors face intense competition as they seek financial support from their institutions, foundations, and government agencies for their research activities; and as they confront burgeoning expenses and dwindling resources, some universities are now pondering the elimination of entire departments in order to focus their limited funds on the disciplines that attract the greatest numbers of students. Economics, then, is very much on the minds of contemporary scholars, at least while contemplating their own, sometimes precarious positions within the university community.

Still, in the field of literary studies, scholars have generally remained unwilling to examine authors as they now must examine themselves: namely, as workers in a competitive marketplace, constantly obliged to address their own economic interests while pursuing their own careers. (Even some contributors to this volume, urged to emphasize the economic implications of their analyses, seemed reluctant to do so, as if that would violate some unspoken taboo.) By and large, we suspect, critics consciously or subconsciously continue to embrace another stereotypical attitude: that the writers who merit scrutiny must be solely motivated by a desire to produce the very best literature possible, so they are willing to spend years supporting themselves with menial jobs until they can finally garner the attention and respect that they deserve from the nabobs of the literary establishment. The scholars who study contemporary poets, playwrights, and other contributors to literary magazines may be justified in clinging to this time-honored belief while analyzing their works, since some of these writers may indeed still match the standard image of the aspiring literary author. But critics of science fiction have no excuse for failing to analyze the economic pressures that have shaped many of the genre's texts—because, as one of the editors of this volume observed over twenty years ago, science fiction is, almost uniquely, "a literary genre born of the marketplace."[1]

Surveying the past two centuries, one can identify several occasions when it seemed like a form of science fiction was emerging as a distinct category of literature: the Gothic novels of the early nineteenth century that strayed into science-fictional territory, most notably Mary Shelley's *Frankenstein; or, The Modern Prometheus* (1818, 1831); the "future war" stories that imitated George Tomkyns Chesney's popular *The Battle of Dorking* (1871); the late nineteenth-century American "dime novels" largely inspired by bowdlerized translations of Jules Verne; the singular stories of Robert Duncan Milne which entertained readers in old San Francisco; the many utopias written in response to Edward Bellamy's *Looking Backward: 2000–1887* (1888); and the British "scientific romances" influenced by the groundbreaking novels and stories of H.G. Wells. But none of these embryonic literary movements endured to become a permanent fixture of the publishing industry. It was only when a profit-hungry editor and publisher named Hugo Gernsback launched a magazine of "scientifiction," *Amazing Stories*, in 1926, and persuaded the world that a new sort of literature he soon rechristened "science fiction" actually existed, that there was forged a strong, genuine community of science fiction publishers, editors, writers, fans, and readers.

The authors of these science fiction stories did not seek, and could never have obtained, any support from a literary establishment that then regarded their work as worthless trash; instead, they had to write the material that was most likely to appeal to the paying markets of pulp magazines. In the 1950s, other options did become available for them—books from small presses and major publishers, young adult fiction, films and television, comic books— but most science fiction writers were still struggling to achieve a comfortable income. By the 1980s, as science fiction became a dominant force in the media landscape, a few science fiction writers were able to become millionaires, though the vast majority of writers never achieved the same level of success. Today, some talented writers have been forced to write *Star Trek* novels, *Star Wars* novels, and novelizations of video games in order to support themselves, while others piece together a tolerable income from magazine stories, small press publications, and any other assignments they can garner.

Compounding their problems is the fact that, as one science fiction writer informed us in conversation, many science fiction writers are simply not very good at making business decisions—a judgment also provided by Harlan Ellison in a fiery speech announcing his resignation from the Science Fiction Writers of America, published as "How You Stupidly Blew $15 Million a Week, Avoided Having an Adenoid-Shaped Swimming Pool in Your Back Yard, Missed the Opportunity to Have a Mutually Destructive Love Affair with Clint Eastwood and/or Raquel Welch, and Otherwise Pissed Me Off."[2] As a result, some veteran writers now find themselves in financial distress, even though they had long ago earned enough money to seemingly provide them with lifelong security. Perhaps, writers were always impractical people, as evidenced by their initial resolve to enter a profession with very uncertain rewards, so that their economic incompetence precedes their work as a science fiction writer. Perhaps, science fiction's unusual demand for constant creativity forces writers to concentrate exclusively on the fiction they are writing, instead of everyday concerns, so that economic incompetence is a result of becoming a science fiction writer.

We would like to make mention of a term from contributor Charles Platt's compilation of interviews with science fiction authors, *Dreammakers: Science Fiction and Fantasy Writers at Work* (1983), to suggest that science fiction writers may find themselves in a fundamentally paradoxical situation, engaged in the "business of dreammaking." In any event, this may help to explain one common attribute of science fiction that some essays in this volume will address: numerous works of science fiction simply ignore economic issues, and when writers do speculate about the future of the discipline, their views regularly seem naïve.

Based on these observations, one could conclude that there are two aspects of economics that science fiction scholars need to consider: what science fiction writers have had to say about economics, and how economic factors have influenced what they have written. We would add a third area of interest, harkening back to our initial comments: the ways in which science fiction scholarship is itself a business, with its work shaped by economic considerations in the same way that the texts scholars examine are shaped by economic considerations. The essays in the three sections of this volume will address, in various ways, these three concerns.

The first topic—whether and to what extent science fiction authors have addressed economic issues—was discussed in a 2003 column in the British science fiction magazine *Interzone* by one of our editors, Gary Westfahl, entitled "In Search of Dismal Science Fiction," lamenting the fact that science fiction, while dedicated to providing speculations about our scientific and social futures, only rarely offered stimulating ideas about our economic futures.[3] That column may or may not have been read by Annalee Newitz, then an aspiring science fiction writer possibly interested in *Interzone* as a potential market for her stories. Whether she read the column or not, she did write and publish in 2016 an article that might be construed as a response to the column, if only because of its title—"The Rise of Dismal Science Fiction"—though she easily could have coined the term "dismal science fiction" independently, or borrowed it from other commentators who have used the phrase during the last decade (an internet search turned up at least three of them). Her article maintains in essence that Westfahl's search has been fulfilled: after the economic recession of 2008 and 2009, she claims, writers and filmmakers began in earnest to create science fiction works that were related to the subject of economics.

Still, there are crucial limitations in her argument. As an aside, one notes that a few of her examples—like George R.R. Martin's *Game of Thrones* novels and Max Gladstone's novel *Three Parts Dead* (2012)—are actually fantasies, not science fiction, and while fantasies can certainly provide interesting commentaries on economics, the genre is hardly a good vehicle for proposing specific changes in our world's economic system, or predicting our future economic systems. More broadly, as suggested by her subtitle, "To Understand Our Economic System, We Need Speculative Stories," and by the title used in the article's web address—"How Science Fiction Helps Us Understand Our Economic System"—she is praising "dismal science fiction" primarily as an educational tool. Thus, just as Hugo Gernsback argued that science fiction in the 1920s could provide readers with a scientific education, Newitz argues that science fiction in the twenty-first century can provide readers with an economic education. (As it happens, the idea can be traced back to 1894, when Adeline Knapp published a collection of science fiction stories specifically designed to convey lessons about economics, *One Thousand Dollars a Day: Studies in Economic Education*.)

This is all well and good; but Gernsback's more powerful argument for science fiction was that it could also provide predictions of our scientific future, even helpful ideas that could inspire salutary scientific innovations—which parallels Westfahl's desire for "dismal science fiction" that proposed imaginative solutions to current economic problems. Yet Newitz does not defend "dismal science fiction" on such grounds, lamely concluding only that "Maybe by confronting our problems in metaphors and thought experiments, we equip ourselves to solve them in the real world."[4] In contrast, Westfahl's column expressed a longing for science fiction that would actually offer some specific ways to solve our problems, not merely make its readers better able to do that work themselves.

So, resuming the search for science fiction stories that might help to improve the world's economies, the editors followed one obvious vector, identifying authors who are qualified to address economic issues, and there happens to be such an individual: Richard A. Lovett, who in 1981 earned a Ph.D. in economics from the University of Michigan with a dissertation entitled "The Role of the Forest Service in Ski Resort Development: A Proposal for More Efficient National Forest Management." Perhaps, one might suppose, his stories would foreground proposals for more efficient use of other natural resources. However, as a regular contributor to the magazine *Analog: Science Fiction/Science Fact*, both his stories and his articles appear to be focused on speculative science, not speculative economics, and numerous other publications suggest that his true passion is running marathons. Even a potentially relevant article entitled "The Invisible Hand," published in a 2017 issue of *New Scientist*, turns out to be about the hypothesized Planet Nine, not Adam Smith. Thus, even authors with a background in economics may prove reluctant to draw upon that expertise in crafting science fiction.

Despite Newitz's conclusions, then, the editors remain convinced that science fiction has insufficiently addressed economic issues, or has done so in only a superficial manner. One might point to several recent counterexamples like the film *In Time* (2010), which fascinatingly hypothesizes a future world wherein the time one has to live represents the principal form of currency, or to the novels of writers like Kim Stanley Robinson (discussed below) and Cixin Liu, who consistently consider economic matters while crafting their intriguing future worlds; but such texts, we believe, remain relatively rare.

Still, the authors in our first section do examine how science fiction writers, however inadequately, have dealt with economic matters. Gregory Benford's "Economics and Science Fiction: An Introduction" both analyzes a number of texts and critiques their weaknesses in addressing economics, while Steven Postrel's "An Underutilized Resource—Economics in Science Fiction" offers the perspective of an economics professor in responding to Benford's comments and explores how economic issues have been and might be considered in science fiction stories. Joey Eschrich's "Complicating the Frankenstein Barrier: Science Fiction Futures and Social Transformation" disputes George Slusser's interpretation of Mary Shelley's *Frankenstein; or, The Modern Prometheus* (1818, 1831) to argue that its author was actually interested in her society's social and economic future, not its scientific future. Bradford Lyau's "Robert A. Heinlein Revisited: A Response to George Slusser's Calvinist Interpretation of His Works" draws upon history and philosophy to identify the true beliefs of an author sometimes associated with theologian John Calvin, including comments on the economic implications of his beliefs. David Brin's "The Emperor—and Heretic—of Point of View" employs the *Dune* novels of Frank Herbert to critique many authors' lingering fondness for the ancient political and economic system of feudalism. Finally, two essays consider the economic and social impact of the new technology of virtual reality: Jonathan Alexander's "Counterfeit Worlds: *Simulacron-3* on Film and Television" considers how virtual worlds might be exploited for commercial purposes as observed in Daniel F. Galouye's 1964 novel and its two film adaptations, while Howard V. Hendrix's "Millions Seek the Egg: Replicative Technofuturism in *Ready Player One* and *Armada*" analyzes the recent young adult science fiction of Ernest Cline from a political and economic perspective.

Our second topic, "The Business of Science Fiction," has manifestly been inadequately explored in analyses of science fiction, except for a volume of essays that two of our editors contributed to—Westfahl, George Slusser, and Eric S. Rabkin's *Science Fiction and Market Realities* (1996)—which had the expressed intent of sparking greater interest in that subject. Yet there is little evidence that the book had any impact on the community of science fiction scholars. Indeed, it is significant that out of the numerous "handbooks" and "companions" to science fiction that began appearing in 2003 (discussed in the final essay), only one of them—Rob Latham's *The Oxford Handbook of Science Fiction* (2014)—devoted a chapter to "The Marketplace," written by coeditor Westfahl. Another valuable text devoted to this topic is Mike Resnick and Barry N. Malzberg's collection of columns, *The Business of Science Fiction: Two Insiders Discuss Writing and Publishing* (2010). For the most part, however, the material one encounters in searching for titles with words like "economics," "business," or "market" tends to focus on giving advice to writers on how to earn more money—and while there is nothing wrong with that, such material also sidesteps the issue of how science fiction writers' perpetual quest for money might be affecting what they write.

To address this deficiency in the literature, this section of the volume first offers Gary K. Wolfe's "Science Fiction: The Age of Perspective," wherein the veteran scholar provides an overview of the history of twentieth-century science fiction and its different eras, sometimes referencing the shifts in the marketplace that influenced its evolution. Charles Platt's "You Can't Get There from Here: Unrealistic Expectations Among the Practitioners of Science Fiction" ponders the reason why so many science fiction writers fail to achieve the sort of lasting success that they hope for. Next come two case studies of particular science fiction marketplaces: Ari Brin's "Negotiating Fear and Optimism: Surveillance in Early Science Fiction" examines how the introduction of new technology into everyday life during the nineteenth century engendered a particular form of science fiction best observed in the pioneering stories of San Francisco author Robert Duncan Milne, while George Slusser's "The Pulp Cauldron of the 1960s: Ace Books and Ursula K. Le Guin" considers the impact of one celebrated series of twentieth-century science fiction publications, the Ace Doubles. The examination of American science fiction concludes with Westfahl's "The Homeostatic Culture Machine Revisited, or, The Contemporary Wordmills of Science Fiction," providing his assessment of the current science fiction marketplace based on a thoroughgoing examination of the science fiction books available for purchase in a bookstore in 2018. The section then shifts to Russia with two essays about the development of Russian science fiction: Slusser's "Father of the Strugatskys: The Origins of Russian Science Fantasy" documents the unique circumstances that gave rise to the tradition of science fiction represented by Arkady and Boris Strugatsky, who adapted to the peculiarities of a repressive society by devising an elliptical method to convey ambiguous messages, while Stephen W. Potts's "Looking Backward: Soviet Utopianism and Post-Soviet Dystopias" offers an updated look at how Russian authors have responded to the changing conditions of science fiction publishing after the collapse of the Soviet Union. Finally, Lisa Raphals's "Chinese Science Fiction and Its Doubles" chronicles the history of Chinese science fiction as it evolved during several tumultuous upheavals in Chinese history.

The third section, "The Business of Science Fiction Scholarship," deals with a sensitive topic that the available literature almost never addresses— the ways that the economics of working as a science fiction scholar affects their work; even worthwhile analyses of current critical trends like Tom Shippey's "Gatekeepers and the Fabril Tradition," included in the critical anthology coedited by Westfahl and George Slusser, *Science Fiction, Canonization, Marginalization, and the Academy* (2002), only tangentially explore how economic considerations have influenced science fiction scholarship. The editors freely acknowledge that the essays in this section represent only preliminary ventures into this important but significantly unexplored subject; in addition, since the authors are sometimes discussing activities that they themselves participated in, the essays in this section at times have an unusually personal tone, though this in no way diminishes their value as analyses of the issues facing contemporary scholars.

The section begins with Alvaro Zinos-Amaro's "The Slusser Test for Generic Identity: Reflections on George Slusser's 'Reflections on Style in Science Fiction,'" which explains how promising, though expensive, new technologies may radically transform the ways that scholars examine literature— including studies of the economic factors that influence particular texts. The volume's focus then shifts to the career of one noteworthy science fiction scholar, George Slusser: Julia D. Ree's "The Early Life of the Eaton Collection and Dr. George Slusser's Invaluable Contributions" conveys an insider's perspective on how Slusser found the resources to expand and improve what is now one of the world's largest collection of science fiction and fantasy literature; and Robert L. Heath's "The Odd Couple: Blending Disciplines of Science and

Humanities Through Teaching" describes Slusser and Heath's uniquely inter-disciplinary approach to the teaching of science fiction, supported by a timely grant. Slusser's career also comes up in a final essay, Westfahl's "Profiting from Prophecies: Science Fiction Scholars and Their Textbooks," which offers an historical survey of the anthologies and handbooks designed to serve as textbooks for science fiction classes and the various degrees of success that they have achieved in the academic marketplace.

Needless to say, the contents of this single volume necessarily do not provide a comprehensive overview of the many ways in which science fiction and economics interact; but we hope that the information and insights pro-vided by these authors, as well as our concluding bibliography of "Primary and Secondary Works Related to Science Fiction and Economics"—which seeks to list all relevant novels and stories, films and television programs, and secondary works involving this subject—will inspire other scholars to further examine this valuable and neglected aspect of science fiction and its critical literature.

There are individuals and institutions too numerous to name that have contributed in some way to the creation of this volume, but the editors must express their special thanks to the Office of the Campus Writing Coordinator of the University of California, Irvine, which sponsored and supported the 2018 George Slusser Conference on Science Fiction and Fantasy where most of the essays in this volume were originally presented as papers. And of course, the editors must acknowledge their enormous debt to the late George Slusser himself, whose J. Lloyd Eaton Conferences on Science Fiction and Fantasy Literature and resulting Eaton volumes long helped to shape the evo-lution of science fiction criticism and provided stimulating models for both our own conference and this volume.

NOTES

1. Gary Westfahl, "Against Agoraphobia: Confronting the Idea of Marketplaces," *Science Fiction and Market Realities*, edited by Westfahl, George Slusser, and Eric S. Rabkin (Athens: University of Georgia Press, 1996), 4.

2. Harlan Ellison, "How You Stupidly Blew $15 Million a Week, Avoided Having an Adenoid-Shaped Swimming Pool in Your Back Yard, Missed the Opportunity to Have a Mutually Destructive Love Affair with Clint Eastwood and/or Raquel Welch, and Otherwise Pissed Me Off," 1978, *Sleepless Nights in the Procrustean Bed: Essays by Harlan Ellison*, edited by Marty Clark (San Bernardino, CA: Borgo Press, 1984), 87–98.

3. Westfahl, "In Search of Dismal Science Fiction," 2003, *An Alien Abroad: Science Fiction Columns from Interzone* (Holicong, PA: Wildside Press, 2016), 220–225.

4. Annalee Newitz, "The Rise of Dismal Science Fiction: To Understand Our Economic System, We Need Speculative Stories," *Slate*, March 13, 2018 (Emagazine), at https://slate.com/technology/2018/03/how-science-fiction-helps-us-understand-our-economic-system.html.

PART ONE

The Business
in Science Fiction

Economics and Science Fiction

An Introduction

GREGORY BENFORD

Scientific and technical assumptions that violate normal science, such as faster-than-light travel, can sometimes make for very good stories. The same is true of economics, because economics after all is a science in a way—it's quantitative, empirical; there is a Nobel Prize for it. And so normal economics made me think about the assumptions behind many of the future worlds sf builds.

Physics isn't exactly thrilling to read if you're not a physicist, so we writers manage to work that stuff into drama. So the dry nature of much economic writing shouldn't be a big barrier, though one must understand it first. Friends like Vernor Vinge and Charlie Stross write about economics through the social lens they choose and they are all very aware of these things. Vernor and I are libertarian and he treats those ideas well, whereas I avoid politics in most of my work; it seems a poor investment in the long run, when it will often go out of date. Economics, maybe less so.

Sf writers are often thinking about economics as a frame for a person-centered plot, and libertarians are very often self-propelled folk, so they fit the narrative thrust. One notable example is Poul Anderson's Nicholas van Rijn stories and novels. These stories are clearly informed by Poul's libertarian economic views and the market-centric economists. The driving force behind each of the stories is that of the free trader and all that implies, demonstrated in active detail, not lectures. (A notable shortcoming of much economics-centered sf is the expository lump.)

Thomas Carlisle called economics the dismal science because it was inherently about scarcity. I recalled this because my senior Dallas public high school thesis was on his *Sartor Resartus* (1836). I found it to be a confusing, arch satire, not a set of ideas. Carlisle seemed vexed about poverty, as though it was a disease. Yet scarcity is inherent in dynamic systems. Markets move to minimize it. To minimize it means you must first understand it: economics, then act. But can avoiding poverty be the central goal of society? Science fiction should use such notions to envision futures, yet it seldom does.

Let me reprise my meandering education in such matters. One of the first sf writers I met was Mack Reynolds, whose stories such as "Compounded Interest" (1956) and "The Business as Usual" (1952) interested me in futurist economics. Visiting him in 1965 Mexico, Reynolds said to me, "The dominant economic system in the future might not be capitalism, or socialism either. My main complaint about American science fiction was that so few writers develop new economic systems to fit the future worlds they have created. Face reality, man! Long live the Class Struggle!" He advocated the Minimum Basic Allowance; first time I'd heard the idea.

So I soon saw that the genre is inherently interested in economics, but often unconsciously. (It's impolite to talk about money, you know.) Yet most people in the literary world are fearful of economics or want to just forget about a solid fact: that there are scarcities and tradeoffs happening whether you wanted to see it or not.

What's also striking about many space operas and future societies is that one seldom sees any economics. You can hardly ever figure out how anybody makes money. The extreme form is Iain Banks's anarchist future in which, essentially, it costs nothing to manufacture anything, and everybody is rich.

I link such thinking to the old *Star Trek* future without money. You have to ask yourself, "How did they carry out transactions? Or plan real costs?"

Future Economics

I've known Kim Stanley Robinson ever since he was a graduate student working for Fredric Jameson at the University of California, San Diego, so I looked particularly at Stan's and Iain Banks's ideas because they reflect a left-wing view of future economics beyond what we know. From the left wing much social pressure comes, despite the fact that various economic disasters over the last century have largely came from left-wing economics: the Soviet Union, Venezuela, North Korea, Cuba, etc.

What is to be learned from studying the future depictions of ideas already subjected to so much, shall we say, experiment? I've closely followed Stan's works and notes the narrative tics he keeps returning to, which tend to wed together in a social picture.

In many of Robinson's futuristic novels you find a long walk-about, showing off the scenery that really doesn't do much for the story. He uses in places a somewhat John Dos Passos–style novel of apparatus. (In *Aurora* [2015] there's a computer narrator. In *2312* [2012], AIs run the whole planetary solar system. In *New York 2140* [2017] there's an argument about the evil banks because currency itself is a trap.) There is in many Robinson novels at least one even-handed economic debate in which the liberal voices tend to win. (I agree with the British critic Roz Kaveney that "if there is a weakness in Robinson's work, it is perhaps this; his characters are so intelligent that they never shut up."[1] Alas a truth about many of us…)

In Stan's Mars trilogy there is talk of alternatives to capitalism, such as the gift economy and eco-economics accounting. In that background, Earth-side, our current transnational corporations become first partners of states, then overlords of states, and finally transcend states entirely into something like meta-national rivalries. But!—no World State, as such luminaries as Albert Einstein and Bertrand Russell said was essential. He shows neo-Marxist and neo-anarchist ideas but not much of the emotional side of politics and economics. His people seem afraid of markets because markets favor certain abilities, give some advantages over others. Alas, life isn't fair, but maybe government can remedy that. This tends toward some bureau or collective allocating income, not supply and demand. In this future, no Apple or Google, I expect.

In a speech last year, Stan begins by saying the only way to solve our environmental problem is to end capitalism—the personal use of assets for personal gain. He never says what comes after capitalism (nor does his audience ask, tellingly; they just cheer). But you can tell from his novels and views of economics that he believes that small worker collectives organized together can create a better economy that's more equitable. This, in the face of a simple fact: capitalism and globalization have done more to improve living standards than any other economic arrangement. But is democracy a necessary ingredient? Not in China, so far. State capitalism works, too … until it doesn't (see: USSR).

This is a struggle suffusing much social sf: Ursula K. Le Guin's *Always Coming Home* (1985), Cory Doctorow's *Walkaway* (2017), Michael Moorcock's *The Steel Tsar* (1981), Ken MacLeod's Fall Revolution series, Eric Frank Russell's "…And Then There Were None" (1951), Robert A. Heinlein's *The Moon Is a Harsh Mistress* (1966), L. Neil Smith's *The Probability Broach* (1980), J. Neil Schulman's *Alongside Night* (1979), Victor Koman's *Kings of the High Frontier* (1996), Mack Reynolds's many stories.

Some love the British writers into alternative economics, like Ian R. MacLeod and Ian McDonald in his Luna series. Americans checking in are represented by Andy Weir's *Artemis* (2017) with its corporate colony, John Varley's *Steel Beach* (1992), John Kessel's *The Moon and the Other* (2017).

There is much clashing in the economics of rapacious managers and imperialism as Heinlein saw it in *The Moon Is a Harsh Mistress*. Notably, Le Guin's *The Dispossessed* (1974) saw anarchism as leading to virtuous poverty ruled by social pressure and guilt. Indeed, Marxist socialist countries have often turned out to be poverty-stricken prisons, in reality. She said to me once she thought that virtuous societies may have to be poor ones. I said, but poverty is not a virtue. It's destabilizing without social pressure, which indeed *The Dispossessed* implies.

The phrase from Alan Greenspan, irrational exuberance, means economists must talk about emotion. But they mostly talk about equations, while the market is both—useful for writers! Can we have a mathematically decodable view of a chimpanzee-mind-driven market? The nano-plenty, robotic future is a post-scarcity world, but there's always something that's scarce. Space tourism, unique experiences, prime real estate, for example.

I think narrow economic models run afoul of experience. Asked to write a sequel to Asimov's *Foundation* trilogy I saw he had said that psychohistory was like the perfect gas law as a model. I had already pointed out to Isaac that in the gas law there is no memory in the system. That's why it works. So it couldn't be predictive! So politics and economics can't be predicted. He had not thought of that. Something like that is true of Charles Stross. He puts in fantasy elements I suspect to add confusion to computation. It's complexifying the market with fantasy elements so that it takes longer to do the computation. That's good for plot, bad for economics—so it would be weeded out in a real, non-fantasy world, if possible.

Some sf writers have invoked state capitalism, not collectivism, because it seems at times to work. China's mixed system of state-directed capitalism has produced stunning results: in just one generation, China has moved 300 million people out of poverty.

If proponents of liberal democracy don't figure out how to fix what's broken, systems like China's could become more prevalent, with severe implications for individual liberties. Still, democratic capitalism generated a 30-fold rise in earnings throughout the 20th century, an unchallenged record. Can collectivism do as well?

Historically, there are certain cases where you can get an anarchistic experiment to work for a short while, but it's very fragile if you tweak it a little bit, or challenge it. Anarchist societies during the Spanish civil war fell apart. Wherever anarchists have tried to revolutionize the land they were living on (e.g., Ukraine, Bavaria, Spain), they disarmed the ruling classes by an armed uprising of the populace. Their idea was that anarchy is power spread thin, neither a legitimate concentration in a sovereign power nor scattered to war lords or tribes.

Even the current structures in Spain, like the Mondragon Corporation experiment in a town of that name, have survived but with some management problems. They tried to have as little hierarchy as possible and founding ideas like agreed-upon wage ratios between executive work and field or factory work. They feature too the empowerment of ordinary laborers in decision-making, and a measure of equality for female workers. They started having trouble making decisions around the 100,000 member level. Those who came in early, the founders, didn't want to share the increasing profit margin with the latest who just walked in the door. How to solve this? Create a Founders Group? How is that not like the shareholders who came in with money and help at the early, lower stock value—as happens in companies. (I've seen this happen in companies I founded.) So maybe such collectives will evolve into modified companies? In Robinson's *2312*, Mondragon Corporation has evolved into a planned economy system called the Mondragon Accord, attempting to graft the present into future socioeconomics.

The fact that cooperatives have often failed historically doesn't figure much in Stan's work. There's a sidewise acknowledgment of this in *Aurora*. Aboard a starship with no captain or ship officers, everything is done by consensus in classic collectivist mode. But they slowly starve. When things go awry, they differ over goals. Half of the crew murders the other half. Nobody knows how to stop this (no Captain, no discipline method). There is no reflection on why this arose or how to fix it, much less the smart AIs controlling the craft.

AIs also run economics in Robinson's future history novels. Essentially, AIs = gods, because they sweep aside all the messy human aspects of economics. This assumption is opposite to Lenin's ignorant early theories, inherited from Marx ("Any cook should be able to run the country"[2]). But mostly, it eliminates human agency, so economics is in the end handled by artificial intelligences, AI.

Robinson has this in common with Banks, who also has sentient artificial intelligence running a galactic economy in the presumptively titled Culture. This seems to appear often in future sf to make it seem plausible that the human science of economics could be objective and not subject to great emotional surges. Nobody questions what the AIs think about taxes or distribution. Nobody much wonders how you know the AIs aren't running the world to benefit.... AIs? Stuff just appears because the AIs apparently know what will be needed before humans even know themselves. So you get these implausible AI futures that have plentitude, with all the economic magic done off stage.

In *2312* the Mondragon Accord is crucially controlled by means of a network of AIs running on quantum computers, as though this solves the knotty human aspects of economics. In Iain Banks, this means you end up fighting over the age-old things which echo medieval plots—kings and queens, tribes and passions rule. But struggles are not about economics because everybody has everything they want. This reflects ignorance of real economics because there's always some scarcity—Beatles tickets, high fashion, good ocean views, fame, etc.

Maybe that's why there's so much love of AI future economies—you build an AI with no motives or biases, to be *fair*. Can't trust those pesky humans! I said to my old friend Marvin Minsky long ago, can you build an AI that's really intelligent without its own motives *and* can you build one without an unconscious? A big issue, because much of our emotion funnels through the unconscious, which we cannot inspect rationally at all. He said, "I don't know the answer about either of those." And nobody does now, decades later. So… AIs should run economics? This is an empty dodge.

Such futures are akin to soft dreaming, ignorant of biology. We are really plain old smart chimpanzees. We have a lot of historically inherited, genetic loading for the Chimpanzee Paradigm. The common chimp has a power pyramidal system with an Alpha male at the top. The bonobo chimps mediate disputes with intense sex, while they dine in the deepest forests. We're the evolved chimps who solely got out of Africa.

In Robinson's near future New York City, there are no racial or ethnic partisanship groups endlessly feuding; it just doesn't happen, unlike today—a miracle by author's fiat. The tribal tensions that dominate New York City today, like the near-collapse of systems such as the subway, don't happen in his future ecosphere. Finance capital gets blamed instead. If you get rid of the banks, everything would be fine—which opens the old problem of how to make new ideas work, since there's apparently no organized borrowing—no market in money, which after all is just a fluid commodity.

Many sf writers don't like extreme wealth. Some ask, who is the man behind the curtain that you should ignore? Must be a conspiracy of some kind.…

And that man is the fear of economics being ruled by passions, as it always has been in alliance with such mechanisms. John Stuart Mill believed that worker-run and -owned cooperatives would eventually displace traditional capital-managed firms in the competitive market economy, due to their superior efficiency and stronger incentive structure. This proved wrong. Why?

Both Mill and Karl Marx thought that democratic worker management could be more efficient in the long run compared with hierarchical management. At times, though, Marx was not hopeful about the prospects of labor-managed and -owned firms as a means to displace traditional capitalist firms in the market economy, even though they would counter his idea of worker alienation. Marx maybe saw what the trouble is—eventually divisive groups arise and paralyze efficiency (it's not clear if he thought this through much).

So, why do people keep writing such utopias or even dystopias? Because our desires to run our lives have limits, which maybe society can correct. Labor-managed firms strive to maximize net income for all their members, while traditional capitalist firms maximize profit for owners. Labor-managed firms create an incentive to limit employment to boost the net income of the firm's existing members. An economy of labor-managed firms tends to under-utilize labor and have high rates of unemployment. That's a contending ineffi-ciency that markets have historically weeded out. Indeed, the Bolsheviks and Marx thought a full transformation of the work process could only occur after technical progress has eliminated dreary and repetitive work—which hasn't happened yet, even in the advanced Western economies. (Grading freshman essays, for example.)

This goes way back to Edward Bellamy and economist Pierre-Joseph Proudhon ("mutualism" in contrast to the "parasitism" of capitalist society) and others in the 19th century, who thought scaling up small units like farms would yield better results if run by the workers. Thinking about the future is almost always governed by the things you want, rather than the things you know.

That's my not short introduction. Now a real economist will speak.

NOTES

1. Roz Kaveney, "After the Black Death, 700 Years of New Life," review of *The Years of Rice and Salt* by Kim Stanley Robinson, *The Independent*, March 5, 2002, 5, available at https://www.independent.co.uk/arts-entertainment/books/reviews/the-years-of-rice-and-salt-by-kim-stanley-robinson-9240192.html .

2. Vladimir Lenin, cited in Kelly O'Connell, "Vladimir Lenin: Russia's Original Cold-Blooded Communist Revolutionary," *Canada Free Press*, posted January 31, 2010, at https://canadafreepress.com/article/vladimir-lenin-russias-original-cold-blooded-communist-revolutionary.

An Underutilized Resource

Economics in Science Fiction

STEVEN POSTREL

A Response to Gregory Benford

As someone who started out doing industrial organization economics—monopoly, oligopoly, antitrust policy, and all that—and then quickly migrated to teaching business strategy over in the management schools, one thing that has jumped out to me about science fiction is that there isn't usually much space or thought given to the hard problems of management.

Operational stuff, maybe, like how to turn the inputs into outputs, but almost nothing about marketing or strategy, figuring out what we should be doing and what we should stay out of, how to design and position our products given what everybody else is doing, etc. But one of the biggest problems that planned economies and cooperatives both tend to have is making good decisions about products and strategies, because the role of "corporate politics" is orders of magnitude stronger in such systems than inside actual corporations (which can be plenty political).

With respect to the moral dimensions of hostility to capitalism among many left-oriented sf writers—and it really pops out at times in Kim Stanley Robinson's work—there is a useful framework due to an anthropologist at UCLA named Alan Fiske. He and his many students and coworkers have come up with a "relational model theory" that describes the four modes with which people mentally classify any relationship: Authority Ranking (A tells B what to do), Equality Matching (A and B alternate providing like services or direction), Communal Sharing (from each according to his ability, to each according to his need), and Market Pricing (A and B agree on a common ratio scale by which they exchange dissimilar things). The last of these is the only one found in humans but not in other animals.

Different societies (and individuals within societies) have different beliefs about which sorts of things ought to be governed in which mode, and these disagreements can cause strong political conflict. For example, I've noticed lots of people who find the idea of providing medical care by anything other than communal sharing to be repugnant. Others (like me) see it more as an ordinary service like getting your car fixed that ought to be governed by market pricing. But even people like me think that interactions within our families ought to be governed by communal sharing (or maybe equality matching, depending on the subject). So we might at least be able to agree on what people are disagreeing about by adopting Fiske's framework.

Economics in Science Fiction

In most science fiction, economics is not part of the science and plays only a small role in the fiction. Firmly in the background, commerce and production follow whatever sketchy analogies with the past or present the author finds congenial: something like contemporary business life, perhaps, or a variation on feudalism. But whether the barons in question be of the corporate or lordly type, problems of scarcity and resource allocation don't intrude much on the story's characters or action.

On those occasions when the economic aspects of a science fiction scenario do take center stage, they tend to do so in terms of what economists call "comparative systems." Authors, intending pointed commentary on the real economies in which they live, spin out their utopian, dystopian, or satiric visions of how some fictional society might answer the classic economic questions: what is to be produced, how it is to be produced, who is to get what, and how will it all be decided?

I find this state of affairs a bit disappointing. Even when such visions don't violate known economic principles, the greatest thematic and story-telling resources of economics are not being used. Most of what economic science comprehends isn't about holistic matters of political economy, where historical irreversibility makes each case unique, but rather about more-generalizable, less grand-scale, patterns of resource allocation and distribution. That's why "comparative systems" is not a high-prestige subfield in economics, despite some very fine theoretical and empirical work. Since the fall of communism (and the intense interest in the "transition economies" it engendered), one would be hard pressed today to find an article on the subject in a top journal.

There are some examples of science fiction, though, where speculations about economics do play a central role, creating an economic subspecies of "hard" science fiction. In standard hard science fiction, a typical move is to imagine something (an environment or technology or phenomenon) that has not been discovered but that also does not directly contradict known empirical laws, and then to play out the implications of that thing for a story's characters, society, or ecosystem. "Hard economic" science fiction does a very similar thing.

In order to understand these sorts of sf stories, it's helpful to grasp in broad terms how economists organize their thinking. The general structure of an economic model includes three sets of "exogenous" elements (things assumed rather than explained) and a set of "endogenous" variables that get determined by the interaction of gain-seeking agents who take the exogenous elements as given. The canonical example would be the endogenous emergence of equilibrium price and quantity in a supply and demand model, taking as given the *preferences* determining demand, the *technology and input prices* determining supply, and the *institutions* of property rights and free competition that allow the equilibrium to emerge.

These three sets of exogenous elements—

1. Technology and the relative scarcities of primary (unproduced) inputs,
2. Individual preferences and social norms, and
3. Institutional rules for agent interaction

—provide the raw material for speculative fiction. Hard economic sf works by positing some interesting change in one of these areas, then tracing out its impact on human behavior. That behavior includes relative prices and quantities (what becomes scarce and what becomes abundant), organizational structures, careers, foci of innovation, etc., all traced out in accordance with standard economic principles.

The most obvious type of speculation for hard economic sf is to imagine a new technology and then to trace out its economic effects. Damon Knight's *A for Anything*, also published as *The People Maker* (1959), is a classic example. The Gismo can costlessly, instantly duplicate any inanimate object, including another Gismo. As a result, shortly after its viral release to society by its idealistic inventor (overcoming the apparently villainous forces that seek to suppress it), all material objects lose their scarcity value and most productive industry becomes superfluous. With characteristic ironic bite, Knight presents this new material Eden as a social catastrophe (validating the concerns of the "villain"): In this new world where anyone can have any inanimate object at a near-zero price, the only things that have value are animate objects, namely human slaves, and the most far-seeing and ruthless individuals quickly enslave the majority population of more-docile and fearful folk, forming the basis of a new aristocratic class. The old order collapses within the first few hours of the introduction of the Gismo; apparently Knight believed (or postulated) that people only conform to moral norms and perform their social roles in order to meet their material needs, under the expectation that others will do so as well. Once those needs and expectations vanish, it's every man for himself and all institutions disintegrate. (Neal Stephenson's *The Diamond Age* [1995] employs a related premise, where pervasive nanotechnology somehow hollows out the nation-state, with human loyalty and identification shifting to tribes and "phyles.")

Another ought-to-be touchstone story of new technology overturning the economic order is Bruce Sterling's "The Beautiful and the Sublime" (1986). Here the postulate is that a form of narrow artificial intelligence has enabled the automation of almost all work in science and technology. As a result, except for the surviving older inventors of this AI (who were able to cash in), the wages and social status of technologists have collapsed—their skills are now superfluous. In this new world of material and technical abundance, what is relatively scarce is the ability to create art and narrative and to make the world seem interesting, beautiful, and meaningful. Those with status and access to resources are thespians and artists and writers; the remaining engineers are relegated to the social margins, much as starving artists have been in our world. The mores and virtues of the artistic class (which Sterling amusingly portrays as a version of 19th-century European romanticism, replete with grand gestures and displays of emotion) are the "respectable" ones. Prudence, practicality, attention to detail, and scientific curiosity are embarrassing traits to be kept out of polite society.

Both *A for Anything* and "The Beautiful and the Sublime" start with a speculation about how technological advances might change the relative scarcities of things, and thus their relative economic value. Such changes in scarcity and relative value lie at the heart of hard economic sf. But both tales do even more, going beyond standard economic theory to show how this change in technology can in turn alter the other supposedly "exogenous" elements, namely preferences and institutions. *A for Anything* depicts complete institutional collapse when material scarcity disappears, and later describes how the class of aristocratic slaveholders evolves its own complex honor culture, full of tests of courage and physical prowess, featuring finely graded levels of status and privilege. "The Beautiful and the Sublime" lays out an inversion of cultural status norms as a result of changing the relative scarcity of "practical" and "artistic" goods.

While these specific new institutions and norms may not be accurate predictions about how things would play out, they do reflect what I believe is a general principle about economic change: *Merit tracks value with a lag.* By "merit" I mean the kinds of personal characteristics and actions that people find laudable. By "value" I mean what is scarcest relative to demand. A historical example[1] occurred after the decline of the Western Roman Empire, as bandits and brigands roamed the countryside. Anyone who was willing and able to use violence to provide physical security to the local population was highly valuable. Such individuals displayed a lesser fear of death in combat, a greater commitment to martial prowess and glory, a pugnacious determination to defend their territory, and a lack of squeamishness in enforcing discipline and inflicting punishment on friend and foe. These traits, unlovely as they may have been at the time when they first became so important, soon became central to the perceived merit of what evolved into the noble class, eventually being refined into concepts of honor and chivalry. Centuries later, when local bandits and Viking raiders were no longer a major threat but local prosperity depended on growing more food per acre, making higher-quality and lower-cost goods for trade, assembling capital, and finding good trading partners, what became scarce and hence valuable were the characteristics of the bourgeoisie—productivity, industry, frugality, honesty, ingenuity. These characteristics gradually grew in perceived merit, largely (but not completely) replacing the older esteem for aggressive bullyboys offering protection.

We can see similar, though less sweeping, changes within our own capitalist system over the decades. The economic value of creative and entrepreneurial executives waxed, waned, and then waxed again in the United States from 1870 to 2018, and we saw the picture of the meritorious businessperson track that value with a lag: the innovative Carnegies and swashbuckling Vanderbilts were gradually replaced in esteem by the loyal and responsible Organization Men, only to be superseded by the creative, disruptive technology and media operators of the late twentieth and early twenty-first centuries. Because of the value-merit lag, the newly scarce, valuable class tends to be resented at first, not only because of envy but also for their seeming lack of merit—why do these people deserve to get rich and powerful when they conspicuously lack the virtues we've come to hold dear? A new understanding of what is meritorious has to be fashioned to conform to the new realities of economic value and relative scarcity. (Economic historian Deirdre McCloskey, I should note, argues the reverse of this thesis, claiming that the economic takeoff of the modern world, initiated in northwest Europe in the late 17th century, was actually caused by new public ideas of what was meritorious—bourgeois innovation, trade, and accumulation—leading directly to leaps in productivity and market growth.[2])

Turning to the second type of hard economic sf story, one that starts from a shock to preferences rather than technology, another clear example also comes from Damon Knight: "The Big Pat Boom" (1963). Here we have enigmatic advanced alien visitors who start buying up ordinary cowpats at high prices. This injection of demand for a previously zero or negatively priced item leads to a massive shift in economic resources toward manufacturing, collecting, and merchandising them. Secondary and tertiary markets develop, a form of connoisseurship springs up classifying and valuing cowpats according to their color, texture, and curl, and people's lives become devoted to working in the industry. So we can see how a shift in preferences not only affects resource allocation but also induces change in market organization within the broader exogenous institutional structure.[3]

Knight probably had the famous Dutch tulip mania in mind when he wrote this story (interestingly, modern scholarship has greatly reduced estimates of the size of this bubble and its financial impact). His depiction of eventual ruin for many when the aliens cease their "experiment" (portrayed more as a practical joke) parallels what really happens when surges of demand enter and leave a market, particularly when resale is an important possibility.

It turns out that in markets for *assets* (objects that are not consumed but used to generate income, where the possibility of resale is important), bubbles are perfectly normal, unlike ordinary consumption goods. We know this because of economic experiments, where people are put in a lab and allowed to buy and sell things for real money. Vernon Smith, an economist now at Chapman University, won the Nobel Prize partly for showing that in experimental markets for consumption goods, supply and demand not only works as the textbooks say, it works better! Forget all that stuff about perfect competition, perfect information, large numbers of buyers and sellers, etc. Markets converge quickly to the theoretical equilibrium with just a few buyers and sellers making bids and offers, even when these experimental subjects only have very limited information—in fact convergence to equilibrium tends to get screwed up if they have too much information.

But with experiments on assets, where, say, you have a simple, tradable security that pays a certain amount to its owner each period, with a known finite number of periods so that the "fundamental" value of the asset is known to all, you see bubbles almost every time. The price goes above the value of its remaining payment stream and then crashes. Why is that? My favorite guess is that it has to do with a lack of "common knowledge," the technical term in economics for infinite repetition of an "I know that you know that I know..." sequence. With a finite number of "I know that's" about the true remaining value of the asset, traders may think that "overpaying" for the asset is sensible if someone else is going to "overpay" even more later in hopes of in turn finding a still "greater fool." And it turns out that the people who make the most money in these experiments are not the ones who only trade based on the fundamental value, but rather the ones who guess most accurately when the bubble will burst (while the worst performers are the ones who try to time it and fail).[4]

But asset bubbles are far from the only way in which economic outcomes depend on preferences. If a change in exogenous norms and preferences were drastic enough, lots of products and practices we take for granted today would disappear and other new ones arise. Suppose people started reading Epicurus (not the hedonistic caricature but the original text) and decided that he was right about how to live the good life, that is, in small communes of good friends eating simple food together, wearing simple clothes, and having great conversations. How would that affect what was relatively scarce, and how would people apply technology and management to get more of it? What would happen to the supply of skilled labor? What would happen to the people and resources previously dedicated to making luxuries and other products whose demand had collapsed? What new products and services would evolve?

Thinking about these questions while keeping them firmly embedded within a modern market economy, rather than following the lazy analogy of "simple material life = Arcadian or feudal past," is what makes for a hard economic sf approach.[5] In an American context one can well imagine that this Epicurean turn might entail a great deal of commercial and technical innovation aimed at improving the convenience, status differentiation, and authenticity of the experience. Epicurus's emphasis on avoiding discomfort and mental distress would mesh nicely with our society's health, therapy, and self-help obsessions, and the industries focused on those areas would likely see a great efflorescence, though focused more on feeling good than living longer, as the great philosopher disdained the fear of death itself. All sorts of different communal/residential setups would be attempted, with rules varying as much as do those for today's condominiums and master-planned communities, to cater to the wide range of tastes for individual privacy vs. interaction, levels and styles of "simple" physical facilities, etc. These might be branded and form chains, with self-selecting population types becoming associated with each brand, much as Internet dating services do now. Others might have boards that selected applicants, and there might be elaborate status distinctions (not necessarily jointly agreed by all groups) associated with which type or specific commune one lived in. Some might even specialize in people interested in science, or even a specific area of science, and then the whole vexed question of work-life balance, as well as the degree to which laboratories ought to be treated as proper professional workspaces rather than personal tree houses would take on new dimensions.

Positing a shock to the last of the three exogenous parts of an economic model—basic institutions and rules of economic interaction—resembles most the utopian, dystopian, and satiric tales to which I referred above. But in a hard economic sf story, the impact of such changes in the rules has to be traced through somewhat realistic implications for how resources get directed, where innovation appears, what sources of new value are stimulated, and how the distribution of that value is affected. Something like Jerry Pournelle's CoDominium Series, with its assumption that a global U.S.–Soviet alliance has prohibited technological innovation outside of its control, could have generated such a story, but the author's interests lay elsewhere.

To some extent, William Gibson and Bruce Sterling's *The Difference Engine* (1990), the alternate history that famously "invented" steampunk, pursues this course.[6] The novel sticks to the technology that existed when Charles Babbage[7] proposed his mechanical computers, and changes history by having him complete his machine. This changes the institutions that allocate resources, putting into power a faction of "Industrial Radicals" who direct R&D into pre-electronic computing and raise technologists to political power. From there, some of the economic implications are spun out in the background of the picaresque plot—the Radicals form an alliance with rising industrial labor unions, while ruthlessly crushing the resistance of non-mechanized workers, causing an even more rapid industrialization than happened historically. This advanced rate of investment at an earlier period, before electricity, leads to a great flowering of advanced steam-powered technology (along with even more enormous pollution problems). But the definitive institutional-innovation hard economic sf story is still to be written, in my (possibly ignorant) opinion.

Economic science could also be used in science fiction without forming the mainspring of the action. There are a host of clever mechanisms and ideas developed by economists, often ones not especially central to everyday research, that create intriguing thought experiments and paradoxes. Game theory, for example, tosses out all sorts of conundrums about what it means to be "rational" when interacting with other thinking people in contexts that combine cooperation, coordination, and competition, Many educated people have heard of the Prisoner's Dilemma, in my opinion one of the more overused models, but one which presents the problem of cooperation most starkly: Payoffs are arranged such that each player ought to "defect" rather than "cooperate" *regardless of what the other player does* (so defecting is what is called a "dominant strategy") but the players would both be better off if they could restrain themselves from defecting—both of them cooperating gives each one a higher payoff than they receive when both defect. The PD is a metaphor for a variety of collective action problems, such as the instability of a world where nuclear first strikes are decisive, or individuals deciding whether to pollute the commons when each one's damage is small and the private cost of not polluting is high.

Philosophers have wasted countless words trying to explain why it is somehow "rational" to cooperate here, but in a one-shot PD game it simply is not—defecting always pays better. But what if the same two players play a Prisoner's Dilemma for a known finite number of periods, say 100 times? Surely they could find a way to cooperate given the "shadow of the future," where playing nice might induce the other player to reciprocate—and in fact, in experiments, they do. But this presents a logical paradox, because in the 100th period we are back to a one-shot game, which means defecting is the dominant strategy. Then in the 99th period, both players know that both will defect next period, so they may as well defect now. Repeating the argument—what game theorists call "backward induction"—leads to the conclusion that defecting is the only "rational" strategy in every period, starting from the first. Being completely "rational" appears to lead to worse outcomes than when one eschews backward induction.

The fundamental equilibrium concept in standard game theory, though, is not the dominant strategy equilibrium found in the Prisoner's Dilemma (because it fails to be possible in most games). Instead the workhorse is the Nash equilibrium, which won John Nash a belated Nobel award in economics, as depicted in the movie *A Beautiful Mind* (2001). (Interestingly, the film completely botched the description of Nash equilibrium, even though it is a simple concept that is easy to explain. My supposition is that the concept's fundamentally selfish character wasn't congenial to the Hollywood mindset, which wanted to turn the actually quite-competitive Nash into a paragon of dreamy romanticism.) A Nash equilibrium is simply an assignment of strategies to the players where no one wants to change his strategy given what the others are doing.[8] Once you're at such a point, no one wants to unilaterally deviate from what they're doing.

Fine so far, but this simple concept doesn't always map to observed outcomes. Consider the following game played in a room with twenty or more people: Everyone chooses a number between 0 and 100, and the person whose number is closest to two-thirds of the average of all the numbers picked wins a prize. When you actually play this game you get a range of answers and the winning number tends to be around 35–45. But the only Nash equilibrium of this game is for everybody to pick zero, as can be readily seen by a reduction argument: Even if everybody else picked 100, the best response would be 66, so the Nash point has to be at or below 66. But if everyone picked 66, then the best response would be 44, and so on, until everyone has picked zero.

One explanation for actual behavior in this game, posited by Colin Camerer of Caltech, is that people are "k-rational," where k is a parameter that differs across the population and describes how many stages of the above argument a player goes through mentally. A k=0 player chooses a random number, a k=1 player chooses 66, a k=2 player chooses 44, and so on. It turns out that the best response for a "fully rational" k = infinity player depends on the distribution of k-types among the population playing the game—overestimating their k levels leads to suboptimal results. The empirical results seem to suggest that a plurality of players are at k=1, the next biggest group at k=2, then k = 3 or above, with a smattering of k = 0 types, but this research is still in its early phases.[9]

These conundrums of rationality (and many others that could be mined from game theory) seem to present great possibilities for science fiction. What happens to a world where the distribution of k shifts drastically upwards across all contexts? Would our social norms break down or mutate? Are there k-distributions that lead to better or worse outcomes? Could we design populations of interacting AIs with deliberately limited k-levels in order to engineer superior results? Can a world of Big Data enable analysts to better characterize individuals' k-levels across contexts in order to manipulate their behavior? If the end of the world is ever convincingly predicted some years ahead, at what point before that end would backward induction kick in and cooperative norms collapse when defection is one-shot dominant?[10]

Economics as a science has many such corners where fundamental questions about human capacities and how people interact could be spun into science fiction stories. Moreover, the practice of economics as a science could be as easily cast into the center of a science fiction plot as could a biology lab or a physics experiment. What if someone discovered a way to exactly predict the effect of taxes on prices and output? What if a hidden, long-term quasi-periodic attractor were discovered to exist in economic data, so that seemingly unrelated aspects of the economy were actually bound together in long-wave cycles?

There is even plenty of experimental economics nowadays, along with "field experiments" where researchers recruit subjects over the Internet or intervene in real online markets to test hypotheses and estimate the size of different effects. Maybe an imaginative writer could conceive of one of these field experiments somehow getting out of control in an interesting way.

So, perhaps optimistically, I look forward to sf writers perusing *The Journal of Economic Perspectives* much as they do *IEEE Spectrum* or *Quanta*, *Econometrica* much as they do *Physical Review*. The opportunities for the entrepreneurial writer are there. We economists tend to believe that dollar bills don't lie on the sidewalk for long.

NOTES

1. This is obviously a very simplified caricature.
2. See Deirdre N. McCloskey, *The Bourgeois Virtues: Ethics for an Age of Commerce* (Chicago: University of Chicago Press, 2010).
3. Gregory Benford says: "I talked once about that with Damon. He had heard that cowpats were a commercial commodity in India. When I went to India, I saw it in the large scale because they were used for cooking fuel or heating. There was a market and once carefully pancaked, they were plastered to a wall to dry out. When they fell off, they were marketable. So it wasn't that sciffy after all."
4. Repeating the game with the same players doesn't make the bubble go away, although it tends to pop sooner and at a lower price. But if one then makes any tweak to the experiment, say, changing the size of the dividend paid, that tends to reestablish the bubble at its original larger size.
For more information about bubbles, see Virginia Postrel, "Pop Psychology: Why Asset

Bubbles Are a Part of the Human Condition That Regulation Can't Cure," *Atlantic Monthly*, 302:5 (December 2008), 40–43, available at https://www.theatlantic.com/magazine/archive/2008/12/pop-psychology/307135/.

5. Neal Stephenson's *Anathem* (2008) tries out a post-apocalyptic scenario containing philosophy-and-math-but-no-tech simple-life communes scattered about a shabby materialist outer world that has technology but no philosophy or science, but it doesn't do much with the economic implications.

6. Though Gregory Benford informs me that Tim Powers and Jim Blaylock, as well as K.W. Jeter, wrote steampunk before the publication of Gibson and Sterling's megahit.

7. Interestingly, Babbage himself was an insightful writer on economics and industrial organization, making contributions to understanding the division of labor and how mechanization affected cost functions.

8. This is a weaker requirement than dominant strategy equilibrium; every dominant-strategy equilibrium is Nash, but most Nash equilibria are not dominant-strategy equilibria.

9. For more information about k-rationality, see Colin F Camerer, Teck-Hua Ho, and Juin-Kuan Chong, "A Cognitive Hierarchy Model of Games," *The Quarterly Journal of Economics*, 119:3 (August 2004), 861–898, and the papers presented at a session held January 5, 2018, on "Bounded Rationality, Level-k Reasoning, and Cognitive Hierarchies" at the Annual Meeting of the American Economic Association, posted at https://www.aeaweb.org/conference/2018/preliminary/2087?q=eNqrVipOLS7OzM8LqSxIVbKqhnGVrAxrawGlCArI.

10. Economic theory is full of paradoxes of self-reference, where agents' knowledge of the theory that explains the system affects their behavior and makes the theory either true or false. The proposition that the stock market is efficient in the weak sense, i.e., that the past pattern of prices cannot be used to predict future prices, is based on the notion that any such theory would be a self-negating prophecy—those seeking to exploit the pattern would destroy it if it previously existed, as they bid up the price of what the theory claimed to be undervalued. But the strong sense of market efficiency, that there is also no trading gain to be had from fundamental research into company prospects, cannot be strictly true because if taken seriously there would be no one doing such research and then research would pay—nobody doing research is not a Nash equilibrium.

Complicating
the Frankenstein Barrier

Science Fiction Futures
and Social Transformation

Joey Eschrich

"If science is now able to offer a real sense of things to come, literature must find a means of presenting them to us," writes science fiction critic and historian George Slusser in his 1992 essay "The Frankenstein Barrier."[1] For Slusser, a key role for science fiction is translating scientific discoveries and making them legible, finding ways to "integrate them into existing human systems" (47). But the essay, so stylistically assured and precisely argued, is also haunted, anxious: Slusser is concerned about whether science fiction can actually fulfill this charge of helping us wrap our collective heads around futures rendered unrecognizable by scientific and technological change. Does Mary Shelley's *Frankenstein; or, The Modern Prometheus* (1818, 1831), situated at the inception of the modern science fiction tradition, make our possible scientific future more tractable, or does it compound our foggy confusion about what's to come? What is science fiction if it falls short of this task, colliding with an insuperable imaginative obstacle, a mute lack?

Slusser approaches these challenges of futurity in terms of science and technology. But *Frankenstein*, which for Slusser suggests the possible limitations of science fiction, also opens up another path for the genre's acuity. In *Frankenstein*, I believe that Mary Shelley performs a unique feat of future imagination, but on a distinctively social, political, and economic plane. I'll begin by examining and unpacking Slusser's "Frankenstein Barrier," then describe how Shelley's *Frankenstein* charts a different course for how science fiction relates to possible futures. I'll conclude by considering how the

29

Frankenstein Barrier, and Shelley's evasion of its strictures, might help us think more precisely about contemporary science fiction literature and its goals for proposing, envisioning, and realizing human futures.

"The Frankenstein Barrier" is demanding, ranging from René Descartes and Sigmund Freud to the novel and film *A Clockwork Orange* (1962, 1971) and the philosopher J.D. Bernal, to Carl Sagan and William Gibson and Bruce Sterling, who appears as a kind of cool, laconic, mirror-shaded, jargon-spouting Greek chorus throughout the piece. The jumping-off point is Slusser's observation that in *Frankenstein*, Victor Frankenstein "makes, for the first time in a literary work, a true thing of future possibility" (48), drawing on the actual modern science of the day. This thing of future possibility is what Victor himself calls "a new species," built from human parts but transcending human limitations. Indeed, the creature is an incredibly fast learner, physically powerful, fleet of foot, resistant to the ravages of cold and hunger and wind.

But this excitement doesn't last long. When Victor beholds the thing he has created, as it groans and stirs, he recoils in horror and flees. Later, when the creature confronts Victor and demands that he create him a mate, Victor initially agrees, but changes his mind at the last minute and tears the in-process female creature to bits. At the end of the novel, Victor and the creature are in the frozen Arctic wastes, chasing each other around on foot and on sledges. All is white and blank—and crucially for Slusser, as we'll see later, all is physical. Victor has transmuted his new species from luminescent idea to fleshy reality, and now it's killed nearly everyone he loves, and it's playing deadly hide-and-seek with him in one of the most bleak, punishing environments imaginable.

For Slusser, Shelley's novel, a foundation of the genre, displays a tendency in two movements that will be repeated time and again for 200 years. The first movement: glimpsing a radically imaginative future that is thrilling and invigorating and truly different than our present: a disjuncture, a break with history. The second movement: Hitting a barrier and seeing that moment of discovery and profound change slide back into what he calls "the white wastes of some blank and mute present" (48–49). This, writes Slusser, is the specter of "a rational future forever held back by an atavistic present" (54).

Sf sets up thrilling future vistas, but they always end up bottoming out in the same old oppositions and problems and limitations. As much as we try to push our narrative premises into the future, their resolutions always run into this Frankenstein Barrier, which makes its presence known in images like the bleak whiteness of Mary Shelley's Arctic or the "white room at the end of humankind's quest for the infinite" (64) in Stanley Kubrick's *2001: A Space Odyssey* (1968), and a host of others that emphasize deathlike stasis or impenetrable irrationality.

And this is where Descartes and Bernal come in: For Slusser, our inability to imagine a transcendent technological future is rooted in a Cartesian duality where pure, rational mind is held back by the flesh. The future is cognitive, and thus limitless. The present is physical, heavy, natural, organic, the body that hungers and thirsts and rages and groans and oozes.

The obduracy of material things, their dull "thingness" and implacability, holds back our movement beyond the confines of the human form and the physical world's limitations and finite resources. Slusser expands on this through a discussion of Carl Sagan's 1977 book *The Dragons of Eden*,[2] where the author posits that the evolution of human intelligence is structured so that our higher rational faculties, which evolved later, are always warring with our monstrous instinctual impulses.

Slusser finds Sagan's conclusions frightening, and more so because they echo the gloomy, late-in-life ideas of another prodigious thinker from a very different background, Sigmund Freud. Sagan's and Freud's writings suggest that the Frankenstein Barrier is innate, part of our evolutionary legacy, an inescapable "impediment to the rational creation of a genuine future" (59)—a future that doesn't just recapitulate the challenges and limitations of the present.

The stakes are high for Slusser here: He begins his essay by pondering the relationship between visions of the future in science fiction and actual possible achievable futures. The key question here is, "How compatible are traditional descriptive processes of fiction with this desire to create new, hence future, things?" (46) That is, can our science fictional explorations actually be a meaningful part of the project to shape futures? Does telling sf stories have any relevance or force with respect to reality? Or are we just in the entertainment business, or perhaps the business of reflecting the present back to itself in imaginative terms?

It's noteworthy that Slusser doesn't lay his cards on the table as to what kind of future he wants. He refers to morality and law as forces in the present that impede change, which implies perhaps a radically different way of managing social relations and resources and property, or a redefinition—perhaps a technological one—of what it means to be human.

Slusser ends the essay by riffing on the same theme, asking "whether sf's vaunted 'sense of wonder,' that which caused Victor Frankenstein to want to create new things in the first place" (71), is hopelessly blocked by this barrier. So it's a big question, and like Slusser's introduction, it ties together sf with the actual practice of science and technology. Can we conquer our primal impulses and stop being irrational? Can we imagine things truly different than they are? Are our grandest sf dreams merely our current sociopolitical and sociotechnical dramas dressed up in fanciful costumes?

*   *   *

Reading "The Frankenstein Barrier" helped clarify for me what I like so much about *Frankenstein*: that it doesn't actually spend very much time with Victor as an inventor. The parts of the novel about fabricating the creature and working on its mate are brief. Near the end of the novel, when another character asks Victor for details about the process of animating the creature, Victor erupts into cautionary, fourth-wall breaking hysterics, saying:

> Are you mad, my friend? [...] or whither does your senseless curiosity lead you?
> Would you also create for yourself and the world a demoniacal enemy? [...] Peace,
> peace! learn my miseries, and do not seek to increase your own.[3]

Indeed, the lion's share of the novel is spent in humanistic and relational pursuits: letters exchanged among loved ones; a kind magistrate tending to a shipwrecked traveler; wedding planning; a crisis of faith; the creature eavesdropping on a loving family in the woods, and learning to read from John Milton and Plutarch and Johann Goethe; torturous ethical self-examinations from Victor; endless procrastination in the face of duty, also by Victor; philosophical debates between the creature and its creator; and Victor and his friend Henry Clerval bushwhacking around Europe.

Slusser produces a sharp critical reading of the largest and most culturally resonant arc in the novel: that is, a scientific saga of staggering ambition, followed by unholy creation, followed by a murderous campaign for vengeance, followed by oblivion on the Arctic ice. So what I want to do here, to complement his argument, is to provide a few examples of how well Mary Shelley uses *Frankenstein* to provide glimpses of a social, political, and economic future that is markedly different than her present. On this front, she doesn't encounter a barrier; her sense of what the future could and should be is clear.

Shelley skillfully interpolates women's voices in what at a glance seems to be an entirely male-dominated novel. Captain Walton, the nautical explorer who provides the beginning-and-end frame narrative for the novel, is turned away from certain disaster through his written correspondence with his sister Margaret. Walton, who is on a scientific voyage in search of the North Pole, nearly puts his entire crew in harm's way in the face of inclement weather, risking their lives and almost igniting a mutiny. We only read Walton's side of the interchange, but it's apparent from his responses that Margaret helps talk him down, stressing the importance of human life over glory and celebrity and giving him something tangible to come home to. Elizabeth, Victor's doomed lover and wife, performs a similar role but onscreen, making an argument in her letter in Volume I, Chapter V for a work life connected to happiness, the restorative energies of the natural world, and positive interactions with other people, instead of the furtive, solitary, and ultimately disastrous road he walks. We might think of this as a cultural-feminist critique of the nascent scientific enterprise, or of the male world of commerce and governance more broadly. Implicitly, through little glints and glances, Shelley is showing us a more ethical world driven by collaboration and comity between men and women.

Another woman communicates Shelley's unease with the justice system and with organized religion. Justine Moritz, a loyal servant of the Frankenstein family, is framed by the creature for the murder of Victor's young brother William. Justine is wracked by misplaced Catholic guilt and dismayed by the suspicion of her employers and protectors, and she falsely confesses and is put to death. Victor stands by miserably, unwilling to intercede; he is terrified that everyone will think he's insane—which is too big of a blow for his ego to sustain.

But before all of this tragedy, Justine is someone in a subordinate position who is treated kindly and humanely by her employers. We might think of her as a symbol for an imagined rapprochement between social classes put into open antagonism by the economic upheavals and escalating greed of the Industrial Revolution. Indeed, Shelley, in Elizabeth's letter to Victor, writes of Justine:

> The republican institutions of our country have produced simpler and happier manners than those which prevail in the great monarchies that surround it. Hence there is less distinction between the several classes of its inhabitants; and the lower orders being neither so poor nor so despised, their manners are more refined and moral. [...] Justine, thus received in our family, learned the duties of a servant; a condition which, in our fortunate country, does not include the idea of ignorance, and a sacrifice of the dignity of a human being [48–49].

In a more general sense, *Frankenstein*'s epistolary structure and its continual shuttling between viewpoints shatter the novel's traditional reification of the unified individual self, that unassailably rational and closed Enlightenment subject. The literary scholar Mary A. Favret writes of *Frankenstein*:

> This novel works to show the limits of that individuality and to replace the individual voice with a network of voices. The principle of life is not individual, nor does it proceed in a straight line. Rather, life becomes, in the novelist's hands, a production of multiple correspondences, always overlapping, revealing connections [....] In spite of its title, *Frankenstein* refuses to be solely Victor Frankenstein's story. The novel has a new task, which requires combination and confusion of identity. Like Frankenstein's monster, the novel is a representation of human life which exceeds the dimensions of any one individual.[4]

Thus, in its literary structure, *Frankenstein* insists on the importance of communities and relationships to social harmony, ethics, and psychological well-being. When a man goes it alone in the novel, things break bad. Shelley insists on a society defined by collectivity rather than unrestrained individual ambition.

These ideas reflect the thinking of Shelley's parents, the philosophers Mary Wollstonecraft and William Godwin. Both were social constructionists with a strong belief in the power of relationships, social norms, and institutions to determine people's character and behavior. In her *A Vindication of the Rights of Woman* (1792) and other writings, Wollstonecraft argued for the importance of education, especially for women, and for the importance of the family. These institutions, the school and the family, shaped people into rational adults and good citizens able to take care of themselves, comport themselves with virtue, and contribute to the overall well-being of society. Wollstonecraft argued that women, who at the time could not legally own property or vote,[5] functioned as "convenient slaves," "immured in their families, groping in the dark."[6] In order to achieve self-determination and exert a positive influence on society, women therefore needed access to the same educational opportunities afforded to men. Wollstonecraft's radical perspectives on women's marginalization and proper social roles paralleled her opposition to slavery, an overwhelmingly lucrative economic engine in late eighteenth-century Europe, which she termed an "abominable mischief."[7] In *Frankenstein*, the figure of the benighted creature stands in for the masses of dispossessed and oppressed people of all stripes: reviled for his unusual looks and unfortunate biology, barred from social interchange, unable to achieve self-actualization and contribute to the common good.

William Godwin, in his most influential book, *Enquiry Concerning Political Justice and Its Influence on Morals and Happiness* (1793), writes: "If justice have any meaning, it is just that I should contribute everything in my power to the benefit of the whole."[8] Victor abandons mundane, applied scientific work at his university (such as improving instruments for chemistry) to undertake his Promethean project, without any specific positive social benefits in mind—just a vague, hand-wavy sense that he might conquer death and an explicit desire that a new race would revere him as its creator. The women in the novel contravene this tendency, pointing to a social order in which mutual enrichment would guide our actions, not selfish ambition. Godwin's principle of equality holds that all people have the capacity for reason, if it's nurtured, regardless of social status. His radical opposition to "accumulated property"[9] beyond one's basic needs reflects his idea that both extreme wealth and poverty impair people's ability to act justly and think beyond self-interest about the good of the community. People's capacities for intellectual achievement and virtue are determined by circumstance, not fixed by birth; a more equitable disposition of property would lead to a flowering of prosocial behavior and "sentiments of generosity and public good."[10] Building on these ideas, Mary charts the creature's intellectual development and innately kind and virtuous nature being vitiated by physical hardship and continuous mistreatment. Meanwhile, Justine reflects Mary Shelley's progressive, though paternalistic and decidedly *not* radical idea that relations between classes need not be exploitative, that people of humble birth could be educated and treated with dignity even while they occupy less prestigious social roles.

* * *

Approaching science fiction via Slusser's idea of an imaginative barrier—and Shelley's skirting of the logic of the barrier and emphasis on the social, political, and economic aspects of our shared future—provides an opportunity to reexamine our habitual ways of thinking about the future. Slusser's essay, and a close look at *Frankenstein* in its light, suggests some realignments of how we view a constellation of issues: science fiction writers' varying strategies and goals towards the future, the relationship between emerging technology and meaningful social change, and the interplay between our present and the possible futures we imagine.

First, perhaps we should be thinking about sf writers, or at least certain sf writers, explicitly as social thinkers and critics as much as storytellers. With the Frankenstein Barrier, Slusser enlists authors into Victor Frankenstein's Promethean struggle, grappling with seemingly insurmountable imaginative obstacles to conjure up radical technological futures for us. But some writers today, from Kim Stanley Robinson and Madeline Ashby to Paolo Bacigalupi and many more, already present themselves almost primarily as social thinkers, and their fiction as potent commentary, in dialogue with nonfiction and political discourse as much as other future fiction. Mary Shelley may not have been able to surmount Slusser's barrier in terms of imagining a posthumanist, biopunk future. But she did marshal her talent and resources to imagine a near-future social order that values women's voices, mitigates abuses based on social class, and centers community and conversation over trailblazing, perilous ambition. So, perhaps social acuity is a marker of sf achievement, not just heroic feats of technological imagination.

Second, Slusser's barrier assumes that there is something on the other side: namely, a technology that will get us out of our familiar problems caused by class strife, racism, misogyny, short-term over long-term thinking, environmental degradation, and the like. But, as the perspicacious cybersecurity expert and designer Eleanor Saitta writes, "All technical problems of sufficient scope or impact are actually political problems first."[11] As we've started to see with artificial intelligence, who controls the data and who decides which information is included in the training sets is immensely important in terms of social outcomes. And as we've seen with climate change, we can have all of the technological solutions lined up nicely and neatly. That doesn't mean that entrenched interests are going to invest in a transition or acquiesce to change. Slusser leaves the kind of futurity, the kind of change he's hoping for undefined, but it's pretty clear it's about scientific discovery and technological ingenuity. But even after that leap, we'll still be grappling with class antagonism, rising and acidifying oceans, and we'll still need to be thinking in terms of a transformation of philosophical consciousness and social relations.

Finally, on a related note, the barrier argument focuses on disjuncture: change that is radically transformative. The cyberpunk grounding of the piece means that many of Slusser's examples are about transcending human limitations, extending the body, building a bridge between biology and the sublime world of information. That's all very millennial and seismic in terms of changing the basic conditions of human existence. But the kind of social change that Mary Shelley is interested in is built upon a long history of relationships, values, and inequalities—so there is continuity between the past, the present, and the future. *Frankenstein* reminds us that if we don't grapple with our social foibles now and in the near future, we'll remain haunted by them no matter what fantastical technologies we create on the other side of the barrier.

I suspect that the Frankenstein Barrier might be an appealing challenge for a certain kind of sf mind: someone who wants to blow us away with something unforeseen—to implant a wholly new idea into the heads of inventors and bring a technological problem from beyond the horizon into our field of vision. But maybe there are multiple sets of goalposts, and not all of our best science fictional minds are toiling in the shadow of the barrier. And ironically, I think Mary Shelley was just fine not being able to see over that imaginary wall, because she was preoccupied with the injustices and inadequacies and abuses that she saw in her day-to-day life. If she wanted to think incisively about the detailed future of science and technology, she would have baked more of that into the book, instead of deliberately avoiding it, and telling us that she was doing so.

So maybe there's more than one kind of project for fiction that looks into the future. And maybe we're limiting ourselves if we fall back unthinkingly onto the assumption that all authors are pursuing the "sense of wonder" that Slusser closes his essay with. Perched at the yawning front gate of a new genre two centuries ago, *Frankenstein* might help us more accurately map 200 years of creativity, and let us see better what our friends and colleagues are up to now.

Notes

1. George Slusser, "The Frankenstein Barrier," *Fiction Two Thousand: Cyberpunk and the Future of Narrative*, edited by Slusser and Tom Shippey (Athens: University of Georgia Press, 1992), 46. Page references are to this edition.

2. Carl Sagan, *The Dragons of Eden: Speculations on the Evolution of Human Intelligence*, 1977 (New York: Ballantine Books, 1992).

3. Mary Shelley, *Frankenstein: Annotated for Scientists, Engineers, and Creators of All*

Kinds, edited by David H. Guston, Ed Finn, and Jason Scott Robert (Cambridge: MIT Press, 2017), 174. Page references are to this edition.

4. Mary A. Favret, "The Letters of *Frankenstein,*" 1987, in *Romantic Correspondence: Women, Politics and the Fiction of Letters* (Cambridge: Cambridge University Press, 1993), 178.

5. For more on women's roles and limitations during Mary Shelley's life, see literary historian Charlotte Gordon's talk as part of the "Spawn of Frankenstein" event hosted by Future Tense, Washington, D.C., February 2017, at www.newamerica.org/future-tense/events/spawn-frankenstein.

6. Mary Wollstonecraft, "A Vindication of the Rights of Men," 1790, *A Vindication of the Rights of Men and a Vindication of the Rights of Woman,* edited by Sylvana Tomaselli (Cambridge: Cambridge University Press, 1995), 53.

7. Wollstonecraft, "A Vindication of the Rights of Woman," 1792, *A Vindication of the Rights of Men and a Vindication of the Rights of Woman,* 69.

8. William Godwin, "Book II: Principles of Society, Chapter II: Of Justice," 1793, *Enquiry Concerning Political Justice and its Influence on Morals and Happiness, Frankenstein: The Pennsylvania Electronic Edition,* edited by Stuart Curran, The University of Pennsylvania, 1997, at knarf.english.upenn.edu/Godwin/pj22.html.

9. Godwin, "Book VIII: Of Property, Chapter I: Genuine System of Property Delineated," *Enquiry Concerning Political Justice and its Influence on Morals and Happiness, Frankenstein: The Pennsylvania Electronic Edition,* at knarf.english.upenn.edu/Godwin/pj81.html.

10. Godwin, "Book VIII: Of Property, Chapter II: Benefits Arising from the Genuine System of Property," *Enquiry Concerning Political Justice and its Influence on Morals and Happiness, Frankenstein: The Pennsylvania Electronic Edition,* at knarf.english.upenn.edu/Godwin/pj82.html.

11. Eleanor Saitta (aka Dymaxion), "Repeat after me: all technical problems of sufficient scope or impact are actually political problems first," May 8, 2014, 10:59 p.m. Tweet, at twitter.com/Dymaxion/status/464645883100139521.

Robert A. Heinlein Revisited

A Response to George Slusser's Calvinist Interpretation of His Works

BRADFORD LYAU

Robert A. Heinlein is the most influential American writer in twentieth-century science fiction. This observation should be unquestioned. His ideas, on the other hand, raise polarizing reactions—one either loves them or hates them. As expected, the resulting analyses, academic or otherwise, of his works tend to be equally controversial.

An example would be George Slusser's *Robert A. Heinlein: Stranger in His Own Land* (1976, 1977), in which he argues how Heinlein, in spite of his advocacy of a rational world view based on science and expressed through advancing technology and a classical liberal philosophy, actually reveals in his fiction a Calvinist view of the world. Slusser concedes that Heinlein may not even be aware of this tendency, but Slusser claims nevertheless that a close reading of Heinlein's works shows patterns of Calvinist thinking and characteristics that are integral parts of America's collective national myth. What Heinlein describes as the use of serendipity in his stories Slusser identifies as Heinlein's resorting to the Calvinist central precepts of predestination and grace.[1]

My contention, back when I read Slusser's book when it came out and still now, is that Slusser misses the mark. Although Heinlein treats themes with which Calvinism became associated as it integrated into American thought and culture, similarity does not equal identity. Toward the end of this essay, I will suggest the parts of Calvinism where Slusser's analysis could apply to Heinlein and will respond accordingly.

I will address this issue by placing Heinlein in the mainstream of American thought, based on categories of thought from the eighteenth-century Enlightenment and filtered through major themes which are associated with Calvinism, developed through the nineteenth century, and are relevant to both Heinlein and Slusser's analysis of him. This analysis falls into two parts: (1) Heinlein's place in the intellectual tradition emerging from the eighteenth-century Enlightenment, and (2) Heinlein's treatment of themes associated with Calvinist thought as they developed through the nineteenth century and Heinlein's lifetime. In my concluding remarks I will attempt to tie these two parts together and from my conclusions of my critique of Slusser's assertions of Calvinism in Heinlein's thought.

The text I use as the basis of introducing the categories of thought in the eighteenth-century Enlightenment is Jonathan I. Israel's recent interpretation of this era. Before the appearance of Israel's magisterial three-volume work,[2] the Enlightenment was usually analyzed in two ways: (1) by country and (2) by theme—particularly the impact of new philosophical approaches and the Scientific Revolution on other disciplines. Most readers—having studied primarily the French, Scottish, and American versions, and then being made aware of the Dutch, German, Italian, *et. al*—are probably familiar with the first category. In the second category, students are often introduced to the *philosophes'* attempts to search for laws or guidelines in politics, societies, economics, philosophy, religion, etc., that possessed the same level of certainty as the discovered laws in the natural sciences. Later, as Enlightenment studies have developed, the scope of study has expanded to include sociological and bibliographic analyses as well as the more contemporary concerns of feminism, non–Western perspectives, and post-colonial viewpoints.

What Israel contributes to this subject, basically, is an overall reexamination of the Enlightenment that results in his dividing its participants into two competing camps: the Moderates and the Radicals. Using most of the substance and methods of earlier studies while adamantly maintaining the supremacy of intellectual history, he traces in meticulous detail how, despite the national and social particularities of the Enlightenment participants, one could break down the intellectual discourse into these two groups. To begin with, Israel defines the Enlightenment as

> a partly unitary phenomenon operative on both sides of the Atlantic, and eventually everywhere, consciously committed to the notion of bettering humanity in this world through a fundamental, revolutionary transformation discarding the ideas, habits, and tradition of the past either wholly or partially.

From this definition he describes this all-important epoch as best characterized as the quest for human amelioration occurring between 1680 and 1800, driven principally by "philosophy," that is what we would term philosophy, science, and political and social science including the new science of economics lumped together, leading to revolutions in ideas and attitudes first, and actual practical revolutions second, or else the other way around, both sets of revolutions seeking universal recipes for all mankind and, ultimately, in its radical manifestation, laying the foundations of modern basic human rights and freedoms and representative democracy.[3]

How to achieve this goal of human amelioration becomes the dividing line, according to Israel, between the Moderates and Radicals.

Israel's Moderates include the names of those individuals popularly recognized as the most influential of the Enlightenment thinkers: Newton, Locke, Leibniz, Voltaire, Hume, and Smith. These thinkers contended that new ideas could be accommodated to existing philosophies and theologies and even applied in a reform-minded spirit to existing political institutions, which were mostly monarchical, aristocratic, and anti-democratic at the time. Most of the Moderates warned that sudden and total change was not advisable and that measured reform would be the way to go. Among these thinkers, some viewed history as having demonstrated that the existing hierarchical structures were part of the natural course of events and that certain people belong on top while others ought to be ruled at the bottom—and that reform only by society's superiors (in ability and not necessarily by birth) would be the best way to improve civilization. If equality and fairness are to be attained, they must be initiated by an elite level of society.

In contrast, Israel describes the Radicals as the purveyors of what a present-day person might label as a purer version of the Enlightenment, including the abolishment of religious authority from political and social spheres; the use of reason—rational thought—alone as the basis for knowledge and policy; the absolute equality of all people regardless of race, gender, and class; absolute freedom of speech and action both in private and public spheres; and—most important—universal representative democracy. Partisans of this camp called for "no compromise" in attaining these goals. The goals were both clear and immediate, and policy must follow accordingly. The significant figures in the Radical camp of the Enlightenment are probably less known to the general public, but their achievements remain no less significant. Israel's list begins with one person, Spinoza, whose role Israel identifies as central to this wing of the Enlightenment. Baruch Spinoza's core concept—of God and nature being no more than two names for the one substance that comprises existence—became the basis for the concepts of reason, equality, and freedom. Major figures who elaborated upon Spinoza's ideas include Bayle, Vico, Toland, Holbach, and d'Alembert.

Overall, Israel views the Moderates as having been the dominant wing of this ideological rivalry. But he concludes that it is now time for the contemporary world to adopt the ideas and principles of the Radical Enlightenment.

Before proceeding further, we should note that, as Israel examines in almost 3000 pages the differences and competition between these two camps, he repeatedly reminds the reader of two points: (1) Both of these groups were revolutionary in theory and impact, and (2) the biggest threat against them remained the forces of the Counter Enlightenment, the protectors and arbiters of the old paradigm of thinking.

In an earlier paper[4] I concluded that Heinlein in his post–Navy career started out in the radical camp, with his involvement with Sinclair Lewis's California gubernatorial campaign in 1934, but ended in the moderate camp, becoming more politically conservative as he grew older and placing the responsibility of a successful future on the shoulders of fewer and fewer people. On the surface this reliance on the dwindling number of people destined to direct humanity's future may suggest a Calvinist leaning, but the remainder of this essay will prove otherwise.

Calvinism continued throughout American history as well. Its basic characteristics, in addition to the most commonly known one of predestination, include: (1) the inherent sinfulness and weakness of individuals, (2) the encouragement of industrious altruism—and not economic individualism, (3) prosperity and success as not necessarily signs of salvation, and (4) democracy which elects an aristocracy (based on ability and piety, not birth) of magistrates as the preferred form of government. Through this last characteristic, Calvinism found its political expression in the desired autonomy of churches, which fit well with the American brand of republicanism.[5]

American Calvinism was going through a significant transformation by the time of Heinlein's youth (he was born in 1907). From the years 1870 to1920 American society was going through a process of increased secularization. Although most Calvinists supported the separation of church and state, they were not in favor of the secularization of society. The competing religious movements (Social Gospel; subjectivity in an individual's approach to faith; and an emphasis on the love of God over concerns about transcendence, scriptural literalness, and which laws must be followed strictly) of this period also called for the separation of church and state, but these competing movements were for secularization—partly influenced by their championing of the First Amendment. This period witnessed Calvinism on the losing side of this disagreement.[6]

For the most part America remained secular during Heinlein's adult life but basic features of Calvinism persisted in various parts of American culture and society. In particular, three Calvinist themes persisted in the broader culture: (1) the notion of human depravity and the subsequent need for redemption, (2) independence from materialist thought, and (3) alienation and anxiety. This last point can be seen in twentieth-century American literature, which provides many examples of alienation from God, nature, or society. Even some political leftist ideologies offer an austere, "Calvinist" approach to social reform or redemption.[7]

The Enlightenment and Calvinism form two major pillars of American thought and culture. While Heinlein views himself as belonging to the former, Slusser claims he really falls into the latter—regardless of Heinlein's own claims or probable lack of awareness of his Calvinist leanings.

Three major themes in American history that are usually associated with Calvinism, whether accurately or not—Manifest Destiny, patriotism, and Social Darwinism—are important to our analysis of Heinlein's stands and Slusser's Calvinist claims. The concept of Manifest Destiny is often associated with the Calvinistic notion of predestination, but it should not be. Besides Calvinism's tenet of the inherent sinfulness and depravity of human nature, this belief system also warns against the notion that outward signs of success constitute "proof" that a person is saved, much less that a nation is "destined" for greatness. Be that as it may, the association persists. The more traditional reasons of national chauvinism, racism, economic and political greed and corruption, and xenophobia can explain with much more certainty the roots of Manifest Destiny. In fact, most historians argue that Manifest Destiny may have been a useful fiction to justify certain actions and that the continent-wide expansion of the United States was in no way guaranteed or inevitable.[8]

Heinlein always expressed his pride in America's accomplishments, but he never stated that his country's successful standing in the world was inevitable or that its future was guaranteed. In his Guest of Honor Speech at the 1976 World Science Fiction convention in Kansas City, he noted that America—celebrating the 200th anniversary of its Declaration of Independence—had been at war for 199 of its 200 years, and then declared that there would be more to come in the future, even with the use of nuclear weapons because, according to Heinlein, war is the natural state of humanity. He also mentioned that the future in space would not necessarily be an American one.[9] This state of affairs was how America came to be, not some destiny or preordained direction of history. In some respects, Heinlein's words sounded less like John Calvin's and more like Thomas Hobbes's observation that human life is nasty, brutish, and short.

This attitude about America's future in space is not a singular occurrence. In front of his largest audience, his interview with Walter Cronkite—along with Arthur C. Clarke—on CBS during the Apollo 11 Moon landing, Heinlein stated that all of humanity would be traveling into space. He made a point of stating that all races and nationalities will be taking part in this great expansion. America is a part of this development, but it is not destined to be the only one or necessarily the leading one.[10]

The role of assimilation plays a role in the concept of Manifest Destiny. Joining a society that was primarily Anglo-Saxon in its culture was considered a prerequisite for all those wishing to become part of America's special mission of civilizing the "lesser peoples," whether immigrant or native.[11] An argument can be made that Heinlein's ideas may be understood under this part of the "destiny" concept. In his novel, *Space Cadet* (1948), Heinlein writes of the adventures of a young man going through the Space Academy (probably based on Heinlein's experience as a midshipman at Annapolis). A point is made of the diversity of the entering cadets and their eventual assimilation into the culture of the Space Patrol, which protects the Solar System's Federation.[12] One could argue here that this scenario is a replay of nineteenth-century American expansion and the immigrant experience. However, in the protagonist's encounter with native Venusians later in the novel, the assumption of human superiority due to humanity's perceived unmatched triumphs in technological achievements is tossed out the window. From this part of the novel a reader might assume that this story is also a critique of America's nineteenth-century westward expansion.

Perhaps a more convincing evidence of assimilation is Heinlein's speculation at the end of his collection of fiction and non-fiction, *Expanded Universe: The New Worlds of Robert A. Heinlein*, in the essay entitled, "The Happy Days Ahead."[13] The first part of this essay details his criticisms of what is wrong in America and how the country can fall into a permanent decline without the help of any external forces. The second part describes how to solve the country's problems. In Heinlein's scenario an African American woman Vice President becomes President after the President's unexpected death. She states categorically during the early days of her administration that no special attention will be given to any particular group based on ethnicity or gender because all are Americans and as such are equal, and all citizens of the country must work together and solve the nation's problems. Heinlein never really describes how to resolve issues of privilege based in ethnicity or gender. Instead, he appears to "solve" the problems by simply urging a change of attitude.

In one of his later novels, *Friday* (1981), Heinlein does offer a portrait of an America where this type of assimilation fails to sustain itself beyond his present. What was the United States of America has become a polyglot of smaller nations, each apparently possessing a particular political structure and culture.[14] Examples would be the "Chicago Imperium" (141) and California being the only place one will "find the clear-quill, raw-gum, two-hundred-proof, undiluted democracy" (145). The latter Heinlein describes in satirical manner, with the protagonist refusing to pass judgment on this government except to say that she did observe that "Democracy is probably all right used in sparing amounts" (145). Of course, this is the viewpoint of one of his fictional characters and should not be taken as Heinlein's own—as he has warned his readers constantly in his nonfiction. However, this presentation does illustrate his pessimistic view of the United States ceasing to be united.

But what does bring Americans of diverse background together? Heinlein's Guest of Honor speech at the World Science Fiction Convention of 1941 in Denver gives more than a hint. For him, what draws us together is the scientific method. Influenced in large part by the ideas of general semantics espoused by Alfred Korzybski (1879–1950), Heinlein introduces the concept of time-binding and the nature of facts, and how the scientific method can be applied to these facts. Even the subject of anti–Semitism is treated under these ideas.[15] So even if Heinlein's view of assimilation is viewed through the lens of Manifest Destiny, it still clearly falls back on the scientific method and not an ontological—or even "Whiggish"—view of history.

If Heinlein expressed a future in terms of faith or destiny, he applied it to the whole human race, not just America. In a 1952 national radio broadcast with Edward R. Murrow, Heinlein proclaims,

> I believe in—I am proud to belong to—the United States. Despite shortcomings, from lynchings to bad faith in high places, our nation has had the most decent and kindly internal practices and foreign policies to be found anywhere in history.
> And finally, I believe in my whole race. Yellow, white, black, red, brown—in the honesty, courage, intelligence, durability ... and *goodness* ... of the overwhelming majority of my brothers and sisters everywhere on this planet. I am proud to be a human being. I believe that we have come this far by the skin of our teeth, that we always make it just by the skin of our teeth—but that we will always make it ... survive ... endure. I believe that this hairless embryo with the aching, oversize brain case and the opposable thumb, this animal barely up from the apes, will endure—will endure longer than his home planet, will spread out to the other planets, to the stars, and beyond, carrying with him his honesty, his insatiable curiosity, his unlimited courage—and his noble essential decency.
> This I believe with all my heart.[16]

Whatever his views on humanity, Heinlein remained proud to be an American. The theme of patriotism is perhaps the best place to consider his views about being a citizen of the United States.

Though most people do not associate patriotism with Calvinism, some of American patriotism's roots come from Puritan/Calvinistic ideas. Some historians consider patriotism to be a conflation of the sacred and secular or, more particularly, between eschatology and chauvinism—which in this context makes patriotism an expression of Manifest Destiny. From this conflation a ritual of dissent emerges, in which dissent occurs and then is resolved when opposing parties are absorbed back into the American mainstream—which fits in with the assimilation aspect of Manifest Destiny. This could be a reason why many people can view both Martin Luther King, Jr., and Ronald Reagan as patriots in the diverse American tapestry.[17]

By 1800 patriotism could be said to be made up of two components: constitutional principles and a sense of biblical mission. Throughout subsequent history, when people criticized patriotism they often did so in an anti–Puritan manner, while paradoxically reaffirming the Puritanism/Calvinist influence. From the mid-to-late nineteenth century challenges to patriotism emerged, primarily due to the influx of new immigrants and to the native-born citizens feeling ever more marginalized in an industrializing and expanding nation. For example, in the latter nineteenth century in the northern United States, the newer immigrants were the growing numbers of Catholics from Europe, while the native born included Protestants in the South still coming to grips with the Civil War, as well as Northern labor groups fighting among themselves in the face of industrialization and immigration. For many new immigrants oftentimes patriotism replaced the old nationalisms of their countries of origin, but their acceptance by mainstream America varied. People of color were not included in this conversation, especially the African Americans who saw the promises of Reconstruction fade away after the presidential election of 1876. The social/economic dislocations of the Gilded Age challenged patriotic feelings in most sectors of society.[18]

During the period just before and during Heinlein's youth, patriotism experienced a rebound. The Progressive movement of the late nineteenth century reinvigorated patriotism due in part to the religious inspiration that accompanied its struggle to include women, farmers, and industrial wage workers in the mainstream of society. Just before Heinlein reached his teenage years, World War I galvanized patriotic fervor, with Woodrow Wilson leading the way through his internationalizing of many Progressive goals, including the bringing of his Fourteen Points to Versailles. It was during this period that patriotism could be said to become nationalized, or standardized. Instead of localized expressions of national loyalty, patriotic events and monuments were now meant to display a more abstract version of nationality under which local expressions were subsumed.

During Heinlein's early adult years, patriotism experienced a downturn due to the disillusionment of the post–World War I era and the onset of the Great Depression, then saw an uplift upon America's entrance into World War II and the subsequent Cold War. American patriotism further endured a challenge during the Sixties, and experienced something of a revival during Heinlein's last years (he died in 1988).[19]

Heinlein never denied that he was a patriot, and often discussed his patriotism in relation to the military. He held that, regardless of the weapons America produces or the fairness of its conscription policy, if its citizens are not patriotic—willing to sacrifice for their country—then the United States is doomed. When explaining his opposition to conscription, Heinlein describes his understanding of patriotism this way:

> A lottery [for a fair conscription process], even meticulously fair, *cannot* make a man willing to charge a machine gun nest in the face of almost certain death. That sort of drive comes from emotional sources. Esprit de corps and patriotism *cannot* be drawn in a lottery.
>
> Conscription works (among free men) only when it is not needed. I have seen two world wars; we used the draft in each ... but in each case it was a means of straightening out the manpower situation; it was *not* needed to make men fight. Both wars were popular.
>
> Since then we have had two non–Wars—Korea and Nam—in "peacetime" and using conscript troops. **And each non–War was a scandalous disaster.**[20]

Here Heinlein talks about emotional sources. Is this a hint of something beyond the rational world view he has been promulgating? Can the Puritan/Calvinist influence emerge here? The answer can be found in the third and last theme of American thought to be examined here—where Heinlein links patriotism with Darwinian thinking.

Social Darwinism may provide the key to understanding Heinlein in this analysis. From the Gilded Age through World War II, this view of human nature and society garnered significant influence in America. Though not supported by Darwin himself, this ideology borrowed—or better yet, co-opted—Darwin's biological terms and applied them to human societies as a way of ranking which peoples or cultures were superior to others. It should be said that Social Darwinism comes from Herbert Spencer, not Charles Darwin,[21] and the ideas of laissez-faire capitalism, industrial capacity, and military superiority were especially significant for explaining or justifying the global empire building by the European powers and America in modern times, and by other powers in earlier periods of history.

Heinlein once said of himself that, as a boy in his native Butler, Missouri, he was steeped in the attitudes of the Bible Belt and thus prey to the "most bigoted" opinions, until he encountered Darwin at the age of thirteen.[22] A few years later, in his *Expanded Universe* (1980) he mentions Charles Galton Darwin (grandson of Charles Darwin) and his book, *The Next Million Years* (1952), as a follow-up to *On the Origin of Species* (1859) and one of the most important books of the twentieth century.[23] This book resurrects the Malthusian problem of overpopulation and concludes pessimistically that the human condition ultimately cannot be improved and therefore human nature must be improved instead. Whoever can do so, their society will endure.[24] Eugenics is the solution proposed. Heinlein's mention of the book can be seen as part of the revival of Social Darwinist themes in American thought.[25] Though Heinlein observes that eugenics is unlikely to occur (he claims it is against human nature), human nature will still improve the usual way—through the survival of those best adaptable to their changing environments.[26]

In his James Forrestal Memorial Lecture in 1973 at the United States Naval Academy,[27] Heinlein makes clear what he thinks is the basis of human social development. The title Heinlein chose, "The Pragmatics of Patriotism," indicates which direction he is heading. He explains patriotism in evolutionary terms as part of humanity's evolutionary make-up. Patriotism's goal is survival, whether of a family, nation, or a whole species—and this becomes the basis of morality. Patriotism may be a feeling, but it is a feeling grounded in the material world where living beings survive or do not survive. Survival means protection as well as propagation and, since war is part of the struggle for survival, any pacifist—following Heinlein's line of logic—must be considered an evolutionary dead end. Using the example of a male baboon standing watch up on a tree to warn his fellow baboons on the ground below that a predator is nearing them, Heinlein asserts that this baboon is more moral than the pacifist. As provocative as this statement is, it nonetheless refutes any non-materialistic explanation for how society works.

This approach by Heinlein fits in with my earlier conclusion that he shifted from the Radical wing to the Moderate wing of the Enlightenment as Jonathan Israel interprets those groups. One might suggest that Heinlein's going over to the Moderate wing—in his case, meaning that only certain qualified people, a kind of rational elite, should govern and operate society— was a cover for Calvinist leanings. It is hoped that the above analysis disproves such a suggestion.

Even though Heinlein treats themes in both his fiction and non-fiction that are associated with Calvinist thought—including predestination, human imperfection and depravity, scriptural authority, and God's inscrutability— his fallback explanations behind his stories or commentaries on human society reside in the scientific method and its application to human society. His success in using this rational method is a matter deserving a separate analysis.

Perhaps if Slusser had changed his focus away from Calvinist predestination and turned it to the Calvinist theme of human shortcomings and sinfulness, he might have made a better case for Calvinist thought in Heinlein's works. However, even then Heinlein would likely have responded by explaining that, despite the fact that humanity has developed a mentality seemingly sophisticated beyond the purview of nature, humanity is still part of nature and therefore subject to evolutionary development.

Furthermore, another part of Heinlein's response to the Calvinist notion of human imperfection and inherent sinfulness is outright rejection, for he also focuses on what is good about being a human being. His long novel, *Time Enough for Love: The Lives of Lazarus Long* (1973), presents many aspects of human life, but—as the title suggests—centers on human relationships, especially between men and women, and argues that they are good and worth living for, as there exist so many variations of love—and sex. Various social taboos against certain sexual relations are brought up and dismissed one by one as the novel progresses. Each time, the only reason given for not having a sexual liaison is biological, specifically genetic. If unwanted pregnancies or genetically defective progeny will not be the result of a sexual encounter, then why not engage in that sexual encounter? Heinlein even goes so far as to have his Lazarus Long character go back in time and pursue a relationship with his own mother. She is already expecting a child, so she—not Long—insists that they consummate their mutual attraction for each other.[28] So human nature is good and worth living for, even in the context of violating the incest taboo.

This essay is not a defense of Heinlein's ideas and opinions. It attempts to explain the basis of his ideas as they manifest themselves in his stories and commentaries. Slusser is correct to reveal certain Calvinistic themes in Heinlein's works, but my disagreement with his Calvinistic interpretation remains the same. Heinlein may treat themes associated with Calvinism, but this observation does not translate into him supporting Calvinist ideas. Quite the contrary. Heinlein's singular use of Enlightenment ideas to buttress his opinions could even be seen as his outright refutation of Calvinism—or of religion in general. The more common perception of Heinlein the rational thinker remains the correct one.

On a more positive note, Slusser and I both agree that Heinlein, due to his importance to the field of science fiction and his influence on society at large, must be examined within the mainstream of American thought and culture and be seen as an important example and contributor to them.

Your turn, George.

Notes

1. George Slusser, *Robert A. Heinlein: Stranger in His Own Land*, Second Edition, 1977 ([Rockville, MD]: Wildside Press, 2006). The first edition of this book, published by Borgo Press in 1976, should be avoided as it was edited and published without Slusser's approval, so he preferred the Second Edition.
2. Jonathan I. Israel, *Radical Enlightenment: Philosophy and the Making of Modernity 1650–1750* (Oxford: Oxford University Press, 2001); *Enlightenment Contested: Philosophy, Modernity, and the Emancipation of Man 1670–1752* (Oxford: Oxford University Press, 2006); and *Democratic Enlightenment: Philosophy, Revolution, and Human Rights 1750–1790* (Oxford: Oxford University Press, 2011).
3. Israel, *Democratic Enlightenment*, 7.
4. Bradford Lyau, "Robert A. Heinlein Revisited: His Place in the Enlightenment Tradition," academic track, 74th World Science Fiction Convention, Kansas City, Missouri, August 2016.
5. See John T. McNeill, *The History and Character of Calvinism* (New York: Oxford University Press, 1957), 201–225.

6. See Gary Scott Smith, *The Seeds of Secularization: Calvinism, Culture, and Pluralism in America 1870–1915* (Grand Rapids, MI: Christian University Press, 1985).

7. See Aliki Barnstone, Michael Tomasek Manson, and Carol Singley, editors, *The Calvinist Roots of the Modern Era* (Hanover: University Press of New England, 1997), especially xiii–xxxii.

8. See Jeremy Black, *Fighting for America: The Struggle for Mastery in North America, 1519–1871* (Bloomington: Indiana University Press, 2011).

9. Robert A. Heinlein, "Guest of Honor Speech at the XXXIVth World Science Fiction Convention—Kansas City, 1976," *Requiem: New Collected Works by Robert A. Heinlein and Tributes to the Grand Master*, edited by Yoji Kondo (New York: Tor Books, 1992), 205–213. Video of speech available at https://www.youtube.com/watch?v=LoSnjYLw2A0.

10. Heinlein, "Mondo Cult Presents Walter Cronkite Apollo 11 Interview with Robert A. Heinlein & Arthur C. Clarke" (New York: CBS-TV, July 20, 1969), at https://www.youtube.com/watch?v=xMAmk5Rpltk.

11. See Natsu Taylor Saito, *Meeting the Enemy: American Exceptionalism and International Law* (New York: New York University Press, 2010), 120–121. For a general background, see Richard White, *The Republic for Which It Stands: The United States During Reconstruction and the Gilded Age, 1865–1896* (New York: Oxford University Press, 2017), part of The Oxford History of the United States series.

12. See Heinlein, *Space Cadet*, 1948 (New York: Ace Books, 1971), especially 40–48.

13. Heinlein, "The Happy Days Ahead," *Expanded Universe: The New Worlds of Robert A. Heinlein* (New York: Grosset & Dunlap, 1980), 514–582.

14. Heinlein, *Friday* (New York: Holt, Rinehart and Winston, 1981). Page references are to this edition.

15. Heinlein, "Guest of Honor Speech at the Third World Science Fiction Convention—Denver, 1941," *Requiem*, 153–168. This text, and two alternate versions of the speech, are available at David Wright, Sr., editor, "A Revised Transcript of Robert A. Heinlein's 1941 Guest of Honor Speech," at http://home.windstream.net/dwrighsr/General%20Semantics/Compare%20GOH%20SPEECH-04.pdf.

16. Heinlein, "This I Believe," *This I Believe*, hosted by Edward R. Murrow (New York: CBS-Radio, December 1, 1952). Text available at http://www.heinleinsociety.org/rah/thisibelieve.html.

17. See Sacvan Bercovitch, *The Rites of Assent: Transformations in the Symbolic Construction of America* (New York: Routledge, 1993).

18. See George McKenna, *The Puritan Origins of American Patriotism* (New Haven: Yale University Press, 2007), 1–163, and Cecelia Elizabeth O'Leary, "Blood Brotherhood: The Racialization of Patriotism, 1815–1918," *Bonds of Affection: Americans Define Their Patriotism*, edited by John Bodnard. (Princeton: Princeton University Press, 1996), 53–81.

19. See McKenna, 350–374; Andrew Neather, "Labor Republicanism, Race, and Popular Patriotism in the Era of Empire, 1890–1914," *Bonds of Affection*, 82–101; Stuart McConnell, "Reading the Flag: A Reconsideration of the Patriotic Cults of the 1890s," *Bonds of Affection*, 102–119; Kimberly Jensen, "Women, Citizenship, and the Civic Sacrifice: Engendering Patriotism in the First World War," *Bonds of Affection*, 139–159; and Simon Hall, *American Patriotism, American Protest: Social Movements since the Sixties* (Philadelphia: University of Pennsylvania Press, 2011).

20. Heinlein, "The Happy Days Ahead," 540. The italics, bold type, and ellipsis are Heinlein's.

21. See Carl N. Degler, *In Search of Human Nature: The Decline and Revival of Darwinism in American Social Thought* (New York: Oxford University Press, 1991), and Richard Hofstadter, *Social Darwinism in American Thought*, introduction by Eric Foner (1944; Boston: Beacon Press, 1992).

22. Heinlein, "The Happy Days Ahead," 545. See also Curt Suplee, "In the Strange Land of Robert Heinlein," *Washington Post*, September 5, 1984, at https://www.washingtonpost.com/archive/lifestyle/1984/09/05/in-the-strange-land-of-robert-heinlein/b7a2ee22-0a6e-4c29-8fc1-88b3e68ec08c/?utm_term=.56f87245c20c.

23. Heinlein, 1980 endnote to "The Third Millennium Opens," *Expanded Universe*, 385.

Article originally published as "As I See Tomorrow…. The Third Millennium Opens," *Amazing Stories*, 30:4 (April 1956).

24. Charles Galton Darwin, *The Next Million Years* (New York: Doubleday, 1953).

25. See Degler, 216–349.

26. Heinlein, "The Third Millennium Opens," 382–383.

27. Published as Heinlein, "Guest Editorial: Channel Markers," *Analog Science Fiction/Science Fact*, 92:5 (January 1974), 5–10, 166–178; edited version by Heinlein published as "The Pragmatics of Patriotism," *Expanded Universe*, 459–470.

28. See Heinlein, *Time Enough for Love: The Lives of Lazarus Long* (New York: G.P. Putnam's Sons, 1973), especially 546–592. Many reviewers criticized Heinlein for his apparent obsession with sex. They may have a point, but when viewed in light of Heinlein's attempt to explore variations on the theme of love and his attempts to establish scientific bases for human conduct, a logic and reason can be found behind his novel-long focus on the matter.

The Emperor—and Heretic— of Point of View

David Brin

Science fiction is a complex genre. Oh, sure, the massive bulk of "sci-fi" production—in novels, games and Hollywood—gushes with simple goals: manic entertainment and generating cash. But many sf-creators often do show genuine ambition. Like adventurers on unknown seas, they aim for something more.

What is storytelling, after all? I've called it exercise for our prefrontal lobes, those "lamps upon the brow" where humans perform thought-experiments like: "how might things be different than they are?" This trait seems qualitatively unique to us, rather than just quantitatively enlarged. Asking "what if...?" led to our prodigious inventiveness, both in pragmatic crafts and in art. Moreover, no activity stretches and exercises those prefrontals like science fiction, poking at every assumption of contemporary life.

This fascination with change led to our most important works, those *self-preventing prophecies* that so stir a reader or viewer that millions close the book or leave the theater driven to act! To help stave off the terrifying future they were just shown. Among these effective warnings was *Soylent Green* (1973), which recruited millions of environmentalists to the cause of saving their world. *Dr. Strangelove* (1964) and *On the Beach* (1959) we now know helped to prevent nuclear war. And the grand-daddy of self preventing prophecies—George Orwell's *Nineteen Eighty-Four* (1949)—girded many tens of millions to denounce potential Big Brothers.

Warnings don't have to be set in a plausible near-future. Through exaggeration, a far off era can either chill the heart or inspire, as we've seen in works of Clarke, Asimov, Stapledon, and ... yes ... Frank Herbert, whose many, varied sf *gedanken experiments* culminated in the popular *Dune* epic we're discussing here. That richly textured and complex future human civilization invites the visitor to ponder quandaries that grow more pertinent daily—like our relationship with "intelligent" machines, or under-exploited powers that may lurk in human minds.

And feudalism, the way of life that dominated nearly all of our ancestors for the last 6000 years or more. Everywhere humans developed agriculture—and likely long before—similar social patterns emerged. Large males would gather in tight bands, pick up metal or stone implements, and use them to crush potential rivals, taking from the losers anything they wanted. In a simple extrapolation of the battle for reproductive advantage that occurs in countless animal species, feudalism amplified the genetic rewards spectacularly, as these "lords" structured society to favor their sons, and their sons' sons. We are all descended from the harems of jerks who pulled off this trick. And, as we'll see, feudal themes have drawn on that long inheritance, alluring writers, directors and consumers for a very long time.

In the *Dune* universe—culminating especially with *God Emperor of Dune* (1981)—we get feudalism exponentiated to its likely outcome, if lordly castes ever come to monopolize tools of technology and the mind. Tools of manipulation and suasion. Tools that amplify their assertion of raw power over those below them on a rigid pyramid. And then to *justify* the hierarchy, as feudal regimes have always done—through religion, mythology, tribalism, politics … and war.

> "When religion and politics travel in the same cart, the riders believe nothing can stand in their way. Their movement becomes headlong—faster and faster and faster. They put aside all thought of obstacles and forget that a precipice does not show itself to the man in a blind rush until it's too late."
> —*Dune*, Frank Herbert, 1965[1]

In his introduction to *Dune Messiah* (1969), Gregory Benford tells how he knew Frank Herbert as a colleague. I am of a later wave that barely overlapped with such legends. While honored to call Ray Bradbury, Frederik Pohl and Poul Anderson my friends, I exchanged mere correspondence with Clarke and Asimov. As for Heinlein and Herbert, I can only say "we met and spoke for a while, once." Still, I feel part of a grand conversation with all of them, and with so many others in both science and science fiction, across a dazzling civilization that has broken away from those old, feudal traps. To us, the grand *terra incognita* of tomorrow is no narrow path defined by kings, priests and adepts, but a vast horizon filled with dangers and opportunities and decisions that may involve all of us, with solutions that depend on *any* of us.

And beyond those horizons? More horizons, still.

But, in order to cross this expanse, we'll need to detect the landmines, snake-pits, quicksand and other traps that may have snared previous sapient species, across the galaxy leaving it so (apparently) empty. Brave authors plunge into these minefields, issuing warnings about environmental calamity, or ill-motivated artificial intelligence (AI), or misused genetic science. Alas though, all too often, the worst failure mode of all, one that plagued our ancestors and cauterized our growth—feudalism—gets *romanticized*.

At least half-seriously, Mark Twain blamed the 1860s Confederacy on southern romantics, devouring books by Sir Walter Scott that glorified the lords and ladies of Europe's dark ages. Likewise, I see similar roots in today's phase of America's re-ignited Civil War.

Something deep inside resonates with Aragorn and his snooty, immortal elf-pals. It's a deep well of feeling that goes back to Gilgamesh and Achilles, found in the *Vedas* and *Journey to the West*, and every legend or ballad catalogued by Joseph Campbell *et al.* During science fiction's Golden Age, the great master of chosen-one sf was A.E. van Vogt, whose protagonists were always Nietzchean *ubermenschen* supermen, qualitatively far above normal humanity. It's an ancient motif, most prevalent today in comics, but continuing also in the demigod-worshipping propaganda of George Lucas and Orson Scott Card.

Oh, this storytelling tradition is a winner, all right. It uses point-of-view to flatter the reader or viewer, who thinks: "I too am an undiscovered *Homo superior,* persecuted for all the ways that I'm inherently greater and destined to rule, once I finally tap into my hidden powers." Who can compete with that? Compared to rule by some mystical or sword-wielding chosen one, our modern, accountable institutions seem dry. And yes, unromantic. Even though they freed us from our ancestors' living hell.

Not every creator accepts this devil's bargain. A few choose not to romanticize feudalism, but instead challenge and interrogate it, as George R.R. Martin does, in his *A Song of Ice and Fire* series (better known as *Game of Thrones.*) But it is Frank Herbert's *Dune* epic that transports us to a future when feudalism is extrapolated and tech-enhanced. Its age-old, capricious unfairness and cruelty is undiminished by future advances. In fact, they are augmented to a terrifying degree, never imagined by Orwell.

Damien Broderick points out in *The Cambridge Companion to Science Fiction* (2003) that the "deep irony of *Dune*'s popular triumph, and that of its many sequels, is Herbert's own declared intention to undermine exactly that besotted identification with the van Vogtian superman-hero."[2] Science fiction scholar Stephen W. Potts said to me in a conversation that Herbert is "undercutting the whole hero myth archetype, by having the characters consciously use—and abuse—it."

Remember that Herbert had lived through the horrors of Nazism and

Stalinism and *caudillo* dictatorships to the south. In very recent memory—while the *Dune* saga took form—came revelations of the Cambodian holocaust led by Pol Pot, which emptied every city, eliminating the nation's knowledge castes as enemies of the idealized Khmer Path to hyper–Maoist purity. With the fell date 1984 itself looming, just ahead, the warnings of George Orwell were very much in Frank Herbert's mind as he wrote his own tale of warning.

The hero-protagonists in these stories are no democrats, nor are they idealists, nor even particularly "good." Only somewhat less horrible than their rivals. That is the slender reed upon which Herbert draws reader and viewer identification ... and upon that reed he builds a masterpiece!

Not one to slavishly follow any formula, Herbert took the classic "Hero's Journey" prescriptions the way any good sf writer should ... as a *dare* to do things differently.

Which brings us to the core point of this essay...

Many fans of *Dune* dump on the Dino De Laurentis–David Lynch movie (1984). And yes, by necessity the film leaves out many complex issues of religion, politics, and ecology explored in the book. Yet I found it faithful overall. Indeed, one problem may boil down to a difference in story-telling arcs, between novel and film.

Full-length books deeply immerse a reader in the characters' perspective or *point of view* (POV). When reading a good novel, you suspend disbelief to get drawn in, and that requires empathizing with the main characters. A good writer will get you identifying with the protagonist, adopting—or trying on for size—even a villain's take on ethics, politics, and the story's conflicts. At least for the span of a chapter, you classify good and evil the way he or she does. It's incredibly powerful, this POV magic, and more would-be authors are stymied by it than any other trick of the trade.

When a brilliant craftsman like Frank Herbert leads you to identify with Lady Jessica or Paul Atreides, you take on their vendetta against the hated Harkonnens. Similarly, in J.R.R. Tolkien's *Lord of the Rings* (1955–1956), the reader identifies with Aragorn or the elves, without questioning any moral ambiguity on their part.

However, when watching a movie, there simply isn't time for you, the viewer, to fully immerse yourself into the characters' point of view, let alone experience their internalized thoughts. You're watching from *outside*, observing their actions, rather than feeling their motives. As a result, something magical that happens in a book cannot occur in the screen adaptation.

Sure, *Dune*'s Harkonnen villains and Emperor are vile (and portrayed as physically ugly), but it occurs to some viewers that the Atreides do many of the same things, just less gruesomely, less sadistically. Perhaps Duke Leto is an admirable person in his context, but he's not setting out to establish freedom and equality in his realm. As in *Star Wars* (1977) and *Lord of the Rings,* goodness is telegraphed with physical surface beauty. But in the *Dune* film, it's not enough. (Note that the Atreides troops even dress like Nazis.)

In Herbert's novels, there are no visuals, but those the reader creates out of authorial prompting. Instead, it is the characters' *thoughts* that draw you in. And when protagonist perspective is conveyed by a master, the magic is to make you, briefly, willing to credit their rationalized reasons.

When reading these works—not just the original *Dune,* but sequels, especially *God Emperor of Dune*—watch how skillfully Herbert *switches narrative perspective.* Most authors either stick to one character's point-of-view and inner voice per book, or at least per chapter. (That is certainly how I do it! Even when the varied POVs are different versions of the same person, as in *Kiln People* [2002].) There are reasons; switching back and forth can jar and confuse the reader. But Herbert was so confident in his skill that point of view might hop among two, or three or more characters, even in neighboring paragraphs!

This artfulness reaches its pinnacle in *God Emperor of Dune.* With apparent effortlessness, Herbert conveys to the reader on a single page how deeply suspicious these manipulative lords, savants, and rebels are of the emperor, and of each other—a task made even more difficult by the posited existence of prescience and some types of telepathy! This is master-level writing craft. Don't try it at home ... till you are as good a writer as Herbert.

Oh, these characters have reasons! In the *Dune* universe, certain technologies have been outlawed due to a traumatic "Butlerian Jihad" thousands of years earlier—a war against Artificial Intelligence that prompted the victorious lords to renounce technology and vow never again to allow egalitarian-open-scientific civilization. Herbert isn't the only author to portray a future that turns its back on enlightenment-style renaissance. In Isaac Asimov's Foundation and Robots cosmos, it is the "devoted" AIs that rationalize exactly the same thing prescription—as I clarify in the very last book of the series: *Foundation's Triumph* (1999).

"Renunciation" stands for belief that we must turn our backs on so-called "progress," lest it kill us all, and it was official policy in countless kingdoms of the past. A modern equivalent—the Taliban—calls for renunciation quite openly, while elements of American society have always expressed contempt for all enlightenment notions of improvability in either society or humanity. Indeed, reverting to feudalism has—for half a dozen millennia—proved an effective way to stymie advancement of science, technology or competitive ambition rising from the lower orders.

So much for the situation that Leto and Paul and Jessica find themselves in, as the *Dune* epic commences. Rigid, perpetual feudalism has its justification (according to the testimony and inner thoughts of those at the top of the pyramid, our protagonists). But Frank Herbert then doubles down, harkening to an even older mythology of the *god-king*. Paul Atreides is superior to all other members of his species—the Kwisatz-Haderach—a chosen one demigod who can see into the future and control many currents of fate. In *Dune Messiah*, Paul wields temporal power as emperor, conqueror and leader of a galaxy-spanning jihad. But it is on the religious and supernatural plane that he awes and daunts all …

… and it is on that plane that he proclaims justification for a new, more intense kind of feudalism. "It's right because I say so."

Which brings us back around to *The God Emperor of Dune*. It is 3000 years later. Paul's son, Leto II has been both emperor and living deity over humanity's realm for nearly all that time. Transforming himself into the physiology of an Arrakis sand-worm, Leto also molded civilization, emptying or eliminating most cities, higher education or cosmopolitan life, even quashing most technology—except for the interstellar transportation Guild, the bio-hackers of Tleilaxu, and the always suspect tech wizards of Ix. (I use the word "wizards" purposely, because the fairytale purpose of these two "towers" could not be more clear.) Every aspect of modernity is deemed loathsome by Leto, if it does not suit one of his cryptic purposes. Moreover, while he needs the wizards for certain things, he also knows they are laboring to bring his own downfall.

Across the course of a book filled with taunts and harsh lectures, Leto issues the chief justification for his hyper-feudal rule—that humanity *would have* killed itself off without him. That his prophetic foresight—though limited in obscure ways—has shown him a "Golden Path" that skirts this doom, a path that necessitates every horror and repression. Humanity achieved the stars, only to crouch under a medieval lash. But for its own good.

Does the reader start to sniff Frank Herbert's true intent?

Oh, others have explored this territory. Take J.R.R. Tolkien, whose own epic tale calls modernization inevitable, if regrettable, even lamentable. In explanatory writings, Tolkien avowed the necessity of an end to the morally-challenged, if beautiful, Elfish oligarchy. He makes us choose then, between two versions of modernity: one of clanking smoke—Mordor—and one of doughty rustic yeomen—dwellers of the Shire. (I go into this in detail, elsewhere.)

If Tolkien is an honest romantic, open about the pros and cons, then George Lucas and O.S. Card give us legends that unabashedly preach rule by mutant demigods … and more demigods all the way down … proclaiming it to be the natural and good order. (That is, Lucas pushed this theme as long as that narrative universe remained under his control. See my argument as "prosecutor" in *Star Wars on Trial* [2006]. And one can see, with some relief, that Disney is pulling away from such obsessions in the new *Star Wars* films.)

In contrast, Frank Herbert's *Dune* epic strips away any sugar coating and offers a refreshing splash of despair. He portrays our own era's brief escape from feudalism as ephemeral, lasting just long enough to scatter humanity's seed across the stars, before resuming our habitual addiction to oligarchy, in which our sole choice will be between sadism and noblesse oblige.

I mentioned a latter-day parallel—George R.R. Martin's *Song of Ice and Fire* series, in which the clear best option for all the people of Westeros would be a lethal plague upon all noble houses. But that series is set in a past-like parallel fantasy world. One can imagine that an infusion of the right technologies might liberate the suffering peasant, as happens in Anne McCaffrey's unabashedly optimistic *Dragonriders* series, when the medieval trap is shattered and the people of Pern rediscover their scientific heritage.

And hence we get to my own hypothesis about the *Dune* saga. That Frank Herbert was testing us! A test that reached its culmination in *God Emperor of Dune*. He clearly knew that humanity was speeding toward a crisis of confidence—our brash civilization's confrontation with renunciation and all of the romantic temptations of restored feudalism. By showing us an extremum of where it might all lead, he makes the choice stark. No spoon of sugar.

This is where it may all lead, if you let it.

I am less subtle—known for railing that our only hope for prolonging this grand experiment of Enlightenment depends on harnessing and unleashing humanity's freedom, diversity, open accountability and—yes—competitiveness. By shining light upon all elites, we force them to share with us those very tools that they would otherwise use, to bring down eons of darkness. We might flourish—elevating the *Dune* series to the high honor of Self-Preventing Prophecy—by empowering most people to create, innovate, benefit from work, and hold each other (even the rich and mighty) accountable.

I am perhaps too strident in shouting Cassandra warnings about resurgent feudalism.

Frank was more subtle.

He presents us with a possible, all-too plausible destiny. A form of governance that 99 percent of our ancestors would recognize, far better than any of our forebears would understand us.

Whereupon Frank Herbert demands:

Choose.

NOTES

1. Frank Herbert, *Dune* (New York: Ace Books, 1965), 393.
2. Damien Broderick, "New Wave and Backlash: 1960–1980," *The Cambridge Companion to Science Fiction*, edited by Edward James and Farah Mendlesohn (Cambridge: Cambridge University Press, 2003), 51.

Counterfeit Worlds

Simulacron-3 *on Film and Television*

Jonathan Alexander

For several years now, I have been working on a genealogy of the concept of virtuality, focusing in particular on the ways in which various fictional and media works have represented the virtual, especially immersive virtualities. My goal has been to analyze the different ways in which the virtual has been constructed in relation to changing historical and ideological pressures and demands. In fleshing out this long history of the virtual, I want better to understand what "work" the virtual has been doing in both the development of science fiction as a genre, but also as a way of knowing and theorizing about the world.

I turn attention in this essay to Daniel F. Galouye's *Simulacron-3*, first published in 1964, which offers a compelling case in point, particularly as it details the creation of a simulated world in which "units" are designed to be as "realistic" as possible and are observed as part of a marketing research plan to track and predict consumer interest. The book was likely influenced by Frederik Pohl's "The Tunnel Under the World" (1955), about a similar kind of marketing research, and Philip K. Dick's 1959 novel *Time Out of Joint*, about a man who slowly realizes that he's living in a simulation. Galouye's novel combines both strains into a gripping if periodically convoluted narrative, accenting the digital and philosophical dimensions of simulated realities. It's a compelling enough tale that it's been adapted into two different films, Rainer Werner Fassbinder's *Welt am Draht* (1973) and Josef Rusnak's *The Thirteenth Floor* (1999), released the same year as *The Matrix*.[1] Indeed, even *The Matrix* and the film *The Truman Show* (1998) bear striking resonances with *Simulacron-3*, even if they are not directly based on it; in the former case, the creation of a computer simulation to control people virtually dominates the narrative, while in the latter case a reality television simulation is created around an individual who doesn't know he's in a simulation, even if the frequent product placements might signal that something strange is going on. There may also be little moments of homage here: in both *Simulacron-3* and *The Matrix*, telephones figure as one connecting point in and out of the simulations, and in *The Truman Show*, a falling klieg light that's supposed to be the star Sirius nearly gives away the fact that Truman is in a vast simulation—a scene reminiscent of one in which Doug Hall, the narrator hero of *Simulacron-3*, looks up at the stars and wonders if they are in fact real or themselves only digitally simulated.

The reach of the book and its durability in the sf imaginary is unquestioned. But its complex intertwining of the virtual and the economic seems particularly prescient and relevant for contemporary concerns. So tracing out the narrative and its adaptation across the last fifty years may be informative about shifting understandings of the virtual vis-à-vis economic and other political and ideological pressures.

The Epistemic Convolutions of a Plot

Plot summaries, such as this one from Wikipedia, attempt to boil the narrative down to its most essential parts:

> *Simulacron 3* is the story of a virtual city (total environment simulator) for marketing research, developed by a scientist to reduce the need for opinion polls. The computer-generated city simulation is so well-programmed, that, although the inhabitants have their own consciousness, they are unaware, except for one, that they are only electronic impulses in a computer.
>
> The simulator's lead scientist, Hannon Fuller, dies mysteriously, and a co-worker, Morton Lynch, vanishes. The protagonist, Douglas Hall, is with Lynch when he vanishes, and Hall subsequently struggles to suppress his inchoate madness. As time and events unwind, he progressively grasps that his own world is probably not "real" and might be only a computer-generated simulation.[2]

While concise, this description belies the sometimes bewildering ride that *Simulacron-3* takes its readers on in its relatively short 170 pages. Doug careens from theory to theory as he tries to figure out what's "real" as well as *who* in his world is "real" and who is a simulation. He slowly figures out that Jinx Fuller, Dr. Fuller's daughter, is the "contact unit" for the reality "above" his own, just as *his* simulation had a "contact unit," a simulated being who was aware that his reality wasn't in fact real—a plot point concocted to bridge the various realities and pawned off as "necessary" to make the simulations actually work. Complicating Doug's existential dilemmas—what is real? am *I* real?—are the various narrative intrigues and conspiracies played out by Siskin, the corporate executive who owns the Simulacron machine and who has ostensibly been using it for market research but is actually planning to use it to predict political opinions so that he can mastermind his own ascendancy to power. In the process, Siskin has to deal with the pollsters union, which will essentially be put out of business if the simulation can start predicting consumer trends, by pitching the simulation to the public as a platform for experimenting with social policies and the possible creation of utopia—which was Doug and Dr. Fuller's earlier plan that Siskin suppressed so he could tout the simulation as marketing research to cover his use of it for political machinations.

Confused yet? If anything, the plot convulsions, with existential and conspiratorial twists and turns mounting, reflects the many different ideological and epistemological pressures surrounding the imagination of virtual and the re-imagination of the real triggered by the creation of virtual realities.

On one hand, the creation of the simulation machine and the monitoring of individuals reacting to different marketing stimuli come nearly directly from the then-popular psychological theories of behaviorism, with Simulacron seeming like a digital Skinner Box. As it's described, with Simulacron, "We can electronically simulate a social environment. We can populate it with subjective analogs—reactional identity units. By manipulating the environment, by prodding the ID units, we can estimate behavior in hypothetical situations."[3] As such, Simulacron is an "electromathematical model of an average community [that] permits long-range behavior forecasts" (9) since the units inside it will "respond to any reaction-seeking stimuli" (24). This is the language of behaviorism, and, unsurprisingly, the staff psychologist describes himself as a "pure psychologist—[with] behaviorist leanings" (30).

Behavioral psychology is quickly matched by existential and philosophical wondering, as Doug muses in one lyrical passage:

> I was nothing—merely a package of vital simulectronic charges. Nevertheless I *had* to exist. Simple logic demanded no less. I think, therefore I am. But then I wasn't the *first* person to solipsists, the Berkeleians, the transcendentalists? Throughout the ages, objective reality had been held up to the closest scrutiny. Subjectivists were far from the exception in efforts to understand the true nature of existence. And even pure science had swung heavily to phenomenalism, with its principle of indeterminacy, its concept that the observed is inseparable from the observer.

Philosophy turns to physics as Doug further contemplates at one point how *any* reality, whether simulated or not, is "composed, in the final analysis, of 'subatomic' particles, which were actually only immaterial 'charges'" (87).

The quickly shifting epistemologies here—what can we know and how can we know it?—reflect Doug's quickly shifting strategies as he tries to figure out not only who killed Fuller but how he (and then he and Jinx) might subvert Siskin's Machiavellian plans to use the simulation for his own selfish political purposes. Beyond the plot twists, the shifting epistemologies prompt us—and Doug—to wonder what is actually real, and what *grounds* reality. At one point, Doug asserts, hopefully: "If this is a simulectronic creation, you'll tell yourself, then there must be someone with total knowledge of the setup working on the inside" (90). And when the contact unit, Ashton, in Doug's simulation is able to make it out of Simulacron into Doug's reality, he proclaims, "I'm a step closer to the real reality! You've got to let me go on and find the material world!" (84). Curiously, in Fassbinder's version of this same scene, Ashton is named *Einstein*, in recognition of the shifting and multiple realities of time and space.

Saturating all of this is yet a *further* set of possible groundings in *economic* realities. Simulacron had been built to measure consumer responses to marketing, and Doug wonders at one point if *his* own reality isn't just a marketing research experiment: "[O]n a higher plane, our entire world, the simulectronic creation in which I existed as an ID reaction unit, was but a question-and-answer device for the edification of producers, manufacturers, marketers, retailers in that Higher Reality!" (110). The problem of the economic is quite pressing in Galouye's novel in that, if successful, the Simulacron computer will put thousands and thousands of pollsters out of work. Siskin puts it mildly: "But when automation fully takes over in opinion sampling, some adjustments will have to be made in employment practices" (8), but contemporaneous fears of technological advances and automation seem only even more pressing today. Interestingly, in Fassbinder's *Welt am Draht*, Simulacron is supposed to be used by the State purely for social research, but Fassbinder's Siskin has his own secret plans to use it to help him predict various commodities futures, such as the future price of steel. Fassbinder's version, which is otherwise fairly faithful to the original novel, flips the script to show how corporate and financial interests use public goods and technologies to further their own agendas and wealth development.

In general, then, the drama of the narrative is about finding out what's "real" in terms of the plot, but also what's really *real*—as in what forces actually propel or guide human activity: existential and philosophical inquiry? behavioral conditioning? market and economic forces? or some complex mixture of all of them?

Questions of Economy

Perhaps unsurprisingly, the economic dimensions of this narrative have attracted the most critical attention. Richard Swope's article in *Science Fiction Studies*, "Science Fiction Cinema and the Crime of Social-Spatial Reality" (2002), is an excellent case in point. Swope focuses on both the films *Dark*

City and *The Thirteenth Floor*, and it is his treatment of the latter that interests us here. For Swope, the "moment of 'truth'" in both Galouye's novel and *The Thirteenth Floor* "arrives when [Hall] become[s] aware that the space [he] imagine[s himself] to inhabit is not at all what [he] had presumed it to be."[4] Swope connects this indeterminacy via the work of Henri Lefebvre to how "late capitalism has conceived or socially produced an increasingly 'abstract space,' 'founded on the vast network of banks, business centres and major productive entities, as also on motorways, airports and information lattices'" (223). Cyberspace and virtual realities are just one more profound extension of such abstract spatialization; following the cyberpunk tradition of William Gibson's *Neuromancer* (1984), Swope references critic David Brande to assert how cyberspace "is a dream of late-capitalist ideology" (233). In one way, cyberspace and virtual realities are an extension of a "world that could be both known (solved) and controlled" (233). But even further, Swope argues that such virtual reality or cyberspace "reflects or offers a metonymic vision of the larger cultural logic of late capitalism" (236)—cyberspace "allows us to imagine the kind of limitless space that capitalism ultimately demands" (236), creating a virtual "spatial fix," in the words of David Harvey (as cited in Swope).

The need for capital to have a limitless frontier of expansion finds its narrative apotheosis in the film *The Thirteenth Floor*. What had begun as a simulation for market research to better predict patterns of consumer spending in response to marketing becomes in the film the creation of *thousands* of simulations. But curiously, the creation of the simulation in the film doesn't come from a market corporation but rather a *computer* corporation—a subtle shift that signals the ways in which capitalism often seeks to cover its tracks. As Swope puts it:

> While the increasing loss of real-world space supplies the impetus for the creation of thousands of simulated worlds, in turn those virtual spaces mask the ecological and geographical consequences of market expansion. Rather than feeling the pressures of the increasing scarcity of space, the inhabitants of this world are allowed to enter a cyber-fantasy, or reenter a re-circulated fantasy of an endless "frontier," which in turn constructs for them a new "social reality" in which there are, in effect, no spatial dilemmas—or to put this in terms of the detective story, no crimes to solve [237].

Or, as Robert Markley suggests, "Cyberspace is the ultimate capitalist fantasy because it promises to exploit our own desires as the inexhaustible material of consumption," transforming the self into a "thoroughly efficient desiring machine."[5]

Following this line from Galouye through Fassbinder's and then to Rusnak's films, we can track the ongoing concern with shifting economic circumstances throughout the latter half of the twentieth century: from the concern in the novel with increasing automation and the rise of ubiquitous marketing as a dominant feature of contemporary life; to the problem in the Fassbinder film of corporate interests manipulating state-controlled resources set aside for the common good; to more recent concerns with the proliferation of virtual technologies as an expanded (and potentially limitless) frontier for commercial and financial growth, albeit one that masks its own use of all-too-limited natural and material resources. In terms of the latter, Swope has a lovely reading of the end of *The Thirteenth Floor* when, as Doug makes his way through to the "real" reality, he's confronted with a Los Angeles business skyline that has literally expanded *into* the ocean, suggesting the further incursion of not just digital but material capitalist expansion.

Economics, Aesthetics, Sexuality

As compelling as this economic reading of the Simulacron narrative is, I find that it steadily elides consideration of both aesthetic and sexual dimensions of the narrative, and the original novel in particular, that offer some potential counter epistemologies.

Surely, the sexual is at play in *The Thirteenth Floor*, early in the film's narrative, in which we learn that Fuller, who has created the simulation, has been porting into a reconstruction of the 1937 Los Angeles of his youth to have sex with cocktail waitresses. This use of the virtual seemed pretty predictable by 1999, the year of the film's release, in which the never-ending capitalist expansion envisioned within cyberspace was perhaps only matched by the id which could now use the virtual as its ever-expanding playground for fantastical desire. Indeed, when the detective investigating Fuller's death in the film version is introduced to the simulation computer, the very first question he asks about it is if the self-learning cyborg units in it can "fuck." And in *The Thirteenth Floor*, just as in *Welt am Draht* and *Simulacron-3*, it is ultimately Jane's or Eva's or Jinx's love for Doug or Fred that saves him (and her and the virtual world) from destruction by her lover/husband who has lost his mind playing god with his simulated units, controlling their lives and even torturing them, with a particular fetish for torturing his own simulation counterpart. All three narrative versions play out this love story, which resonates with the climactic scene in *The Matrix* in which Trinity's love for—and kiss of—Neo is able to revive him across real and virtual worlds—as though love is the transcendent epistemology that unites analog and digital platforms.

Articulated this way, one need not wonder why the relatively simplistic amorous or sexual dimensions of the narrative haven't drawn much critical attention. But the original novel's attention to sexuality is more intense than we see it in the subsequent versions, particularly at the level of language. In the last third of the novel, we hear more and more about "couplings," with the Controller in the real world "coupling" with is simulacrum double, and perhaps others, just as Doug "couples" with units in his simulation, in order to see through their eyes, experience their world. *Welt am Draht* nicely plays out one such scene, and the coupling in all the versions is understood as potentially dangerous—the danger of coupling with another—as the simulation unit could potentially backtrack up into *your* consciousness. Talk about losing yourself in another "person."

The *erotic* dimensions of this coupling are brought to the fore in *Simulacron-3*. Jinx reveals that the Operator is a sadist, frequently coupling with Doug and toying with him, enjoying his pain and confusion. As she puts it, "I suppose he realized how much pleasure he was getting from putting you through your paces. And suddenly he didn't want to do away with you—not too quickly, anyway. ... There was too much perverted gratification to be had by letting you come close to Fuller's secret, then pushing you away" (143). There's something definitely a little bit *queer* here—particularly with someone creating a simulated likeness and then "coupling" with it to torture it. The text even draws attention to the queerness here, having Jinx call the Operator's creation of a simulation in his likeness a "Dorian Gray effect" or "masochistic expedient" in an attempt to alleviate his guilty feelings for having created a whole world of sentient simulations (148). *The Thirteenth Floor* completely tempers this queerness by showing us "David," the sadist in the "real" world, downloading into Doug and confronting Jane (aka "Jinx") in the simulation. He tries to seduce her, then attacks her when she realizes he's not Doug. He's going to kill her because he's jealous of her interest in the simulation Doug, but he's killed first (by the detective slowly piecing everything together). The homoerotically charged masochistic coupling of the novel becomes heteronormative possessiveness.

If we stick with the queerness, though, we quickly realize that there's something very queer about Jinx/Jane/Eva falling in love with a simulation, which is what happens in all three versions of the narrative. "I want to be with you, darling" (142), she says in the novel. And Doug/Fred queries her about the strangeness of the situation, its fundamental queerness, but the queerness is quickly dismissed as the narrative finds a way for the two to be together in the "real" world—thus again eliding the original queerness of a real person falling in love with a virtual person.

But that final elision occurs with a critical difference in the film versions. In both *Welt am Draht* and *The Thirteenth Floor*, the narrative propulsion is toward getting the couple together in the real world, with final scenes in both films focusing increasingly on them and their happy union in reality. In the novel, however, the plot revolves not just around getting Doug safely into the "above" but also, just as importantly, around keeping the simulation going.

In Galouye's narrative, the Operator will wipe the entire simulation if he can't manipulate the demise of the simulation that the units have themselves created—the simulation within the simulation. Jinx and Doug want to save both simulations, however. As Doug puts it, "All we have to do is see that REIN is used only for research into sociological problems.... They would see that it was used for nothing but research into human relations" (161). In the film versions, the simulation is largely forgotten, and in *Welt am Draht*, the final scene shifts back and forth between Fred happily discovering the pleasure of the new world while his dead body languishes in the simulation: the real is valorized over the virtual. But the original novel retains the possibility of using virtualities for the common good. Even Jinx proclaims, "It's the intellect that counts" (155), and Doug muses "For self-awareness is the only true measure of existence" (156). They are committed to the counterfeit worlds and the "realities" that are possible to learn in and through them.

In the novel and film versions, pretty much everyone sees the simulation as just an opportunity for further control, either economically or politically or even psychologically through the Operator's sadism. But Jinx sees it differently—perhaps because she has fallen in love. And it's this difference which seems crucial in opening up an understanding of what the virtual *could* do and the uses to which it *could* be put.

While the film versions shy away from such speculation, the novel's narrative keeps it open, particularly in a curious scene absent in both films. In the novel, fleeing the police, Doug temporarily finds refuge at a poetry reading, featuring "The Foremost Abstract Poetrycaster of Our Times—Ragir Rojasta." Donning a participation skullcap, Doug experiences a virtual reality of shifting sights and sounds, all focused around a few lines from Thomas Gray's "Elegy Written in a Country Churchyard" (1751):

> Full many a gem of purest ray serene,
> The dark, unforthom'd caves of ocean bear;
> Full many a flower is born to blush unseen,
> And waste its sweetness on the desert air [118].

What is seen, and what is not yet seen—these are crucial questions enabled and prompted by the experience of virtuality. During this virtual and aesthetic experience, Doug realizes that "[t]his entire world would have to be wiped clean so a new behavior-predicting simulectronic complex could be programmed" if it's revealed to the Controller that he and others know they are in a simulation (119). In the process, any creative, generative, or alternative possibilities stemming from the experience of virtuality would be lost.

The intrusion of the aesthetic here is a reminder that the virtual reality simulation could be put to other uses—not just control through behavior prediction. The unseen is both what isn't being paid attention to *now* in the simulation but also what *might yet occur* in the simulation if it's allowed to continue running. This version thus borders on what Ernst Bloch called utopian anticipatory consciousness.[6] Indeed, as Doug in the novel reminds us, "to Fuller [Simulacron] was an intriguing and promising doorway whose portals were soon to open on a new and better world" (10). Working with Siskin was never only a "financial expedient" since the real purpose of the virtual reality simulator "would also be fully exploring the unpredictable fields of social interactions and human relations as a means of suggesting a more orderly society, from the bottom up" (10). Even the simulation units want their own simulation "because they believe his simulator is going to transform their world" (157).

This vision suggests, to borrow from Ruth Levitas, a version of "utopia as method," or an approach to the possibilities of the virtual that doesn't see it necessarily as a form of control or, in the film versions, as ultimately competing with "real" life.[7] Virtuality is rather an epistemology itself worth exploring for what it might yet tell us. Curiously, queernesses in the original novel bring this possibility to light, with Doug and Jinx not only finding love in the virtual world but remaining committed to maintaining the virtual reality. José Esteban Muñoz argues that "queerness as utopian formation is a formation based on an economy of desire and desiring. This desire is always directed at that thing that is not yet here, objects and moments that burn with anticipation and promise."[8] It's worth asking at this point why later versions of this same story seem somewhat less invested in this queer utopian formation.

NOTES

1. *Welt am Draht* [*World on a Wire*] (Janus Films, 1973); *The Thirteenth Floor* (Columbia Pictures, 1999); *The Matrix* (Warner Brothers. 1999).
2. "*Simulacron-3*," Wikipedia, last edited July 29, 2018, at https://en.wikipedia.org/wiki/Simulacron-3.
3. Daniel F. Galouye, *Simulacron-3* (1964; Rockville, MD: Phoenix Pick, 1999), 9. Page references are to this edition.
4. Richard Swope, "Science Fiction Cinema and the Crime of Social-Spatial Reality," *Science Fiction Studies*, 29: 2 (July 2002), 221–246. Page references are to this edition.
5. Robert Markley, "Boundaries: Mathematics, Alienation, and the Metaphysics of Cyberspace," *Virtual Realities and Their Discontents*, edited by Markley (Baltimore, MD: Johns Hopkins University Press, 1996), 74.
6. See Ernst Bloch, *Literary Essays*, translated by Andrew Joron, Frank Mecklenburg, Helga Wild, and Jack Zipes (Stanford, CA: Stanford University Press, 1998).
7. See Ruth Levitas, *The Concept of Utopia* (Syracuse: Syracuse University Press, 1991).
8. José Esteban Muñoz, *Cruising Utopia: The Then and There of Queer Futurity* (New York: New York University Press, 2009), 26.

Millions Seek the Egg

Replicative Technofuturism in Ready Player One *and* Armada

Howard V. Hendrix

In "The Forever Child: *Ender's Game* and the Mythic Universe of Science Fiction" (1999), George Slusser contends that,

> As earlier myths extend human narratives to include natural forces and gods, sf defines itself as narrative through its central epic tropes of life extension and immortality. At this level, the science fiction narrative is less interested in the middle of *Bildung* and formation than in the extremes of beginning and end.[1]

When literary critics of—and writers in—science fiction get around to discussing the origin of the genre (which, concerned as we are with beginnings and ends, we eventually always do), we offer a number of dates and circumstances—Hugo Gernsback in 1926, Mary Shelley in 1818, Lucian of Samosata in the second century, the list goes on. While not specifically weighing in on the genre-origins question in his "Forever Child" essay, Slusser *does* describe Victor Frankenstein as "the [scientific] originator of sf's quest for bodily immortality" (88). Yet in this quest for origins, one can of course stray much further back in time than the early nineteenth century, or even the latter second century.

Noting Slusser's idea that, in the mythic universe of science fiction, "Death is deferred in the search for immortality," one can make a strong argument that the first science fiction story might as well be the almost-4000-year-old *Epic of Gilgamesh*, as Robert Silverberg does in his introduction to the 2013 re-issue of his 1984 novel *Gilgamesh the King* when he remarks that the Gilgamesh legend "must be the earliest science-fiction story still in existence, for surely the tale of a quest for an immortality serum qualifies as science fiction."[2]

One may quibble that Gilgamesh himself does not find an "immortality serum" but rather a plant that is presumed to provide immortality through rejuvenation—returning the eater of the plant, back and back, to his youth. Slusser's scientific "originator," Victor Frankenstein—in wanting not only to rejuvenate aged flesh but to reanimate the flesh of the deceased—goes a good deal further in *Frankenstein; or, The Modern Prometheus* (1818, 1831) than the plot of *Gilgamesh*, yet the impulse is the same: the preservation of something in the flesh that doesn't die, that is not merely mortal.

It is curious, therefore, that the final break between Victor and his creation occurs when Victor denies the female helpmate his "creature" insists Victor create—denies, in other words, his creation's demand for an Other with which to engage in procreation. This Victor does specifically on the grounds that the monstrous progeny of such reproduction might displace us humans from our lofty perch, at least, and perhaps drive us from the face of the Earth. (Think about our own cultural fears today, of self-reproducing robots, AI, synthetic life, and more.)

This Frankensteinian fear of being overwhelmed by replication and procreation—especially when coupled with the issue of longevity and immortality—brings up another, somewhat more recent specter that haunts science fiction, namely the "Malthusian specter" of overpopulation, including not only that of our "monstrous creations" but also our own (see Harry Harrison's 1966 novel *Make Room! Make Room!* for what is perhaps the most salient science fictional example).

Mary Wollstonecraft Shelley, author of *Frankenstein*, had much opportunity to be familiar, from a very young age, with issues of birth, death, procreation, overpopulation, and immortality—not only from her mother's writings and death soon after young Mary's birth, and Mary's already having lost a child before she wrote *Frankenstein* at age 18 but also because Mary's father, proto-anarchist writer and philosopher William Godwin, was one of those optimists on the future development of society against whom that supposedly "dismal" philosopher of economics, Thomas Malthus, had written his *Essay on the Principle of Population* (1798). The wranglings of the two men concerning population growth, scarcity, and humanity's economic future were a persistent background to Mary's formative years.[3]

The complexities of procreation and population, of birth and death, mortality and immortality that surrounded Mary Shelley's writing of *Frankenstein* have haunted science fiction from her day to ours. Silverberg provides a long list of immortality-themed works by twentieth century science fiction writers. In a note to his "Forever Child" essay, however, Slusser takes a different tack, calling our attention back and back again to beginnings, to what he calls "a wonderful description of birth as the Fall" in Ray Bradbury's story from *The October Country* entitled "The Small Assassin" (1946):

What is more at peace, more dreamfully content, at ease, at rest, fed, comforted, unbothered, than an unborn child? Nothing. It floats in a sleepy, timeless wonder of nourishment and silence. Then suddenly, it is asked to give up its berth, is forced to vacate, rushed out into a noisy, uncaring, selfish world where it is asked to shift for itself, to hunt, to feed … to seek after a vanishing love that was once its unquestionable right … and the child *resents* it [quoted in Slusser 90].

Although that quote powerfully tempts me to shift into full Lacanian overdrive, I'd like to juxtapose it, here, with this. Early in Ernest Cline's *Ready Player One* (2011) our protagonist Wade Watts (aka Parzival, his avatar "handle") remarks, "I gradually began to figure out that pretty much *everyone* had been lying to me about pretty much *everything* since the moment I emerged from my mother's womb."[4]

For Wade, the world, the big Other that birth introduced him to, seems a lie and a failure, or at least radically fails to live up to his hopes and expectations. His hope for sanity and truth lies in retreating from that world, into a self-contained secondary reality, the cybernetic pocket universe that is OASIS (Ontological Anthropocentric Sensory Immersive Simulation), "the magical place where anything was possible" (18). In the OASIS videogames have achieved their long-awaited apotheosis as virtuality. The videogame ceases to be an inadequate version of reality and reality instead becomes an inadequate version of the videogame. OASIS is that virtual "other place" less radical in its otherness than the Big Other of the Law of the Father. The OASIS virtuality is a more comforting and dreamful "matrix" (Latin for "womb," with all its hints of lost union with the mother).

As someone trained as a biologist, and following a hint from Baudrillard,[5] I'd like to suggest that Paradise was lost much, much earlier than our lapsarian expulsion from the pocket universe of the womb. Slusser writes of the transcendent power located in psychological regression—"from a genital stage to the 'archaic' preadolescent stages of anality and orality" (75)—and, after raising the issue of the Death-deferring immortality quest, in the very next line of his essay goes on to wonder, "But by the same token, might not birth also be retarded, in the sense that we prolong that moment of fall into the common day of formation that Wordsworth [in his *Intimations* ode] decried?" (74). Slusser's idea of endless deferral—of the power that comes from going back and back, from adolescence to childhood to the womb— drives Wade all the way back to the Egg in *Ready Player One*, and even that may be a couple billion years too recent.

Consider: The products of asexual reproduction via symmetric binary fission are identical and immortal so long as optimal growing conditions continue to supply their needs. The asexually reproducing "parent" cell is immortal in its potentially endless division into "daughter" cells identical to itself, a situation known to biologists as "replicative immortality"—also one of the hallmarks of cancer cells. In contrast, the products of procreation, of sexual reproduction via sperm and egg (gamete fusion), are genetically distinct and varying but also inherently mortal. Sexual reproduction allowed for the ingression, into genetic replication, of change and novelty in sectors ranging from size to intelligence, but at the cost of "replicative senescence," of aging and mortality at levels from cell to organism—George C. Williams's "antagonistic pleiotropy" writ large.[6] The advantageous carries the deleterious along with it.

Across innumerable iterations, evolution calculates, DNA performs risk/benefit analyses. T.B.L. Kirkwood's "disposable soma"[7] explanation for mortality illustrates this well: statistically speaking, the less likely it is that you're still alive at a certain age, the more likely it is that your genes no longer much care about you at that age; the more likely it is that your genes no longer much care about you at a certain age, the less likely it is that you're still alive at that age. Yes, the reasoning is circular, ouroboric, eating its own tail here, but that's less important than the fact of what can be learned through the process of traversing that circle.

More broadly, from the genetic trait's point of view, and from the perspective of the assemblage of genes we choose to call a species, high mortality rates and low fertility rates look virtually indistinguishable, as do low mortality rates and high fertility rates. This in part accounts for the dilemma that—for most populations of most species on a clearly finite Earth, and all other things being equal (a rarely observed condition)—longevity looks like a compromise between fertility and mortality rates, the crux point on the graph where the rate lines cross.

This is the primordial chiasmus, the X that marks the spot of the Fall in which we "sinned all"—in which we lost the immortal self-identity of asexual reproduction to the distinct mortalities inherent in sexual reproduction. This is the heart of our paradox, in that the paradise of immortality lost *to* procreation we seek to regain *through* procreation—via the sort of immortality provided through children. The result? The current global birthrate among humans (as measured by the number of live births per second) is significantly more than double the current global death rate among humans (as measured by the number of deaths per second).[8]

Yet, somewhere in our cells, we seem to remember that billions-years-lost immortal self-identity, or think we do, or at least feel nostalgia for such a thing. Following Lacan, Žižek, Edelman, and Ruti,[9] we can say, however, that to the extent that what's been lost is imaginary, that lost "thing" can only be reached for in other things, never grasped in itself. That lost imaginary thing's ultimate, unreachable replacement is the future itself, the future that (at least politically) is hypostatized in the figure of the child (Edelman 3, 115). That's why traditionally we "believe the children are our future," as the song

"The Greatest Love of All" (1977) says, despite the fact that that future always already only provides a "sort of" immortality, a "sort of" self-identity—immortality through the continuing reproduction of mortality, via progeny not quite self-identical to ourselves.

That song—"The Greatest Love of All," written by Linda Creed and Michael Masser and variously recorded by Shirley Bassey, George Benson, and Whitney Houston—is riven by the tensions outlined above, for although its first line and twenty fifth lines are "I believe the children are our future," it goes on to insist "I learned to depend on me" (line 10) and, repeatedly, claims "Learning to love yourself is the greatest love of all" (lines 23–24, 43–44). Alas, obsolescence and senescence are programmed into the genes of this self each of us most greatly loves. For mortal beings, the future necessarily implies death. Time to come is also always time to go. Death lives on Future Street. A few doors down from hope.

Those tensions bring us squarely to all those science fiction dreams of vastly increased longevity or even immortality in one's own flesh, or genetically self-identical posterity through cloning, or algorithmically self-identical posterity through uploading of human mind to vast machine or downloading to robotic bodies. These lattermost two (mind-uploading and robotic download) are ways in which geek fiction, despite swapping space helmet for 3D head-mounted display, continues science fiction's obsession with what I here—extending Edelman's idea of "reproductive futurism" (3) to include science fiction—will call "replicative technofuturism."

Fundamentally, this is the belief that human population growth and resource consumption can never outstrip technological progress—not even if consumption is amped up by population growth coupled to increasing birthrates and/or decreasing death rates. Replicative technofuturists like "optimistic economist" (and anti–Malthusian) Julian Simon[10] have asserted that (in a rare instance of synergistic pleiotropy) more conceptions in the flesh mean more conceptions of the mind, more geniuses for innovation and progress: boundless reproduction of human (or transhuman or posthuman) beings to people space and time, boundless production of goods, services, and information to use and consume, boundless accumulation of capital and wealth. Forward to the fantastic future forever!

To speak against such boundless optimism seems almost mean-spirited and miserly somehow, the sort of thing that might have been said by Ebenezer Scrooge who—before his great conversion to what Lee Edelman calls second fatherhood (47)—was a Dickensian avatar of Malthusianism. The pre-conversion Scrooge in *A Christmas Carol* (1843) says, among other things, "If [the poor and destitute] would rather die … they had better do it, and decrease the surplus population."[11] In Dickens's story commemorating the commemoration of Christ's birth, Scrooge, the lifelong bachelor and business partner of the late lifelong bachelor Jacob Marley, becomes "second father" (116) to Tiny Tim, but only after his Christmas night visions.

Similarly, in *Ready Player One*, the digital avatar of the late lifelong bachelor and videogaming genius James Halliday, co-creator of that world-wide multiplayer game/reality, the OASIS, ultimately serves as second father for the orphaned Wade Watts. Halliday's still-living but estranged business partner, the widowed Ogden Morrow, plays fairy godmother to Wade in his quest. Together Halliday and Morrow are described as a male pairing like "Jobs and Wozniak, or Lennon and McCartney" (53). Cline in *Ready Player One*, however, takes pains to point out that, perhaps unlike Scrooge, Halliday (although agoraphobic, socially maladroit, and Aspergerish) is definitely heterosexual. Halliday's estrangement from his business partner Morrow, we are told, is the result of his having lost Karen "Kira" Underwood, the secret love of Halliday's life, to that same business partner.

That more business-oriented partner, Og Morrow, marries but remains childless (more by accident than by choice). Throughout the novel's backstory, Morrow, having been primarily involved with his wife Kira in creating educational software and content for the OASIS, has taken the more traditionally "female" role of "rearing the next generation." Halliday, the better programmer of the two men, is the more solitarily masculine and Scrooge-like in the sense of being inward-turned, reclusive, the hoard-dragon, the Minotaur at the heart of his maze—and, although Halliday's mind has not literally been uploaded to OASIS (in the book, as opposed to the film), it is Halliday's mindset that is most clearly baked into that megamachine virtuality's algorithms.

For all the grandiloquence of that term "virtuality," virtual reality or VR is neither more nor less than CPU—not "central processing unit," but "cybernetic pocket universe." The globe-girdling OASIS, like the worldwide web and internet from which it is descended, is likewise a cyberspatial (and therefore potentially infinite) pocket universe, simultaneously both "smaller" than our physical world and "larger"—rather like the "It's bigger on the inside" Tardis of *Doctor Who*. The pocket universe is a popular trope in texts ranging from *Twilight Zone* episodes to Dr. Seuss's *Horton Hears a Who!* (1954) but the most important early science fictional version of the (pre-cyber) "pocket universe" concept can be found in Theodore Sturgeon's 1941 novelette "Microcosmic God." The novelette features another male technological pairing— the brilliant scientist Kidder and eminently capable engineer Johansen who, like Morrow and Halliday in the OASIS, are ghosts in the shell. Unlike the user interface "shell" of the OASIS in *Ready Player One*, however, the "shell" in "Microcosmic God" is literal: an impenetrable miraculous gray shell invented by the Neoterics, the race of "little people" push-evolved by Kidder.

Like Kidder and Johansen or Scrooge and Marley, the widowed Morrow and the deceased Halliday are equally childless in the biological sense—but together Halliday and Morrow have achieved a remarkable replicative tech-nofuturist feat. Their posterity is not genetic, but algorithmic. The OASIS built by the two men, like many another cyberpunk "matrix," is a phallic womb. A more comprehensible/less Otherly digital reification of the law of the father, the OASIS functions very much like that "second womb" of patri-archal culture through which the quester-initiate is "born again" *from males*. The hunt for Halliday's Easter egg echoes both puberty initiation rites for the egg hunters and, for the system's creators, couvade (the cultural custom of an adult male counterpart to pregnancy, confinement and "labor," particularly in expectant fathers, surrounding the time of the woman's actually giving birth, and which may be a cultural sign of male parturition envy).

Male birthing (and self-birthing) similarly figures in Slusser's compar-ison of Robert Heinlein's character Lazarus Long and Orson Scott Card's character Ender:

> Though called an "ender," his power in fact comes from never beginning, from end-lessly deferring the move into the light of common day. Where Lazarus controls the conscious realm of his [paternal] final cause, Ender probes the mystery of the uncon-scious maternal first cause.... In becoming [the lost mother's] "guardian," Ender relo-cates the child *before* the mother [88].

That such a reading should apply not only to Card's *Ender's Game* (1985) but also to Cline's texts *Ready Player One* and *Armada* (2015) should not surprise us. Cline readily acknowledges his special debt to Card and Card's work not only by name but also by plot points. *Armada*, in particular, is a book that, in its closing chapters, reads increasingly like the love child of Card's *Ender's Game* and a stripped down version of Homer's *Odyssey*.

Cline goes his literary precursors one better, however, and not just by "solving" in *Armada* the problem of miscommunication with the alien that figures so prominently in the novel of *Ender's Game*—or by just simplifying the *Odyssey*'s long-absent-father dynamic (of the Odysseus/Penelope/Tele-machus triad) into the Xavier Ulysses Lightman/Pamela Lightman/ Zackary Ulysses Lightman family dynamic of *Armada*. No, the most important way in which Cline, in both *Ready Player One* and *Armada*, goes his literary pre-cursors one better involves an egg, in each case.

In *Armada*, Pamela and Xavier Ulysses don't just have joyous long-deferred reunion sex like Penelope and Odysseus do in the *Odyssey*. Although Xavier Ulysses Lightman may not be the Bowman that Odysseus is, he undeniably plays Mister Sure-Shot to Pamela's Mrs. Target, in that the Lightmans' ecstatic one-nighter—sandwiched into the plot space between their reunion and Xavier Ulysses Lightman's death while "sav[ing] humanity from total annihila-tion" (348)—precipitates in Pamela's pregnancy and, later, the birth of Xavier Ulysses Lightman, Jr., Zackary Ulysses Lightman's much younger brother.

The egg at the end of Xavier Ulysses Senior's Night Sea Journey is thus encountered "offstage" in *Armada*, but it's center stage in *Ready Player One*. Cline goes Card one better in that the power that comes from going back and back Cline here pushes all the way back to the egg—to Halliday's Egg and its treasures, the goal of the myriads of egg hunters or "gunters" participating in the Easter Egg Hunt. Travelling inside the matrix of OASIS and through the ordeal of the game, the gunters seek the Easter Egg, the male ovum symbolic of both James Halliday's legacy and Jesus Christ's resurrection (talk about the child before the mother!), to (yes, like sperm) fertilize the Egg's promise of re-birth and resurrection—and incidentally win the Egg's treasures, including Halliday's fortune of a quarter of a trillion dollars.

All this Parzival/Wade achieves, but only after proving himself individualistic white knight (who has nonetheless learned to play well with others) and true vassal to Halliday and Morrow's "good-parent" megacorporation, Gregarious Simulation Systems (GSS, an intriguing homophone for "Jesus"). Not only does Parzival/Wade defeat in single combat dark-knight usurper Nolan Sorrento, leader of the faceless corporate Sixer-hacks of "bad-parent" megacorporation Innovative Online Industries (IOI, 1-0-1) but also, after Wade's avatar Parzival is killed by IOI machinations, Parzival/Wade's Messianic nature is further underlined by Parzival's being literally resurrected, the only player in the game to have won the "extra life" quarter during the course of his quest. The friendly takeover of Halliday and Morrow's megacorporation by Wade Watts—true son and subsidiary of parent corporation GSS—could hardly stand in starker contrast to the potential "outside" hostile takeover of GSS by Sorrento and IOI. Still more stark, however, is the vision of the future suggested by this situation, namely that the only real "freedom of choice" we have is which megacorporation we choose to align ourselves with.

The nature of the Easter Egg Hunt in *Ready Player One* provides proof for Slusser's contention that, at the mythic level, science fiction narrative is less interested in the middle of *Bildung* (self-cultivation, formation, maturation) than in the extremes of beginning and end. The vast videogame of the Easter Egg Hunt is designed by James Halliday in his final years, but to win the game in the 2040s a gunter must become radically familiar with the beloved popular culture of Halliday's first years, his childhood and youth, particularly the 1980s.

Hallidayan pop culture and the history of videogaming, in this context, serve as stand-ins for the cultural collective and for history itself. As the "second womb" of culture from which the quester-initiate Wade/Parzival is "born again," the cybernetic pocket universe OASIS is womb with room enough for the second birth of all Earth's billions—Halliday's children. Yet the full riches of that second birth from culture and father, after the first birth from nature and mother, can be grasped only by our hero, for only Wade has managed to penetrate to the heart of the Egg and re-father himself by identifying so thoroughly with the womb-world OASIS's father/creator that Wade is able to make possible not only his own rebirth, but also that of the world.

The snake eats its tail here. Halliday's fictional Egg Hunt in *Ready Player One* begins with the historical fact of the first videogame Easter egg, the words "Created by Warren Robinett" hidden inside a secret room that Robinett covertly programmed into the Atari game *Adventure* (1979). Finding Robinett's grey pixel dot Easter egg for the first time was, as Halliday puts it, "one of the coolest videogaming experiences of my life" (5)—the book's "Rosebud," from which all things come and to which they all return.

By the time Wade obtains Halliday's egg, the Easter egg is no longer Robinett's grey pixel dot but a silver (not the movie's golden) egg. In Greek Orphic mythology the silver cosmic egg, created by Time/Aion, is the orb out of which bursts Phanes, the "first born," ouroboric deity of light and divinity of procreation. Once Parzival/Wade places this silver egg into a perfectly size-matched and extremely Holy Grail–like golden chalice—thereby completing a conjoint symbol of both procreation and immortality—a fanfare sounds. All of Halliday's powers and treasures are transferred to Wade, who also becomes the new Anorak, god of this cybernetic pocket universe. (Less so in the film, with both child and aged Halliday still in frame, like David Bowman's *2001* apotheoses.)

Wade/Parzival now also becomes the only person whose avatar can access the secret room that is the Easter egg *inside* Halliday's Easter egg *inside* the OASIS—the holiest of holies that houses the Big Red Button that will launch the worm to shut down the OASIS forever, if Wade judges it necessary to do so in order to save humanity, by returning it, cold-turkey, from virtuality to reality.

In *Armada* the retreat from the Big Other is still more desperate. Zack fears he will go crazy like his father and succumb to his father's conspiracy theory of history: namely, that there is an Other of the Big Other, an alien invasion that is being covered up by those in the know, those behind the curtain, who are pulling the strings of the great social puppet-show. This problem is solved when Zack—a great videogamer like his father—learns that what Zack thought was his father's conspiracy theory of history is in fact the true secret history of the preceding fifty years. The pocket universe this time is the matrix of conspiracy theory, the covert network of bases and actions of the Earth Defense Alliance, that the world as a whole only learns of when the "aliens" (who mirror our culture) actually arrive, as part of a grand test that will determine humanity's future.

The development of videogames, it turns out, has been secretly arranged to train warriors to fight the aliens. As Zack notes soon after being swept up and away into the Earth Defense Alliance:

We hadn't used up all of our oil and ravaged our planet in a mindless pursuit of consumerism, but in preparation for a dark day that most of us hadn't even known was coming. Even humanity's lack of concern for its rampant overpopulation problem now made a terrible kind of sense. What difference did it make if our planet was capable of supporting all seven billion of us in the long term when a far greater threat was waiting in the wings? And despite the overwhelming odds, humanity had done what was necessary to ensure its survival.[12]

The parallel to this passage in *Ready Player One* occurs when Parzival/Wade is asked by his cybercrush Art3mis/Samantha what he plans to do with Halliday's vast fortune in the event that he, Wade, wins. His answer—"have a nuclear powered interstellar spacecraft constructed in Earth's orbit," fully stock it with everything he might want, "get the hell out of Dodge" and "start looking for an extrasolar Earthlike planet" (97–98)—is juxtaposed to Art3mis's answer—that she's "going to make sure everyone on [Earth] has enough to eat," then "figure out how to fix the environment and solve the energy crisis" (98).

In *Ready Player One*, our hero wins in virtual reality but ultimately decides to return to reality, along with the fortune he is dividing up with his three friends, to face the challenges there. The egg-and-chalice completion of the game foreshadows Wade's own potential role as avatar of Phanes, god of procreation. His exit from the OASIS into the real is potentially the end of his endless deferral, his being born again into the light of common day— including the reality of his budding affair with Samantha/Art3mis, his longtime avatar love-interest, and their implied future of procreation.

Implied, but not yet realized, as is also the case in *Armada*.

True journey is return to the real, but in *Armada* the conspiracy theory matrix ceases to be an inadequate version of history and, instead, history becomes an inadequate version of the conspiracy theory matrix. Humanity, having passed its test from the alien Emissary, is showered with gifts and fixes by the alien federation called the Sodality. All humanity's problems— including the longevity/population dilemma—turn out to be non-problems in the face of the Sodality's hyper-advanced technology. Curiously, however, Zack Lightman in the end remains skeptical of the seemingly too-good-to-be-true alien advent, having seen history displaced once already by conspiracy theory.

This skepticism is understandable. The books and their main characters, like humanity itself, all stand in the gap between the "dismal" (and too simplistic) economics of population growth promulgated by Thomas Malthus, and the "optimistic" (and too simplistic) economics of technological panacea promulgated by Julian Simon. This may be why, for the long-orphaned but second-fathered Wade/Parzival and the mostly fatherless (but briefly father-son reunited) Zackary Ulysses—the virgin heroes of *Ready Player One* and

Armada, respectively—for them, the reality of procreation, even of sexual intercourse, like the solution to the longevity/population dilemma or the believability of that solution, is still always already deferred to after the end of each book, and before the beginning.

NOTES

1. George Slusser, "The Forever Child: *Ender's Game* and the Mythic Universe of Science Fiction," *Nursery Realms: Children in the Worlds of Science Fiction, Fantasy, and Horror*, edited by Gary Westfahl and Slusser (Athens: University of Georgia Press, 1999), 74. Page references are to this edition.

2. Robert Silverberg, *Gilgamesh the King* (1984; New York: Open Road Integrated Media, 2013), xiii.

3. See particularly Maureen Noelle McLane's "Literate Species: Populations, 'Humanities,' and *Frankenstein*," *ELH*, 63:4 (Winter, 1996), 959–988.

4. Ernest Cline, *Ready Player One* (New York: Broadway Books, 2011), 16. Page references are to this edition.

5. See Jean Baudrillard's "The Final Solution, or the Revenge of the Immortals" in his essay collection *Impossible Exchange*, translated by Chris Turner (London: Verso, 2001), 26–39.

6. For the full initial rendition of the "antagonistic pleiotropy" concept, see George C. Williams's "Pleiotropy, Natural Selection, and the Evolution of Senescence," *Evolution: International Journal of Organic Evolution*, 11:4 (December 1957), 398–411. Available at https://doi.org/10.1111/j.1558-5646.1957.tb02911.x

7. For the full initial rendition of the "disposable soma" theory (much more than my thumbnail summary here), see T.B.L. Kirkwood's "Evolution of Ageing," *Nature*, 270 (November 24, 1977), 301–304.

8. From "World Birth and Death Rates." Ecology Global Network, January 5, 2016, www.ecology.com/birth-death: "Sources: *Population Reference Bureau* & *The World Factbook* (Central Intelligence Agency)."

9. Regarding Jacques Lacan, I am indebted to the discussion of the sinthome in Paul Verhaeghe and Frédéric Declercq's "Lacan's Analytical Goal: Le Sinthome or the Feminine Way" in *Re-Inventing the Symptom: Essays on the Final Lacan*, edited by Luke Thurston (New York: The Other Press, 2002), 59–83. Regarding Slavoj Žižek, see the film *Slavoj Žižek: Signs from the Future*, a recording of his presentation in Zagreb at the "2012 Subversive Forum: The Future of Europe," available at https://www.youtube.com/watch?v=pOTufvP9-6U. Regarding Lee Edelman's elaborations on Lacan and Žižek and his concept of "reproductive futurism" and its political role, I am indebted to Edelman's *No Future: Queer Theory and the Death Drive* (Durham: Duke University Press, 2004); Edelman page references are to this edition. That Edelman only mentions science fiction tangentially in a footnote in his text led me to extend and amplify Edelman's approach to encompass what I have here called replicative technofuturism. For Mari Ruti's responses to Žižek and Edelman and her re-inscriptions of Lacan I am indebted to *The Singularity of Being: Lacan and the Immortal Within* (New York: Fordham University Press, 2012).

10. Of his many books, see particularly Simon's *The Ultimate Resource* (Second Edition, Princeton: Princeton University Press, 1996), *Hoodwinking the Nation* (New Brunswick, NJ: Transaction Press, 1999), and *The Ultimate Resource 2* (Princeton: Princeton University Press, 1998).

11. Charles Dickens, *A Christmas Carol* (1843; New York: Hodder and Stoughton, 1911), 18. Page references are to this edition.

12. Cline, *Armada* (New York: Broadway Books, 2015), 101.

PART TWO

The Business
of Science Fiction

Science Fiction

The Age of Perspective

Gary K. Wolfe

In his 1979 study *The World of Science Fiction: The History of a Subculture*, Lester del Rey identified what he called the "five ages of science fiction": the "Age of Wonder" from 1926–1937, the "Golden Age" from 1938–1949, the "Age of Acceptance" from 1950–1961, the "Age of Rebellion" from 1962–1973, and the "Fifth Age" from 1974 until the appearance of his book. Del Rey's historical survey is of course now quite dated, covering a little over a half-century of a genre which—even if we date its beginnings as a commercial genre from the launching of Hugo Gernsback's *Amazing Stories* in 1926—passed its ninetieth birthday in 2016, and del Rey's approach was somewhat parochial even in 1979, although it remains of interest by offering the perspective of a major author whose career spanned much of that history.

Yet his formulation represented a kind of consensus history of the field in the 20th century, which has been echoed in various forms in later histories ranging from Brian W. Aldiss and David Wingrove's *Trillion Year Spree: The History of Science Fiction* (1986) to Edward James's *Science Fiction in the 20th Century* (1994) and Adam Roberts's *History of Science Fiction* (2006, revised 2016), even though each of these studies took a considerable broader and deeper view of the field's history and prehistory. Roberts, for example, doesn't even arrive at the twentieth century until Chapter Eight (which considers "high modernists" like Karel Čapek, Evgeny Zamiatin, and Olaf Stapledon), and only beginning in Chapter Nine—halfway through the book—does he discuss the post–1926 era which was the whole of del Rey's formulation. But then his periods begin to look familiar: the pulp era of the 1920s and 1930s, the "Golden Age" of 1940–1960, the "New Wave" and post–New Wave era of the 1960s and 1970s. After that, he rather abandons labels in the face of the genre's growing diversification and multimedia impact, titling one chapter simply "Prose Science Fiction 1970s–1990s." He does discuss the cyberpunk movement of the 1980s and a few not-easily-classifiable writers such as Gene Wolfe and Octavia E. Butler. Other critics and scholars have identified additional post–1980s movements, such as the "humanists" of the 1980s and 1990s and the "New Space Opera" of the 1990s and early 2000s, but in general, the rapid diversification (some might even say balkanization) of the field over the past twenty years, along with its growing interpenetration with related genres such as horror and fantasy, has resisted the kind of simplistic labeling of eras that del Rey posited nearly forty years ago.

Nevertheless, it is just such a simplistic labeling which I am proposing here, in arguing that the current period of science fiction might well be termed the Age of Perspective. Much of what I'm about to say is implicit in recent histories of the field by Roberts, Roger Luckhurst, Mike Ashley, and others, going all the way back to Aldiss and del Rey, so in a sense this is an exercise in synthesis rather than effort to build a new historical paradigm. I'm not trying to suggest that each of these different periods *replaces* the preceding one, but rather builds upon it by introducing a newer angle of vision, shared by a significant number of writers. As always, there will be outliers— writers who anticipate later developments, sometimes by decades, and writers who cheerfully and unironically hearken back to earlier eras. There will also be many works that seem to fit into two or more of these eras. But one problem with these earlier proposals for the different stages of science fiction and fantasy history is that they conflate radically different ways of measuring literary history. Some "eras" are labeled by modes of publication (pulp magazines, paperbacks), some by developing markets (such as the rise of the full-length science fiction novel in the 1950s), some by the influence of particular editors (Gernsback, John W. Campbell, Jr., Michael Moorcock), some by writers' manifestoes (cyberpunk, with its chief theorist Bruce Sterling, or the rise of feminist science fiction under the influence of Joanna Russ or Ursula K. Le Guin), some driven by nostalgia (such as ideas of the "golden age"), some by shifting and broadening demographics of readers and writers (such as current discussions of the field's growing diversity in terms of gender and culture). In formulating the various eras which I propose to describe, I want to briefly revisit the last century or so of sf history from a slightly different perspective—not in terms of themes, techniques, major writers or editors, or publishing venues, but rather in terms of how the genre talks to itself, what readers come to expect, and how writers seek to build on what has gone before. Broadly, then, these eras describe what readers and writers were *thinking about* as they defined the science fiction of their particular era.

Let me begin with the present Age of Perspective by mentioning a few recent stories and novels. In 2010, Peter Watts, one of our more formidable practitioners of biological hard sf, published a story in *Clarkesworld* titled "The Things." It's told from the point of view of an alien—a self-described "explorer, an ambassador, a missionary"—whose spacecraft crash lands on Earth, near what we quickly recognize as an Antarctic research station.[1] A kind of hive mind which sees all biomass as interchangeable, it's rather amazed at the individual biological units which it encounters and which it eventually inhabits—units with names like MacReady, Blair, Copper, and Childs. If we had any doubt as to what Watts is doing here, those character names, taken directly from John Carpenter's 1982 film *The Thing*, and before that of the 1951 film *The Thing (from Another World)* and before *that* of John W. Campbell, Jr.'s famous 1938 story "Who Goes There?" make it quite clear: Watts is essentially retelling the story—mostly the Carpenter version—from the perspective of the Thing itself (with apologies to Immanuel Kant).

Six years later, the young writer Sam J. Miller published, again in *Clarkesworld*, "Things with Beards," which he himself described as a "fanfic sequel" to Carpenter's movie.[2] It concerns the main human character, MacReady, surviving his earlier experience and now dealing with the AIDS epidemic and police brutality in his own community—all the while wondering if he himself is a Thing, a kind of alien observer. Even chronologically, the 1980s setting suggests the events of the story were concurrent with the release date of Carpenter's film.

Something similar has been going on in horror fiction. In 2016, the same year as Miller's story, Victor LaValle published the novella *The Ballad of Black Tom*, which re-imagines H.P. Lovecraft's 1927 "The Horror at Red Hook," long notorious as one of his most vitriolic and racist stories, from the point of view of a black con man and bad musician who gets involved with some of Lovecraft's more eldritch supernatural figures. Also that same year, Kij Johnson published "The Dream Quest of Vellitt Boe," a reworking of Lovecraft's "The Dream-Quest of Unknown Kadath" (1943), but featuring a woman protagonist (and a middle-aged one at that) of the sort so noticeably absent from Lovecraft's own work. Less than a year later, Ruthanna Emrys reworked parts of Lovecraft's "The Shadow over Innsmouth"(1936) from the point of view of one the fish-like inhabitants of Innsmouth, who are treated as unspeakable horrors in Lovecraft's original, but who become victims in Emrys's tale. I could go on at length about the many other aspects of what we might call the Lovecraft Rebuild, which has been going on for the past few years, but I chose these examples because they each respond to a specific earlier story, essentially reinventing it by shifting the narrative perspective.

Moving over to fantasy for a moment, Kij Johnson's name comes up again, with 2017's *The River Bank*, a kind of sequel to Kenneth Grahame's *The Wind in the Willows* (1908), but again introducing female characters, as well as some themes of class and privilege, that were notably invisible in

Grahame's original. Also in 2017, two debut novels offered new perspectives on Victorian-era classics. Molly Tanzer revisited Oscar Wilde's *The Picture of Dorian Gray* (1890) in her debut novel *Creatures of Will and Temper*, but with Dorian transformed into the provincial teenager Dorina Gray and Lord Henry Wotton gender-shifted into Henrietta Wotton. Theodora Goss, in *The Strange Case of the Alchemist's Daughter*, created a kind of league of extraordinary women out of the female survivors of the stories of Robert Louis Stevenson's *Strange Case of Dr. Jekyll and Mr. Hyde* (1886) Mary Shelley's *Frankenstein; or, The Modern Prometheus* (1818, 1831), H.G. Wells's *The Island of Doctor Moreau* (1896), and Nathaniel Hawthorne's "Rappaccini's Daughter" (1844). The sequel, *European Travel for the Monstrous Gentlewoman*, appeared in 2018 and re-envisions still more figures from Victorian fiction, including Bram Stoker's *Dracula* (1897) and Sheridan Le Fanu's *Carmilla* (1871, 1872).

Now, all of this could easily be dismissed as a sudden outbreak of "fanfic," the sort of fan-generated fiction often written simply to celebrate favorite stories or authors, but I think something much broader is happening. If we widen the discussion to include works that revisit long-familiar tropes, and not just specific works, the number of possible titles increases dramatically. Rivers Solomon's debut novel from 2017, *An Unkindness of Ghosts*, will strike many veteran sf readers as a variation on the familiar generation starship tale, and some elements of it even recall the most famous early example of the form, Robert A. Heinlein's "Universe," from the May 1941 issue of Campbell's *Astounding Science-Fiction*. As in Heinlein's tale, the main character, Aster, befriends a young renegade who knows secret passages around the ship and dramatically reveals to her the stars as seen only from a forbidden upper deck. The actual management of the ship has been largely reduced to superstitious ritual, but old documents may reveal forgotten details about the real nature of the journey. I have no idea if Solomon was familiar with Heinlein's old story—though I rather doubt it—but at least some familiarity with the generation-ship tradition seems evident. What lends the novel its considerable power, however, is that the protagonist Aster is a neuroatypical if highly competent figure, and the social divisions aboard the ship itself are a brutal and blatant analogue of racism, slavery, and economic inequality.

Other examples abound. Kameron Hurley described her 2017 novel *The Stars Are Legion* as a traditional space opera, which it is, except that there are no male characters at all. Catherynne Valente actually titled her 2018 novel *Space Opera*, but it's less a homage to the classic space opera tradition than to Douglas Adams's *The Hitchhiker's Guide to the Galaxy* (1979) and to—of all things—the annual Eurovision song contest. Nnedi Okorafor's *Lagoon* (2014) is in many ways a familiar invasion of Earth scenario, with the aliens landing offshore from a major city, but the city is Lagos, Nigeria, and the culture that initially confronts the aliens is the complex society of Nigeria—as well as, bizarrely, such nonhuman viewpoints as a swordfish, a bat, a tarantula, and a spider. Lavie Tidhar's *Central Station* (2016, based largely on stories published earlier) depicts a giant spaceport located in a far-future metropolis, but the metropolis in question is Tel Aviv, and the political environment surrounding the station invokes some classic issues of Israeli culture and history. Future space programs are mounted by Nigeria in Deji Bryce Olukotun's *After the Flare* and by the Czech Republic in Jaroslav Kalfar's *Spaceman of Bohemia* (both 2017).

What all these and many other works have in common is not only that they address earlier works or traditions, but that they do so from particular perspectives that were largely absent from those traditions, whether they involve culture, gender, sexual orientation, class, or even species. Of course, there have always been science fiction and fantasy works which respond to earlier works—as Samuel R. Delany once noted, one could build a small shelf of responses to Heinlein's *Starship Troopers* (1959), from his own *Fall of the Towers* trilogy (1963–1965) to works by Harry Harrison, Joe Haldeman, and others. In this sense, science fiction has always been in dialogue with itself, but my argument is that this issue of new, reversed, or shifting perspectives represents a particular *kind* of dialogue, and one that is especially significant to the present moment in the history of the genre. This is why I'm labeling this present era as the Age of Perspective.

But how does this build upon and relate to earlier eras of science fiction's development, and why do I think it's a logical outgrowth of those eras? In order to answer that question, we need to ask the same question of earlier periods: what were the authors thinking about (apart from the obvious concerns of what they could sell to editors), and how did the genre express itself rhetorically? Given these questions, here is my list of seven successive periods or eras or ages of sf, deliberate cast as a version of del Rey's old formulation. (A few historical-minded readers may recognize that some of these labels are also borrowed from an old series of Mentor paperback anthologies on the history of philosophy.)

- The Age of Adventure, from the early pulps through the height of pulp fiction popularity in the 1930s;
- The Age of Reason, or what is sometimes referred to as the Golden Age or the Campbell era—or what Roger Luckhurst refers to as the "engineer paradigm" in his *Science Fiction* (2005)[3];
- The Age of Irony, or the development of more skeptical social or satirical themes in the 1950s and later;
- The Age of Style, or the growth of modernist or postmodernist techniques during the period of the New Wave and after;
- The Age of Attitude, or a shift toward street sensibilities and

more hardboiled character paradigms in cyberpunk and its offshoots;
- The Age of Complexity, characterized by narratives of enormous scale—multivolume novels, extensively recomplicated series, and ambitious, planned future histories;
- Finally, the Age of Perspective, which is what I am terming the present moment.

The Age of Adventure

The first age, then, was simply the age of adventure, with fiction ranging from Edgar Rice Burroughs and the Munsey authors to E.E. "Doc" Smith, Edmond Hamilton, the early Jack Williamson, and the first great period of classic, galaxy-busting space operas. I might well have called this the Age of Excess, since as Adam Roberts wrote of Doc Smith, "The extravagance and excess is, in an important sense, the *whole* of Smith's space adventure tales."[4] This is not, to put it mildly, a period of conscientious verisimilitude. Burroughs may have borrowed a few of Percival Lowell's ideas about Mars and seemed aware of Mars's gravity and thin atmosphere, but showed little interest in thinking these ideas through, beyond the extent to which they provided John Carter with his comic-book-like superpowers. Certainly, many of the classic tropes were laid out during this era, from interstellar travel to super-weapons, mad scientists, telepathy, galactic empires, alien civilizations, etc.—but all were viewed almost exclusively as devices for the ever-increasing scale and melodrama of what Roberts described as "fantasies of ... empowerment."

But even relatively early in the pulp era, some editors and writers began to suspect that some of these ideas might be worth examining *as ideas* rather than as enabling devices for ever-expanding fantasies of scale. In 1933, *Astounding* editor F. Orlin Tremaine introduced a policy of including in each issue what he called "thought-variant" stories. The early examples, such as Nat Schachner's "Ancestral Voices" (1933) or Donald Wandrei's "Colossus" (1934) weren't exactly examples of rigorous extrapolation, but they helped lay the groundwork for the next era. Charles Hornig, the editor at *Wonder Stories,* adopted a similar idea, which led most famously to Stanley Weinbaum's classic "A Martian Odyssey" in 1934. But the most important development was John W. Campbell, Jr., assuming the editorship of *Astounding* in 1937, first introducing whole issues of what he called "mutant" science fiction, deliberately signaling new directions in sf, and of course eventually collaborating in developing a new, more analytical approach to how sf would treat its ideas, through the fiction of Heinlein, Isaac Asimov, A.E. van Vogt, and others. Since Campbell, starting in 1938, titled the monthly feature in which readers would vote on their favorite stories "The Analytical Laboratory," it seemed reasonable to call this era, not the Golden Age, but perhaps the Age of Analysis, or the Age of Reason, which matches one of the titles in those old Mentor philosophy paperbacks.

The Age of Reason

Virtually all histories of science fiction recognize the role Campbell, Heinlein, Asimov, and others played in bringing some of science fiction's favorite themes into the arena of rational speculation, and Campbell's sometimes wobbly insistence on scientific verisimilitude. Just looking at some of the most familiar titles from the late 1930s and early 1940s gives some sense of the new emphasis on evidence-based extrapolation: Asimov's "Trends" (1939), "Reason" (1941), and "Evidence" (1946); Heinlein's "Common Sense" (1941) and "If This Goes On—" (1940); Hal Clement's "Proof" (1942) and "Technical Error" (1944); and so on. Of course, classic space opera continued to appear side by side with these more analytical tales; the serialization of Doc Smith's *Gray Lensman* was by far the most popular item in the "Analytical Laboratory" for October 1939, while van Vogt's rollercoaster plots hardly seemed as disciplined as Campbell might have called for; but even van Vogt, for all his appeal to the supermen and invincible alien fantasies of the earlier pulp era, made some effort to establish at least quasi-credible rationales for the aliens in "Black Destroyer" and "Discord in Scarlet" (both 1939) through an invented science he called Nexialism. My point is that this new period didn't replace or even fully displace the space opera form, but rather added to it a layer of reason, analysis, and rational social and technological extrapolation. Even more complex social, economic, and political layers would be added a few decades later, with what came to be called the New Space Opera.

The Age of Irony

There were, of course, some serious fault lines in the Age of Reason, and some of them could be laid at the feet of Campbell himself, with his serial passions for pseudoscientific notions like psionics, the Hieronymus Machine, the Dean Drive, and most famously L. Ron Hubbard's Dianetics. Campbell was, or at least pretended to be, a hard-headed rationalist, demanding stringently logical futures of both scientific and social verisimilitude, but on the other hand, he was fatally attracted to the impossibilities of fantasy, even to the point of starting an alternative magazine, *Unknown*, to accommodate the good story ideas his authors came up with that couldn't fit his vision of *Astounding*. But even that magazine often tried to reclaim fantasy's impossibilities for sf, such as Jack Williamson's "Darker Than You Think" (1940), with its rather contorted ethnological explanation for werewolves, or Eric Frank Russell's *Sinister Barrier* (1939), with its appeal to Charles Fort's almost anti-scientific view of anomalous phenomena. Oddly, though, when ideas of telepathy or other psychic powers showed up in the work of van Vogt and others, they were more likely to appear in *Astounding* rather than *Unknown*.

One reason for this may be that when Campbell briefly attended Duke University, a faculty member there named J.B. Rhine had already set up his laboratory to investigate ESP, telekinesis, and the like, so it's entirely possible Campbell could have gotten the notion that there was some sort of science behind ESP on the basis of those experiments, which later turned out to be thoroughly unreplicable. As a student at Duke, Campbell apparently met Rhine and participated briefly and unsuccessfully in his experiments with "reading" the cards used in ESP tests,[5] so there were plenty of notable blind spots in his championing of reason and scientific methodology. (Andy Duncan's story "New Frontiers of the Mind" in the July 2018 issue of *Analog Science Fiction/Science Fact* fictionalized this encounter between Campbell and Rhine.)

Quite apart from Campbell's apparent blind spots, more and more writers began to see a darker underside to the rationalizable futures of Heinlein or Asimov. Jack Williamson—perhaps one of the most adaptable writers the genre has ever seen, starting his career in those large-scale space operas—darkly answered Asimov's robots with his Humanoids in "With Folded Hands" (*Astounding*, July 1947). Writers as varied as Frederik Pohl, C.M. Kornbluth, Robert Sheckley, and even Ray Bradbury and Kurt Vonnegut, Jr., discovered profound ironies in the odd mix of the postwar consumerist culture, nuclear anxiety, and McCarthyist threats to free speech, resulting in works as varied as Pohl and Kornbluth's *The Space Merchants*(1953), Vonnegut's *The Sirens of Titan* (1959), Bradbury's *Fahrenheit 451* (1953), and even more or less mainstream parodies of science fiction themes in novels like Bernard Wolfe's *Limbo* (1952) and films like *Dr. Strangelove, or How I Learned to Stop Worrying and Love the Bomb* (1964). Stylistically, though, the writers from within the ranks of sf tended to present these darker visions in the same sort of efficient, transparent prose that had become the de facto standard during the Campbell era, with a few important exceptions such as Bradbury, Sturgeon, and Cordwainer Smith (Paul Linebarger). The shift in sensibility during the 1950s and 1960s for the most part didn't quite seemed matched by a similar shift in style or presentation, so the stage was set for the next phase, in which the very language and narrative structure of sf stories were reinvented—at least in the minds of some of the New Wave practitioners.

The Age of Style

In their editorials, earlier editors like Gernsback and Campbell had presented what amounted to manifestoes for the kind of fiction they wanted to see, Gernsback focusing largely on the idea of science fiction itself, Campbell on a more credible, realistic approach to the fiction that had dominated sf pulps in the 1930s. But perhaps the most famous call to revolution was that presented by Michael Moorcock in his first editorial in *New Worlds*. The previous editor, John Carnell, had already published several of the authors who would later be associated with Britain's New Wave, such as J.G. Ballard and Brian W. Aldiss, but when Carnell recommended the young Moorcock for the editorship of the then-fading magazine, Moorcock quickly made it a platform for his promise of a renaissance of style in science fiction writing. The model for that renaissance, celebrated in an essay by J.G. Ballard in Moorcock's first issue, was the controversial and deliberately transgressive work of William S. Burroughs, the American author whose experimental forms, including hallucinatory celebrations of drug culture, had gained notoriety mostly through the publication of *Naked Lunch* in 1959. Only a few years later, Burroughs's 1964 novel *Nova Express* looked enough like the new model of science fiction to earn a nomination for a Nebula Award from the Science Fiction Writers of America.

But the emerging emphasis on style wasn't confined to the self-consciously literary experiments of Ballard, Aldiss, Barrington J. Bayley, and others in England. American writers like Harlan Ellison, Roger Zelazny, Samuel R. Delany, Joanna Russ, and Thomas M. Disch had established reputations based in large part on the stylistic innovations they had already brought to the field—Ellison's street-smart, deliberately confrontational prose, Zelazny's rhapsodic flights, Delany's sophisticated linguistic borrowings from modernism, and so forth. Ellison may have disavowed the term New Wave in his famous *Dangerous Visions* anthologies (though he did embrace *nouvelle vague*, as though the term were OK as long as it was in French), but it was clear that he was inviting authors to submit work that was stylistically more innovative, and more transgressive, than what they felt they could get away with in the magazines. That was a bit unfair, of course, since editors such as Cele Goldsmith and Terry Carr were already publishing some fiction that looked radically experimental in comparison to only a few years earlier, and this included not only writers who wanted to free up the stylistic possibilities of the genre, but writers like R.A. Lafferty or David R. Bunch, whose idiosyncratic styles were so integral to their work that their stories could hardly have been told in any other manner.

But there was far more to this shift than simply language and style. Emerging along with it was an entirely new attitude toward the genre and toward the worlds and characters it portrayed—characters who, for the most part, were neither targets of satire nor paragons of competence. These characters, I think, largely defined the next phase of sf, which I call the Age of Attitude.

The Age of Attitude

This overlaps largely with the period that is usually called cyberpunk, with all its offshoots from post-cyberpunk to steampunk, biopunk, diesel-punk, nanopunk, atompunk, even elfpunk. The root which all these variants have in common is, of course, punk, and it's my argument that even in the original cyberpunk, punk is really the defining part of the term. Bruce Sterling, in his *Cheap Truth* fanzine, wrote of William Gibson's story "Burning Chrome" (1982) that "THIS is the shape for science fiction in the 1980's: fast-moving, sharply extrapolated, technologically literate, and as brilliant and coherent as a laser. Gibson's focussed and powerful attack is our best chance yet to awaken a genre that has been half-asleep since the early 1970's."[6] A lot of writers could and did take issue with Sterling's complaint that science fiction had been half-asleep, but in effect Sterling was simply using the 1970s as a whipping boy much as Moorcock had used the 1950s. Like Moorcock, he wanted to reinvent the whole genre, but surprisingly few of what he cited as examples were as groundbreaking as he made them out to be.

"Burning Chrome" did introduce the term "cyberspace," which Gibson defined as the "electronic consensus-hallucination" of the online world, and produced a famous line—"the street finds its own uses for things"—which encapsulated much of the cyberpunk aesthetic, the idea that technological developments could be co-opted by bright young—well, punks—in ways that such developments were never originally intended.[7] But it was also a caper story with grungy, street-level hackers outsmarting big shot gangsters. That was hardly new, and much of what was seen as revolutionary in Gibson's movement-defining novel *Neuromancer* (1984) wasn't entirely new, either: we'd seen people escaping into virtual worlds of one sort or another as far back as Arthur C. Clarke's *The City and the Stars* (1956) or even E.M. Forster's "The Machine Stops" (1909).

What really did feel new in cyberpunk was its complex of attitudes: the attitude of the author toward the reader, of the characters toward their world and toward each other: deeply cynical, hardboiled, improvisatory, immediate, survivalist. In *Neuromancer*, Case is a small-time hustler and drug addict who was nevertheless a skilled hacker, Molly Millions a self-described "street samurai" with weapon-like body modifications and mirror lenses implanted in her eyes. Again, we had seen similar characters before in the work of writers ranging from Alfred Bester to Ellison to Philip K. Dick, but now it seemed to have become a dominant aesthetic. Writers like John Shirley, Rudy Rucker,

Lewis Shiner, Pat Cadigan, Tom Maddox, and Greg Bear were all included in Sterling's more or less "official" cyberpunk anthology *Mirrorshades* in 1986—even though more than half the stories in that anthology dated from before Gibson's novel.

Neuromancer, of course, became the first novel in a trilogy, called the Sprawl trilogy, which occupied much of the 1980s (*Count Zero*, 1986; *Mona Lisa Overdrive*, 1988), and that in turn was followed by his "Bridge" Trilogy (*Virtual Light*, 1993; *Idoru*, 1996; *All Tomorrow's Parties*, 1999), which occupied much of the 1990s, and by the "Blue Ant" or Hubert Bigend novels which occupied much of the 2000s (*Pattern Recognition*, 2003; *Spook Country*, 2007; *Zero History*, 2010).These novels also prefigure another age, and one which overlaps in significant ways with the previous two, but which became much more highly visible in the 1990s and later. This is what I'm calling the Age of Complexity.

The Age of Complexity

"Complexity" in this sense doesn't necessarily mean that earlier works were somehow more thematically simple than the books covered under this rubric, but rather refers more to structure and scope than to theme. This age is characterized by large, architectonic works whose narrative structure may range over multivolume novels or connected series with a common narrative arc. There had been such large structures before, but seldom so narratively complicated as now, and it's important to distinguish between what I'm discussing here and earlier sequels and franchises. Frank Herbert's *Dune* (1965), Isaac Asimov's original "Foundation" stories (1942–1950), Anne McCaffrey's *Dragonflight* (1968), and Arthur C. Clarke's *Rendezvous with Rama* (1973) were not necessarily conceived to become multivolume series of the sort they eventually metastasized into, often involving additional authors and collaborators. But beginning mostly in the 1970s, we begin to get series of novels in complex dialogue with themselves and pointedly deepening and recomplicating their narrative worlds.

Some examples might include Aldiss's Helliconia series from 1982 to1985; Gregory Benford's Galactic Center novels, which began with *In the Ocean of Night* (1977) and continued through *Sailing Bright Eternity* (1996); Iain Banks's Culture series, which began with *Consider Phlebus* in 1987 and continued through nine novels, ending with *The Hydrogen Sonata* in 2012; and perhaps most complexly of all Gene Wolfe, whose four-volume novel *Book of the New Sun* in the 1980s turned out to be only the first section of a vast narrative that later included *The Book of the Long Sun*—four more volumes in the 1990s— and finally the three-volume *Book of the Short Sun* between 1999 and 2001.

More recent examples might be China Miéville's Bas-Lag novels, beginning with *Perdido Street Station* in 2000, and N.K. Jemisin's "Broken Earth" series, which won successive Hugo awards for *The Fifth Season* (2015) and *The Obelisk Gate* (2016), with the third volume, *The Stone Sky* (2017) also nominated. I'm less certain about the many novels in C.J. Cherryh's Alliance/Union universe or Lois McMaster Bujold's Vorkosigan saga, since most of these are essentially standalone narratives in a common universe, though certainly some deepening and complicating of that setting goes on here as well.

Almost certainly, there are economic and publishing considerations that made such large-scale structures possible. Just as the growth of the science fiction book market in the 1950s permitted writers to conceive sf novels *as novels*, and not as magazine story fix-ups or expansions, so did the spectacular success of J.R.R. Tolkien's *Lord of the Rings* trilogy in its 1960s paperback incarnation and of Herbert's *Dune* novels in the same period helped reveal a market for far larger fictional projects. But while some sf and fantasy writers took advantage of this growing market to simply develop a franchise or brand, others saw an opportunity to build a metafictional structure as rich and complex as Faulkner's Yoknapatawpha county or Tolkien's Middle-Earth.

All of these earlier ages are still with us, of course, and still in dialogue with one another in much the same way that science fiction has always talked to itself. But in most of them, the variety of voices and perspectives has been fairly limited, in terms of economic and social structures, race, gender, capacity, and culture. It's no surprise to anyone that for most of its history, sf has largely imagined worlds from the perspective of Anglo-American culture and classic Western liberal values. This has begun to change radically over the past twenty years or so, and it's why I've called the current age, which I began with, the Age of Perspective.

The Age of Perspective

Some commentators, including myself, have referred to the period since 2000 or so as the Age of Diversity, but I've chosen instead the Age of Perspective for a couple of reasons. For one thing, while diversity is certainly to be celebrated, the term more readily describes the diversity of writers and readers, rather than a general characteristic of the fiction itself. It's encouraging that the sf and fantasy world has embraced Nigerian-American writers like Nnedi Okorafor or Deji Bryce Olukaton, Caribbean writers like Karen Lord or Tobias Buckell, or Nalo Hopkinson (actually Caribbean Canadian), Malaysian writers like Zen Cho, or Chinese writers like Cixin Liu, gay or lesbian or nonbinary writers like Yoon Ha Lee or Sam J. Miller—but I'm using perspective to refer to something else: the perspectives and points of view of the fiction itself. Ian McDonald, a British author living in Belfast, has sought to portray futures from the perspective of India, Brazil, and Turkey, and another British author, Paul McAuley, portrayed outer solar system colonies seeking independence from the superpowers back on Earth—but the most powerful of those superpowers is Greater Brazil. Increasingly, characters from non–Western backgrounds, characters who are neuroatypical, genderfluid, nonbinary, or even disembodied entirely, are presented not as a variety of the Other, but as figures with both viewpoints and significant agency—and not only in fiction by authors who share some of these qualities. At times, such a trend seems to raise the specter of cultural appropriation, although most of the minority writers I've spoken with seem to feel that avoiding issues of appropriation is largely one of sensitivity and homework. In some cases, a shift toward another cultural perspective may be demanded by the nature of science fictional extrapolation itself; when Kim Stanley Robinson populates his 2018 novel *Red Moon* with mostly Chinese characters, it's less an arbitrary choice than an outgrowth of his reasoned speculation that China may be best positioned to establish moon colonies by the mid–21st century.

My point, though, is that this new age of perspective is not really a trend at all, but that it simply represents the latest era in science fiction's maturation—and, like all the other ages I've mentioned, it invites readers to reconsider and authors to reinvigorate the conventions of the earlier eras. New perspectives can return us to the space operas, rationalist futures, satires, stylistic experiments, and punk movements, and make them seem fresh, simply by offering us a different angle of vision. Like all the eras I've described, it doesn't subsume or replace all that went before, but offers a way to reinvent it, and to do so in a way that is perhaps more inclusive than the field has ever been. This might not have always been true in the past, but today, no one *owns* science fiction—or fantasy or horror fiction, for that matter.

Notes

1. Peter Watts, "The Things," *Clarkesworld*, No. 40 (January 2010), at http://clarkesworldmagazine.com/watts_01_10/.

2. Sam J. Miller, "New Story: 'Things with Beards,'" Sam J. Miller, posted June 9, 2016, at http://samjmiller.com/new-story-things-with-beards/.

3. Roger Luckhurst, *Science Fiction* (Cambridge, UK: Polity Press, 2005), 73.

4. Adam Roberts, *The History of Science Fiction*, Second Edition (London: Palgrave Macmillan, 2016), 267. A later Roberts quotation in the text is on this page.

5. See Alec Nevala-Lee, *Astounding: John W. Campbell, Isaac Asimov, Robert A. Heinlein, L. Ron Hubbard, and the Golden Age of Science Fiction* (New York: William Morrow Dey Street, 2018), 56.

6. Bruce Sterling (as by Vincent Omniaveritas), "Editorial: Dirt Cheap Literary Criticism With the Honesty of Complete Desperation," *Cheap Truth*, 2 (1983), available at http://www.skepticfiles.org/ezine/cheap002.htm.

7. William Gibson, "Burning Chrome," 1982, *Burning Chrome* (1986; New York: Ace Books, 1987), 170, 186.

You Can't Get There from Here

Unrealistic Expectations Among the Practitioners of Science Fiction

CHARLES PLATT

Science fiction is full of grandiose ideas. We don't just have happy endings; we vanquish alien invasions and travel to the stars. Therefore I think it is unsurprising that some science fiction writers have pursued unrealistically ambitious goals in their personal lives, never imagining that they can't get there from here. I will examine this syndrome and its consequences, illustrating it with case histories.

My first encounter with big ambitions in science fiction was in the late 1960s, when I was a teenage college dropout working for Michael Moorcock on *New Worlds* magazine. Often I would sit on the floor in Moorcock's living room, listening to him play the guitar rather badly while he told us that we were going to change the face of science fiction and could even exert some influence on modern literature.

Moorcock was about 24 years old at the time. His experience included writing comic strips for Fleetway Publications and stories for *Science Fantasy* magazine. Still, many people, including myself, were willing to believe him. I don't think it's coincidental that all of us had grown up suspending our disbelief in stories where one courageous individual could defeat a tyrant or travel through time. We didn't recognize limits that seem self-evident to most people in the everyday world.

Literary Ambitions

While Moorcock had a somewhat contentious attitude toward the literary establishment, others simply wanted to become a part of it. During the 1970s, especially, a number of writers aspired to find recognition in what they often referred to as "mainstream literature." I will cite seven examples.

First, the two Phils: **Philip Jose Farmer** and **Philip K. Dick**. Farmer often used to tell me that he would be lionized by the literati when his novel *Pearl Diving in Old Peoria* was published. We cannot assess the outcome of this ambition because I don't think he ever finished writing the book. Still, I doubt that it would have achieved its goal, if Philip K. Dick is a relevant example.

Dick wrote at least six novels outside of science fiction and was unable to sell any of them at that time. This represents a prodigious investment of energy, and may be the most remarkable example of a successful science fiction writer who tried and failed to escape from the genre. While the books were eventually published in small-press editions, obviously that was not what Dick was aiming for.

Ironically, the stories and novels that he wrote inside science fiction were the ones that spawned numerous motion pictures. While he was alive, however, he suffered disappointments within the field. After *The Man in the High Castle* (1962) won a Hugo Award, he told me that he expected his monetary value as a writer to increase dramatically. Yet in 1970, when Doubleday tried to sell paperback rights to *Flow My Tears, the Policeman Said*, the only offer came from Donald A. Wollheim of DAW books. I recall that it was $1,250. As Dick said to me rather bitterly at that time, he used to receive about that much from Wollheim for half of an Ace Double in the 1960s. Perhaps stung by this disappointment, he didn't publish any more science fiction novels for the next three years.

Other writers who nursed literary ambitions included **Thomas M. Disch**, **Norman Spinrad**, and the ones I think of as the two bergs: **Barry Malzberg** and **Robert Silverberg**. Malzberg once told me that when he started writing, he hoped to win the Nobel Prize for Literature. Silverberg was a little more realistic, simply hoping for acclaim as a serious contemporary novelist. Neither Spinrad nor the bergs were rewarded as they had hoped. Disch was more successful, but not on a sustainable basis.

Another writer who felt he deserved greater renown was **Harlan Ellison**, who remarked to me in the early 1970s that he felt he should be as well-known as Hemingway. When a writer makes this kind of confession, it is most often in a tone of regret, late at night, when cherished dreams have sustained damage from which recovery is unlikely.

Ellison seemed to feel that his existing body of work at that time ought to be sufficient to win the recognition that he deserved. So why should he create more? Unfortunately, somewhat like the bergs, he was averse to rewriting and believed that a first draft with a few pen corrections was more than adequate. This turned out not to be the case.

Even Ellison's *Again, Dangerous Visions* collection (1972) failed to find a receptive audience outside of science fiction. Anthony Burgess described it as "mostly a jejune, hack, etoliated, unvisionary, certainly undangerous collection of droppings from the crupper of a jade which, somewhat feebly jet-propelled by its own windbreaks, considers that it's related to Pegasus."[1] Seldom has the gulf between category fiction and the literary establishment been more painfully apparent.

The Magic Triad

Science fiction writers have a much better track record of achieving success within their own area of expertise: writing science fiction. Before I name some examples, I will suggest three prerequisites, which I refer to as the magic triad.

> There must be a "big simple idea."
> There must be a "good mix."
> There must be a "good fit."

These attributes are necessary, but not sufficient, as some talent is also required. But if any element of the magic triad is missing, the work is unlikely to enjoy great success, and the writer won't "get there from here."

I will explain my terminology by referring to the work of Alfred Bester, beginning with his first novel, *The Demolished Man*. The big simple idea in this book can be summarized as, "protagonist tries to get away with murder in a society of telepaths." Like all great ideas, it makes one wonder why no one had thought of it before. The only question is how much of it can be ascribed to Bester.

In his essay "My Affair with Science Fiction" (1974), published in his collection *Star Light, Star Bright* (1976), he mentions that he originally planned to write about a crime committed in a world where time travel would allow police to go back and see what happened.[2] However, while he was planning the novel, he enjoyed frequent conversations with H.L. Gold of *Galaxy* magazine, who felt there had been too many time-travel stories. It was Gold who suggested a telepathic society.

This is a fine example of a "good mix" between a writer and an editor. A very successful writer almost always has synergistic support from an editor, or a literary agent, or a collaborator, or some other person with a solid, practical grasp of publishing. Gold also seems to have exerted a general anchoring force, demanding that Bester's flights of fancy should be internally plausible and should make sense.

In addition to the idea and the mix, *The Demolished Man* (1952) was a "good fit," by which I mean it fit well with the mood of the times and the interests of its potential audience. Many science fiction writers have difficulty achieving a good fit, because—well, they are misfits. But when *The Demolished Man* was published, the science fiction field had just matured sufficiently to be receptive to an innovator who went beyond genre conventions, and this was Bester's strong suit.

When I was a teenage science fiction reader, I revered Alfred Bester. In fact, I wanted to *be* Alfred Bester. I never remotely imagined that anyone could be as successful as he was, yet might fail.

Alas, not only he but numerous successful writers have experienced what I call the slow slide into obscurity.

The Slow Slide into Obscurity

After Bester wrote his first two science fiction novels, he enjoyed a long sojourn at *Holiday* magazine. Then in the 1970s he needed cataract surgery, which was not a trivial matter in those days. The lenses of his eyes were removed, and he had to wear special eyeglasses with a very limited depth of focus. They restricted his mobility and compelled him to spend time at home, where he resumed writing science fiction after a break that had lasted almost 20 years. At this point, the magic triad was missing.

He had no big simple idea.

He did not have a good mix. Much as I admired David Hartwell, he was not the right editor for Bester. Where Gold had demanded solid practicality, Hartwell permitted self-indulgence.

Nor was there a good fit. Bester was still very much a 1950s writer, but the year was now 1979, and there is no worse fate for an innovator than to seem out of date.

By this time I had become friends with him and was distressed by his situation. In the last year of his life, when I visited him in his farm house in rural Pennsylvania, he told me that he blamed his audience. "They just don't understand," he said.

Personally, I don't think readers have any obligation to understand the writer. It is the writer's job to understand his readers. Bester was now estranged from them.

His last published novel, *Tender Loving Rage* (1991), would not have been published at all if I hadn't rescued it from a shelf in his office. I gave it to a small press, and this marked the end point of his slow slide.

I do hope that no one was expecting my discussion, here, to be upbeat and cheerful. Actually I have some relatively encouraging case histories, but before I get to them, I'll mention a few other writers who have suffered the slow slide. In no particular order:

Piers Anthony. I used to think of him as the Del Rey Books reincarnation of Lewis Carroll, but his days as a *New York Times* bestseller seem to have passed. He is now mostly writing eBooks for Open Road Media.

John Brunner. He won a Hugo Award for *Stand on Zanzibar* (1968), but never managed to build upon that success.

Philip Jose Farmer. *Riverworld* was a brilliant big simple idea, but most of his subsequent ideas were a bit wacky. I loved his work, but only *Riverworld* had the magic triad.

Harry Harrison. Ten years after *Make Room, Make Room!* (1966) had been made into *Soylent Green* (1973), which added the crucial big simple idea of cannibalism, Harrison told me in a phone call that he had come up with a killer concept to revive his fortunes. "I can tell it to you in two words," he said. "Talking dinosaurs." Well, it was indeed a big simple idea, but not a good fit with the potential audience. I don't think people really wanted to read about talking dinosaurs. They wanted to read about talking people. Sadly, Harrison suffered the slow slide.

Algis Budrys is my final example. I revered his writing, and I don't think he ever wrote a bad story. But *Rogue Moon* (1960) failed to win the Hugo Award, and even though Budrys said he wasn't angry or bitter, I think he was. He did what I call the sidestep, which is what some writers do when their ambitions have not been fulfilled on the scale that they imagined. He sidestepped into advertising, public relations, and writing sales literature for a truck manufacturer.

After *Michaelmas* (1977), which I thought was an amazingly prescient novel, he made a final sidestep and became the primary enabler for Writers of the Future. At that time L. Ron Hubbard was still alive, and Writers of the Future was widely regarded as an attempt to rehabilitate his reputation. I told Budrys that I thought he had made a shrewd move, but I asked if he felt good about it. "Whatever you think of Scientologists," he said, "they are the most honest, straight-shooting people I have ever met. And Charlie, you wouldn't believe how much they are paying me." Fair enough: If you're going to do a sidestep, make it pay.

I can think of only one writer who made a major comeback from the slow slide into obscurity, and that is Robert Silverberg. As he saw his old titles gradually disappearing from bookstores, while some of his friends were doing rather well writing large fantasy novels, Silverberg said he wanted to find out how much he was worth in book publishing of the late 1970s. He came up with a big simple idea, in two parts. First: "Very large planet with normal gravity." This was a good start, because it always helps if a big simple idea entails a large object. But the second part of the idea clinched it: "Protagonist is a juggler." This was a concept that most writers would have rejected as far too silly, if they had thought of it at all. But it was an inspired choice, creating endless possibilities for costumes in science-fiction conventions.

Steady State Status

Needless to say, not all writers suffer the mortification of the slow slide. The fortunate ones reach what I call steady state status. Their old work stays in print and earns royalties, while they enjoy some speaking engagements and convention appearances. Thus they sustain a reasonably comfortable lifestyle.

My premiere example is Ray Bradbury. First, of course, he enjoyed great success by coming up with a big simple idea. I am not referring to *The Martian Chronicles* (1950), which I see as a vapid conceit. Bradbury's idea was, "Firefighters burning books."

This made no sense at all. Even in a totalitarian future, firefighters will be needed to *put out fires*. They will be expensively trained and highly skilled. Maintaining their equipment will also cost money. By comparison, any idiot can burn books, and you won't have to pay him more than minimum wage.

Still, big simple ideas that don't make sense can be just as popular as big simple ideas that do make sense. After *Fahrenheit 451* (1953), Ray wrote some of the world's worst poetry, which he told me was some of the world's best poetry, but whatever it was, it didn't matter. His name had become a brand that was synonymous with science fiction. He was a charming man, everyone loved him, and he gave great speeches. He enjoyed steady state status that never faded away.

Some other examples:

Frederik Pohl, who simply never stopped writing.

Gregory Benford, same as Pohl.

Arthur C. Clarke, who never stopped subcontracting. (Incidentally, "Rama" was a big simple idea that did well for him.)

Isaac Asimov, same as Clarke. Asimov had two big simple ideas at the very beginning of his career: "three laws of robotics" and "psychohistory." Later he sidestepped into nonfiction, which was easier for him to write, but his publisher saw the financial possibilities of his fiction franchise, and orchestrated his return to the field. This was a very good mix.

Larry Niven. *Ringworld* (1970) showed once again that a big simple idea can work well if it entails a large object.

World-Changing Ambitions

Some writers have ventured not only outside of science fiction, but outside of the written word altogether. These brave adventurers have pursued what I refer to as world-changing ambitions.

H.G. Wells was the pioneer. Not content with being an internationally famous writer of scientific romances, he wanted to establish a world government. He was serious about this, and had meetings with Stalin and Roosevelt. Online, you can find a transcript of his meeting with Stalin, in which he complains that the dictator is not a purist about socialism. Unfortunately Wells didn't seem to understand that world leaders (or craven power junkies, as I prefer to think of them) are unlikely to be interested in aggregating power on a collaborative basis. They are more likely to want to annihilate each other.

I don't think Wells ever got over the disappointment of World War II, but let us pay tribute to his amazing run of big simple ideas, including "Mars invades Earth," and "machine travels through time," and "man makes himself invisible," and "gravity shielding." We may shake our heads in envy at his great good fortune to be writing when these ideas were still fresh and new, just lying around and waiting for someone to pick them up. Big simple ideas are much harder to find these days.

Getting back from big simple ideas to world-changing ideas, legendary editor John W. Campbell, Jr., had no shortage of them. "Psionics" was one—the scientific study of paranormal phenomena. This was not successful for Campbell, although it worked for me as a topic for a general paper that I wrote when I was applying to study at Cambridge University. Yes, implausible as it may seem, I got into Cambridge by rewriting the editorial from the January 1959 issue of *Astounding Science Fiction*.

"Hieronymus machine, detects eloptic radiation" was another of Campbell's enthusiasms. I built one, and it didn't work. "Dowsing rods"—they didn't work for me either. But the most memorable of his enthusiasms was his ambition to go to Mars in a submarine. You see, if you have *unlimited power* (a possibility that any good science fiction reader might find plausible) you don't need to build your own airtight vessel. Just pull one off the shelf—or out of the ocean. Bolt a bunch of Dean drives to it, and off you go! Campbell even put a picture of a submarine arriving at Mars on the cover of his magazine. Unfortunately, the Dean Drive didn't work.

At least one of Campbell's writers suffered similar disappointments. Frank Herbert defied orthodox wisdom in book publishing, which said that a novel as long as *Dune* (1965) could not be sold profitably at that time. Obviously, it could. Emboldened, Herbert seemed to feel that he could defy orthodox wisdom in other fields, such as aerodynamics. He designed a wind turbine that consisted of vertical blades revolving around a vertical axis. He even paid for a prototype, and tested it.

Undeterred by the disappointing outcome, in 1979 Herbert decided to build his own computer. He paid someone to create a motherboard from the chips up. His own concept for word processing, and his own programming language, were to be included as firmware. He sold an outline for a nonfiction book about computers titled *Without Me, You're Nothing*, and planned to write it on the computer of his own design.

Jerry Pournelle, who actually knew a bit about the subject, warned Herbert that the project was a bit ambitious. Designing your own computer was difficult, and—well, it might not work at all. Herbert (according to Pournelle) was unimpressed. "Jerry, you just have to spend more money," he said. Alas, he ended up writing his book about computers on a typewriter.

Barrington J. Bayley, a British writer whom I knew well, had a world-changing idea in the field of physics. He believed that gravity is a force of repulsion, and the only reason we remain on the surface of planet Earth is that gravitational force from stars is holding us down. Therefore, to get into space, we might put gravitational shielding above our heads instead of beneath our feet.

Bayley could have written a science fiction novel about this, but he thought he had made a huge discovery, so he spent several months writing a paper. This was difficult for him, as he had no background in mathematics. I persuaded him to let me show it to a scientist friend, and the first line in the scientist's response was, "I hope Mr. Bayley realizes that this is not an original idea." Thus, it was not only wacky, but second-hand. When I relayed the bad news back to Bayley, he shook his head and said, in these precise words, "This is typical of the blinkered scientific establishment."

Philip Jose Farmer had a world-changing idea, which he propounded in a keynote speech at a science-fiction convention in 1968. Farmer had bought into Paul Ehrlich's doom scenario regarding global resources, and was convinced that humanity was running out of everything. He announced a bold initiative to be called REAP, which was an acronym, although I have forgotten what it stood for and have been unable to dig up this information online. I do recall the goal, however. Farmer wanted all serious writers of science fiction to join together and guide humanity into a resource-depleted future.

This idea was not a good fit, because most science fiction writers would rather transcend limits than confine themselves within them. They ignored Farmer's invitation, but this didn't matter, because Paul Ehrlich was wrong, and his prediction that 65 million Americans would die of starvation between 1980 and1989 erred on the side of pessimism. So, we didn't need REAP after all.

Another global initiative with an ecological message was named Viridian by Bruce Sterling, who established it in 1998. Sterling wanted to encourage the development of sustainable consumer products that would be so utterly cool and beautiful, people would buy them for that reason, not just because they were sustainable. According to a brief Wikipedia entry, he formally ended Viridian ten years after he started it, because it had succeeded in its objectives.

This was a truly brilliant exit strategy. If only Michael Moorcock had thought of it in the 1970s, he could have announced that the so-called new wave had achieved its goals of reforming modern literature, freeing us to deal with other matters. But Moorcock was British, whereas Sterling was a Texan. It helps to have a bit of braggadocio when your world-changing idea doesn't quite live up to expectations.

Viridian was actually Sterling's second ambition on a global scale. Academics who study the history of science fiction may view cyberpunk as a minor deviation from the main thread of imaginative literature, but Sterling didn't see it that way at all. I was in correspondence with him when he was the primary promoter of cyberpunk, and in a letter that he wrote to me, he referred to it as "a fucking juggernaut." He seemed to feel it would infect movies, music, fashion—in fact, all the arts, with its idiosyncratic mix of futuristic technology and punk chic.

Unfortunately cyberpunk was not a big simple idea, and there was no mix. Only about half-a-dozen writers were active in the movement, and two of them (Rucker and Kadrey) tended to make embarrassing public statements that might be summarized as, "Actually we're not really sure what it is, and we're not convinced that we write it." The only editor they could really claim was Ellen Datlow of *Omni* magazine, who seemed to think of it along the lines, "I really like these guys, and sometimes I publish their stories." William Gibson is probably still regarded as a cyberpunk writer, but his work preceded the label, and he avoided making any grandiose claims. Ironically steampunk, a tongue-in-cheek, retro riff on the aesthetic, has survived more tenaciously than cyberpunk.

Sterling still remains a highly regarded science fiction writer, but none of his books had a big simple idea (unlike Gibson, whose big simple idea could be summarized in one word: "cyberspace"). Sterling had big complicated ideas, which are never as popular as simple ideas. After a sidestep into nonfiction about computers and hackers, he returned to science fiction on an intermittent basis, while also sidestepping into public speaking. He is an unusually gifted public speaker; people stand and cheer at the end of his speeches. Thus he has achieved a kind of steady state status.

Ambitions Fulfilled

I can think of only two examples where world-changing ambitions have been at least partially fulfilled. The first is L. Ron Hubbard, for whom Dianetics was a success. Since this was really a science-fictional concept, we can examine it to see if it has the magic triad, and indeed it does. Big simple idea: "Psychiatry is bogus. We're going to make it scientific." Good fit: Yes. People were very skeptical about psychiatry in the 1950s, and were positively predisposed toward a "more scientific" alternative. Hubbard also had a good mix with John W. Campbell, who promoted Dianetics for him.

Too bad that Campbell's own ideas were so easily debunked. He should have come up with something in a soft science such as psychiatry, where a concept is not so easily disproven.

The second example of a successful world-changing idea was generated by the Citizens' Advisory Council on National Space Policy during the 1980s. This group was created by Jerry Pournelle with several other writers, including Gregory Benford and Larry Niven. Benford told me about it in June 1981, and I heard about it from Pournelle in September of the same year. Pournelle had always wanted to promote his personal ideology, and not just in his fiction. He had obtained a Ph.D. in political science, "to study politics and learn how to manipulate those levers," as he put it when I interviewed him.

He told me that the Citizens' Advisory Council was established with the ulterior motive of reviving the space program. He believed that a larger budget for NASA would achieve nothing, whereas military spending could have civilian spinoff in the long term. After some lively, contentious meetings, the Citizens' Advisory Council came up with a big simple idea: "Develop a system to shoot down incoming nuclear missiles."

Imagine my surprise when I saw Ronald Reagan referring to this concept as the Strategic Defense Initiative on television a couple of years later. Did this mean that science fiction writers were now establishing U.S. military spending priorities? Well, yes, it did. To be fair, the Citizens' Advisory Council included members from the aerospace industry, and at least one astronaut. This must have enhanced their credibility. Still, it was a science-fictional idea that did have world-changing potential. In this rare instance, writers proved that they could, in fact, get there from here.

Failure

I chose the topic for this discussion because although failed ambitions are an undeniable reality, people generally don't address the subject. Personally,

I like to analyze other people's folly in the unrealistic hope of avoiding it myself.

My choice of topic should not be interpreted to mean that I am pessimistic. On the contrary, I love the grandiose concepts in science fiction, and have contributed my own time and energy to at least two of the goals or movements that I have mentioned above. In addition I have sidestepped into cryonics, which is a science-fictional concept even though its real-world implementation originated with a school teacher. I tend to think that human cryopreservation, as it is done now, will not be reversible in the future, but that hasn't discouraged me from working on it.

The more grandiose an ambition is, the less likely it can be fulfilled, and in most of the cases that I have mentioned, you really can't get there from here. Nevertheless, attempting to do so can be interesting and even pleasurable, so long as one remains mentally prepared to deal with the very high risk of failure.

NOTES

1. Anthony Burgess, "Science Fiction Still in the Literary Mainstream" (review of *Again, Dangerous Visions* edited by Harlan Ellison), *Los Angeles Times*, July 16, 1972, W1.
2. Alfred Bester, "My Affair with Science Fiction," 1974, *Star Light, Star Bright* (New York: Berkley, 1976), 220–248.

Negotiating Fear and Optimism

Surveillance in Early Science Fiction

ARI BRIN

For a newly empowered generation of illustrious travelers and tourists, San Francisco in the 1870s would have certainly appeared the ideal place to make a fresh start. Its population had doubled in just seven years to almost 150,000 people, comprising a majority of California residents at the time.[1] Detached from the Civil War, teeming with diversity, and placed within an enviable natural harbor, the city throbbed with ambition and enterprise. It was upon this setting that the young Scottish expatriate Robert Duncan Milne arrived in August 1874. He was well-dressed, was Oxford-educated, and had recently acquired a patent for a new type of rotary steam engine. While the twenty-seven-year-old Milne could immediately appreciate the local ingenuity of San Francisco—exemplified by Andrew Hallidie's brand new cable-car system—he was yet struck by something else: its vast scientific ignorance.

Despite a host of intellectual figures appearing in San Francisco in the mid- to late 1800s (such as Ambrose Bierce, John Muir, Eadweard Muybridge, Robert Louis Stevenson, and Mark Twain), San Francisco was not a scholarly community in the mid-nineteenth century, and rather housed a "prodigious appetite for the occult."[2] The gap between the educated and uneducated population was enormous—as most immigrants to the city had come, in some way, connected to the gold prospecting trade. California was perhaps the first state to be born alongside the late nineteenth-century technological boom, yet it was not immediately a recipient of its conveniences. The telegraph, the first system to ever transmit instantaneous electrical impulses in the form of language long-distance, was in widespread use in New York in the mid–1850s, yet the Pony Express was the only means for long-distance communication in California until 1861. It would take forty years from the announcement of the telephone in 1877 for the first transcontinental phone call to reach California.[3] One might say that California, especially its most populous city of San Francisco, was occupied by people more accustomed to speculation than to technological reality.

These inequalities of access were paired with a widespread cultural shift that encouraged the reading of daily papers, and precipitated literacy rates of 90 percent from San Francisco to New York.[4] Interest in scientific achievements was growing, regardless of actual scientific understanding, and many writers were beginning to exploit this gap between the intellectual class and the majority readership. In the middle of the 19th century, elements of realism in the form of believable hoaxes could bring significant attention to a story, thus enabling it the rare honor of being reprinted. Richard Adams Locke's famous *The Moon Hoax* (1835, 1853) had boasted that telescopic advancements had made it possible to see whole civilizations in detail on the Moon. It had set New York into a frenzy, and swelled the circulation of New York's fledgling *The Sun* newspaper. That, in turn, had inspired Edgar Allan Poe's "The Balloon-Hoax" (1844), which would later inspire Jules Verne to write his early stories about flying machines.[5] These sorts of stories were required to be convincing, if not actually scientific, in order to convince the largest body of readership possible of their claims. Perhaps no other genre was so formative to the creation of modern science fiction. In 1874, George Cary Eggleston would offer a striking explanation for why this subgenre experienced so much success in nineteenth-century Britain and New York:

> We want wonder stories quite as our forefathers did, but we cannot get up the pseudo-belief in them which is absolutely necessary to their enjoyment. Science has destroyed the work of the classic wonder-mongers, not by proving the stories impossible, for we knew that already, but by creating in us mental habits fatal to their enjoyment.[6]

Eggleston remarks here that beyond disproving fantasy narratives, the newfound importance of science in day-to-day life was creating a more analytical, skeptical populace at large.

This view sheds contemporary light on what many historians see as a massive cultural shift in the late nineteenth century. Christopher White argues that even the growth of Spiritualist communities such as the one in San Francisco showcased a demand for "more reasonable forms of religious enchantment and wonder."[7] It was not only the radically transformational nature of technologies, but that these technologies were quickly becoming ordinary objects that almost anyone could own. The electric light, the camera, the telegraph, and subsequently the telephone were beginning to transform the daily lives of people across the world. These inventions in turn transformed the very nature of progress from something that felt distant and reserved for a select few to something that directly affected millions of ordinary lives.

The reactions to this transformation (and to a rapidly vanishing way of life) are what I will examine in this essay. San Francisco in particular, and the nascent community of science fiction that developed there, represented a microcosm of a larger literary shift towards rational wonder stories. Utilizing the hoax genre, Milne (alongside others) bestrode the middle ground between utopia and dystopia, carving out a particular form of response to technology that had the power to predict, forewarn, and allay potential concerns. California, as an isolated place on the brink of this technological future, was a prime place from which to synthesize the encroaching reality of a technological future. And one writer was an ideal figure to make the leap from exploiting this scientific gap to engaging with its consequences.

Negotiating Fear

Since the invention of the camera in 1839, dormant anxieties about surveillance were bubbling up to the surface. These technological changes would prove disruptive to more than just the philosophical manner in which people viewed time; they would have profound consequences for privacy. Amid an age of rising secularism, especially in Britain,[8] this was an especially powerful notion. The ancient fear of always being watched had been bestowed for generations by religion, in which God provided an omniscience, even to acts committed outside the presence of any potential human oversight. Indeed, this "surveillance" was intended to enact a moral influence on society.[9] Photography was a surveillance of a totally different kind, exacting pressures that the secular could not ignore. By the later decades of the nineteenth century, one's image could be captured instantaneously, and more importantly, without one's consent. From expensive, time-consuming, irreproducible daguerreotypes came the camera that could capture fleeting moments for mass reproduction. From this enhanced invention surfaced the lurid photograph and the paparazzi image.[10]

Before these surveillance technologies were commonplace (and any long-term consequences still potentialities), many in positions of power fostered a hopeful attitude toward their development. In the 1880s, a popular suggestion among the scientific elite was that the camera might assist in eliminating human bias in recollection. While a human may misremember, "Photography has no such weakness. It records just what falls upon the prepared plate [...] the photographic eye is found to be trustworthy where the human eye is too often unreliable, or even deceptive."[11] It seemed that the camera might be able to protect the innocent, by replacing eyewitness accounts, which may be flawed or subject to manipulation. These technologies perfected recollections, and removed human error in ways that transcended earlier memory prosthetics such as writing and printing. Thus, alongside incipient anxieties about surveillance, a faith was developing in the superhuman abilities of new inventions.

Milne's oeuvre reflects a consistent belief in the ability of technology to bring justice to a world in which human fallibility reigned. By centering a number of his stories around crime, Milne posited that the correction of human error was something not just attainable through a hypothetical invention, but by means of inventions to which his contemporaries already had access. In his stories, Milne hypothesizes the utilization of time-disruptive technologies in assisting detectives to unmask villains whose crimes have escaped human senses. Milne asserted that technology could correct witness bias, espousing a type of technological positivism that would come to be a hallmark of early American science fiction.[12]

Milne's "A Dead Man's Ring" (1883) is a detective tale that anticipates the rational deduction of Arthur Conan Doyle's Sherlock Holmes series, by using the technology of its time as a tool for uncovering the unseen.[13] The story might additionally serve as the first instance of "enhancing" a photograph in detective work, now a familiar trope to any fan of police procedural fiction. The story is set after the murder of the prominent Mr. Ainsley during a public parade. After a series of false leads and setbacks, the detective in charge of the case spots a display of photographs along the parade's thoroughfare. Upon further inspection, he notices that the backdrop of one of the photographs is the very hotel in which the man was murdered. While Mr. Ainsley's window is minuscule, it is yet visible. Struck by an idea that the picture might hold the clue to the murderer's identity, the detective purchases the photograph with the intention of examining it under a microscope.

Of course, the microscope is unable to add resolution where there is none, and the white oblong dot apparent in Mr. Ainsley's window still appears blurry upon a closer look. The science-fictional aspect of the story materializes when the detective brings his photograph to the studio of Professor Whipple, who has devised a complex mechanism for re-focusing upon any element of a negative by utilizing a process involving "convergent rays."[14] Whipple manages to refocus the image, and at last clarifies it. To the detective's shock, the oblong dot is revealed as a raised arm holding a dagger, with a set of rings that assist in the eventual identification of the criminal.

Here, there is no need for a literal time machine in order to retrospectively witness a murder. While the mechanism by which Whipple re-focuses the image is impossible, the implications are pertinent to the time of Milne's writing. The emerging concept of the information footprint—or the "sum of semiotic clues by which one is identified, tracked, measured, classified, and adjudicated"—had become increasingly relevant for the ordinary individual by the end of the nineteenth century.[15] New technologies had become a sort of time machine, with the ability to replay the past in detail. This is most obviously seen in the camera, but advancements in trick imagery such as magic lanterns and Pepper's ghost were utilized throughout the nineteenth century to display phantasmic images that seemed to come from another time.[16]

Six years later, the San Francisco journal *The Argonaut* published another Milne story, "The Silent Witness" (1889), which again portrays technology as a key to correcting human fallibility. In the story, a man has just been accused of murdering his uncle. The evidence is stacked against him; he was just cut off from his uncle's money, and a witness in the room next door testified to hearing an argument between the two men just before the estimated time of murder. But just before the jury is set to make its final deliberation, a new piece of evidence is brought forward. It is a phonograph. Conveniently, the next-door neighbor has just returned from his six-month long vacation to find that his audio equipment had been left recording. In this time, it surreptitiously captured audio of the murder. The audio is played to the shocked jury, and offers conclusive proof that the criminal was rather the uncle's jilted lover. In a defense of the machine as a superior witness, the neighbor declares:

> Though you can't swear it, you can swear by it, for the phonograph is the George Washington of science—it can not tell a lie.[17]

It is important to note that while phonographs existed at the time, they could not record without human oversight and could not hold much more than three minutes of audio. While "The Silent Witness" would have worked as a successful hoax to its contemporary readership, a modern lens shows it to be a science fiction story through and through. The characters are reliant on modern technologies at a level unusual for the nineteenth century. News is read from the "telegraphic columns" of the *Call*. A detective checks his watch to make sure that he is not late for his "three-thirty" going East. A man hops on a train on a whim to traverse the country. And a phonograph—a piece of technology—is the hero, bringing justice to a fallible world.

A recurring theme within Milne's works is clear: privacy may no longer be presumed as the normative state. The camera and the phonograph's potential uses as tools of surveillance are underscored, but here it is not with the conscious intention to frighten. Milne's conclusion is rather that technology may lead to a correct prognosis that humans alone are unable to uncover. Writers of American science fiction at this time tended to mirror Milne's stance of technological optimism. Several stories from the nineteenth century are imbued with faith that technologies would bring good into the world: more justice, more fairness, and more accountability. But as consequences began to concretize, and new power imbalances sharpened, a reliance on technology seemed to encourage a mistrust of the human. Simple optimism no longer seemed a sustainable path for science fiction.

Negotiating Over-Optimism

Though the phonograph was invented by Thomas Edison in 1877, the device was not optimized for several years, and had barely entered the commercial market before the close of the nineteenth century.[18] Yet, since the first rumors spread of a voice-recorder, the public reactions were swift and intense, ranging from amazement to disbelief. The East Coast science fiction writer Edward Page Mitchell's "The Soul Spectroscope" (1875), published just two years before news of the phonograph emerged, provides a clear picture as to how unanticipated Edison's mode of sound recording was to the general public. In Mitchell's story, Professor Dummkopf muses on how the elusive qualities of sound might potentially be captured.

> When I have pictorially captured smell, the most palpable of the senses, the next thing will be to imprison sound [....] Catch it in a bottle, then its circumference cannot extend. You may keep the sound wave forever if you will only keep it corked up tight. The only difficulty is in bottling it in the first place.[19]

Lauer claims, in his history of the early phonograph, that "unlike photography, which had prehistoric precursors in pictorial representation, the inscription of sound did not."[20] The public's familiarity with the camera was used to make the phonograph seem more palatable. In an 1888 defense of the phonograph, which remained largely misunderstood by the public ten years after its invention, Edison drew parallels with the nature of the photograph. He declared that the phonograph would simply accomplish "the same thing in respect of conversation which instantaneous photography does for moving objects." Edison furthermore claimed that the phonograph would have a positive moral effect on society: by "retain[ing] a perfect mechanical memory" of what we say, "it will teach us to be careful what we say ... exerting thus a decidedly moral influence."[21] Lauer places Edison in a larger context of myopic, over-optimistic inventors, in seeing "only the salutory [sic] effects of his disciplinary apparatus."[22]

Edison was certainly not alone in his relentless scientific optimism. In 1888, the wildly popular novel *Looking Backward: 2000–1887* had solidified Edward Bellamy as an important writer of "the American utopian movement," consisting, as E.F. Bleiler claims, of authors illiterate in the sciences, but considering "themselves in possession of social knowledge that would offer easy, specific remedies for the ills of the world."[23] *Looking Backward* depicted a future utopia in which money, crime, and war have been eradicated, and the normal system of trial by jury has been overturned. This vision of a fairer world, made possible by innovation, persisted in late-nineteenth century American imagination.

We can see hints of a similar over-optimism in Milne's "The Silent Witness" and in several other early stories about surveillance technology. In an 1879 story (one of the first he ever wrote) entitled "The Great Electrical Diaphragm," Milne's narrator visits a rich Baron who has invented a type of cellular phone that can communicate across vast distances. Milne uncommonly anticipates an age in which millions—not just the very rich—would have access to telephonic communication.

But concerns about privacy were not at the forefront of this particular early narrative. An observer of the Baron's experiment asks if eavesdropping might become a concern, seeing as the proto-wireless technology allows sound waves to pass freely through the atmosphere. The Baron responds that private "lines" may be created by tuning, sending, and receiving frequencies to the same combination—this may be interpreted by a modern reader as encryption. When the observer asks about the possibility of two couples tuning to the same frequencies, the Baron replies:

> You will certainly receive [...] messages not intended for your ears; but as you will be in the same predicament of publishing your private affairs, I imagine that a very little experience will suffice to make you change your combination. Abuse is to some extent unavoidable, but the novelty will soon wear off; and besides the knowledge that you may be haranguing a large audience will make you more careful of what you say— alone a considerable recommendation," continued he, with a dry twinkle of his eye.[24]

Poignant in the above quote is the Baron's belief that members of the public would not care to surveil others once they were in the position of demanding regular privacy themselves. For Milne, there was safety in numbers, especially when gossips, eavesdroppers, and oppressors would be as exposed as anyone else. It's not a very satisfying answer, especially in the age of the Zuckerberg trials, as it is obvious to a modern audience that powerful people with the tools to listen will do so, and with great interest. The novelty, so to speak, has not worn off.

Think once more back to Edison's statement on the benefit of the phonograph, to "teach us to be careful what we say," for how closely the inventor's 1888 statement mirrors Milne's 1879 story. Milne viewed the telephone as a necessarily disciplinary device, for its lines had never been posited as private. By the early 1900s, the telephone was increasingly normalized as a "household item," despite many drawbacks. Lines were often shared between 10 or more people. One could never be certain that others were not silently listening in on private communications, and anxieties regarding the potential for sur- veillance were widely reported. Certainly, some wished to halt the march towards the uncertain future, going so far as to label the telephone the "enemy of peaceable civilization" and calling for the "execution of the inventor of the telephone and the destruction of his work."[25] The telephone did not at first symbolize more private communication, but rather a new potential for sur- veillance over many by a few.

It is no surprise that science fiction itself has often gone the route of calling for the execution, per say, of the inventor. This is in some ways the story of Frankenstein, and of countless dystopian narratives since. Science fiction as a mouthpiece for "the people" is one of the genre's greatest and most persistent usages, tapping into something inside all of us that innately distrusts those with the tools of power. That American science fiction did not often take this route in its earliest years is proof for its divergence from its British counterpart, a thread that has been explored by Brian Stableford, among others. Though the San Francisco science fiction community was born into a uniquely American optimism, it became quickly necessary to engage with the anxieties caused by surveillance tools.

Milne showed a unique willingness to confront such novel topics with a tempered optimism in his stories of scientific wonder. He was able to antic- ipate the cultural disruption that may accompany an age of technological development, however utopian his anticipations may have tended throughout his writing career. Although Milne envisioned a force of potentially great good in technology, he also saw the potential for misuse should the technol- ogy fall into the hands of a few. One thread that continued throughout his work is the insistence of his fictional scientists and inventors that technolog- ical developments should be made transparent and made rapidly available to all. While many other notable writers of scientific fiction in the nineteenth century, such as Mary Shelley, Jules Verne, and H.G. Wells, often posited some degree of elitism as a necessary condition and result of scientific progress,[26] Milne's stories regularly portrayed the opposite. Total distribution of any technology was the only way to ensure that the potentials for abuse would not come to fruition.[27]

In 1881, two years after "The Great Electrical Diaphragm," Milne pub- lished "A Dip into Space," about a super-telescope that allows a viewer to see all of the surface of the planets in detail. Milne's narrator is taken on a visual tour of many celestial wonders, including Saturn's rings. Yet the most remark- able point of the story occurs when Milne's narrator inquires as to the inven- tor's intentions for his incredible device. The inventor replies immediately:

> I propose to relinquish all right to the possession of my discovery, and to make a present of it to the world. Such discoveries as mine are too vast to remain the monopoly and private property of an individual. They are useless unless dissemi-

nated among mankind [....] I hold that all great discoveries are the property of all, and that it is criminal to selfishly withhold them from all.[28]

The inventor's remarkable reply appears to target a perceived tendency of scientific discoveries to be kept hidden from public view. If we imagine the Major to be a mouthpiece for the author himself (a safe bet, given how often Milne's characters repeat similar stances), it is evidence of a strongly held philosophy—that science owes a duty to humanity. In a way similar to H.G. Wells's later mastery of the genre, Milne could alternate between hope and warning, and he presented a collection of dystopian visions should technologies remain privatized and in the hands of a few. His 1891 story "A Question of Reciprocity" explores the devastating consequence when a technologically advanced group of criminals use bomb-equipped drones in order to extort millions from San Francisco's terrified population.[29] Between 1884 and 1888, Milne published a series of stories about radio hypnotism, which are disturbing narratives of unequal access to power.[30]

Milne, as Wells's science-fictional predecessor, engaged with the positives and drawbacks of technological development. It is clear that Milne made the leap from exploiting the scientific ignorance of his audience in scientific hoax stories, to engaging with its consequences on a large scale. He introduced science fiction, a genre distinguished by the presence of a "novum" validated by cognitive logic,[31] to a San Francisco audience at a time when interest in the fantastic was tempered by rising skepticism.

Many early examples of the genre tended to posit technological development within a regime of destructive power, or as the obvious path to absolution of humanity's ills. Milne, in contrast, treats the concept of technological progress as potentially useful, or potentially damaging. Milne might yet prove to be one of the most accurate seers of the past two centuries, for his obsessions—with expanding powers of vision, reach, and transparent accountability—are more pertinent today than ever. Far more clearly than his contemporaries, and many who came after, Milne foresaw that the future's daunting challenges would also come rich with opportunities, and that the difference might be determined by something as simple as giving everyone the chance to see.

NOTES

1. See Henry G. Langley, compiler, *The San Francisco Directory, for the Year Commencing October 1868* (San Francisco: Henry G. Langley, Publisher, 1868), at https://archive.org/stream/sanfranciscodire1868lang#page/n5, and Langley, compiler, *The San Francisco Directory for the Year Commencing December 1, 1869* (San Francisco: Henry G. Langley, Publisher, 1869), at https://archive.org/stream/sanfranciscodire1869langrich#page/n179.

2. Sam Moskowitz, *Science Fiction in Old San Francisco: History of the Movement, 1854–1890*, Volume I (West Kingston, RI: Donald M. Grant Publishers, 1980), 25.

3. "Phone to Pacific from the Atlantic," *New York Times*, January 25, 1915, 1.

4. Cited in Philip Ethington, *The Public City: The Political Construction of Urban Life in San Francisco, 1850–1900* (New York: Cambridge University Press, 1994), 19–20.

5. See Monique Sprout, "The Influence of Poe on Jules Verne," *Revue de Littérature Comparée*; 41:1 (1967), 38.

6. Cited in Moskowitz, "Lost Giant of American Science Fiction: A Biographical Perspective," *The Crystal Man: Stories by Edward Page Mitchell*, edited by Moskowitz (New York: Doubleday, 1973), xxxviii–xxxix.

7. Christopher White, "Seeing Things: Science, the Fourth Dimension, and Modern Enchantment," *The American Historical Review*, 119:5 (December 2014), 1470.

8. See Roger Luckhurst, *The Invention of Telepathy* (Oxford: Oxford University Press, 2002), 14–17 and 21, for the diffusion of scientific secularism in 1870s Britain and attempts to separate religion from education. See Georgina Byrne, *Modern Spiritualism and the Church of England, 1850–1939* (Woodbridge: Boydell Press, 2010), for additional evidence of British secularization in the late nineteenth century.

9. See David Lyon, "Surveillance and the Eye of God," *Studies in Christian Ethics*, 27:1 (February 2014), 21–32, for a comparison of modern surveillance with the disciplinary nature of "God's eye."

10. See Josh Lauer, "Surveillance History and the History of New Media: An Evidential Paradigm," *New Media & Society*. 14:4 (2012), 566–582.

11. Richard A. Proctor, "The Photographic Eyes of Science," *Longman's Magazine*, 1:4 (February 1883), 461.

12. Brian Stableford, *Scientific Romance in Britain: 1890–1950* (New York: St. Martin's Press, 1985), 25.

13. Beginning in the late 1880s, the Sherlock Holmes stories pioneered an interest in the forensic potentials of the "informational footprint." Arthur Conan Doyle viewed evidence such as the footprint and photography as means of revealing truth, though this fervent faith resulted in his humiliation in the case of the Cottingley Fairies. See Philip Ball, *Invisible: The Dangerous Allure of the Unseen* (London: Bodley Head, 2014), 68–71.

14. The basic principle is nearly identical to that of Milne's 1881 story "A Dip into Space," wherein convergent light rays are used to focus infinitely on any point of a planet. This vague scientific jargon would have likely been believed as possible by San Francisco's readership at the time.

15. Lauer, 578.

16. See Ball, 76–80, for a history of these phantasmagoria.

17. Robert Duncan Milne, "The Silent Witness," 1889, *Into the Sun and Other Stories*, edited by Moskowitz (West Kingston, RI: Donald M. Grant Publishers), 1980, 214.

18. See Leslie J. Newville, *Development of the Phonograph at Alexander Graham Bell's Volta Laboratory* (Washington, D.C.: Smithsonian Institution, 1959), available at http://www.gutenberg.org/files/30112/30112-h/30112-h.htm.

19. Edward Page Mitchell, "The Soul Spectroscope," 1875, *The Crystal Man*, 158; a page reference in a note below is to this edition. Story originally published in *The Sun* (December 1875) and available at http://www.forgottenfutures.com/game/ff9/tachypmp.htm#soul .The use of "pictorially" shows how the camera served as a useful analogy in describing the capture of non-visual senses.

20. Lauer, 574.

21. Thomas Alva Edison, "The Perfected Phonograph," 1888, cited in *Edison and His Inventions*, edited by J.B. McClure (Chicago: Rhodes & McClure Publishing Company, 1889), 225, 228.

22. Lauer, 576.

23. E.F. Bleiler, with Richard Bleiler. *Science-Fiction: The Early Years: A Full Description of More Than 3, 000 Science-Fiction Stories from Earliest Times to the Appearance of Genre Magazines in 1930* (Kent, OH: Kent State University Press, 1990), xxi.

24. Milne, "The Great Electrical Diaphragm," *The Argonaut*, May 24, 1879, 3.

25. *San Francisco Bulletin*, March 3, 1877. Reprinted in the Jefferson City, Missouri *State Journal*, March 30, 1877, 2. Though we cannot know with certainty, the unattributed opinion piece does not appear to be printed in jest.

26. Relevant examples include Shelley's *Frankenstein; or, The Modern Prometheus* (1818, 1831), Verne's *20,000 Leagues Under the Sea* (1870), and Wells's *The Time Machine* (1895) and *The Island of Doctor Moreau* (1896).

27. It must be noted that Edward Page Mitchell's "The Soul Spectroscope" from *The Sun* (December 1875) is a notable exception, as Professor Dummkopf imagines his lie-detector invention dispersed into society at large, "bring[ing] about a millennium of truth and sincerity" (160).

28. Milne, "A Dip into Space," *The Argonaut*, August 27, 1881, 1.

29. See "A Question of Reciprocity," *Into the Sun and Other Stories*, 217–253.

30. I examine these stories in great detail in my master's dissertation, The Veil of the Future: Technological Optimism and Anxiety in the Works of Robert Duncan Milne, University of Liverpool, 2017.

31. See Darko Suvin, *Metamorphoses of Science Fiction: On the Poetics and History of a Literary Genre* (New Haven: Yale University Press, 1979). Suvin later employed the term "novum" to summarize what he described here as "an imaginative framework alternative to the author's empirical environment" (8)—or, more generally, a novelty or innovation.

The Pulp Cauldron
of the 1960s

Ace Books and Ursula K. Le Guin

GEORGE SLUSSER

[Editor's note: this manuscript, which Gary Westfahl found in George Slusser's papers, has never been published in English, although a Danish translation, entitled "1960s Pulp-Kedel: Ace Books og Ursula K. Le Guin," appeared in the Danish journal *Passage—Tidsskrift for Litteratur og Kritik* in 1997. Its relative brevity, and the presence of a few errors in the text, strongly suggest that Slusser regarded it solely as a draft, which he chose to never revise for proper publication; instead, one guesses, he offered it as a courtesy to a Danish scholar associated with the journal that he encountered at a European conference. In editing the manuscript to be published here, Westfahl retained virtually all of Slusser's language while silently correcting the errors.]

American science fiction in the 1960s was, to use a semi-appropriate metaphor, a cauldron of creative activity. As with the hippie "counterculture" in the streets, the surge of creativity in science fiction was a product of a sudden and rapid expansion of technological means to do things. In terms of means of publication and dissemination of sf narratives, this decade saw the rise to dominance of the paperback. Sf had, from its inception in the American pulp magazines, been an ungoverned and "unpoliced" genre. It cultivated the gaudy, even tawdry, in its shameless desire to purvey stories about the great adventure of this century—that of scientific advancement. The format of the magazine however to some extent reined in the energy of sf by restricting its narratives to the short story or serialized novella forms. The rise of paperbacks as preferred medium in the 1960s however unleashed the creative energy of sf, gave it versatility, power, and (most important) scope and diversity.

The most significant of paperback lines in the 1960s was Ace Books, and in particular the "Ace Double" series. Side by side in the prodigious production of Ace Books were old pulpsters and new writers, many of whom were to lead the "new wave" of American sf in the 1970s and even 1980s. I have chosen here the case of one newcomer—Ursula K. Le Guin. Le Guin's exuberances of the 1960s are especially significant, both for the redirection of sf, and for a sense of the literary and cultural legacy of the 1960s in general. Coming from a very un-pulpish background—the daughter of two eminent university professors of anthropology at Berkeley—Le Guin sought liberation in the pulp cauldron of Ace Books. Then, in the next decade, as a now-established sf writer, she renounces her pulp excesses in favor of more conventional and "literary" forms of narrative.

Le Guin's trajectory here is in many ways an exemplary one. A writer who, given her intellectual milieu, ten years earlier would have sought expression in "little" poetry magazines (indeed Le Guin has and continues to write poetry), Le Guin plunges into pulp sf, producing in rapid succession a "trilogy" of novels—*Rocannon's World* (1966), *Planet of Exile* (1966), and *City of Illusions* (1967). In these novels, she sets forth, in the organic fashion of the open-ended pulp "space opera" series, the parameters of a "universe"—that of the Hainish League of All Worlds, later to become the Ekumen of the novel (also published by Ace) that is considered her first "significant" work, *The Left Hand of Darkness* (1969). Conventional wisdom has discounted these early novels as a workshop, nothing more. I myself, in awe perhaps at what I thought I saw emerging then in *The Left Hand of Darkness*, made such a statement in 1976:

> These early novels, however skillfully written, remain verbal skeletons, too stylized and bound by the conventions of space adventure to be truly effective. In *The Left Hand of Darkness*, Le Guin takes a bold step, for here the Hainish saga is transposed into concrete terms—recognizable societies, with men instead of symbols. *The Left Hand of Darkness* is far more complex than its predecessors.[1]

It is clear, from the titles of the novels alone, that Le Guin moves away from the pulp tradition. *Planet of Exile* or *City of Illusions* have the classic formula ring, as if they could interchangeably fit on any number of paperback novels written in the 1960s. *The Left Hand of Darkness* not only offers "literary" resonances (Emerson, Hawthorne, Melville) alien to pulp space opera, but in its Taoist overtones makes specific reference to actual contemporary cultural "reality," in this case the hippie fascination with things Eastern. This latter is an absolutely new accent for a pulp genre that had generated its own linguistic and cultural conventions, and worked almost hermetically within them, producing titles that refer back to the core of space adventure, not outward to immediate cultural or social matters. I do not mean to minimize the achievement of *The Left Hand of Darkness*, nor to find fault with the need, within any narrative genre, to create more complex structures. What I would argue however is that "complexity" in literature need not be measured automatically in terms of "men" rather than formulas or symbols. Understandably, it must have been tempting for writers like Le Guin, Samuel R. Delany, or even Philip K. Dick—all of whom made their literary debut in Ace Books— to move from pulp fiction to the respectable complexity of more conventional modes. Yet in the case of each of these writers, when one measures later narratives against the early pulp novels—for Delany the later Tales of Neveryon against a work like *The Einstein Intersection* (Ace 1967) or in Dick's case the late *VALIS* (1981) with his first novel *Solar Lottery* (Ace 1955)—one sees just how much energy and creativity was lost. Of all these writers, Le Guin is most vocal in repudiating her pulp beginnings. This reputation has been subsequently amplified in the many mouths of her feminist admirers, who despite their "radical" pretensions prefer in terms of literary allies the more conventional and consecrated forms of "utopia," and even "fantasy." Her case therefore can stand, in terms of sixties' rebellion and seventies' realignment, as exemplary.

Before I discuss the nature of Le Guin's first Ace trilogy, it is necessary to contextualize them as products of the Ace publishing phenomenon. Since its creation in 1953, the U.S. paperback house Ace Books has specialized in science fiction. During the 1960s, two notable editors—Donald A. Wollheim and Terry Carr—were behind the prodigious output of Ace; Wollheim had a marked taste for classic sf adventure fiction, but also an interest in broader categories of writing (after 1972, when he left Ace to form his own company, DAW Books, Wollheim was the rare publisher to offer translations of foreign-language sf, notably works of the Strugatsky brothers). Wollheim and Carr had an uncanny ability to discover new talent.[2] During the 1960s, first works by a host of writers later to become famous as the "new wave" were produced. In the Ace list, we find works of old pulpsters like Ray Cummings, Murray Leinster, and Otis Adelbert Kline, the sword and sorcery by Robert E. Howard, and novels of Isaac Asimov (*Foundation* [1951] and *Foundation and Empire* [1952], which Wollheim retitled *The 1,000 Year Plan* and *The Man Who Upset the Universe*) next to novels by new-name writers: Dick, Delany, Le Guin, John Brunner, Thomas M. Disch, Robert Silverberg, and Roger Zelazny. Reading the Ace list of titles and authors, one has the impression of worlds colliding, of a fermenting cauldron of old and new. Results are often surprising: from this forced fusion of styles and forms there might emerge new sf experiments (Delany's *Babel-17* [1966]), or new forms of old pulp (Gordon Dickson's *The Genetic General* [1960] or works of H. Beam Piper).

Almost as if it were a purposeful means of forcing collisions between generations of sf writers, Ace Books devised a unique paperback form—the so-called Ace Double. The format linked two short novels, sometimes by a same author but usually by two separate writers, often of glaringly disparate natures and styles, back to back, with separate covers and texts upside down in relation to each other. Whichever novel one begins with is read to its end in the middle of the book, then the book is turned over and upside down, and the second novel is read. One finds such unusual linkages as Samuel R. Delany's first novel *The Jewels of Aptor* (1962) with James White's *Second Ending* (1962), where in the same book two very different forms of pulp adventure form an invisible continuity. Or there is new writer Robert Silverberg's *Collision Course* coupled with Leigh Brackett's *The Nemesis from Terra* (1961), again two different generational variations on shared space opera formulas, or Dick's surrealist *Solar Lottery* linked with another Leigh Brackett story, *The Big Jump* (1955). Reading and handling these two novels back to back, one literally feels that the conventional "jump" to Barnard's Star in Brackett is being challenged by the innovative imagination of Dick, who would introduce fantastic telekinetic displacements to other planets, unaided by rockets, in later novels like *The Simulacra* (1964). These are the sorts of jumps that will become the trademark of his zany variations on pulp conventions, now deemed "postmodern" inventions by critics.

It is significant that Le Guin's first novel, *Rocannon's World*, appeared back to back with Avram Davidson's *The Kar-Chee Reign* (1966). Davidson's pulp adventure is a stock tale of alien invasion, of the "strange monstrous Kar-Chee from the depths of the stars," and of the rebirth of human resistance on mother Earth left behind and depleted in our race to galactic empire.[3] As if in dialectical response to Davidson, Le Guin's story presents Earth members of the Galactic League not in the act of "invading" other worlds, but of bringing to them new technologies, in this case telepathy. The threat here is no longer to some sacred Earth stock, but rather to the environmental balance of the entire galactic system, the system that, by sustaining order on all worlds, maintains the equilibrium needed for humankind to exist at all. Le Guin has drawn energy from endless pulp retellings of the alien menace story, and in telling her variation on the story pushed the envelope, adding a new sense to the dynamics of intergalactic involvement. This collaborative sense, of writers not directly influencing each other, but sharing a common epic "matter" of situations and conventions, is lost if we consider a novel like *Rocannon's World* as simply the early pulp version of a later "literary" masterpiece.

We find the same sort of osmotic link between Le Guin's next novel, *Planet of Exile*, and its inverted Siamese twin, in this case Thomas M. Disch's first novel *Mankind Under the Leash* (1966), later republished as *The Puppies of Terra* and "White Fang Goes Dingo." Disch's work is itself an elaborate, literary-picaresque version of the alien master story, where the human pet White Fang rebels by "going dingo," investing the forms of the ruling Dingo race—a cross between space opera and Cervantes's "Dialogue of the Dogs" (1613). In Le Guin's novel, the treatment of this same alien master scenario is equally open to external or extra-formulaic concerns. These however are not the parodic concerns of mock-epic, with its overlay of literary and stylistic allusions; instead Le Guin's story makes clear gestures to the contemporary political reality of America's invasion of Vietnam. In this novel, we find Terrans of the same magnanimous but misguided League of All Worlds caught in the invasion of a "primitive" planet by a powerful alien race, the Gaals. Driven to take common cause with the people of this Planet of Exile, the Terrans begin to succumb to native infections, losing their former immunity to "alien" bacteria. Simultaneously, however, the infections that bring death also bring a new promise of life, and the means of overthrowing the Gaal masters. Just as in Disch's novel a human becomes a pet, a White Fang, so that in the end he can become a Dingo, and in this roundabout way hope to free a subjugated humanity, so in Le Guin it is through Terrans growing biologically closer to what was thought a primitive race that a dynamic and liberating fusion can occur. This is the same "new future" promised in endless stories of this sort; but the ways of getting there, and thus the nature of that future itself, have changed significantly. Again, the significance of the change can only be measured in relation to the tradition of the pulp space epic that drives that change.

This pulp tradition is clearly the force that, via the early Ace trilogy, nourishes *The Left Hand of Darkness*. But there are other emerging elements as well in this substantially larger novel, elements that begin to be reflected in the Ace presentation itself, perhaps as internal marks of the increasingly "literary" nature and status of the narrative itself. *Rocannon's World* and *Planet of Exile* appeared in double format, their covers adorned with (in both cases) fascinating yet formulaic icons of space adventure—Rocannon astride a giant dragon holding aloft a torch in Gerald McConnell's cover, or Rolery, the primitive heroine of *Planet*, depicted as a fur-clad "savage" in a landscape where galaxies and suns vie with what appear to be runic or primitive circular scratchings, in the magnificent cover by Jerome Podwill. The third novel, *City of Illusions*, is significantly an Ace Single. Although the novel also betrays its pulp roots, as Le Guin's variation on the classic theme of a future Earth conquered by sinister aliens, its cover features a painting by sf artist Jack Gaughan that de-emphasizes icons of galactic travels and primitive encounters to place full focus on half a human face with a probing yellow eye. In this composition, spaceships and "aliens" have been reduced to abstract motifs, mere decorations surrounding the giant face. The Ace edition of *The Left Hand of Darkness* is, more than a single, an "Ace Science Fiction Special."

In its cover painting, the pulp icons have altogether given way to stylized human faces and abstract bubble motifs. Departing from the pulp tradition, wherein noteworthy artists were cherished for illustrating the works of numerous science fiction writers, the Ace Science Fiction Specials had covers by Leo and Diane Dillon, artists favored by Harlan Ellison who otherwise avoided science fiction to focus on illustrating children's books. Lacking a following in the field, these artists could not draw attention away from what has now become a work of literature in itself. The ties to the collective pulp tradition that nourishes and sustains Le Guin's novel have been severed.

The question to ask here is: what sort of narrative is *The Left Hand of Darkness* in relation to the "pulpier" novels that precede it? On an obvious level, the changes seem to be in the direction away from adventure toward a more comprehensive world building. This same tendency occurs (slightly earlier in the decade) in the work of Frank Herbert, if we measure the distance between a work like *Under Pressure*, also known as *Dragon in the Sea* (1955), with *Dune*, which appeared in 1965. In *The Left Hand of Darkness* (as in *Dune*), subtle shifts away from the pulp adventure genre permit a deepening contextualization of "action." The result is both a profusion of didactic elements on multiple levels of the narrative, and a corollary immobilizing of the action, its transformation into something to be observed rather than vicariously experienced. For example, the Planet of Exile had winters thirty years long, a hardship the protagonist(s) must endure and overcome. In *The Left Hand of Darkness*, however, the planet itself is Winter. The observer from the Ekumen, Genly Ai, coming to Winter, must adapt to its unrelenting ecology. And to adapt, he must describe its milieu, the complex interrelations between climate, geography, and denizens. In this self-contained world, all vestiges of interplanetary invasions, winged or fuzzy "aliens," "primitive" and "advanced" cultures, are gone. There are two rival societies—Karhide, an ineffectual monarchy, and Orgoreyn, a socialist dystopia—and beneath these, the rich Gethenian culture, with its myths and religions. Social relations are rendered problematic, not through alien invasion, but from within, as a result of androgynous Gethenian sexuality, where each individual is alternately male and female.

Le Guin has created a self-generating dynamic that permits, like *Dune*, the elaboration of a multi-layered world, a process that comes to fruition in 1960s sf, and demands the greater length of the hardback format (*Dune*), or more prophetically perhaps the expanded Ace Special paperback format. Indeed, toward the end of this decade, the thick paperback emerges, and with it the triumph of didactic world-elaboration, the process that eventually allowed Heinlein's publishers to produce the much lengthier, uncut version of his *Stranger in a Strange Land* (1961) as a paperback best-seller in 1991. However admirable Le Guin's world-building in *The Left Hand of Darkness*, it permits at the same time a subtle shift away from the pulp origins toward (in this case) a concerted gentrification of sf. Within the frame of the Hainish League of Worlds, and its promise of intergalactic adventure, Le Guin allows conventional literary forms and "genres" to proliferate. Genly Ai is a new Gulliver or Prendick, the outside observer who embraces the alien culture to such a degree that he in turn is alienated from his initial world. Orgoreyn is the classic dystopia; Karhide a comic opera kingdom; and the Handdara "fastness circle" that underlies this culture provides its utopian substratum, the conservative sense that in folk myth and culture, buried by technological "advancement," lies the true order of things, an order *a priori* humane because "organic." Just as conservative are the Hemingwayesque overtones of the central "adventure" of the narrative—Ai's and Estraven's heroic trek over the ice. For what is implied by this ritual of bonding is all too conventional—that truth in human relations (and the characters here are distressingly human despite their anomalies) is only found in extreme struggle and communion with harsh nature. The pulp adventure of an early Le Guin hero like Rocannon has now become adventure worthy of *Argosy* magazine.

It seems then that a significant transformation was taking place in the 1960s within the vital stream of pulp fiction, in organic fashion, as reflected in the development of Ace Books from the Doubles to the Specials. If what is being created is a "new wave," then (to extend the metaphor) this wave is but one of many within the flow of pulp. Le Guin, however, in the very act of generating her new wave masterpiece from this pulp stream, is quick to renounce it. Le Guin calls this stream "the saurian ooze." The term comes from an essay she wrote called "A Citizen of Mondath," published in the British journal *Foundation: The Review of Science Fiction* in 1973. She describes her early contact with magazine sf, and her tone is one of bemused condescension:

> I liked "Lewis Padgett" best and looked for his stories, but we looked for the trashiest magazines, mostly, because we liked trash. I recall one story that began, "In the beginning was the Bird." We really dug that bird. And the closing line from another (or the same?)—"Back to the saurian ooze from whence it sprung."[4]

Le Guin goes on to tell how she "got off science fiction some time in the late forties":

> It seemed to be all about hardware and soldiers. Besides I was busy with Tolstoy and things. I did not read any science fiction at all for about fifteen years, just about that period which people call the Golden Age.... I almost totally missed Heinlein, et al. If I glanced at a magazine, it still seemed to be all about starship captains in black with lean rugged faces and a lot of fancy artillery [27].

This is obviously a pose, the classic litany many utter in relation to sf: it is a literature for children, and thank god it is trash, for this makes it easier to put away child's things and grow up. Far from the Olympian height of "Tolstoy and stuff," sf never grows up. It is ever playing with war toys, and drawing lantern-jawed "starship captains," who gaze into the depths of the cosmos. But why did Le Guin, who so successfully used these same pulp icons, so flippantly disparage them?

In subsequent editions of her early pulp novels, Le Guin provides new introductions that subtly disavow their pulp source. In the "Introduction" to the 1978 edition of *Planet of Exile*, for example, Le Guin recontextualizes pulp adventure in terms of the Tao and feminism. She claims the way of this book is "both in one: or two making a whole," yin and yang. The central constant theme of her work (as of this date) is, she tells us, "marriage":

> I haven't yet written a book worthy of that tremendous (and staggeringly unfashionable) theme. I haven't figured out yet what I meant. But rereading this early, easygoing adventure story, I think the theme is there—not clear, not strong, but being striven toward. "I learn by going where I have to go."[5]

This description gives the feel of the flow of that same sf current that her "easygoing" narrative, in all three Ace novels, is moving through. But Le Guin is once again driven, in retrospect, to immobilize this flow. For she seeks, in this "Introduction," to qualify the particular marriage in *Planet of Exile* in the dualist sense of yin and yang:

> Taoism got to me earlier than modern feminism did. Where some see only a dominant Hero and a passive Little Woman, I saw, and still see, the essential wastefulness and futility of aggression, and the profound effectiveness of *wu wei*, "action through stillness" [141].

There is a fascinating, no doubt subliminal, dialectic going on here between flow and stasis, and with it a gradual hardening of the fluid categories both of pulp adventure and the Tao into rigid duality. From the discussion of flow and change, essentialist and separatist categories begin to emerge. Pulp is now caught up in the canonized sequence of mainstream English prose, and both pulp and Virginia Woolf (when immobilized in this manner) prove "unsuited to the description of feminine being and doing." The solution Le Guin proposes to this impasse is a complete remaking of narrative that seems to oppose all "drift" of conventional forms:

> It is hard to break from tradition … hard to remake one's mother tongue. One drifts along and takes the easy way. Nothing can rouse one to go against the stream, to choose the hard way, but a profoundly stirred, and probably an angry, conscience [141].

Yet it is precisely by not going against the stream, by reshaping male and female relations from within the confines of pulp types and expectations, that Le Guin succeeds so admirably, in her early Ace sf adventures, in conveying precisely this sense of continuity, of "both in one." She seems, in her retrospective "Introduction," to be looking back in anger, drawing very un–Tao-like battle lines. On the contrary, however, it is the early Hainish trilogy that reveals the "easy" to be the hard way, the way that works, from deep within the sf stream, to prove the profound effectiveness of "action through stillness."

In conclusion, Le Guin's early Ace novels are, for most critics, overshadowed by *The Left Hand of Darkness*. Probably, they are ignored by critics because Le Guin herself looks back in embarrassment on them—or rather, as I have tried to show, with deep ambiguity as to her own sf origins. We have seen that these novels, once re-placed in the context of Ace Books and the deep flow of creativity emerging from its "saurian ooze" in the 1960s, are no mere preamble to more experimental narratives. Instead they are, if seen in the pulp context, significant experiments themselves. Le Guin's trilogy stands, with Delany's *Fall of the Towers* (Ace Books, 1963–1965) as a stunning example of space-opera trilogy, impositions of the magic number three on otherwise boundless adventure.

NOTES

1. George Slusser, *The Farthest Shores of Ursula K. Le Guin* (San Bernardino, CA: Borgo Press, 1976), 16. The "farthest shores" at that time did not reach very far from the Ace decade, as far as *The Dispossessed* (1974). As a reader with his nose too close on one hand to the "literary" renaissance of sf by means of writers like Le Guin, Delany, Ellison, Dick, Silverberg and others, most of whom were part of the Ace new wave, and on the other too far by virtue of my own 60s generation from the pulp Golden Age, I was at that time an uncritical recipient of the "elevation" of pulp sf to the status of "literature" as measured in terms of creating "real men" (i.e., "round" characters in the realist tradition of fiction) rather than "symbols" (i.e., the vaguely symbolic fantasy names of sf space opera). Now, more than twenty years later, and having observed the further shores of writers like Le Guin and Delany, I am skeptical of the benefits of this "elevation" of sf.

2. Carr rejoined Ace as Editor in 1984, and began a series of Ace Specials that featured first novels. Among the works he commissioned from new writers who had never written novels were William Gibson's *Neuromancer* (1984), Kim Stanley Robinson's *The Wild Shore* (1984), and Lucius Shepard's *Green Eyes* (1984).

3. Avram Davidson, *The Kar-Chee Reign*, published dos-à-dos with Le Guin's *Rocannon's World* (New York: Ace Books, 1966), blurb on the first page of Davidson's half of the book.

4. Ursula K. Le Guin, "A Citizen of Mondath,"1973, *The Language of the Night: Essays on Fantasy and Science Fiction*, edited by Susan Wood (1979; New York: Harper Collins), 1992, 22. Page references are to this edition.

5. Le Guin, "Introduction" to *Planet of Exile*, 1978, in *Language of the Night*, 143. Page references are to this edition.

The Homeostatic Culture Machine Revisited, or, the Contemporary Wordmills of Science Fiction

Gary Westfahl

I have always maintained that all science fiction scholars face one basic choice: they can invent science fiction, or they can study science fiction. To invent science fiction, scholars may assemble all the texts that they like, devise a definition of science fiction that includes all their favorites and excludes all the texts they dislike, arrange the selected works in chronological order, and draw upon general historical trends or purported textual clues to discern within the preferred works a coherent literary "tradition." This was the approach expressly employed in Darko Suvin's *Metamorphoses of Science Fiction: On the Poetics and History of a Literary Genre* (1979), which has inexplicably remained an admired and influential critical work despite my energetic efforts to condemn its manifest and innumerable flaws.

To study science fiction, scholars must begin with some key questions: at what time did people begin to identify certain works as "science fiction," and who were the people who thought of themselves as science fiction writers and science fiction readers? How did these individuals communicate and interact, and how did they tangibly influence the genre of science fiction as it evolved and matured? These are questions that can be answered by means of research and documentation, not creative writing, and such labors—which necessarily focus on the actual twentieth-century tradition of science fiction founded by Hugo Gernsback—have long been my central preoccupation as a science fiction scholar. And, to extend one's study of science fiction into contemporary times, scholars cannot limit themselves to the books being reviewed in *Locus* magazine or those that have attracted the interest of their colleagues; instead, they must visit a bookstore and examine all the books in the "Science Fiction and Fantasy" section—something I have now done on three occasions.

Demonstrating the remarkable breadth of his scholarship, George Slusser placed himself firmly on both sides of the critical debate I have outlined. On one hand, he enthusiastically praised *Metamorphoses of Science Fiction* when it was first published,[1] and in later writings about the origins and early history of science fiction, Slusser argued that the individuals who contributed key intellectual ideas to the genre were effectively part of its history; thus, he repeatedly discussed several figures—including René Descartes, Blaise Pascal, Benjamin Constant, Thomas De Quincey, E.T.A. Hoffmann, and Honoré de Balzac—who are rarely if ever mentioned in other histories of science fiction. I understand his reasoning, but all of this sounds suspiciously like another ingenious effort to invent science fiction—and, not incidentally, to bolster its image by adding some impressive names to its heritage. On the other hand, Slusser also understood the importance of Gernsback and the series of science fiction pulp magazines that he brought into existence, and he was regularly willing to study and write about texts from that milieu that lofty critics like Suvin would never deign to examine. For example, he was fascinated by the way that Gernsback re-invented Jules Verne while presenting his works to American readers, and he repeatedly analyzed the works of Robert A. Heinlein, one of the many authors nurtured and shaped by the pulp tradition, along with other writers of his era. And, when he undertook to examine the state of contemporary science fiction, he also went to the marketplace to see what books had just been published—although instead of traveling to a bookstore, he examined "the distribution racks of a local magazine warehouse, which circulates new books, and retrieves and remainders what does not sell,"[2] undoubtedly during one of his many missions to purchase books for the Eaton Collection.

Slusser's visit was inspired by the theme of the 1990 J. Lloyd Eaton Conference on Science Fiction and Fantasy Literature, "Science Fiction and Market Realities," a topic chosen in response to innumerable complaints around that time that the once-variegated and thought-provoking genre of science fiction was being inundated, and disastrously transformed, by repetitive sequels and series. Speaker after speaker passionately denounced this horrendous development, berated all the villains who were purportedly responsible for this degradation of the genre, and demanded vigorous action to eradicate these iterative invaders and restore science fiction to its original, uncorrupted nature.

Characteristically, Slusser refused to follow the script. Instead, in his fascinating contribution to the conference volume, "The Homeostatic Culture

Machine," Slusser described the "homeopape," a newspaper written by a machine in Philip K. Dick's story "If There Was No Benny Cemoli" (1963), in order to argue that the state of contemporary science fiction was not a matter of "agency" (79); instead, science fiction was now being produced not by human beings, but by a similar sort of machine. Much later, as it happens, I developed an interest in science fiction stories about devices like the home-opape, such as the novel-writing machine envisioned in R.K. Narayan's *The Vendor of Sweets* (1967), and I drafted an entry for the online Encyclopedia of Science Fiction on that topic entitled "Writing Machines." However, co-editor David Langford and I agreed that that term, which has other meanings, was not a good choice, and after that erudite editor added several additional examples to my entry, he suggested that we borrow the term for novel-writing machines used in Fritz Leiber's *The Silver Eggheads* (1959), "wordmills," as the heading for what was posted as our jointly written entry.[3] If this becomes the standard term, we can now rephrase the question that Slusser raised: are the science fiction and fantasy books now available in bookstores being produced by people, or by wordmills?

As Slusser himself realized, his daring conceit was not at the time, and is not today, literally true: contemporary computers have grown rather adept at generating poetry, some of it strangely appealing, and researchers are undoubtedly working to train computers to work in other literary genres. But we can be confident that science fiction novels are still being written, edited, and copyedited by human beings. Still, although Slusser himself would not have defended his idea in this manner, I can discern one way in which his argument might be validated. As major publishing companies grow larger and larger, and as the decisions of their employees are increasingly constrained by more and more extensive, and more and more detailed, market research, there may indeed come a time when the process of creating a work, and gradually shaping and preparing it as it moves from an author's computer to the shelves of Barnes and Noble, will effectively become a purely mechanical operation, proceeding almost automatically, even if this novel-writing "machine" consists entirely of human components. Writers, knowing what publishers prefer, and perhaps provided with extensive guidelines and instructions, can only be creative within certain prescribed parameters; agents, even more knowledgeable about publishing practices, may further prod writers to limit themselves to safe, market-friendly decisions; editors may reject works that do not precisely match the expectations imposed by superiors, or demand revisions so that the book touches all of the bases deemed essential to financial success; and even some readers, preconditioned to look for certain sorts of products, may avoid the occasional idiosyncratic text that somehow slips through the cracks, leading to dismal sales that either drive the rebellious writers out of the marketplace altogether or force them back to more predictable and palatable pathways. It is even possible to imagine, as Slusser did, that the impetus for the production of science fiction will cease to involve purely "economic forces" (95); for as long as books are earning enough money to justify their publication, the executives of conglomerates may be content to let the science fiction machine continue operating as it always has, declining to investigate ways to further boost their profits while focusing on other aspects of their vast and multifaceted businesses.

Still, the history of economics is filled with examples of guaranteed formulas for success that eventually failed due to changing conditions, as I noted in my own contribution to the conference volume *Science Fiction and Market Realities*,[4] creating the hope that monolithic megacorporations might someday be forced to abandon their rules and again engage in creative experiments to address unanticipated shifts in readers' preferences that led to sales so disappointing that they could not be ignored. So, I suggested, fears of the corporate homogenization of science fiction may have been overblown, as the genre might evolve back to its original state, either due to inevitable changes in the marketplace—my argument—or as a result of its own unpredictable, self-directed evolution—Slusser's argument.

Twenty-two years after *Science Fiction and Market Realities* was published, it seems a good time to assess the current state of science fiction to see if these hopes have been fulfilled. So, on April 18, 2018, I entered the Barnes and Noble bookstore in Montclair, California, to closely examine the books available in its "Science Fiction and Fantasy" section.

In focusing solely on the 96 shelves of that section—divided into the subcategories of anthologies, general fiction, books based on role-playing games, and other media-inspired series—I should first note that I was neglecting to examine four other sections related to science fiction: the 54 shelves devoted to "Teen Fantasy/Adventure," the 8 shelves for "Gaming," the 30 shelves for "Graphic Novels," and the 56 shelves for "Manga." Though numbers of shelves do not necessarily correlate to numbers of books, it is interesting that the total amount of space allocated for these publications—all traditionally regarded as unworthy of critical attention—far exceeds the amount of space allocated for adult science fiction and fantasy, though it is increasingly the case that talented authors are moving into the fields of young-adult fiction and graphic novels, making scholars more and more willing to study these forms of literature. Some time in the future, then, interested scholars may be obliged to include these sections in their bookstore surveys, but I thought it best at this time to limit myself to the smaller, but still substantial, section devoted to adult science fiction and fantasy.

As another caveat, part of my plan was to draw conclusions from counting the number of books in different sections, but I found that a significant number of books had been incorrectly shelved. One might blame customers indifferently reshelving books that they had decided not to buy in the wrong place, but clueless employees must be blamed as well. For example, several books by Ursula K. Le Guin in the "G" section were surely put there by an employee who didn't know any better, though most of her books were in the "L" section where they belonged. Because I intended to pay special attention to anthologies, the problem of anthologies incorrectly shelved with novels particularly bothered me, so much so that I actually moved three of them into the proper section and adjusted my statistics accordingly. However, quickly realizing that I was tampering with my data, I made no further effort to correct shelving errors, though I took note of them. Thus, I can report that three books in the "Science Fiction and Fantasy" section were not science fiction or fantasy at all: Ernest Hemingway's story collection *In Our Time* (1925); Norman Doidge's nonfictional *The Brain's Way of Healing: Remarkable Discoveries and Recoveries from the Frontiers of Neuroplasticity* (2015); and Jessi Klein's autobiographical *You'll Grow Out of It* (2016). Perhaps some employee thought that Hemingway's and Doidge's titles sounded science-fictional, but I have no idea why Klein's book ended up in this section. More significantly, there were over 20 books in the general section that clearly belonged with the series, including several adaptations of *The Walking Dead* (2010–), a *Doctor Who* book, a *Star Wars* book, and a World of Warcraft book.

I began my survey by simply counting all the books in this section, not counting duplicate copies or different editions of the same book—but I quickly encountered another problem. Today, authors are not only writing long series of similar books, but they are giving their books almost-identical titles, and publishers are providing them all with almost-identical covers. Thus, it could be surprisingly difficult to distinguish one book in a series from another. Consider the output of John G. Hemry, who writes as Jack Campbell, one of the innumerable prolific authors I encountered that I had never heard of, and one that has never to my knowledge been mentioned by a science fiction scholar. (I confirmed this by visiting the Science Fiction and Fantasy Research Database, which endeavors to list every critical book and article written about science fiction, searching for both his real name and his pseudonym, and obtaining no results.) One can also be confident that his pseudonym was not chosen as a way to pay tribute to innovative editor John W. Campbell, Jr., who surely would have rejected in an instant all of his redundant "military science fiction" novels as possible serials in *Analog: Science Fiction/Science Fact*. His original Lost Fleet series consists of six books—*The Lost Fleet: Dauntless* (2006), *The Lost Fleet: Fearless* (2007), *The Lost Fleet: Courageous* (2007), *The Lost Fleet: Valiant* (2008), *The Lost Fleet: Relentless* (2009), and *The Lost Fleet: Victorious* (2010)—all but one on display at Barnes and Noble with extremely similar covers. He went on to write another series of five related books, *The Lost Fleet: Beyond the Frontier: Dreadnaught* (2011),

The Lost Fleet: Beyond the Frontier: Invincible (2012), *The Lost Fleet: Beyond the Frontier: Guardian* (2013), *The Lost Fleet: Beyond the Frontier: Steadfast* (2014), and *The Lost Fleet: Beyond the Frontier: Leviathan* (2015)—all available in equally similar covers. As an aid for confused readers, the usual strategy for publishers is to employ different background colors for each book in a series, but there are only so many colors in the rainbow, and I also encountered instances of the same book available in two different, but almost identical covers. Such books indeed seem to be the products of machines, and one has to wonder whether this is really a viable publishing strategy; surely, there must come a point when even Campbell's most dedicated fans look for the latest installment of their favorite series, pick up a Campbell book they don't recognize, and then ask themselves: wait a minute, haven't I read this book before?

So, acknowledging that the data may be distorted by flawed shelving decisions or my own failure to distinguish different novels that look almost exactly the same, I offer these statistics, adjusted to the best of my ability to acknowledge the discrepancies noted above: there were a total of 1663 science fiction and fantasy books on the 96 examined shelves. There were 39 anthologies, 1309 general novels, and 315 installments of media-related series. In terms of percentages, 81 percent of the books were shelved as the original works of authors (novels and anthologies), while only 19 percent were shelved as adaptations of role-playing games, video games, films, or television programs. On the face of it, this appears to represent heartening news for commentators in the 1990s who worried that science fiction was being taken over by media franchises; original science fiction, it would seem, is alive and well, and still dominating the market. Yet many of the "original" works of science fiction, of course, are installments in series creating by individual authors that, in most cases, closely mimic the series based on films, television series, or games, and hence represent only another example of the trends that so alarmed earlier critics.

To estimate how common such series were, I undertook another survey with results that are necessarily only suggestive, not definitive, since I was not obsessive enough to examine each of the 1309 books in the general section to accurately determine whether they were standalone works or part of a series. So, I relied on less reliable criteria: if the titles of the spines of books included some umbrella title, like "Book II of the [blank] Chronicles" or "A [blank] book," if a series of books had the same author and shared the same design, or if the books were by an author known to specialize in interminable series (like Mercedes Lackey), I classified them as "series" books. If books lacked any sort of umbrella title, if they did not resemble any adjacent books, and if the author was not known for an obsession with generating series, I classified them as "standalone" books. Needless to say, these criteria are far from infallible: publishers may republish radically different works with similar designs if they think that might improve sales, books in a series may not necessarily look the same, and even authors famous for their series might occasionally publish an unrelated book. Yet I would guess that my errors all balanced out—that the number of standalone books misclassified as series books was about the same as the number of series books misclassified as standalone books—so I would regard my results as indicative of the general state of science fiction and fantasy, although they cannot be regarded as entirely accurate.

Here are the results: I classified 346 of the 1309 books in the general science fiction and fantasy section as probably standalone books, and the remaining 963 books as probably installments of series. Statistically, that would mean about 26 percent of science fiction and fantasy novels being published as products of a single author's imagination can be considered original works, while 74 percent of the novels not already linked to media franchises can be considered parts of authorial series. (Including the anthologies as original works only slightly improves the percentage to about 29 percent.) To put everything together, combining the number of media-related books and authorial series books, one gets the figure that about 77 percent of all science fiction and fantasy books now being published are installments of series, while only 23 percent are standalone novels or anthologies.

Needless to say, perhaps, I found this survey of contemporary science fiction very depressing, so much so that I was very happy to walk out of the bookstore after my three hours of research—and no, I didn't find any books that I wanted to purchase. As a lifelong reader of science fiction, and a veteran science fiction scholar, it was not heartening to find that a large majority of the books now being published as science fiction and fantasy had been written by authors I had never heard of, and authors I had no desire to read. Looking for reasons to be hopeful, I decided to search the shelves with special care for books that could be considered works of "classic science fiction"—defined as works published before 1980, or later works by authors who became famous before 1980, that would be plausible inclusions in the syllabus of a science fiction class. I found precisely 61 such works. Jules Verne was represented by a single novel, *Journey to the Center of the Earth* (1865), while there were three novels by H.G. Wells—*The Time Machine* (1895), *The Invisible Man* (1897), and *The War of the Worlds* (1898). The "Big Three" science fiction writers of my youth were present—seven books by Isaac Asimov, four by Arthur C. Clarke, and five by Robert A. Heinlein—along with three other authors of their generation: Philip K. Dick (eight books), Frank Herbert (six books), and Ursula K. Le Guin (five books). Other distinguished novels available for purchase included Anthony Burgess's *A Clockwork Orange* (1962), Edgar Rice Burroughs's *A Princess of Mars* (1911) and *Tarzan of the Apes* (1912),

Octavia E. Butler's *Kindred* (1979), Pat Frank's *Alas, Babylon* (1959), Joe Halde-man's *The Forever War* (1974), C.S. Lewis's *Out of the Silent Planet* (1938), Anne McCaffrey's *Dragonflight* (1968), Walter M. Miller, Jr.'s *A Canticle for Leibowitz* (1960), Michael Moorcock's *Behold the Man* (1969), Larry Niven's *Ringworld* (1970), George R. Stewart's *Earth Abides* (1949), and Arkady and Boris Strugatsky's *The Dead Mountaineer's Inn* (1970). I did not compile sta-tistics, but there were also scattered works that might be termed in parallel fashion "classic fantasy," such as Mervyn Peake's *Titus Groan* (1946), an omnibus of Lewis's Narnia novels (1950–1956), and numerous books by H.P. Lovecraft and J.R.R. Tolkien.

While it is heartening to see that many milestones in the history of sci-ence fiction remain available to casual browsers in a contemporary bookstore, one can also bemoan the complete absence of any number of other major contributors to the development of the genre; for my survey of the Barnes and Noble bookshelves found no books by Brian W. Aldiss, Poul Anderson, J.G. Ballard, John Brunner, Hal Clement, Harlan Ellison, Henry Kuttner, Fritz Leiber, Stanislaw Lem, C.L. Moore, Frederik Pohl, Joanna Russ, Robert Sil-verberg, Clifford D. Simak, E.E. "Doc" Smith, Olaf Stapledon, Theodore Stur-geon, A.E. van Vogt, and John Wyndham, and more, equally distinguished names could be added to the list. These are all authors that I became acquainted with by purchasing their books in drugstores and bookstores, and authors that have all received varying degrees of critical attention, but they have now been effectively erased from the genre by modern publishing con-ventions, based on the offerings in bookstores.

One traditional mechanism for introducing older authors to new readers has been the retrospective anthology; but of the relatively small number of anthologies available—39—in the bookstore I visited, 30 consisted of original stories by contemporary writers, 8 were retrospective anthologies (with occasional original stories) focused on specific themes, and only one—Ann VanderMeer and Jeff VanderMeer's *The Big Book of Science Fiction* (2016)—endeavored to provide a comprehensive overview of the genre, with stories by eight of the excluded authors listed above. Indeed, the once-prominent editors of anthologies have now entirely vanished: no one in the 1960s could imagine visiting a bookstore and not seeing an anthology edited by Groff Conklin, and no one in the 1990s could imagine a bookstore without an anthology edited by Martin Harry Greenberg; but neither name could be found in today's Barnes and Noble bookstore, as their herculean efforts to bring superior short fiction to new readers are now, it seems, entirely unknown.

Still, if one is looking for good news, my survey of the books based on media franchises did suggest, interestingly, that these series will not neces-sarily remain popular indefinitely. Back in the 1980s and 1990s, the number one concern of alarmed commentators was the seemingly endless proliferation of *Star Trek* novels; but today, even though a new series is airing episodes and another feature film and another television series have been announced, the bookstore was only offering twelve *Star Trek* novels, indicating that this longstanding publishing juggernaut may finally be losing its appeal. On the other hand, the *Star Wars* franchise seems more robust than ever, represented by 94 books, far more than any other media series. The other franchises that inspired more than ten books in that bookstore were the Warhammer war game (33), its spinoff the Horus Heresy (29), the Halo videogame (17), three variations of the Dungeons and Dragons role-playing game (15), and the television series *Doctor Who* (13), with the *Alien* films just missing the cut with 9 books. Noting that most of the other franchises that inspired fewer than nine books were videogames, and that even the cited film and television series are often experienced by young people primarily by means of licensed videogames, one can readily conclude that games of all kind are now the primary basis for media franchise novels; and while many complain that today's youth are spending too much time playing videogames, those games at least are clearly inspiring many of them to read books—even if they are books that scholars and librarians would not approve of.

In sum, interminable series of related books—whether created by authors or based on films, television programs, or games—may now be entrenched as a permanent and prominent force in the marketplace, but the popularity of particular series, or sorts of series, may constantly change. *Star Trek* fades away, while Warhammer surges. When I last surveyed the science fiction and fantasy section of a Barnes and Noble bookstore, there seemed to be a lot of series of science-fictional detective novels and "steampunk" novels involve fantastic reinventions of Victorian England; this time, I noticed fewer of them, as the pendulum has apparently swung back to space adventures. Fantasy novels were once set almost exclusively in thinly disguised versions of medieval Europe; now, more and more of them take place in modern metropolises. Thus, the novels themselves may be predictable, but the field's novelty may lie in the possible emergence of new sorts of predictable novels, if that is not a contradiction in terms.

As a further bit of good news, it may be distressing that only 23 percent of contemporary science fiction is not a work of series fiction, but that still represents a large number of books—and a large number of very good books. Clearly, there remain a few bookstore browsers who are simply not interested in purchasing and reading long series of virtually identical books, readers who want to read the classic works of famous authors as well as new novels by a few stubborn writers like William Gibson, Kim Stanley Robinson, and Neal Stephenson, who have largely resisted the impulse to focus on interminable series and have instead managed to become successful by writing meritorious individual works. The sort of science fiction that I grew up with, in other words, is not dead; it remains alive and well in contemporary bookstores, though it is now lurking in the niches of shelves otherwise filled with formulaic fiction.

More broadly, bookstores no longer represent the only way—or the best way—to buy books. In the past, one could always order books directly from publishers (which is how I obtained a copy of Ace Books' *The Worlds of Robert A. Heinlein* [1966], a book I had heard of that annoyingly could never be found in any bookstores I frequented), but it was a tedious and time-consuming process; today, one can easily purchase almost any book online, which means that the items available in bookstores no longer represent an accurate picture of the books currently available for customers. Consider the case of Clifford D. Simak, who was long one of my favorite science fiction writers. For decades, I have been visiting bookstores and looking for copies of his books, but there never are any on the shelves, and it was saddening to believe that this once-renowned author had apparently been forgotten. Hence, when a local book club asked me to give a talk about a science fiction novel, and I suggested that they read Simak's *City* (1952), I worried that members might find it difficult to find a copy. But if you visit the Barnes and Noble website instead of one of its bookstores, and do a search for "Clifford D. Simak," you discover that *City* is still in print, along with virtually all of his novels and several collections of his short stories, so those book club members could readily order new, affordable copies of *City* and innumerable other science fiction novels—including books by all the authors listed above whose works were not being displayed in bookstores.

We are witnessing, then, the emergence of an interesting division in the population of people who still like to read science fiction books. If someone is comfortable using the internet, is knowledgeable about science fiction, and prefers particular sorts of books, they will naturally buy virtually all of their books online. The individuals who still frequent bookstores, then, must primarily fall into two categories: either they are unable or unwilling to engage in online shopping, or they know little about science fiction, have no desire to locate specific books, and are therefore required to physically examine books in order to determine whether they would be enjoyable reading material. Bluntly, connoisseurs go to websites, and clods go to bookstores. As a logical result, bookstores would choose to primarily display the science fiction books most appealing to clods—predictable adventures set in familiar imaginary worlds—while connoisseurs obtain copies of the genre's timeless classics or the best modern science fiction from websites.

As I have said before, there is nothing wrong, nothing objectionable, about science fiction that does not meet the high standards of critics and connoisseurs. There have always been numerous people who prefer unchallenging entertainment: in medieval times, people could read the works of Geoffrey Chaucer, but more people chose to watch Punch and Judy shows and laugh uproariously as one hand puppet clobbered another hand puppet; in Renaissance London, the plays of William Shakespeare faced fierce competition from arenas offering bear-baiting; today, the ratings for *Masterpiece Theatre* and *Great Performances* are dwarfed by the ratings for World Wide Wrestling. The only thing unusual about science fiction is that, as I discuss elsewhere,[5] science fiction was settling into a pattern of formulaic fiction during the 1930s when editor John W. Campbell, Jr., and later editors who shared his views, forcefully imposed their own desire for original and variegated stories on the genre, temporarily driving space opera and its relatives into marginal fields like juvenile fiction, film, television, and comic books. Thus, there was a time when, unusually, science fiction for elites represented the norm, not the exception. But inevitably, during the 1980s, the forms of science fiction preferred by most readers soared back into prominence, so that science fiction, probably like most forms of popular fiction, now has a small, well-concealed wing for the elite, where original and imaginative stories still flourish, and a larger, more conspicuous wing for the masses, filled with iterative texts that could fitly be described, in the manner of Slusser, as the products of wordmills, not living authors. All of these books, and similar books in other genres, provide precisely the sort of mindless diversion from everyday life that many people prefer; they are nothing to be annoyed about, nothing to be condemned; they are merely contemporary manifestations of the sorts of less than admirable, but essential, entertainments that have always been a part of human history.

I therefore conclude that George Slusser was both right and wrong: yes, there does exist a contemporary body of science fiction literature seemingly generated by wordmills, a mass of replicative texts that may be strangely evolving in their own, self-directed fashion. Yet there also remain science fiction novels and stories that are visibly hand-crafted by distinctive individual talents, even if they can be hard to find in modern bookstores. Both are legitimate forms of science fiction, and both demand the attention of working science fiction scholars, even if they, like me, will continue to focus solely on only one of its forms for their leisure reading.

NOTES

1. George Slusser, Review of *Metamorphoses of Science Fiction: On the Poetics and History of a Literary Genre* by Darko Suvin, *Nineteenth-Century Fiction*, 35:1 (June 1980), 73–76.

2. Slusser, "The Homeostatic Culture Machine," *Science Fiction and Market Realities*, edited by Gary Westfahl, Slusser, and Eric S. Rabkin (Athens: University of Georgia Press, 1996), 87. Page references are to this edition.

3. Westfahl and David Langford, "Wordmills," *The Encyclopedia of Science Fiction*, Third Edition, edited by John Clute, David Langford, Peter Nicholls (editor emeritus), and

Graham Sleight (managing editor), posted February 14, 2017, at http://sf-encyclopedia.com/entry/wordmills.

4. Westfahl, "Against Agoraphobia: Confronting the Idea of Marketplaces," *Science Fiction and Market Realities*, 7–19.

5. Westfahl, "The Marketplace," *The Oxford Handbook of Science Fiction*, edited by Rob Latham (London: Oxford University Press, 2014), 81–92.

Father of the Strugatskys

The Origins of Russian Science Fantasy

George Slusser

[The following is a chapter from a forthcoming book by the late George Slusser, *Stalkers of the Infinite: Understanding the Science Fiction of the Strugatsky Brothers*. The text, left in draft form, was edited by Gary Kern.]

The English-speaking reader of science fiction too often sees this form through a single lens—its own: English-language sf. The tendency is to measure by a single model all literature that seeks, in Isaac Asimov's famous definition, to represent the impact of scientific and technological advancement on human beings. Yet we see every emerging scientific culture in the Western world striving to create a form of scientific narrative as early as the 18th century, when the impact of modern science and technology began to be felt in an irreversible manner. And we could go even farther back to the 17th century with René Descartes and Blaise Pascal. Throughout the 19th century, parallel developments of scientific narrative arose not just between England and the United States, but in France, Germany and Russia. England produced H.G. Wells, France—Jules Verne, and the U.S.—Edgar Allan Poe. These authors became the three mainstays in the inaugural issues of Hugo Gernsback's *Amazing Stories* (1926). It was here that the term "science fiction" first appeared. If we therefore accept this American magazine as the "birthplace" of modern sf, we are forced to admit a multinational patrimony for the form. Science fiction, such as it exists today, represents a confluence of individual cultural strains.

Absent, it seems, is a Russian "father" for sf. Or for that matter, any East European ancestor. Gernsback has no one to propose. Yet already in 1926 one could find candidates: Konstantin Tsiolkovsky had written the fantasy *On the Moon* (*Na lune*, 1893); Aleksandr Bogdanov—the novel *Red Star* (*Krasnaya zvezda*, 1908); Yevgeny Zamyatin—the novel *We* (*My*, 1924); Alexei Tolstoy—the novel *Aelita* (1923); Mikhail Bulgakov—the novella *The Fatal Eggs* (*Rokovye yaitsa*, 1925); and Aleksandr Belyaev—the story *Professor Dowell's Head* (*Golova Professora Douèllya*, 1925). In Czechoslovakia, Karel Čapek had written the play *R.U.R.* (1920), coined the word *robot*, and raised the specter of robots thinking for themselves and having feelings. Three decades later Stanislaw Lem would begin writing in Poland, and Arkady and Boris Strugatsky in Soviet Russia. All these writers clearly dealt with the themes of science, and with moral, philosophical and physical issues resulting from change brought about by the advancement of scientific learning. Yet to Anglophone readers the shapes or modes this fiction took may appear strange and in need of mediation. The scientific and industrial revolution took an alternate track in this cultural sphere.

This is especially true in Russia. In relation to Europe and its Anglo-French center, Russia occupies a peripheral location analogous to the U.S. in relation to that same Europe. Both Russia and America were latecomers and newcomers to scientific culture. Both had huge resources, and both embraced technology rapidly and radically to make up for lost time. Yet how very different were the ways each of these cultures proceeded to create a technological society. And how different the fictional works that each of these cultures produced.

Our task, then, is to place the Strugatskys in a context that is both international and national, to see them as writers both of "science fiction" in the internationalist sense and in what their culture calls "science-fantasy." Thanks to Roger DeGaris and Macmillan's short-lived but enormously creative "Best of Soviet Science Fiction" series, the major works of the Strugatskys' *opera* were translated and made available to English-speaking readers. Nevertheless, it is clear that very few Strugatsky stories or novels got into the broader sf circuit in the U.S. or England. Their works were largely taken up by the academic critics rather than by fans. Writer Ursula K. Le Guin praised their novel *Hard to Be a God* (1964) as a "thoroughly good book."[1] Her choice of words, however, lifts the authors out of the sf context and their national context. They are neither specifically "Russian" writers, nor "Russian sf writers." They are simply writers of "literature," a category needing no national or genre qualification.

The other and opposite mode of internationalist criticism, of course, is ideological. Here we deal with writers and critics who are less Russian than Marxist. Seen through this lens, the Strugatskys may be judged as dissidents, using science fantasy as means to protest oppressive aspects of Soviet society. On the one hand, as Patrick L. McGuire sees it, their sf embraces in veiled and oblique ways the "forbidden themes and devices" in Soviet society.[2] On the other, as Stephen W. Potts argues, their sf extracts the "best" of Marxist thought from the restrictive Soviet context and elaborates a liberal and humanistic future, one that offers an alternative vision to an American sf often decried as expansionist and racist. Such arguments, however, do not operate on the level of national cultures and their historic forms of response to science and technology. They are the product of warring ideologies. Potts, at one point, softens his ideological approach:

> The social and political content of the Strugatskys' fiction merits discussion primarily because, in its mature phase anyway, it rejects the orthodoxies of *either* side in the Cold War dispute. Unfortunately, here as in their own country, the ideological controversy has tended to eclipse the esthetic concerns of the brothers' work.[3]

Even so, Potts merely sidesteps the question of comparative science fictions and reformulates Le Guin's judgment on the grounds of "literary" or esthetic valuation. Neither approach considers the specifically Russian development of a significant, variant form of scientific fiction. General aesthetic considerations and internationalist ideologies alike are accretions to this national matrix, in which a culturally specific form of sf has taken a unique shape. My purpose here is to examine a few interesting works in the continuity of this Russian tradition. Hopefully, by comparing and contrasting these works with contemporary works in other cultures, I can get a sense of the shape of Russia's particular sense of "things to come."

First, however, a caveat. In the broad history of the development of a "scientific fiction," defined as fiction whose themes and forms arise as a result of some aspect of scientific discovery, there are no hermetic creations. Works like Mary Shelley's *Frankenstein; or, The Modern Prometheus* (1818, 1831) and E.T.A. Hoffmann's "Der Sandmann" (1817) share the "theme" of scientists creating artificial life. But the treatment, as expected in these diverse cultural contexts, is very different. And yet neither work is itself deprived of cross-cultural influences, however oblique. Shelley, for example, repositions the Germanic Faust in the more domestic context of British Gothic. Hoffmann, on the other hand, writes not so much about mechanical creation of life as about the role of perception in the apprehending and "creating" of worlds, an issue very much alive in the near-contemporary fiction of Laurence Sterne (1713–1768).

Moreover, the epistemological theory that underlies Nathanael's woes in "Der Sandmann" is David Hume's idea of the *percept*, the immediate sense perception prior to any conceptual overlay. Hume's idea was challenged by Immanuel Kant and the German idealists at the time Hoffmann was writing his tale. In like manner, while placing the Strugatskys in their Russian/Soviet context, we are aware that this Russian world is itself no island, but rather a stream carrying many islands. This is true for all their Russian precursors who, though moving in this distinct cultural stream, were at the same time negotiating shared currents, acting and reacting, in their own particular way, to works from other cultures. This is the dynamic that Goethe, in the early 19th century, saw operating to create what he envisioned as the "*anmarschierende Weltliteratur*" [advancing world literature] to emerge from the advent of modern science.[4] What he foresaw, in fact, was science fiction taken on an international scale.

On the one hand, we have the general "matter" of science, shared by all modern cultures, just as the "matter of Arthur" was shared by diverse vernacular cultures in the late Middle Ages. On the other, there is the resistance of strong individual national cultures to science's otherwise leveling impact. From the ongoing dialectic between these two impulses, Goethe saw a dynamic and culturally negotiated form of literature emerging. Thus, at the core of science fiction, if seen in this international perspective, we may find a somewhat realized form of Goethe's *Weltliteratur*. Let us examine Russia's contribution to this form through the lens of the Strugatskys and their precursors.

In a 1983 interview, Arkady Strugatsky named a number of writers both foreign and Russian as influences on his and his brother's works. The foreign are not only American writers labeled as sf, but a broad group of "speculators." Among the Americans are Kurt Vonnegut, Jr., Ray Bradbury, Robert Sheckley, and Le Guin. Next to these, three Russians: Alexei Tolstoy, Mikhail Bulgakov and Ivan Yefremov.[5] The latter three were familiar to every Russian reader of the time. By naming them, Arkady gives hints as to why he selected the American writers he did. His list had to take into account the issue of censorship. Some foreign writers slipped through the net in the preceding decades, others did not.

Beginning in the post–Stalin period called the "Thaw" (1957–1972), the progressive and very popular monthly *Innostranaya literatura* [Foreign Literature] published translations of Lem, Sheckley, Kōbō Abe, William Tenn, and many other sf writers. This was due to editors pushing the envelope under the gaze of the censors. If a work was possibly a bit too sensitive for them, it could be prefaced by an introduction that gave it the right Soviet perspective. If a phrase or paragraph was still too daring, it could be softened in translation or excised. Some writers, like Ray Bradbury, could pass censorship on their merits as "poets." His novels, and those of Le Guin, were published in the sixties and seventies in huge Russian editions for all of the Soviet republics. They had enthusiastic fan clubs, and the stability of the state was not endangered. Banned authors were often available in some form from underground sources, such as retypings with carbon copies. Most often, contraband books from abroad circulated in the original language; readers waited for their turn on a long list. The book was transmitted in a plain jacket.

Bradbury might seem an unlikely influence on writers like the Strugatskys, who came of age in the period of Nikita Khrushchev and space-age "realism," exemplified by Ivan Yefremov's *The Andromeda Constellation* (1957).Yet reading Alexei Tolstoy's fanciful account of Mars from 1923, *Aelita*, itself an oddly "poetized" version of Edgar Rice Burroughs's red planet, could prepare a space-age Soviet writer to appreciate Bradbury's equally diaphanous description of the red planet, giving life and form to a place that was otherwise simply a destination for advanced launch systems. In addition, the dark and grotesque humor of other Bradbury stories like "Skeleton" (1945) and "The Man Upstairs" (1947) echoes a similar mix of fantasy and dark reality found in a writer like Mikhail Bulgakov, forbidden in Stalin's time and revived in the 1960s, though in bowdlerized editions. Zamyatin's *We*, however, remained totally forbidden and far too risky for this kind of circulation.

All the same, none of the authors Arkady Strugatsky named in 1983 have the exact *Stimmung* the brothers seek: Sheckley's humor is too raucous, and the social extrapolations of Le Guin are too dry and contrived. Yet some aspect of each resonates at some level in the Strugatskys' work. This resonance will in all cases call for adaptation and fine tuning. The ending of *The Ugly Swans* (1966–1967), for example, could be seen as adapting, in a radically different setting, the ending of Arthur C. Clarke's *Childhood's End* (1953), another writer Arkady mentioned. Likewise, the mystical rationalism or "cruel miracle" of Lem's alien encounters, in novels like *Solaris* (1961) and *The Invincible* (1964), are relocated in a more "domestic," shall we say "Russian," setting in the novel *Roadside Picnic* (1972)—a work whose title suggests domesticity. (The action is supposedly set in Canada.). There are, of course, clear resonances of Lem's texts in the alien "visitation" of this novel. But these have been pitched at a different register, that of satiric irony, resignation, and real human suffering. The Strugatskys, in fact, have shaped Lem's themes into a thoroughly Russian novel. Despite this, Arkady's string of primary influential Russian sf works offers the critic a basic scale from which one can identify and measure the Strugatskys' variations on general sf themes.

Since England has its seminal *Frankenstein*, France—the *Voyages extraordinaires* of Jules Verne—and the U.S.—Poe's scientific mysteries—so we need to anchor the Russian tradition of scientific fantasy in a 19th-century text in order to set the parameters for later development. We must go, if possible, farther back than Gernsback's trio of patriarchs—Wells, Verne, and Poe—to lesser known and less obvious works, works such as Balzac's *Le Centenaire, ou les deux Beringheld* (1822), which perhaps more than Verne is the seminal work of a uniquely French form of sf. In works like this, issues raised by contemporary science began to shape the narrative, becoming its first cause and the motor that drives its resolution.[6]

Attempts such as that of Monique Lebailly to offer an anthology of *La science-fiction avant la SF: Anthologie de l'imaginaire scientifique français du romanticisme à la pataphysique* (1989) are interesting in their desire to fix a point of beginning for the genre. Even so, she offers a list of writers, from Alphonse de Lamartine and Victor Hugo to Ernest Renan to Albert Robida and Alfred Jarry, all of whom she claims have written works in which some aspect of science is a shaping element. This is surely true; it reveals the degree to which scientific matters had at that time impacted the realm of *belles lettres*. But it also indicates the chaotic beginnings of the form. For, as this disparate list shows, it is impossible to find any single work that magically marks the beginning of the genre. It is more a question of degree—how much, in any given work, does science and the scientific worldview "re-write" fictional themes and structures? It is by this yardstick that we will measure the origins of sf in Russia.

One significant starting point for the genre, however, is the moment at which the purely imaginary voyage, itself a meaningful alteration of the actual voyage of discovery, becomes a *scientific* journey. On such a voyage, one ostensibly uses current technological devices to travel to some previously inaccessible part of the world and gather data that will advance scientific knowledge at home. Jules Verne, whose chief works come in the middle and late 19th century, is considered the master of this form. Wells also used it in *The First Men in the Moon* (1901) and greatly stretched its parameters of credibility in an earlier work, *The Time Machine* (1895).

Russian literature, however, has its own, and very early, example of this form: Osip Senkovsky's little-known work, *The Fantastic Journeys of Baron Brambeus (Fantasticheskie puteshestviya barona Brambeusa)*, first published in 1833. Senkovsky (1800–1858) was an ethnic Pole, born in Lithuania, but educated in Russia. As a distinguished Orientalist at the University of Petersburg, he was able to take scientific journeys as a philologist to the Middle East and Asia. When a bookstore owner in Petersburg, Aleksandr Smirdin, invited him to co-edit a new journal, *The Library for Reading*, a main feature of which was the dissemination of new scientific ideas to the layman, he became engaged in a literary project similar to Verne's later collaboration with the popular publisher Pierre-Jules Hetzel.

In the pages of *The Library for Reading*, Senkovsky, using the pen name Baron Brambeus, took up the cause of Russian science against what he saw as intellectual excesses and pedantries of the time, notably Romanticism and German idealism. The irony is that this champion of a fundamentally pragmatic science was later disdained because of the satiric irreverence with which he wrote. The socially progressive critic Vissarion Belinsky (1811–1848) called him "a misanthrope, a hater of his fellow man" who makes "fun of everything and especially persecutes enlightenment."[7] Other socially minded critics followed suit. Immensely popular in his time, Senkovsky fell into obscurity. His

Fantastic Journeys were republished in 1835 and included in his nine-volume collected works in 1858, and these editions went into the collections of his university library in Petersburg and the central library in Moscow (later called the Lenin Library), and possibly elsewhere, but they were not republished again in Russia—the Soviet Union—until 1989, just before the collapse. Interest in Senkovsky nevertheless remained alive among the Formalist critics of the 1920s, and the respected writer Veniamin Kaverin (1902–1989) published his appreciation of Senkovsky in 1929 and 1966. New Russian editions of Senkovsky have appeared in our time. The journeys became available to the English-speaking world only in 1993 through the elegant and scholarly translation of Louis Pedrotti: Osip Senkovsky, *The Fantastic Journeys of Baron Brambeus*.[8]

Senkovsky's *Journeys* will be our touchstone text for the development of Russia's unique form of "science fantasy." Barely known in the West, it is a key work for giving a clear sense of the lineage from which the scientific journey as a literary form derives, and for demonstrating the particular ways in which the insular Russian literary and cultural tradition "domesticated" 19th-century scientific discovery, which was already international in nature. It was first published as four pieces collected in the volume of 1833:

Autumn Boredom
A Poetic Journey Over the Great, Wide World
A Scientific Journey to Bear Island
A Sentimental Journey to Mount Etna

The first piece is an absurdist complaint against St. Petersburg during the wet autumnal season, when the nocturnal darkness begins to return after the summer white nights. The author considers and rejects one after another ridiculous method for fighting the growing boredom: drowning himself in the Neva, getting an appointment as judge, getting married, living with animals, imitating animals, rereading his own works. "Oh, why can't I marry a parrot?" he sighs. "I'd be boundlessly happy with this bird that was created for true friendship and perpetual agreeableness" (7). Intermittently, he criticizes the persistent use of two obsolete pronouns that drive him crazy. Finally he hits on the idea of sharing his writings with the reader, but only on the condition that the reader first read his foreword. It begins:

I've yawned at Nature and at Art. I've eaten roast puppies and paradoxes. I've snacked on Chârost [possibly a dish from a hotel of that name, possibly carrion] and bananas, washing them down with a Madeira that crossed the equator eight times… [11].

All this nonsense serves to produce the right mood for stories of travel. Thus the book consists of a preface and three journeys.

The first and shortest journey, "Over the Great, Wide World," describes the author's trip through the Russian Empire, seen as a literature and culture in thrall to French Romanticism of the most decadent sort, what Senkovsky calls the cult of "frenzied feelings." The baron travels from the frigid north to the sunny south in search of strong emotions, but finds in Moscow only more boredom, regulations, and, in place of a once rugged and healthy people, "a society that drunkenly dances the squat dance." In Ukraine, he rides by rye fields separated by groves, rye fields separated by groves, and so on, but after a torrential rain he runs into "an ocean of mud." His coachman jumps down upon arrival in Odessa and disappears in it. The author is able to leave the coach only by walking across a long plank extended by some citizens from the sidewalk. He presents himself as an important person, a collegiate secretary of the tenth rank, plays cards, wins suspiciously, and escapes a duel by threatening to call the police, explaining that duels are now outlawed; he runs with the money to his hotel and decides to avoid the police by hiding in the quarantine station for people possibly infected with the plague. Here the variety of nationalities—Greeks, Jews, Italians, and Turks—makes him think that he is in a suburb of Constantinople. He goes to his room, and "a black cloud of enormous, emaciated, starving fleas" attacks him. They suck the blood from his body, the peace from his mind, the happiness from his heart, but in his agony and despair he experiences "a strong feeling, but a feeling truly hellish, truly poetic." And comes to a great reversal:

> "Here is sublime poetry!" I exclaim with delight. "That Little Russia mud was noth-ing. Real poetry can be found only in an Odessa quarantine station." [...] The mixed sounds of Turkish, Greek and Italian curl through the air in a cloud of tobacco smoke, rising from the bowls of countless Turkish pipes. The plague, the sultan, Tsar-grad and rods for beating people predominate as subjects of all conversations. All ideas walk around in turbans and yellow slippers. All feelings sit cross-legged on the floor. [...] Add to this also the poetry of paradoxes expounded by travelling observers, and you'll agree there's nothing on earth more pleasant than being infected with the plague and placed under quarantine [23].

After fifteen days he is finally cleared and, inspired by his experience, takes a ship on the Black Sea to the real Constantinople. Informed in advance by a Greek nobleman, Bolvanopoulos (*bolvan* in Russian means "blockhead"), that Turks act intelligently by doing the opposite of what is done in other lands (for example, they read the Koran from the opposite side of the page, make decisions first and seek the reason for them afterwards), and that nine-tenths of the good done in the world is done by mistake, Brambeus embarks on a series of adventures that proceed on the principle of contradiction. He falls in love with the daughter of a certain Signor Petracchi and experiences such fires of passion that he wishes Eugène Sue, Victor Hugo, and Honoré de Balzac were with him to describe it. For example:

I return home in a heavenly rapture from seeing her, leaping over the bloody, decapitated, bluish corpses of executed giaours lying on the street corners in piles of dung, and my heart contracts and palpitates like a frog's leg that is being stimulated by the action of a galvanic cell. [...] In what other land does love provide so many and such lofty and strong poetic feelings? Here my heart experiences incessant irritation. Here I can feel. I'm alive [31].

The lovers are stirred into such a fire of passion that they fail to watch the brazier and set a fire that burns down the entire quarter of the city, destroying 9580 houses. Their first kiss is ineffable, beyond all description, especially when she confesses that she is stricken with the plague, so that the baron exclaims what "happiness this is, what an unearthly feeling [....] With our last kiss we may dissolve into pus, which people will handle with caution and dispose of with disgust" (37).

He wakes up later in another room amid smoldering ashes, smoking borax and straw, covered with cheap olive oil. His beloved's body has been carried away. He is attended by a learned doctor who lectures him on politics and history. "And the stupider I grew," exults the baron, "the more learned I became." At the end of his story he has become a scholar ready to tell about his scientific journey. (38–39)

Obviously the purpose of all these extreme excitations, contradictions, and disasters is to spoof the Romantic vogue for the *ailleurs* and the rash of "italienische Reisen" and "voyages en Orient" that the vogue engendered. The serious message to the Russian reader echoes Emerson's maxim: "The soul is no traveller."[9] And the author's sly purpose is to cleanse the landscape of illusions in order to prepare for the next voyage, clearly scientific this time.

But before we examine the second voyage, let us briefly consider the third, "A Sentimental Journey to Mount Etna." The baron consults the diary of a trip he took to Italy in 1829 and discovers that he married "the divine Signora Patapucci at a station two stops from Naples." How could he have forgotten? No matter, he recalls that he left "Signora Brambeus" in Messina, where she felt at home, and met up with an old Finnish companion, Count B., whereupon he decided to climb Mt. Etna with him, his sister and a Swede. The group hires a guide and mules, and sets off from Nicolasi, a town in the foothills, with "ten pairs of new shoes and thirty bottles of old wine." The narrative combines factual detail, realistic description of the terrain and fanciful events.

On the way, the baron draws closer to the sister, who turns out to be an Italian from Genoa named Giulietta. At the mouth of the volcano, the baron sits hugging Giulietta, and the Swede, who is jealous, pushes him in. The baron slides down cooled lava canals all the way to the center of the earth, where he discovers people who live and move about upside down. He is curious, philosophically, how one can live in an upside-down world, but suddenly loses his weight, crashes around (like an astronaut in zero gravity), and becomes disoriented. The romantic quest has led to hard realities. But again, as in the first journey, he learns to think by the principle of contradiction: if a stupid man is the opposite of an intelligent one, you can turn him upside down, and he will be smart. Brambeus is helped to step down onto the earth that has been a ceiling for him, and at once he understands German and German philosophy. He converses, makes friends and gets married, but then subterranean explosions thrust him upward and out of Mt. Vesuvius, and into a coach riding in Naples. Fortunately, he lands on his wife's suitor, killing him, and is reunited with his above-ground spouse, and they ride on to Rome. Thereafter, he likes to walk on the ceiling after breakfast, but is dissuaded from doing so by the Holy Inquisition, which has begun to regard him as a heretic and Satanist.

This third journey, however ridiculous, responds to real, contemporary scientific issues, such as the interest of the new "earth science" in volcanic upheavals and geologic periods. In its way, it is a precursor to Verne's *Voyage au centre de la terre* (1864). Yet the choice of Etna as the entry point, rather than a barren place like Iceland, evokes certain patently romantic preoccupations of the period—notably, an interest in the "history" of lost civilizations, raised by archeological excavations at Pompeii and Herculaneum in the first decades of the 18th century. A different mode of idealism is at play in the yearning to relocate utopian societies in "antediluvian" places, lost islands of peace and perfection in an otherwise turbulent course of history. Science serves in this context as a magic wand, decoding stones and mysterious markings on caves and walls, bringing to life forgotten worlds before the fall. A vestige of this motive remains with Arne Saknussemm's "runes" in Verne's *Voyage au centre de la terre.*

This motive comes to the fore in the second, not the third journey of Baron Brambeus: "A Scientific Journey to Bear Island." This is the one that primarily concerns us. It is three times longer than the first and twice as long as the third. And, as the only specifically named *scientific* journey, it is framed by two questionably motivated and scientifically absurd excursions. On this journey Baron Brambeus is accompanied by a certain Dr. Spurtzmann, a pedantic scientist of German origin. It follows that German idealism is the target of satire in this voyage. The author aims particularly at the supposedly scientific method of a now very obscure Russian philosopher, philologist and academician, Daniil Vellansky (1774–1847). He was a disciple of Friedrich Schelling (1775–1854), and as the man who introduced Schelling to Russia he was given honorary degrees in subjects he knew nothing about, such as medicine. Nevertheless, he lectured on them, but, as his students complained, very abstractly. His chief work was *Experimental, Observational and Speculative Physics* (*Opytnaya, nablyudatel'naya i umozritel'naya fizika,* 1831). The arguments of Dr. Spurtzmann in the narrative demonstrate that Vellansky's idealist "science" begins its investigation of physical nature from the wrong end, starting with the idea and deducing physical laws from it, rather than inductively constructing hypotheses from the observation of nature. Such a process works only in an upside-down world, a world in which Immanuel Kant and Friedrich Schelling are instantly comprehensible.

The narrative, contrary to the preface and other two journeys, begins in a realistic manner. The tone is comparatively serious—humorous but not preposterous and absurd. Here is the first paragraph in Pedrotti's translation:

> On April 14, 1828, we set off from Irkutsk toward the northeast on the longest of my journeys, and in the first days of June we arrived at the Berendin Station after travelling on horseback for more than a thousand versts [600 miles]. My companion, Doctor of Philosophy Spurtzmann, a distinguished naturalist but a poor rider, had become completely exhausted and could not continue the journey. Nothing more amusing could be imagined than this venerable observer of Nature, hunched over his emaciated horse and laden on all sides with rifles, pistols, barometers, thermometers, snake skins, beaver tails, gophers and birds packed in straw. He had fastened a certain species of hawk on his cap, since he lacked room on his back and chest. In the villages through which we rode the superstitious Yakuts, taking him for a great travelling shaman, reverently offered him *kumiss* [fermented mare's milk] and dried fish, and they tried their best to get him to practice just a bit of shamanism on them. The doctor lost his temper and cursed the Yakuts in German. Assuming that he was speaking to them in the sacred Tibetan tongue and that he did not understand any other language, they showed him even more respect and even more persistently begged him to drive the devil out of them. We couldn't help laughing almost the whole time that we were travelling [41].

Their trek is neither to the romantic south, nor to an inverted world like *Alice's Adventures in Wonderland* (1865), but to a real wasteland, the tundra of Siberia. On the way, the baron tells the doctor about his enthusiasm for the French Egyptologist Jean-François Champollion, the man who deciphered the Rosetta Stone. (His report was published in 1824, but he died in 1832, and his system was not yet in use at the time of Senkovsky's story.) Brambeus claims to have learned the method and tries to teach it to Spurtzmann, but finds that it is hard to do so on horseback. In Yakutsk they proceed north up the Lena River to the Arctic Ocean. Here there is a bay with Bear Island, named after the indigenous polar bear population. Their guide is Ivan Antonovich Strabinskikh, Chief Assayer of Mines, a trained scientist on a mission to survey the surrounding area. Their purpose is to hunt for fossils in a famous cave, accessible only by bear path. They reach it, enter and discover the bones of plesiosaurs and "antediluvian dogs." Brambeus, however, wanders into another chamber and discovers Egyptian hieroglyphs on the walls. Immediately he believes he can read them. He calls in Dr. Spurtzmann, who believes he can read them too. They start arguing over the decipherment;

Spurtzmann tries to make the title correspond to Schelling; Brambeus insists that they read it without adornment, and translates it: *Notes of the Last Antediluvian Man*. With an uncertain agreement, the baron begins to decipher the four long walls of the cave, dictating his translation to the doctor. They stop from time to time to argue over the decipherment and interpret the story. This story from before the flood takes up easily three-quarters of the second journey and forms the heart of the book.

It also follows themes from Mary Shelley's novels. The narrator Walton in *Frankenstein* is seeking a warm or hyperborean land in the midst of the frozen Russian arctic. Brambeus discovers that this same icy North, whose history is now being revealed in hieroglyphs, was at a lost moment in the past a land of palm trees and easy living. And the "historian" of this tale, the antediluvian who wrote on the walls of the cave, claims to be a lone survivor, like the hero of Mary Shelley's *The Last Man* (1826), whose travail at the end of the 21st century is prophesied by a sybil on painted leaves found in a cave near Naples.

The lone survivor in Senkovsky's tale reveals that Bear Island was once a mountain peak; it was turned into an island by a flood, which itself was caused by a cosmic catastrophe: a comet striking the Earth. It happens that the year 1835 was the date of the predicted return of Halley's Comet. This prediction aroused both scientific and popular imaginations at the time, and Senkovsky plays up the occasion, virtually inventing what was to be the later sf theme of disaster-by-comet-impact, where such a body either hits the Earth, or more commonly misses it by just a little. Pedrotti notes that H.G. Wells, in his novel *In the Days of the Comet* (1906), responds to the next predicted return of Halley's comet on its 76-year cycle. American writers Larry Niven and Jerry Pournelle do likewise in *Lucifer's Hammer* (1977), anticipating the next return in 1986. Gregory Benford and David Brin pick up the theme in *Heart of the Comet* (1986). Scientists of Senkovsky's time were beginning to be fascinated by the evolutionary possibility of geological upheavals due to volcanic activity and the impact of extraterrestrial bodies. Beneath such speculation, however, lay the old Biblical paradigm of the Deluge, the fall after the Fall. And in Senkovsky's account there is more than a hint that this lost civilization is simply another Sodom and Gomorrah, a place of ease and sin calling down divine retribution.

Brambeus and Spurtzmann read the tale of the antediluvian last man with relish. They embrace its sad conclusion less out of scientific rigor than a desire for fame, a desire to be both scientific and popular, because the tale is not only scientifically significant, but also simply a "good story." In fact, the reader is tipped off early in the journey to their personal designs and possible lack of objectivity. The two travelers, a bit like Verne's Lidenbrock, are more theoreticians than experimental scientists.

From the Baron's first impressions of Siberia, we sense that he wants to see a warm land:

> The weather was clear and hot. The Lena and its banks had long continued to delight us with their beauty. Here was a genuine panorama formed tastefully from the most peculiar sights to be found in all the universe [49].

Thus, though they pose as objective scientists, Senkovsky's explorers remain romantics and idealists. Comet and cataclysm are real possibilities, but the discovery of an Egyptian climate and culture in northern Siberia is much less plausible.

The same is true for the story of the last survivor that now unfolds. It is told by Shabakhubosaar, a nobleman in Khukhurun, the capital city of Barabia. The country is waging a war against Sakh-Shukh, a black state in the area now called Novaya Zemlya, with the aim of subjugating the blacks, turning them into eunuchs, and using them to keep the untrustworthy Barabian wives at home while the men go out and find younger ones. The hero, not married, is madly in love with the beautiful Sayana, who has many admirers and must be watched every minute. His former teacher and frequent companion is the chief astronomer of the city, the hunchback Shimshik, who has a pointed beard and wears a top hat. He has seen the approaching comet and predicted that it will strike the Earth, but he is more interested in proving himself right against a competitor astronomer than in warning the citizens. Shimshik, in fact, with his logic-twisting pedantry, is almost a mirror image of Dr. Spurtzmann. The readers of these walls seem to be reading about themselves. At one point, Spurtzmann even proposes, in a footnote to the hieroglyphic text, "to write from Irkutsk a report to the University of Göttingen about the scientific services of the Hofrat Shimshik" (108).

As the story goes on, the hero overcomes numerous obstacles to win the hand of Sayana, but after their marriage the comet, which has constantly been growing, crashes into the Earth. The account on the walls describes the ruination of a once happy society: earthquakes, floods, fires, people forming groups and killing each other, then eating each other. The hero, separated from his new wife, heads for high ground, as does she, not without finding a lover on the way; they reunite in the cave on Bear Island. As the stores of food are consumed, the number of survivors dwindles. Sayana dies of starvation in Shabakhubosaar's arms. As the ice closes in around the cave, he— the sole survivor, the last man—is compelled to eat her. His last words: "I'm freezing. I'm dy…" (122)

The story of the Siberian flood is finished. It has taken the two scientists six days of steady work to decipher and transcribe it. They give orders to prepare to depart. Their fame and glory in Europe are assured. They celebrate in the chamber of hieroglyphics with their last two bottles of champagne:

"Now let's drink to the health of genial, scientific and industrious Germany," I said to my companion, pouring out a second glass.

"Well, and now to the health of great, mighty and hospitable Russia," my courteous companion said, resorting to the bottle again.

"Long live floods!" I cried.

"Long live hieroglyphs!" the doctor cried.

"May comparative anatomy and all scientific theories flourish forever!" I exclaimed.

"May all scientific researchers, Bear Island and polar bears flourish!" the doctor exclaimed [124].

The two go on exulting and shouting hurrah, raising toasts to "red-haired mammoths, mastodons and Egyptologists," but strong winds blow up and delay their departure for three days. When the winds die down, the chief assayer, Ivan Antonovich, having completed his surveys elsewhere, arrives by boat from across the bay. They tell him about their great discovery and the ancient history of Siberia revealed on the cave walls. He is amazed and incredulous. He has never seen Egyptian hieroglyphics in Siberia before. They lead him to the cave so that he can see for himself.

Ivan Antonovich bears the surname Strabinskikh—derived from the French word *strabisme*, squinting, near-sighted. (Russian has borrowed the word: *strabizm*.) Therefore he examines the hieroglyphics closely:

He walked around the entire room, pushed his nose right up to each wall, craned his neck back, carefully inspected the ceiling and once again turned to the walls. In his face we read wonderment combined with some kind of mineralogocial joy, and we nudged each other, taking sly pleasure in the impressions that he was experiencing. He adjusted the candle in his lantern and once more walked around the room. We remained silent.

Unexpectedly, the assayer asks where are the hieroglyphs. He receives the reply that they are there, all over the walls. He replies:

"You call these hieroglyphs?" the amazed Ivan Antonovich said with a drawl. "This is the crystallization of a stalagmite that we in mineralogy call *glyphic* or *pictorial*" [127].

The would-be readers of hieroglyphics are stunned. They object, and Ivan Antonovich answers with a full paragraph of scientific fact enumerating in which countries the stalagmites have been found, the different types of designs their crystallization produces, and the numerous false interpretations that have been made of them over the years. The joyful explorers are "completely shattered by this unexpected eruption of lithological erudition," and turn on each other. Spurtzmann accuses Brambeus of propagandizing Champollion and his system, claiming that he never really believed it or the translation that Brambeus was dictating. Brambeus retorts that if he didn't believe in it, Spurtzmann should not have added his commentary and wanted to make Shimshik an honorary fossil member of the University of Göttingen. Meanwhile the assayer begins to chip off stalagmites to take back for scientific display in Petersburg.

Thus romantic reverie shatters on hard facts and hard science, just as foreign theories fall silent when confronted by a real Russian man of the land, his native "drawl" silencing the affected Teutonisms and French imports. Yet the baron is incorrigible:

> It's not my fault if Nature plays around in such a way that considerable good sense can be made of her silly jokes, in accordance with the rules of Champollion's grammar [129].

And Dr. Spurtzmann, despite his indignation, asks to have the translation, which is written in his hand. But Baron Brambeus refuses: he plans to publish it himself (in the very collection being read), and even with the doctor's commentary. Here ends the "scientific journey" and its unmasking of pseudo-science, of which there will be many examples in the next two centuries ahead.

From Senkovsky's "Scientific Journey to Bear Island" we get not only a fantastic, satiric and amusing story, but a sense of what the particular Russian form of "science fantasy" is and will remain, right down to the work of the Strugatskys. Foreign enthusiasms and theories must be put to the test of Nature, in the form of the hard and vast Russian land and its people. Yet we sense that it is only because theories of this sort are calqued on this unlikely terrain that its writers come to see the degree that "Nature plays around" with us, forcing preposterous and yet uncanny synchronicities such as this extended overlapping of Champollion and meaningless natural glyphs. In a crazy way, we go beyond the Cartesian duality of mind and matter, and are asked to consider a both-and form of logic. The marks tell the guide Ivan Antonovich that nature will not be read according to our designs. At the same time they offer a coherent narrative to the two enthusiasts of Champollion. But however comforting this narrative may seem to them, it remains ultimately a fantasy, and as such a story that must eventually bow to the cold equations of fire and material indifference.

If Senkovsky reveals Russian attitudes toward science in the 19th century to be at odds with those of the dominant scientific cultures of Britain and France, he suggests affinities, even parallels, with the other "frontier" culture and land of vast expanses: the United States of America. An important place of such confluence may be a shared response to German metaphysics, or more accurately, to the problem of a conjunction between physics and idea, with which Kant wrestled in such concepts as the "synthetic *a priori*." The encounter of the baron and Ivan Antonovich is echoed in Poe's scientific hoaxes. Here some preposterous hypothesis is set forth in empirical terms, with the goal of bringing a reader to inscribe it into the realm of physical probability. But while the norm here remains a material one, elsewhere in Poe, as in the "occurrences" of Ambrose Bierce, or in the romance quest of dreamers like Ahab to transcend physical limits, we find a similar alternate, and parallel, reading of the book of nature. But if a vision such as Emerson's transcendentalism arises in the U.S., where the move from individual center to ideal circumference is secularized as a dynamic of "undulation," an interplay of power and form, Russian writers drifted toward the form of uncanny co-habitation—"heimlich-unheimlich"—outlined by German philosopher Gotthilf Heinrich von Schubert (1780–1860), author of *Views From the Night Side of the Sciences* (*Ansichten von der Nachtseite der Naturwissenschaften*, 1808).

It is significant that all three journeys of Baron Brambeus are prefaced by a section entitled "The Boredom of Autumn." The physical place that generates all these modes of exploration, even the scientific, is St. Petersburg— "Peter's city." This is Peter the Great's Western Enlightenment construct of cold stone. Through a feat of Western technology, and with the bones of slave labor, the city reclaimed the marshes and broke through—in Pushkin's phrase—a "window on the West," which means a window on modern Europe and modern science.[10] But to Brambeus this city is mechanical and sterile in contrast to Slavic, wooden Moscow. It will be the same to Gogol, Dostoevsky and Andrei Bely, writers who domesticated—or made their own—E.T.A. Hoffmann's sense of the "night side" of bourgeois rationalism in their native rationalist nightmare.

It is surely no accident that in one of their later novels, *Definitely Maybe* (1977), the Strugatskys return from outer space and locales in alternate history to contemporary Leningrad, the name St. Petersburg acquired after Lenin's death in January 1924. (It recovered Peter's name after the Soviet collapse in August 1991.) Here in the novel, side by side, we have the physical ordering of Peter's plan overlaid with Marxist state "rationalism," plus uncontrolled noise in the form of unending white nights, endless dust, trees that grow huge overnight in the confines of dank courtyards. In terms of the relation of theory to nature, we find Brambeus's situation again. For here it seems that so many models for studying and controlling nature have been formulated that nature itself is forced to react to them, disrupting all the theories and systems that seek to read its "text." Brambeus's universe, long before that of this novel's hero, Vecherovsky, is "homeostatic," ultimately forced to restore equilibrium in the face of destabilization, which in this case results from too much scientific theorizing itself.

With Senkovsky as with the Strugatskys, the reader remains suspended inconclusively between two equally inadequate visions. On the one hand, there are the theorists of homeostasis, who turn the inscrutable face of matter into a "good story." On the other, there are the squinty pragmatists like Ivan

Antonovich, flawed by his materialist shortsightedness. This makes the reader hesitate, for which of these is the true "reader" of nature? What if nature's "script" is ultimately inscrutable to human logic? Or worse, what if, as Vecherovsky thinks, those patterns are less random than malevolent, directed specifically *against* human beings and their desire to advance learning?

This same feeling of generalized malevolence—in the form of boredom, official indifference, the stultifying impenetrability of bureaucratic institutions and language—seeps through the rational façades of Peter's city. It is the same force of inertia that besets Brambeus, that frames and closes upon his journeys. But even so—and this is another lesson that Brambeus teaches us—it is better to have an enemy to fight than an intangible "law" against which we can merely protest, and are left to wander in a Kafkaesque maze of theoretical arguments. Vecherovsky decides to leave the city and go to the Pamir mountains, where the processes of mind and life are slower. The Russian title of the novel translated as *Definitely Maybe*—*Za millard let do kontsa sveta*—means "A billion years to the end of the world." And Vecherovsky's last words tell us: "There's a lot … that can be done in a billion years if we don't give up and understand, understand and don't give up."[11]

The English title may not fit this novel, but it does offer an accurate description of the nature of the Russian science fantasy we have been tracing from Senkovsky to the Strugatskys. Here knowledge is not purely a function of reason or ratiocinative powers. It is tied as well to endurance, to surviving the contradictions and paradoxes that beset mankind's attempts to understand its world, a world where natural forces and social contexts interact and intermingle. Scientific advancement occurs here in a slow time (we have billions of years) that permits the search for knowledge to loop endlessly back through primitive or atavistic points of contact. As with Antaeus, son of Poseidon and Gaia, these points provide the means of re-energizing human aspirations when sole adherence to either pole—rational or mystical—tends to stultify such aspirations.

The sf landscape we are exploring remains unclassifiable in terms of good and evil, because it is subject to a process of endless reversal that confounds all such judgments. Why not imagine an antediluvian Egypt nested in the barren rocks and caves of the present-day Siberian wasteland? Or perhaps the resurgence of figures and happenings out of Russian folk legend in a city build by reason in an otherwise improbable location? Or unregenerate barbarism emerging at the center of the Marxist plan to re-engineer in rational manner other interplanetary cultures? Behind such questions lies the paradox of "definitely maybe," where if there is a hope of ever knowing anything, it is dependent on human steadfastness, not "giving up," in the face of the only law possible in such a universe—that of continuous reversal and surprise. This is what, in Russian scientific fiction, links pure reason to animism and anthropocentrism; the world of space travel to that of native forests and tundra; the certainty of technology to fantasy, rational to paranormal phenomena.

In terms of this undulating process, Senkovsky's work contains the seed of the Strugatskys' fiction. In fact, the stages of the brothers' career seem almost to unfold in like order from the domains of the baron's journeys. Their first works are space-opera adaptations, travels over "wide worlds" of space and time to distant solar systems. They range from stories that resemble American "juvenile" sf—for example, the long story "Destination: Amaltheia" (1960) and the space-cadet novel *Space Apprentice* (*Stazhory*, 1962)—to the more troubling stories gathered under the title *Noon: 22nd Century* (1962) and the novel *Far Rainbow* (1963). In parallel with the Baron's "poetic" journey, we find, in a work like *Hard to Be a God* (1964), young idealists pursuing the romantic idea of guiding history in parallel human cultures on distant planets so as to avoid the struggle between capitalism and communism, and bring them bloodlessly to the socialist classless state. But what these idealists discover, for all their efforts, is that human nature remains unpredictable, intractable, perhaps fundamentally evil. Their humanitarian, Sovietizing efforts result in more venality and misery, into which they are physically plunged.

While Senkovsky's tone is universally satirical, the Strugatskys' tone, as befits the *Bildung* model behind these tales of men coming of age, remains sober and didactic, with a tinge of the elegaic. Yet there is an analogous interplay of centrifugal and centripetal impulsions, where outward expansion is inexorably linked to contraction, as the human agent of change comes to grips with the harsh realities and limits of its human condition. The Strugatsky stories, in a manner that conflates the "future history" cycle with the juvenile space epic, present characters that, as they mature, recur from one narrative to the other.

Thus in the story "The Meeting" (in *Noon: 22nd Century*), Pol Gnadykh, whose younger self we have met in previous stories, is now at the end of his adult career as an interplanetary zoologist. His job is to capture or kill specimens on outlying planets. "The Meeting" describes his visit to a museum to visit the remains of a creature he shot years before, when he was a more impulsive or "romantic" youth. He has since been troubled by the thought that this being was not just an animal, but a sentient alien. In the intervening years his youthful companion Sasha, now director of this museum, has sought to convince him that it was just an animal, all the while knowing that Pol is correct, that it was something more—an alien. As they stand over the case containing the skull of the being, Sasha traces in the dust on the case the word *sapiens*.

Granted, stories like this strongly reflect—as youth epics—Marxist-

Leninist ideology, where it is not the far but the near target that counts, and where human progress always takes precedence over more "exotic" issues like an alien encounter. Yet a bitter irony is suggested for the Marxist hand that would trace the words *Homo sapiens* on the face of the universe. For here, as with the lost illusions of Senkovsky's protagonist, the word "knowledge," when associated with mankind and its condition, must invariably be one of contradictions and limits. Where all lives in the universe are modeled on mankind, these lives as well must be nasty, brutish, and short.

This is the lesson another grown-up youth of the Strugatskys, Gorbovsky, learns in *Far Rainbow*. In this novel, he and the crew of "spacers" are trapped on planet Rainbow, which offers striving humankind no pot of gold, but immanent destruction as a mysterious "Wave," caused by scientists pursuing over-the-edge experiments with natural forces, consumes this world. Extreme Science has triggered a real "homeostatic universe" response. Gorbovsky and others must come to grips with their mortality. In accepting to use the little rocket fuel remaining to evacuate the children, and staying behind themselves, they are opting for a future. But this is a future that joins their own youthful past. Instead of following the scientists, and seeking change, expansion of human knowledge and possibility, they choose to confirm, and thus close, the circle of life, with its intrinsic limitations.

Thus neither soul nor body is a traveler in these works. The subsequent group of Strugatsky novels, from *Hard to Be a God* (1964) to the Maxsim Kammerer novels—the fascinating *Prisoners of Power* (*Obitaemyi ostrov*, 1969) and its sequel, *The Time Wanderers* (*Volny gasyat veter*, 1986)—follow Senkovsky both in launching adult heroes on scientific journeys and in sending them not to far planets or places, so much as to alternate historical contexts.[12] The "discovery" on Bear Island is a supposedly lost episode of human history that recorded an Egyptian culture in Siberia before a cataclysm, and its "recovery" and refutation, in a sense, reaffirm the cyclic nature of that history.

And so with a work like *Hard to Be a God*, where spacetime traveling "social engineers," men writing their own hieroglyphs on the walls of worlds, discover a humanoid planet where society appears to be evolving along lines predicted by Marxist theory. This society is at what that theory defines as the early medieval stage, and the opportunity seems ripe to help it evolve to the communist state without going through the upheavals and cataclysms of human history on Earth—the rise of the bourgeoisie, capitalist expansion and the proletarian revolution. The Strugatskys' scientists learn, however, that as with comets and floods there are forces in nature that remain intractable to peaceful transition. What is more, these forces prove ironically to be centered less in material nature or *res extensa* than in human nature itself, something Marxist positivism rejects. The refined proto–Egyptian world of Brambeus learns in the end that a cannibal lurks in the bosom of all mankind. And Strugatsky protagonists like Don Rumata and Maksim discover, beneath whatever veneer their rational science spreads, that human beings are essentially violent, barbarous and unregenerate. In a less than subtle way, Russian tradition overtakes Marxist doctrine in these novels. The "noon" of twenty-second century socialism has reverted to medieval darkness.

The baron's last voyage, after the Bear Island adventure, is the sentimental one. It turns neither outward nor backward, but inward, down Mt. Etna into the boiling world of nature, growth, passion. At the same time, in the upside-down world Brambeus encounters, it associates the natural world of growth and change with folk tale and fantasy. In this way the sentimental journey of Brambeus sets the coordinates for other, later Strugatsky novels, such as *Monday Begins on Saturday* (*Ponedel'nik nachinayetsya v subbotu*, 1965) and *Snail on the Slope* (*Ulitka na sklone*, 1965–1968). In the latter novel, the scientific institution, now called the Directorate, is located in the midst of a primeval forest that is falling under the power of a female entity called The Accession. The interplay between the two interacting worlds—science and primeval fantasy—tends to cancel out impulsions, so that progressive tendencies and the uplifting of human life through rational science are exactly offset by the regressive forces of life forms sinking back into primeval ooze. The dominant image in this work is the slope, and if mankind is going to survive on it, it is as a snail—the slow trek of struggling humanity for the billion years before the end of the world.

This model of entwined, alternate and interacting worlds—scientific and fantastic—dominates the Strugatsky novels of the 1970s: *The Ugly Swans* (*Gadkie lebedi*, 1966–1967), *Roadside Picnic* (*Piknik na obochine*, 1972), and finally *Definitely Maybe* (1977).These works lead naturally back from primeval forest and bog to the quagmires of bureaucratic society, from the vast Russian countryside to the urban landscape of Senkovsky's modern city of Peter. Fantasy no longer needs an abode in nature, for we need only look, as the Strugatskys do in penetrating fashion, at the bureaucratic dictates of Stalin, who declared by fiat that genetics and relativity were erroneous, and backed up his dictates with mass murder. For the Strugatskys, the promise of a Soviet realism yields to the drab streets of Soviet Moscow or Leningrad, where reality is so soul-destroying that it summons up, as a necessary counterpoint, wildly fantastical occurrences.

NOTES

1. Ursula K. Le Guin, cited on the cover of *Hard to Be a God*, by Boris and Arkady Strugatsky (New York: DAW Books, 1974).
2. Patrick L. McGuire, *Red Stars: Political Aspects of Soviet SF* (Ann Arbor: UMI Press, 1984), 14.

3. Stephen W. Potts, *The Second Marxian Invasion: The Fiction of the Strugatsky Brothers* (San Bernardino, CA: Borgo Press, 1991), 14.

4. Johann Wolfgang von Goethe, Letter to Karl Zelter, May 4, 1829, quoted in Fritz Strich, *Goethe and World Literature*, translated by C.A.M. Sym (London: Routledge, 1949), 350.

5. Alexander Fyodorov, "Interview with Arkady Strugatsky," *Soviet Literature* (Spring, 1983), 122.

6. See Honoré de Balzac, *The Centenarian: Or, The Two Beringhelds,* translated and edited by Danièle Chatelain and George Slusser (Middletown, CT: Wesleyan University Press, 2005).

7. Vissarion Belinsky, cited in Louis Pedrotti, "Introduction," *Osip Senkovsky's The Fantastic Journeys of Baron Brambeus*, translation and commentary by Louis Pedrotti (New York: Peter Lang, 1993), xv.

8. Osip Senkovsky, *Osip Senkovsky's The Fantastic Journeys of Baron Brambeus.* Page references are to this edition.

9. Ralph Waldo Emerson, "Self-Reliance," 1841, *Essays and Lectures*, selected and annotated by Joel Porte (New York: Library of America, 1983), 277.

10. Alexander Pushkin, "The Bronze Horseman: A St. Petersburg Story," 1833, translated by John Dewey, *Translation and Literature*, 7:1 (March 2011), 60.

11. Arkady and Boris Strugatsky, *Definitely Maybe*, 1974, translated by Antonina Bouis (New York: Macmillan, 1978), 142.

12. The literal translation of *Obitaemyi ostrov* is *The Inhabited Island*. The title *Prisoners of Power* is a terrible mislabeling of the work and ignores the Robinson Crusoe subtext. The literal translation of *Volny gasyat veter* is *The Waves Still the Wind*.

Looking Backward

Soviet Utopianism and Post-Soviet Dystopias

STEPHEN W. POTTS

A half century has passed since the Golden Age of Soviet science fiction. It began with the so-called Thaw, following the 1956 Twentieth Party Congress where Khrushchev denounced Stalin and commenced de–Stalinization. As part of that process, he produced "a new Party Program including an explicit timetable for Soviet entry into the [final] stage of communism," in part "an attempted remedy for the psychological malaise within the Soviet Party resulting from de–Stalinization and the Party's changing role in managing society." Jerome Gilison finds this project "highly indicative of Khrushchev's leadership style, which was chiefly characterized by perpetual, undaunted optimism, a deep faith in the system he led, and the certainty that any goal could be reached if only people could be sensibly organized to overcome minor, insignificant obstacles."[1] He thus set goals that could only be considered utopian, for example, that the Soviet Union's economy would surpass that of the United States by 1970; income would rise by 150 percent while the work week would shrink to 36 hours (Gilison 93). His timetables, of course, turned out to be overly optimistic and ultimately unachievable. Nevertheless, the utopian promise of Khrushchev's program influenced a generation of Soviet intellectuals who came of age in the 1960s and who embraced the ideal of "socialism with a human face." They are still known as the *shestdesyatniks*, from *shestdesyat'*, the Russian word for "sixty."

In the West we have always associated Soviet socialism with utopianism, but utopianism *per se* is formally discouraged in Marxist theory. In his own time Marx disparaged utopias, whether fictional ones like William Morris's *News from Nowhere* (1890) or real-world efforts like those of Robert Owens.

Marx criticized utopianism as a literary and philosophical movement rooted in pure idealism, in contrast to the scientific basis of communism. As he asserted, "I write no recipes for the cookshops of the future."[2] While utopia sought to dictate social organization, communism would evolve naturally out of historical conditions. Utopia depended on the primacy of the state; communism would lead to the state's "withering away." And while utopias tend to portray a terminal state of static perfection, Marx regarded "communism not as the end but as the beginning of a human history.... [T]he conflict between the forces and relations of production would still continue under communism, even if revolutions themselves would have become a thing of the past."[3]

In the opinion of some modern commentators, however, Marx protests too much. According to Gilison, he in fact "shares with the [utopians] an optimism about the potentiality of human beings for essential perfectability" (29). Marx's vision of the future, for all his denials, "is the only utopia which has ever become the guiding principle for directed, planned social change in a modern mass society" (34). For John Hoffman, Marxism is "utopian simply because it poses an alternative to a particular status quo" (59). Such critics point to theorists Karl Mannheim and Ernst Bloch, contemporaries of Stalin, who argue for the restoration of utopian expectations into Marxist thought, because without them "man would lose his will to shape history and therewith his ability to understand it."[4]

From the beginning, however, Soviet policy had to depart from theory. Lenin recognized he had inherited a nation of peasants with a poorly developed capitalist economy and a poorly organized urban proletariat. He thus justified a strong state with set goals as a means to instill "the elementary rules of social intercourse" in the masses so that they would "become accustomed to observing them without force, without coercion, without subordination, *without the special apparatus* for coercion called the state" (quoted in Gilison 50), thus setting society on the road to perfect stateless communism. Gilison even suggests that "if one gives it credit for utopian aspirations, there is some logic in the attempts of the Soviet regime to isolate the country from foreign, corrupting influences" (31). As Aldous Huxley has one of his characters observe in his utopian *Island* (1962), "So long as it remains out of touch with the rest of the world, an ideal society can be a viable society."[5] Under Khrushchev utopian aspirations were "a motivation for directing social energies" through "the extrapolation of ideal future goals from immediate, present efforts" (Gilison 17); furthermore, "present deprivations can be justified by future compensations, present shortages by future surpluses, present sacrifices by future rewards" (54).

Literature was embraced in the Soviet Union as a means of education and propaganda. As part of his program to modernize the masses, Lenin even promoted science fiction to encourage positive images of future society and technological progress. Not much was published—the bumper year was 1927, with 46 sf titles of all lengths[6]—but among the output were a few communist utopias: Okunev's *Coming World* (1926), Nikol'sky's *In a Thousand Years* (1928), and Larri's *Land of the Happy* (1931). In general, however, Lenin discouraged utopian interpretations of Soviet socialism, as much to lower expectations as to adhere to Marxist orthodoxy. When Stalin came to power, science fiction was one of the many domains that suffered retrenchment, as the regime suppressed long-term speculation about the future in favor of "short-sighted, pedestrian sf which provided popular illustrations of the contributions that Soviet inventors, scientists, and engineers were supposed to be making toward the fulfillment of the current Five-Year Plan."[7]

Khrushchev's liberalization, although directed at economic activity and daily life, inevitably impacted the cultural sphere. After all, Soviet publishing took its cues from the Party, which regularly handed down guidelines on preferred and proscribed topics. To a large extent, however, publishing was self-policing, with the Writers' Union, founded in 1936 and including authors, editors, and publishers, monitoring the output of its members. In pursuit of Khrushchev's agenda, writers were given license to attack the excesses of Stalinism, especially in the dominant mode of socialist realism, which often portrayed scientists as heroes. But Soviet science fiction also responded quickly to the Thaw, not just to the utopian expectations of Khrushchev's economic and social agenda but to the early triumphs of the Soviet space program, especially the 1957 launching of Sputnik and the 1961 flight of Yuri Gagarin. The genre benefited from increased openness to the West, as western fiction, including science fiction, appeared in translation. By the 1960s Russian fans were enjoying Asimov, Bradbury, Sheckley, and Vonnegut, alongside others like Bester, Clarke, Simak, and even Heinlein.

The Soviet Golden Age began when Yefremov's *Andromeda Nebula* was serialized in 1957 in the popular science magazine *Tekhnika molodyozhi* (*Technology for Youth*). The story inspired a typical ideological debate, with a conservative economic journal questioning its utopian assumptions and the Writers' Union organ *Literaturnaya gazeta* defending it. Its hardcover publication in 1958 by Molodaya Gvardia (Young Guard), one of the three educational publishers that handled science fiction, presumes official approval. An English version from the Soviet Foreign Languages Publishing House appeared in 1959 as *Andromeda: A Space-Age Tale*.[8] Yefremov depicts a spacefaring humanity nearly 1000 years in the future, when the Earth has evolved a smoothly running communist society. The civilization enjoys a global computer network that provides international audio-visual connectivity and that allows access to entire libraries, facilitated by a circle of communication satellites in orbit over the Earth's equator. The planet is being engineered for maximum productivity, while spaceships devoted to scientific exploration travel to other stars. While the light-speed barrier has not been conquered, humans are long-lived enough, at 170 years, that committing half a century to a single round trip voyage proves an acceptable sacrifice. Contact has been made with alien species, but mostly via the Great Ring, an audio-visual web spanning the galaxy. Unfortunately, it too is subject to the laws of relativity, meaning that it is not uncommon to receive messages that are hundreds of years old, from civilizations that may already be extinct.

Most of the story is devoted to adventures in space, from encounters with dangerous alien lifeforms to discovery of alien artifacts, and finally to the efforts of a few visionaries to arrange the voyage of a literal lifetime to a beautiful distant planet visualized via the Ring. Yefremov spends more time on science than on dialectical materialism, but interpolates enough to bring this future into line with current ideology. We are told that after the end of our own era—known as the Era of Disunity or Fission Age—the "rebuilding of the world on communist lines entailed a radical economic change accompanied by the disappearance of poverty, hunger and heavy, exhausting toil" (52). Yefremov introduces some specific Marxist notions to this society, such as one from Marx's essay "The German Ideology" (1932), to wit, that the citizen of the communist future will be a polymath capable of pursuing a variety of careers. For example, when starship captain Darr Veter returns to Earth after a long space voyage, he immediately seeks out physical labor as a miner, while the finest interpretive dancer among the characters, Chanda, is also a biologist.

Other classically Marxist elements include the idea, controversial even for classical Marxists, of children being raised and educated in publicly operated schools, preparing them for social responsibility while liberating both men and women, who enjoy perfect equality, for personal fulfillment. In fact, educational institutions have taken the place of government, which has withered away with the state. In a post-scarcity society with the monetary economy in the distant past, individuals get their rewards from scientific exploration, useful labor, and service to the general welfare. In this sense it resembles the world of *Star Trek: The Next Generation* (1987–1994), where Captain Picard can proclaim, "The acquisition of wealth is no longer the driving force in our lives. We work to better ourselves and the rest of humanity."[9] Yefremov employed this utopian future as the backdrop for two more works: the novella *Heart of the Serpent* (1958, 1961) and the novel *Hour of the Bull* (1968). All feature characters who are not only enlightened communists but perfect physical specimens, even approaching the *Übermensch* ideal.[10] In fact, critics have complained of the lack of credible humanity in his characters, a complaint shared even in contemporary Soviet commentary.

Among Yefremov's critics were the Brothers Strugatsky, who offered their own version of the triumph of communism. In the opening years of their writing career, Arkady and Boris Strugatsky also take for granted a future utopia—like Yefremov's (or, again, *Star Trek*'s) a global society liberated from the struggle for material well-being and devoted to progress, scientific exploration, and spiritually satisfying work. This world is the setting for their early story collections *Space Apprentice* (1962, 1981) and *Return* (1961), the latter later revised and released as *Noon: 22nd Century* (1967, 1978). In contrast to Yefremov's perfect world, however, their "future Communist society is deliberately 'unglamorous': despite all the wonders of technology, the abolition of private property, and profound socio-economic transformations, the people are ordinary, even humdrum" (Gomel 365). They seek meaningful work, suffer disappointment in love, struggle to understand the alien, and look forward to the future, sometimes falling into error in the process. As the Strugatskys often asserted, the chief conflict in this idealized world is "between the good and the better."

Specific references to ideology are less evident here than in *Andromeda* but present nonetheless. For instance, the story "Moving Roads" features the cosmonaut Kondratev, who seeks his place in this brave new world after returning from a relativistic space voyage of 150 years. As he travels on one of the slow-moving pedestrian conveyors that cross the park-like landscape, the road become a metaphor for the gradual progress of humankind. The story's climax arrives as he enters a city where he confronts a huge statue of Lenin, "straining ever forward ... [stretching] his arm out over this city and this world, this shining and wonderful world that he had seen two centuries before."[11] The final story, "What You Will Be Like," anticipates the continued evolution of humanity. Here it is Kondratev's fellow cosmonaut Slavin who offers an encomium to Lenin's foresight, concluding with the observation that "the human race began with communism and it returned to communism, and with this return a new turn of the spiral begins, a completely fantastic one" (319).

If literary utopias are inherently ideological, these by Yefremov and the Strugatskys differ in purpose from those of classical tradition—from Plato and More through William Morris and Edward Bellamy—all of which were responding to perceived evils in their own time and thus were "radical critiques of existing society" (Gilison 5). The Russian authors, by contrast, were formally extrapolating from the programmatic promises of Marxism under Khrushchev. Their utopianism is thus "not the product of general alienation *from* society but the project of inculcation *by* society" (Gilison 53). Aside from Yefremov and the Strugatskys, however, few Golden Age authors portrayed fully realized utopias, and then mostly in short stories. The entry on science fiction in the *Great Soviet Encyclopedia* names Genrikh Altov, Georgy Gurevich, and the team of M. Emtsev and E. Parnov as utopian writers, while others point to Sergei Snegov's *Men Like Gods*, published in two parts in 1966 and 1968. Most noteworthy sf practitioners of that generation, however—such as Sever Gansovsky, Anatoly Dneprov, Dmitri Bilenkin, Ilya Varshavsky, Olga Larianova, and Gennady Gor—generally avoided speculation about the political structure of the future, preferring treatments of robots, aliens, time travel, scientific heroism, and technology gone wrong—not unlike their counterparts in the Anglophone science fiction of the time.

Like Yefremov, the Strugatskys continued to use their original future history as background for later stories. Between 1963 and 1965 they reached a pinnacle of productivity with the novels *Far Rainbow* (1963, 1979), *Hard to Be a God* (1964, 1973), *Monday Begins on Saturday* (1965, 1977), and *Predatory Things of the Age* (1965, 1976; published in English as *The Final Circle of Paradise*). They simultaneously established themselves as the most popular science fiction authors in the Soviet Union; all of these novels were listed as favorites in a 1967 poll of Soviet genre fans (Simon 384). Unfortunately, this rise to prominence coincided with Khrushchev's replacement by Brezhnev, who cast a chill on the Thaw and the utopian expectations of his predecessor. Even as they became more popular, and partly for that very reason, the Strugatskys attracted criticism on ideological grounds in Soviet literary reviews. Some of it was undoubtedly motivated by envy, mostly from science fiction hacks from the Stalin era (Simon 386). But much of it represents the "tempest in a teapot" phenomenon alluded to by Patrick McGuire: "the tendency of Soviet ideologists to engage in ferocious battles over virtually meaningless verbal quibbles" (14).

It is true, nonetheless, that in their work of the sixties the Strugatskys were subtly questioning Marxist orthodoxy, if only by presenting societies that fell outside the norms of theory. In *Hard to Be a God* they portray an alien world where feudalism has evolved directly to fascism, in *Predatory Things of the Age* a decadent capitalist enclave surviving within the future communist world. If utopias were becoming ideologically suspect under Brezhnev, dystopias were even more so. Soviet publishers avoided anti-utopias on the grounds they were "either expressions of genuine despair ... that things can only get worse, or else instruments of capitalist propaganda consciously constructed to defame communism" (McGuire 62). As the *Great Soviet Encyclopedia* insists, the science fiction of "the USSR and other socialist countries ... counterposes gloomy Western antiutopian writings with writings inspired by social optimism."[12] Nevertheless, John Glad claims the resurrection of the Russian anti-utopia in 1964 with Emtsev and Parnov's *Soul of the World*, and even asserts that all but one of the novels/novellas produced by the Strugatskys in the 1960s were anti-utopian.[13] Rosalind J. Marsh agrees, maintaining that these "works raise complex issues reflecting disillusionment with the vision of the Utopia conventionally associated with" the Soviet program to advance society through science and technology.[14]

Here is where we need to quibble over semantics, because recent critique on utopias and dystopias has refined terminology. For example, not all dystopias are "anti-utopias," currently defined as fictional societies critical "not just of any particular utopian program but of utopianism in general."[15] Under this definition, *We* (1921) or *Nineteen Eighty-Four* (1949) would be appear to be anti-utopias, although Tom Moylan adds a further refinement: since their authors were not hostile to the socialist mission, only its distortion by Lenin and Stalin, he considers these works "critical anti-utopias."[16] It was Moylan who introduced the concept of "critical utopias" in works which emphasize "the awareness of the limitations of the utopian tradition, so that these texts reject utopia as a blueprint while preserving it as dream"[17]; thus, they recognize "the continuing presence of difference and imperfection within utopian society itself and thus render more recognizable and dynamic alternatives" (1986, 11). Moylan cites as examples novels like Ursula K. Le Guin's *The Dispossessed* (1974) and Delany's *Triton* (1976) that explore the possibility of utopia without idealizing it.

Later, Moylan joined other critics in adding the category of "critical dystopia," which challenges the pessimism of the twentieth-century dystopian tradition by resisting closure and maintaining space for utopian alternatives (Moylan 2000 189). In place of Orwell's jackboot stomping on a face forever, in other words, the critical dystopia presents a worst case scenario in order to suggest meaningful engagement for opposition; examples cited are Margaret Atwood's *The Handmaid's Tale* (1985), Kim Stanley Robinson's *The Gold Coast* (1988), and Octavia E. Butler's *Parable* novels (1993, 1998).

Per these definitions, the novels of the Strugatskys would not be anti-utopian, since they do not attack utopianism *per se*. The furthest they go in that direction may have been *Ugly Swans* from 1967, where utopia appears attainable only after a clean break with the present. By questioning orthodoxy, their novels fit the definitions of critical utopia/dystopia, when they are not outright satires like *Tale of the Troika* (1968, 1977) and *The Second Martian Invasion* (1967, 1970). In fact, there were sympathetic Soviet critics who complimented the Strugatskys on this score, such as A. Lebedev, who in a review of *Snail on a Slope* (1965, 1980) disparaged utopianism as "an error pretending to eternity" and stated "only a theologist is capable of believing in the fatal inevitability of progress"(quoted by Glad 110–111). Despite such critics who saw this social critique as positive, "it became evident to the authorities that science fiction possessed a definite 'dissident' potential" (Glad 197).

Beginning in 1969, the year the Strugatskys were among the first science fiction authors admitted to the Writers' Union, the regime clamped down on the genre. Publishing guidelines under Brezhnev were at best inconsistent, but publishers tended to err on the side of caution. In the 1970s the science

fiction novel and novella gave way to the short story. The Strugatskys' difficulties with the literary bureaucracy are a matter of record.[18] They published
little in the 1970s, even as the official *Great Soviet Encyclopedia* dismissed
attacks on them as mere "polemics" and praised them for their "humanist
ideal of progress" and their commitment to the future (v. 24, 605). Utopia,
however, was no longer on the agenda in the Brezhnev era. Writing at the
time, circa 1975, Gilison wondered how the Soviet state could sustain itself
without explicit expectations of a brighter communist future. The alternative,
in his view, was stricter controls to hold the population on course. He spec-
ulated that the leadership "will preserve their power and privilege, but beyond
that the ideological consequences are difficult to imagine" (187).

A decade later, however, at least one Russian writer imagined such consequences, and not surprisingly he found them dystopian. Dissident Vladimir
Voinovich, after being ejected from the Writers' Union, emigrated to western
Europe, where in 1986 he published *Moscow 2042*. In this dark satire, the
Soviet Union evolves to its natural culmination: a propaganda-driven police
state incapable of meeting the material needs of its people and headed toward
total collapse. Social cohesion is rigorously enforced through a ridiculous
personality cult built around the "Genialissimo," who like Stalin is credited
not only with inspired leadership but with scientific and literary genius. Real
power, however, is wielded by the bureaucracy and the military.

The protagonist, identified by name as the author, visits the Moscow of
2042 by time-traveling from 1982. Not only does Voinovich condemn the
Soviet system, he expresses little faith in his fellow intellectuals, even fellow
dissidents. A colleague with the name Sim Simych, modeled on Alexander
Solzhenitsyn and portrayed as a pompous self-promoter, urges Voinovich to
carry his 36-volume magnum opus into the future. There writers are encouraged to attack each other, though since none of their computers are actually
connected, their diatribes never see print. Meanwhile, scientists serve the
state by creating the Marxist New Man in the lab, an *Übermensch* who turns
out to be asexual and barely human. Simych has himself frozen, and resurrects
in 2042 in time for the collapse of the Soviet state. He becomes the leader of
its successor, a right-wing autocracy allied with the Orthodox Church that
drags the populace back to tsarist times. Protagonist Voinovich finds himself
in prison beside the Genialissimo, who lays the fault with the masses: "if the
people are the majority, then I should tell you that the people are stupider
than any one person. It's much more difficult to convince an individual of an
idiotic idea than an entire people."[19] *Moscow 2042* is distinctly anti-utopian
in attacking Marxist orthodoxy, but it is much more a pointed satire on Brezhnev's Soviet Union, a dystopia in the "if this goes on" mode that "treats the
future as merely a disguise for the present" (Glad 113).

A few years after Voinovich's novel, of course, the Soviet Union did collapse. The Russian Spring emerged under Boris Yeltsin, but typical of Russian springs bad weather left progress bogged down. The police state disappeared, but so did any pretense of support for public welfare. Part of the blame, as Nobel economist Joseph Stiglitz wrote in 2002, rested on the way the West introduced market economics to the new Russia: "The IMF unwittingly connived with a new and wholly unscrupulous elite. The billions of dollars loaned to Russia showed up in Cypriot and Swiss bank accounts," creating the robber baron class we now know as the oligarchs (quoted by Hoffman 151). By the onset of this century, the country saw "a dramatic collapse in living standards, health and security" (Hoffman 144); alcoholism went up, life spans down, and in place of democracy, a kleptocracy reigned.

With literature no longer employed as an educational tool, today's Russian authors are free to write for the market, which presumably serves the tastes of its readers. In her Afterword to *Worlds Apart: An Anthology of Russian Fantasy and Science Fiction* (2007)[20] Sofya Khagi summarizes the range of genre fiction in the new century. Fantasy has emerged as a favorite, inspired by Tolkien but exploiting Russian folklore. Alternate histories are widespread in the fiction of Andrei Lazarchuk, Kir Bulyechev, and others. Popular are escapist action thrillers with space opera or cyberpunk plots. And, also mirroring the West, we find dystopias, although with a uniquely Russian flavor. Alongside *Moscow 2042* Khagi names another in the satirical vein: Tatyana Tolstaya's *Kys'*, published in English in 2003 as *The Slynx*.

Tolstaya's is a dystopia in the post-apocalyptic mode. Here again we must wrestle with semantics. Booker does not regard post-disaster scenarios, even if certainly "bad places," as dystopias, because they "do not generally focus on the details of the imaginary societies they portray so much as on the collapse of the preexisting society" (5). As Moylan among others observes, dystopia and utopia alike are rooted in history (Moylan 2000 274), while the post-apocalyptic tale severs itself from history. *The Slynx*, however, points its satire directly at the Russian and particularly the Soviet past. Two hundred years after a devastating nuclear war, Russians inhabiting the former site of Moscow have returned to neolithic village life and a subsistence economy, with mice as the primary food staple and currency. Mutant lifeforms abound, from the now mostly toxic flora and fauna to the edible glowing figs called "firelings." The villagers themselves have various disfiguring mutations, euphemistically named "Consequences." The "Oldeners," those born before "the Blast," are now immortal until disease, accident, or predators kill them. At the extreme end are the Degenerators, devolved Oldeners with furry hides and a tendency to run on all fours, which has made them convenient draft animals; however, they are bad-tempered and do not serve willingly. The eponymous Slynx is a monster reportedly lurking in the surrounding woods, though it increasingly becomes clear it is a creature of the collective psyche.

The village survives under a nominal autarch, Fyodor Kuzmich, who turns out to be a somewhat good-natured if self-serving dwarf. What passes for governance is the bureaucracy known as the Murza. More feared are the San-iturions, who raid shacks ("izbas") in search of books to confiscate, capture rulebreakers with "the hook," and take them away for "healing" from the "Ill-ness," though none are ever seen again. Despite these sinister elements, the fabulist narrative resonates with humor, pointed historical allusions, and fre-quent literary references, mainly in the form of snatches of verse from Pushkin and other poets.

Protagonist Benedikt and most of his fellow "Golubchiks"—a Russian term that suggests "yokels"—live in ignorance of the past, dominated by superstition. Theirs is a classic village of fools, suggesting that not only civ-ilization but intelligence has suffered a permanent collapse. So has empathy. Most amusements involve physical harm to others, and Benedikt regards it as perfectly natural that the villagers should steal from one another. He passes off as mere "government thinking"[21] that the Paymaster Murza would with-hold salary chits for himself, or that the Tax-Collector Murza would over-charge, or that the Warehouse Murza would keep goods in the warehouse for his own use instead of distributing them. Oldener Nikita Ivanich observes ironically that such mutual theft is "a basic redistribution of personal property holdings" (65). Benedikt cannot grasp Nikita's advocacy of "more-ality."

The Oldeners themselves, while aware of the mistakes of history, seem doomed to repeat them. Though more sympathetic than other characters, they become satirical targets when they drift into nostalgia for the Soviet era. For example, a funeral for one Oldener opens with a ritual call for relics of the time: "Party cards, Komsomol or trade union ID ... State lottery tickets?" (108). When instructions for a meat grinder turn up, Nikita reverences it as "[t]his priceless relic of a bygone era!" (111). Given the opportunity to add his input, the representative dissident Lev Lvovich complains that the meat grinder was "[d]evised long ago by the slaves of the Third Rome. By slaves! And there are no Xeroxes!" (112). But in his reflexive responses, Lev himself proves nostalgic for Soviet days of samizdat and fruitless opposition. Later in the novel, during one of their many comradely disputes, Lev accuses Nikita of Tolstoyan mysticism and nationalism for his support of traditional virtues, a charge that goes back to Lenin's time. At one point Nikita demonstrates his sympathy for the oppressed working class by inviting the Degenerator Teterya into his izba and treating him to drinks as an equal. But when talk turns to the fall of the Soviet Union, the inebriated Teterya rants against Jews and Gorbachev, until his attack on Sakharov prompts Lev to punch him and Nikita to throw him out.

Mired as they are in historical paradigms, the characters cannot escape oligarchy. In the second half of the novel Benedikt gets to experience the

Murza from the inside after marrying the lovely blonde Olenka, the daughter of a Saniturion, whose only mutation is the claws on her feet she has inherited from her parents. We learn that the Saniturions are not merely repressive thought police, confiscating books and their owners like the firemen of *Fahrenheit 451* (1953), but that their purported mission is to preserve history and culture, like the monks of Saint Leibowitz. When Benedikt's Father-in-Law, Kudeyar Kudeyarovich, apprentices him to become a Saniturion, he argues that they are weeding the culture so it can grow, even as he denigrates the masses as superstitious savages. It is hard not to see the Saniturions as an ironic Leninist vanguard.

Benedikt's apprenticeship leads to gluttonous reading, analogous to the gluttonous eating indulged in by his wife's family; nonetheless, he acquires no wisdom from this pursuit. When his Father-in-Law enlists him in the overthrow of Fyodor Kuzmich, Benedikt immediately visits the Great Murza's library. There he discovers all the texts that the deposed ruler plagiarized for his own published tales and poetry, and for his many inventions like nails and boats; like Stalin the dwarf was esteemed as scientist, social theorist, and literary figure. The library, however, reflects the general stupidity of this society in its arbitrary classification system, which shelves together volumes alluding to color like Stendhal's *The Red and the Black* (1830), Scott O'Dell's *Island of the Blue Dolphins* (1960), and works by T.H. White, or anything with the syllable Nin, including Anaïs Nin, *Nineveh: An Archeological Collection*, and *Mutant Ninja Turtles*. The cultural legacy is useless absent some theoretical principle that lends it coherence and meaning.

The New Boss is worse than the Old Boss. No sooner does Kudeyar Kudeyarovich set himself up as General Saniturion than he starts making absurd authoritarian decrees, such as banning leap year as well as all sorcerers except those designated as "government workers" (262), while a half-hearted attempt to codify civil rights is soon abandoned for lack of interest or understanding. Benedikt is named Deputy for Defense and Marine and Oceanic Affairs in this landlocked village. As a former draft animal, Degenerator Teterya becomes Minister of Transport, Oil, and Refineries, and in this role decides to recreate the internal combustion engine and restore the "guzzelean" economy. He proposes executing Nikita Ivanich, who can breathe fire, as unfair competition. The significance of the Slynx emerges when Benedikt gets into an argument with his father-in-law, and they accuse each other of being the Slynx, confirming what Nikita says earlier: "There isn't any Slynx, it's nothing but human ignorance" (21). The Beast lurks within the people themselves.

If dystopias use the future to comment on the present, *The Slynx* does so by satirizing the past and the penchant for repeating it. In fact, the stranglehold of history appears to infuse all current Russian dystopias. That is certainly the case in Dmitry Glukhovsky's *Metro 2033* (2005, 2010). Although also post-apocalyptic, it belongs not to the satirical mode but to the popular genre of action thrillers; indeed, it has inspired an internet video game. The English edition identifies it as an "underground bestseller," appropriately, since most of action occurs in the Moscow subway system. Despite the title, it is not clear that the story actually takes place in 2033; some narrative details and references set it later. All we are sure of is that the remnants of Moscow's population have built communities in the Metro complex a generation or more following a civilization-ending nuclear war. As in *The Slynx,* no mention is made of the identity of the enemy or the reasons for the war; the disaster is simply a pretext for the setting. Violence remains a fact of life in the Metro, however, and gun cartridges are the universal currency.

Protagonist Artyom, a young man around twenty years of age, has grown up in the Metro settlement labeled VDNKh. This station is haunted by "the dark ones," a race of black-skinned mutants with telepathic powers, apparently originating in the radioactive ruins above. Artyom's stepfather Sukhoi sees them as a threat only because they are "the next stage in evolution, better adapted to the environment than us."[22] He says so to Hunter, a "stalker" who, like the stalkers of the Strugatskys' *Roadside Picnic* (1972, 1977), explores the dangerous regions underground or above in "the Zone," so called in another echo of *Roadside Picnic*. Hunter selects Artyom for a quest to the heart of the Metro, a cluster of stations called Gorod, i.e., the City or Polis, to find a military commander named Melnik and enlist him in the fight against the dark ones. The quest will lead Artyom on a sort of Pilgrim's Progress, through various societies, ideologies, and philosophies and the evolution of his own worldview.

Historical analogies abound from the outset. For example, the two great powers of the Metro exist in détente following a struggle that left both exhausted. One is the Sokol or Red Line that cuts diagonally across the entire system, consisting of Soviet revanchists who operate along Stalinist lines. The Red Line intersects a ring route controlled by the Hansa, a capitalist trading network that communicates with most other lines in a manner reminiscent of Yefremov's galactic Great Ring. Under this détente, the Red Line has turned its paranoid security apparatus inward:

> Hundreds of agents of the internal security service, like in the old days, with a certain nostalgia for the KGB, constantly and diligently watched the happy inhabitants of the Red Line, and their interest in guests from other lines was unending. Without the special permission of the management of the "Reds" no one could get to any other station. And the constant monitoring of passports, the total watching and a general clinical suspicion was imposed on the accidental travelers as well as the spies who were sent there [73].

In contrast to this "eternally half-starved" police state (426), the Hansa is the most prosperous of all Metro communities, but it is also highly restrictive. Artyom can only enter by participating in a literal rat race, but when his rat loses, he is condemned to indentured servitude cleaning the latrines. Days at this labor teach Artyom the grim underside of capitalism. While the Hansa is comfortable, and its citizens go about their business without the fear and superstition that characterize other stations, working in the latrines drives Artyom to an existential crisis, convincing him that human life is meaningless and that "man is a clever machine for the decomposition of food and the production of shit"—in short, mere consumers with no "ultimate goal" (227). Within days he manages to escape, exploiting the fact that no one will approach him since he is covered with excrement.

Experiences with other ideologies lead to equally pessimistic conclusions. At one point Artyom stumbles into a settlement controlled by Slavic nationalists who revere the Nazis and call themselves the Fourth Reich; their symbol is a three-hooked cross reminiscent of the swastika. In the name of racial purity they murder the neighboring Chechens or anyone who does not meet the Slavic ideal. Artyom ends up killing a guard and being scheduled for a quick execution. But just as he is losing consciousness at the end of a rope, he is saved by a party of anti-fascist guerrillas. They are members of the International Brigade, a multi-ethnic collective fighting in the name of Che Guevara. Although Marxists, they criticize the Red Line for being Stalinist and ignoring the Interstationist struggle. Of all the subcultures of the Metro, these individuals seem the most sympathetic, if somewhat naïve. They praise the ideological battles of Spain and World War II by rote, and have "funny dialectical arguments" about, for example, the place of mutants in the revolution. They invite Artyom to join their struggle, but assist him on his quest when he refuses. Artyom considers them more mere relics of the past, and "[t]hat magical, wonderful world was long dead" (207).

Among the other philosophies he explicitly rejects is conventional Christianity, as inherently irrational, gaining strength instead in his growing existentialism: "the thought that his life was of no use and that each living thing should resist nonsense and the chaos of life" (237). He later falls in with a pair of old-timers, smoking the ubiquitous mushroom-sourced intoxicant from a hookah. They argue that his journey through the Metro has in fact exhibited purpose, evidenced by the fact he has survived multiple confrontations with death while his many guides have died or disappeared. Convinced, Artyom continues his quest in the belief he is a Chosen One tasked with a great goal. Only when he travels on do we discover that the smokers are postmodern fabulists who do not believe this anthropocentric theory themselves. Artyom encounters similarly artificial belief systems in passing. He hears of a station dominated by Satanists who are digging deeper, expecting to find

Hell. Near the end of his quest he encounters a tribe of naked savages who worship a Great Worm that supposedly built the Metro, and who kidnap children to increase their numbers but eat adults as the only available meat. The Great Worm mythos, however, has been invented by their priests, actually intellectuals who are laying the foundation for a new civilization and who have created the myth because people need something to believe in. In fact, when one of the savages overhears a priest admitting the invention of the Great Worm, he literally dies from existential angst, his last word a mournful "Alone!" (398).

The motif of false belief continues when Artyom finally reaches Polis, where he finds the commander Melnik and the stalker Hunter. Polis sits directly under the heart of Moscow, its symbol the double-headed Romanov eagle, which Artyom mistakes for a mutant. The next step in his quest is to join the commandos on an ascent to the Zone, accompanied by Daniel, a member of an intellectual priesthood called Brahmins. They head for the Lenin Library, the treasury of Russian culture, in search of the Book of the Future, a mythical text with gold letters that reportedly contains all answers, including information that will defeat the dark ones. After Daniel is disemboweled by one of the zombie-like "librarians," which attack anyone who makes a sound, Artyom finds himself in the open facing other mutants. He is literally hypnotized by the sight of the Kremlin, which turns out to host a metastasized life form that draws in its prey telepathically. Thus, both these monuments to Russian history prove lethal. After rescuing Artyom, commander Melnik inspires his troops with a song from the Great Patriotic War before acknowledging that "[i]n our country all eras are much the same" (417).

Given the novel's pattern, it should not come as a surprise that Artyom's quest is also premised on false belief. Having convinced himself that he is a Chosen One, not only through his near miraculous escapes but because of his recurring dream of a dark one trying to communicate with him, he implements the destruction of the dark ones' enclave in a Moscow park. He learns only as nuclear missiles head their way that he has interpreted the clues exactly backwards, leading to tragedy. Once again, the Beast that destroys actually lurks within. Glukhovsky presents a paradox: humans must embrace belief to live meaningful lives, but all belief systems are reductive or destructive. The final page of the U.K. edition sports an advertisement for the computer game, illustrating a corpse or zombie at the window of a Metro train over the words "Fear the Future." The novel, however, shares with Tolstaya's very different *Slynx* the fear that the future will simply repeat the past. There is no escape from the mistakes of history, especially Russian history.

This message is repeated across the Russian science fiction of this century. We find it again in yet another Russian dystopia: Vladimir Sorokin's

Day of the Oprichnik (2006).[23] Reminiscent of *Moscow 2042*, it offers another darkly satirical vision of a near-future Russia that has returned to the autocracy of tsarist times, enforced with futuristic technology. The story follows an "oprichnik," a government agent named after the guards of Ivan the Terrible, over 24 hours as he participates in assassination by death ray, gangrape, and other brutal methods of defending the Motherland. Sorokin produced it at the outset of the Putin era and recently marveled that he had anticipated Russia's return to one-man rule and the Orthodox Church. Already notorious for his surreal satires and pornographic explorations of sadomasochism and bestiality, Sorokin need not worry that his controversial writings will bring him trouble. As reviewer Stephen Kotkin writes, "subversive works in Russia today are essentially impossible. Provocative fiction no longer produces consequences."[24]

So that's the good news. Even as Vladimir Putin clamps down on political opposition, Russian fiction writers are free to criticize, like those in the West, because they no longer matter. And they seem aware of that fact, judging from the tone of cynical resignation that infuses their dystopias. As defined by western critics, the dystopia—and especially the "critical dystopia"—is intended as an awful warning against contemporary trends and a call to correct them. Booker shares the view of many theorists when he writes, "the bleak dystopian world should encourage the reader or viewer to think critically about it, then transfer this critical thinking to his or her own world" (5). Contemporary Russian authors, however, apparently see no hope of meaningful progress. Indeed, critic Aleksandr Chantsev names several others working in what he calls "the antiutopia factory." Chantsev's explanation for this trend is that "the end of the totalitarian system was most certainly attended not only by a joyful feeling of liberation but also by a plunge into social depression, the sense that a new-model authoritarian or repressive society is in the making...."[25] The result is the conviction that the future will be no better than the past. This pessimism is not shared by all Russians. Recent polls conducted by western political scientists have found that "three-quarters or more say they now feel freer than under the Soviet regime," though a significant percentage express some nostalgia for Soviet times.[26] And although only eight percent say they favor dictatorship, a majority believes Putin will make Russia great again.

Starting from the utopian assumptions of Khruschchev's Thaw, Golden Age authors like Yefremov and the Strugatskys explored the premise that the future could be better, sometimes problematically, a fundamental topic in all science fiction traditions. Russian writers half a century later face the quandary expressed by Krishan Kumar: "The waning of the socialist utopia in the second half of the twentieth century posed problems not just for utopia but for anti-utopia. Both saw the disappearance of the hope that had been the source of their vitality, however differently expressed" (63). Indeed, the memory of that hope, even as false hope, contributes to the pessimism of Russian intellectuals in the 21st century. Essayist Lev Anninsky, a self-confessed *shestdesyatnik*, recently wrote that "[t]he system has been destroyed, but those who destroyed it did not recognize that it provided a refuge of sorts, and now we have no refuge and the rain pours straight down on our heads."[27] He shares the conclusion of the dystopian novelists, that the fault is not with a single ideology but with the legacy of the past: "You can't change the character of the Russian people overnight any more than you can rewrite Russian history. It is as it is, and we had better just accept the fact" (217).

In the conclusion of his 1980 study *Three Tomorrows*, John Griffiths lamented the tendency toward dystopian futures in British and American science fiction, finding vigor in the positive visions of the Soviet Golden Age. Now his complaint applies even better to post-millennial Russian sf: "The writers of earlier days were telling Man how to build heaven; today they are content to teach him how to survive in hell."[28]

Notes

1. Jerome M. Gilison, *The Soviet Image of Utopia* (Baltimore: Johns Hopkins University Press, 1975), 5. Page references are to this edition.

2. Quoted in Krishan Kumar, *Utopianism* (Buckingham, UK: Open University Press, 1991), 32. A page reference is to this edition.

3. John Hoffman, *John Gray and the Problem of Utopia* (Cardiff: University of Wales Press, 2008), 96. Page references are to this edition.

4. Karl Mannheim, *Ideology and Utopia* (London: Lund Humphries, 1936), 236.

5. Aldous Huxley, *Island* (New York: Bantam, 1962), 55.

6. Patrick L. McGuire, *Red Stars: Political Aspects of Soviet Science Fiction* (Ann Arbor: UMI Research Press, 1985), 10. Page references are to this edition.

7. Erik Simon, "The Strugatskys in Political Context," *Science Fiction Studies*, 31:3 (November 2004), 378–406; 380. Page references are to this article.

8. Ivan Yefremov, *Andromeda: A Space-Age Tale*, translated by George Hanna (Moscow: Foreign Languages Publishing House, 1959). Page references are to this edition.

9. *Star Trek: First Contact* (Paramount Pictures, 1996).

10. See Elana Gomel, "Gods Like Men: Soviet Science Fiction and Myth Creation in Our Age," *Science Fiction Studies*, 31:3 (November 2004), 358–377; 372.

11. Arkady and Boris Strugatsky, *Noon: The 22nd Century* (New York: Macmillan, 1977), 88. Page references are to this edition.

12. *Great Soviet Encyclopedia*, Third Edition, edited by A.M. Prokhorov (Moscow: Sovetskaia Entsiklopedia Publishing House; 1976; translation published by New York: Macmillan and London: Collier Macmillan, 1980), Volume 17, 678. A page reference is to this edition.

13. John Glad, *Extrapolations from Dystopia: A Critical Study of Soviet Science Fiction* (Princeton, NJ: Kingston Press, n.d.), 116–117. Page references are to this edition.

14. Rosalind J. Marsh, *Soviet Fiction Since Stalin: Science, Politics and Literature* (London: Croom Helm, 1986), 231.

15. M. Keith Booker, editor, *Dystopia* (Ipswich, MA: Salem Press, 2013), 6. Page references are to this edition.

16. Tom Moylan, *Scraps of the Untainted Sky: Science, Utopia, Dystopia* (Boulder, CO: Westview Press, 2000), 161. Page references are to this edition.

17. Moylan, *Demand the Impossible: Science Fiction and the Utopian Imagination* (New York: Methuen, 1986), 10. Page references are to this edition.

18. See, for example, Erik Simon's "The Strugatskys in Political Context," cited above.

19. Quoted by Erika Gottlieb in *Dystopian Fiction East and West: Universe of Terror and Trial* (Montreal: McGill-Queen's University Press, 2001), 254.

20. Sofya Khagi, Afterword, *Worlds Apart: An Anthology of Russian Fantasy and Science Fiction*, edited by Alexander Levitsky, translated by Levitsky and Martha T. Kitchen (New York: Overlook Duckworth, 2007), 645–650.

21. Tatyana Tolstaya, *The Slynx*. translated by Jamey Gambrell (Boston: Houghton Mifflin, 2003), 48. Page references are to this edition.

22. Dmitry Glukhovsky, *Metro 2033* (London: Gollancz, 2011), 36. Page references are to this edition.

23. Vladimir Sorokin, *Day of the Oprichnik*, translated by Jamey Gambrell (New York: Farrar, Straus & Giroux, 2012).

24. Stephen Kotkin, "A Dystopian Tale of Russia's Future," *New York Times Book Review* (March 11, 2011), at https://www.nytimes.com/2011/03/13/books/review/book-review-day-of-the-oprichnik-by-vladimir-sorokin.html.

25. Aleksandr Chantsev, "The Antiutopia Factory: The Dystopian Discourse in Russian Literature in the Mid–2000s." *Russian Science Fiction Literature and Cinema: A Critical Reader*, edited by Anindita Banerjee (Boston: Academic Studies Press 2018), 328–370; 370.

26. Richard Rose, William Mischler, and Neil Munro, *Popular Support for an Undemocratic Regime: The Changing Views of Russians* (Cambridge: Cambridge University Press, 2011), 107.

27. Natasha Perova and Arch Tait, editors, *The Scared Generation: Annual Anthology of New Russian Writing*, No.9 (Moscow: GLAS, 1995), 216. A page reference is to this edition.

28. John Griffiths, *Three Tomorrows: American, British and Soviet Science Fiction* (London: Macmillan, 1980), 115.

Chinese Science Fiction
and Its Doubles

Lisa Raphals

The relation of science to science fiction in the history of Chinese science fiction is closely linked to Western science and ideals of progress, nationalism, and empire.[1] That linkage arose through exposure of Chinese intellectuals to science fiction in the nineteenth century, and to the availability of certain translations. But when we turn to China's long history of philosophical speculation and its own indigenous sciences, a very different picture arises. Themes from these areas appear in other genres of Chinese speculative fiction, but rarely in "science fiction." This essay explores the history of Chinese science fiction, but then swerves toward the "untold science fiction" of the indigenous Chinese sciences, and explores possible relations between the two.

Introduction

The problem of the "science" in Chinese science fiction is complicated by three sets of questions. The first is the question of what counted as "science fiction" (henceforward sf). As with science fiction in general, scholars debate at what point "Chinese science fiction" can be said to have emerged. In particular, should it be seen as a modern phenomenon that arose in the late nineteenth or early twentieth century—at the end of the Qing dynasty (1644–1911)—or can it be traced back to earlier literary genres? The problem also involves questions of genre. Today the genre of "science fiction" (*ke huan* 科幻) is considered distinct from "fantasy" (*qi huan* 奇幻), which includes both fantastic fiction with Chinese supernatural elements (*xuan huan* 玄幻) and magical fiction with Western elements (*mo huan* 魔幻).[2]

If we take the "modernist" view, three further questions arise. What did Qing readers and writers understand as "Western" sf? Which writers were available in translation? What happened to "Western science fiction" over the course of the twentieth century? Did it remain a foreign import or did it become increasingly indigenous? What did the Chinese authors of work we retrospectively recognize as sf consider themselves to be doing? How did they identify themselves and the work they produced? Answers to these questions are complicated by the bumpy history of the genre in the twentieth century, where until recently it was relegated to children's literature concerned with science education, and was of little literary or popular interest. Others argue that Chinese sf was a twentieth-century phenomenon that emerged only in the 1930s, 1950s, or even the post–Mao period. A second set of questions concern the history of science in China. They ask what was understood as the "science" science fiction "fictionalized" in different periods of Chinese history, and how indigenous approaches to understanding the world related— or did not—to "Western" science. Finally, a third set of questions concern the relation between these two histories.

This essay offers a different approach to Chinese sf and its relations to science. It begins with a brief modernist history in which Chinese sf originated in the Qing dynasty and was strongly informed by translations of Western sf. I then turn to another possible history that has been little explored: namely the relation—or lack of it—of Chinese sf to indigenous Chinese sciences. Chinese scientific and philosophical literature offers a long and rich parallel history of speculation on topics that are now staples of science fiction across several genres of Chinese writing since the fourth century BCE. The remaining sections turn to three distinct threads that appear in Chinese philosophical and historico-literary texts from the fifth or fourth centuries BCE to roughly the sixth century CE. From a contemporary point of view, these texts address three important elements that are, in contemporary terms, staple elements of sf. But from the viewpoints of their creators, these genres address practices and theories defined by indigenous Chinese sciences. This essay surveys what might be called a "parallel sf context" in these genres and the practices they draw upon.

The first is accounts of travel in space (above or beyond the earth) and time. In a contemporary context these are "time-travel" narratives. But in the context of indigenous sciences, they address, describe or challenge accounts of the physical nature of the earth as described in indigenous Chinese sciences. The second is what for convenience I will call "transformation accounts," including contact with sentient non-human entities and accounts of transformation between species. Such accounts prominently include the indigenous Chinese genre of "tales of the strange" (zhiguai 志怪). Such tales, traditionally understood as history, rather than fiction, have retained ongoing popularity in both text and film, especially in martial arts fiction, graphic novels, and film. These stand in counterpoint to indigenous life sciences and accounts of evolution or inter-species transformation. The third is accounts of extreme longevity or immortality. These overlap accounts of health and longevity in indigenous traditions of medicine and materia medica. All three Chinese indigenous literary, religions and scientific traditions informed Chinese sf in important ways. In the case of transformation stories, they provided an alternative literary path, one that was in some cases, taken up by the genres of martial arts fiction. I argue that relations between Chinese literary genres, its indigenous scientific traditions, the introduction of Western science, and the introduction and development of science fiction all form a complex network that warrants further study and should not be over-simplified.

A Modernist History of Chinese Science Fiction

This mid-century positioning of science fiction stands between two very different orientations. One was what many consider the origins of science fiction in China: the development of exploratory, typically utopian, science fictional writings in the late Qing dynasty (1644–1911), especially from the last decades of the nineteenth century and the first three decades of the twentieth. The other is the rise of speculative, often dystopian, science fiction since 1989.

The Qing Legacy of Chinese Science Fiction

A range of contemporary scholars are actively exploring the role of sf, both in translation and homegrown versions—in the cultural life of the late Qing dynasty.[3] As Jing Jiang observes, Chinese science fiction and utopian texts are an important site, where "notions of 'Chineseness,' modernity, and human nature were first articulated, expanded, and subsequently consolidated into a vision of modern China."[4]

Several of the key intellectual figures of the period concerned themselves with sf. Both the great Qing statesman Liang Qichao 梁啟超 (1873–1929) and the great writer Lu Xun 魯迅 (1881–1936) translated Western science fiction into Chinese. Liang translated Jules Verne's *Deux ans de vacances* (*A Two Years' Vacation*, 1888), and Lu introduced Verne's *De la terre à la lune* (*From the Earth to the Moon*, 1865) to Chinese audiences. Both thought that science fiction would help spread modern Western knowledge into China.[5]

By 1919, at least fifty sf titles had been translated into Chinese in both books and magazines, translated under rubric of "science fiction"—*kexue xiaoshuo* 科學小說—a term that was not yet in general use in the West.[6] These translations focused on particular authors and themes. Qing translations of Western sf were heavily oriented toward technological fantasy. As the sf author and editor Xu Nianci 徐念慈 (1875–1908) put it: "Trips to the moon, the end of the world, adventures under the sea and journeys to the center of the earth, all these novelties are derived from a scientific ideal, an ideal that aims at transcending Nature and promoting evolution."[7] Jules Verne was especially popular, in multiple titles and translations that included *From the Earth to the Moon*, *Journey to the Center of the Earth* (1864), *Twenty Thousand Leagues Under the Sea* (1870), *The Mysterious Island* (1874), and *Five Weeks in a Balloon* (1863). By contrast, H.G. Wells's *The Outline of History* (1920) had been translated into Chinese, but not his science fiction. Readers of this literature rejected as "unscientific" the indigenous literature that drew on traditional sciences.[8]

Another important element in that picture was a late-nineteenth century utopianism. Utopian literature was represented by early translations of Edward Bellamy's *Looking Backward: 2000–1887* (1888). It was a central concern of the great Qing statesman Liang Qichao, whose *Future of New China* (*Xin Zhongguo weilai* 新中國未來, 1902), an unfinished political novel, imagined a utopian, revitalized Confucian China; and has often been recognized as the origin of Chinese science fiction.[9] That utopianism was linked to evolutionary thinking and confidence in national rejuvenation, which began to dominate modern Chinese intellectual culture at the beginning of the twentieth century. Liang's novel influenced several other early twentieth century utopian works.[10]

Behind both interests was a view that fiction could both civilize and imagine a future for a China defeated by the Opium War and partitioned by Western powers. As Li Boyuan 李伯元 (1867–1906) put it in his founding manifesto for the magazine *Illustrated Fiction* (*Xiuxiang xiaoshuo* 繡像小説):

> The Western countries have used fiction to civilize their people…. [Fiction writers], who are keen observers of significant affairs of the world and have a profound understanding of human wisdom, use such knowledge to analyse the past and predict the future. They then express their opinions in their works with the view of awakening the populace.[11]

At the beginning of the twentieth century, boundaries between these genres were not harshly drawn. Liang and Lu were interested in both science fiction and utopian works. But by the 1950s, the situation had changed. Sf was "science fantasy fiction" (*kexue huanxiang xiaoshuo* 科學幻想小説), a sub-genre of "science belles-lettres" (*kexue wenyi* 科學文藝). Both were distinct from "utopian fiction" (*lixiang xiaoshuo* 理想小説).[12]

Sf Under Mao

After the founding of the People's Republic of China in 1949, the agenda of Chinese science fiction was set by first Marxism and then Maoism. Marxist priorities drew on Soviet theories that science fiction should concentrate on describing two things: (1) the imaginative processes of scientific thinking as the source of techno-scientific development and (2) the imagined future of communist society.[13] Government campaigns for "Marching toward Science" (*xiang kexue jinjun* 向科学进军) in the mid–1950s promoted both sf and popular science. Nonetheless, between 1949 and 1966 Chinese science fiction focused on short stories aimed at young readers, and few works for adults were published in this period.[14] Science popularization was linked to the Chinese Association for the Popularization of Science (*Zhongguo Kexue Puji Xiehui* 中國科學普及協會), founded in Shanghai in 1978. This science popularization was aimed at a young audience of children and young people. The narratives were linear and action-oriented, conspicuously included children, and first appeared in specialized children's magazines and publishing houses oriented toward children and young people. However, the "fantasy" content of this genre was strictly limited to the scientifically plausible, a point that is important for comparison with the use of indigenous Chinese "tales of the strange."[15] Given its primary interest in science education, this period saw little in the way of either indigenous sf or translations of foreign work. As Wu Dingbo has observed, these productions share several common traits. They provide science education through a cast of characters who are scientists. They use patriotism and optimism to resolve conflicts. Their adventures are set in a near—and by implication—possible, future accessible to the reader.[16]

During the Cultural Revolution (1966–1976), sf disappeared from China. The situation changed between 1978 and 1983, with a major resurgence.[17] This period also saw the publication of Rao Zhonghua's 饒忠華 *Compendium of Chinese Science Fiction* (*Zhongguo Kexue Xiaoshuo Daquan* 中國科幻小說大全, 1982), which subsequently became a standard sourcebook for the subject.[18]

New Wave Chinese Sf

Another history focuses on the extraordinary growth of speculative Chinese sf since 1989. This "new wave" rejects both propaganda and utopianism. Song Mingwei identifies the key year as 1989: the year of the Tiananmen massacre and the tragic collapse of the democracy movement. Several of these writers pursue "hard science" themes, but deployed in socially complex and nuanced settings.[19] The three most prominent Chinese science fiction writers are Liu Cixin 劉慈欣 (1963–), Wang Jinkang 王晋康 (1948–), and Han Song

韩松 (1965–). Liu Cixin's *Three-Body Problem* (*Santi* 三体) trilogy imagines a disastrous scenario of the consequences of reckless alien contact, beginning during the Cultural Revolution and ending in a distant future of inter-civilizational and inter-dimensional warfare.[20] Wang Jinkang also focuses on science, but he frames it in the context of ethics.[21] For example, *The Ant Life* (*Yi sheng* 蚁生, 2007) imagines a utopia in which hormones from ants are used to replace human selfish impulses with altruistic ones (the experiment backfires). Han Song 韩松 (1965–) also addresses problems of society and culture, and the implications of science for society, in novels such as *Artificial People* (*Renzao ren* 人造人, 1997), *Cosmic Tombstones* (*Yuzhou mubei* 宇宙墓碑, 1991), and *My Homeland Never Dreams* (*Wo de zuguo bu zuomeng* 我的祖国不做梦, 2007), in which an authoritarian state uses drugs to control its citizens.

China is also a prominent theme. In Wang Jinkang's *Being with Me* (*Yu wu tong zai* 與吾同在, 2011), the Chinese Communist Party unites the world against an alien invasion. In *Six Lines from Samasara* (*Liudao zhongsheng* 六道眾生, 2002), He Xi 何夕 (1971–) imagines Chinese scientists changing the microstructure of matter in order to relocate surplus populations to new worlds. In his "Foreign Land" (*Yiyu* 異域, 1999), Chinese scientists discover a way to speed up time. But younger new wave Chinese science fiction introduces social and political themes and interests that offer indirect critique of government policies in sometimes dystopian visions, the human implications of technology, and issues of government control. Ma Boyong's 馬伯庸 (1980–) "City of Silence" (*Jijing zhi cheng* 寂静之城) addresses the effects of government censorship in an imaginary future in which the internet is used to control people's minds. Chen Qiufan's 陈楸帆 (Stanley Chan, 1981–) "The Flower of Shazui" (2012) examines the growth of Shenzhen. His novel *The Waste Tide* (2013) is focused on recyclers who live off the byproducts of the high-tech industries of Shenzhen. In his "Year of the Rat" (*Shu nian* 鼠年, 2009) university students support themselves as rat catchers in a world where China supports its economic growth by exporting genetically modified rats.

Other authors choose themes from history and legend, sometimes combined with time travel. For example, Zhao Haihong 趙海虹 (1977–), one of the few women authors of Chinese sf, has a longstanding interest in Chinese genres of the short story and martial arts fiction. Her novels include *The Other Side of Time* (*Shijian de bifang* 时间的彼方, 1998) and *Jocasta* (*Yi'ekasida* 伊俄卡斯达, 1999). Fei Dao 飛氘 (pen name of Jia Liyuan 賈立元, 1983–) imagines Confucius returning to Mount Tai to understand the history of Chinese civilization. Xia Jia 夏笳 (pen name of Wang Yao 王瑶, 1984–), another woman sf writer, draws on themes from legend and religion in novels such as *The Demon-Enslaving Flask* (*Guan yaojing de pingzi* 关妖精的瓶子, 2004), *Carmen* (*Kamen* 卡门, 2005), and *Dream of Eternal Being* (*Yong xia zhi meng* 永夏之梦, 2008), a love story between an immortal and a time traveler. (See the appendix for partial listing of authors, stories and translations.) Zhao Haihong, Fei Dao, and Xia Jia have academic backgrounds which link them both to the writing of sf and to its reception through both teaching and critical studies.[22]

In summary, early twentieth-century sf in China, both in Western translations and homegrown, was focused on themes of evolution and technology, with specific interest in helping China gain scientific and technological expertise in the wake of defeats in the Opium War. While it included some of the recognized "classics" of Western sf, others were conspicuously absent, for example, Mary Shelley's *Frankenstein; or, The Modern Prometheus* (1818, 1831) (*Kexue guairen* 科学怪人, literally "science madman"), which would have been inconsistent with the priorities behind early Chinese interest in sf. The Maoist period was equally preoccupied with Western science, but with a marked shift from interest in the power of fiction to promote social change, toward a narrower view of sf as a tool for science education. Liang Qichao's call for a science-fiction literature of national renewal had all but disappeared, leaving only the science. Since 1989, sf has flowered in China, free from these earlier constraints. In some cases—notably Liu Cixin's *The Three-Body Problem* (2006)—it has retained a scientific orientation. But in all these periods, "science" is clearly understood as modern Western science. I now turn to three themes that build, to varying degrees on themes from Chinese philosophy and from the indigenous Chinese sciences.

Sf and the Indigenous Chinese Sciences

As the previous section has shown, a defining feature of the late Qing emergence of Chinese sf was its close engagement with modern science. But as Fan Fa-ti has pointed out, historical actors—including both early twentieth-century Chinese scientists and readers and writers of early Chinese sf—wrestled with binary concepts such as traditional/modern and Chinese/Western, and these binaries and categories informed their practices as producers as readers of both science and sf.[23] Given these orientations, it is no surprise that the authors and audiences of late Qing sf described other fantastic indigenous literature as "mythology" or "superstition." But we are not obliged to base a contemporary history of Chinese sf solely on such assessments. Before turning to an alternative narrative of the origins of Chinese sf, it is necessary to build a (necessarily) brief picture of the relevant Chinese sciences and key philosophical ideas.

Any account of the history of science in China or of the Chinese sciences must address the problem of what disciplines were considered sciences, and where they stood in indigenous hierarchies of knowledge. An ongoing debate on the nature of Chinese science initially arose from the pioneering work of Joseph Needham (1900–1995).[24] Needham approached the history of science in China by trying to fit the Chinese scientific tradition into the categories of twentieth-century Western science. Many later historians of science in China, including some of Needham's own close collaborators, later rejected this "universalist" approach as anachronistic and culturally inappropriate.[25] Part of the problem, as Nathan Sivin has argued, is that indigenous Chinese accounts focused on specific sciences—quantitative and qualitative—rather than on any unified notion of science. In his taxonomy of the Chinese sciences, Sivin categorizes the quantitative sciences as mathematics (*suan* 算), mathematical harmonics or acoustics (*lü* 律, *lülü* 律呂) and mathematical astronomy (*li* 歷, *lifa* 歷法). The qualitative sciences were astronomy (*tianwen* 天文), medicine (*yi* 醫), and siting (*fengshui* 風水). *Tianwen* included celestial and meteorological observation and astrology. An important subcategory of medicine was "Nurturing Life" (*yangsheng* 養生), which included self-cultivation and longevity techniques. Medicine also included materia medica (*bencao* 本草) and internal (*neidan* 內丹) and external (*waidan* 外丹) alchemy.[26] The historical development of these sciences have been extensively explored by historians of science.[27]

The indigenous Chinese sciences put us in a position to ask different questions. Let us imaging an alternative past, in which the early visionaries who first created Chinese sf also took seriously the indigenous sciences of their own tradition. What might such this alternative Chinese sf look like? The next three sections attempt several possible answers.

Travel in Space and Time

Reference to space or time travel is not a widespread element in Chinese philosophical or historical writing, but their early occurrence makes them worthy of note. Both occur in the great Daoist classic, the *Zhuangzi*. One passage describes a sage, the "spirit person of Guyi," who appears to practice diet and breath regulation: "He does not eat the five grains but sucks in the wind and drinks dew." These practices are powerful: "he roams beyond the world" (literally the four seas) and when he concentrates his spirit, it protects living things from plagues and makes the grain ripen.[28]

Time travel also features, expressed as a paradox:

> For there to be a "right" and "wrong" [or alternately, "it's so"; "it's not so"] before they are formed in the heart-mind would be to go to Yue today and arrive yesterday.[29]

This paradox will be familiar to any reader of the limerick "Relativity":

> There was a young lady named Bright
> Whose speed was far faster than light;
> She set off one day
> in a relative way
> And returned home the previous night.[30]

But the *Zhuangzi* paradox seems to be an analogy to an error, rather than a description of actual time travel. The paradox reappears as one of several paradoxes attributed to Zhuangzi's friend (and logical sparring partner) Hui Shi: "I go to Yue today yet arrive yesterday."[31] Here the travel to Yue (contemporary Vietnam) is posed as a paradox, but the idea of time travel is clearly articulated.

Time travel has a complex role in new wave Chinese science fiction. On the one hand it has been perhaps surprisingly absent from Chinese sf. As Robert Price notes in a recent dissertation, the absence of time travel themes from Chinese sf is all the more mysterious because of its early and prominent role in modern sf, not only in H.G. Wells's *The Time Machine* (1895), but even earlier in Mark Twain's *A Connecticut Yankee in King Arthur's Court* (1889).

By contrast, time travel became a prominent element in Chinese historical television dramas, where it provided a plot device for a modern protagonist to travel to and experience the courts of imperial China. The first show of this genre, *Shen Hua* 神話 (The Myth, 2010), was based on a 2005 Jackie Chan movie of the same name.[32] The increase of such dramas eventually prompted the State Administration of Radio, Film, and Television to ban time travel plots from Chinese television on grounds that they "treated [sic] serious history in a frivolous way."[33] But as the *New Yorker* columnist Richard Brody pointed out, Chinese time-travel plots share the notion of escape, specifically escape from contemporary China to the China of an earlier, and in some sense, preferable time.[34] Time travel plots do feature in new wave sf. For example, Qian Lifang's *Tian yi* (The Will of Heaven, 2004) and *Tian ming* (The Command of Heaven, 2011) both feature complex time travel plots that take future technocrats back to Han dynasty China.[35]

Transformation Stories

The idea of one species (or gender) giving birth to, or transforming into, another is also of early origin, and is found across several genres. Stories of this kind include: accounts of human origins, the genre of *zhiguai*, and Buddhist reincarnation stories.

Accounts of Human Origins

Several Warring States period (481/403 BCE–221 BCE) and Han dynasty (206 BCE–220 CE) texts offer accounts of the evolution of living things in two senses: (1) that one kind of living thing is descended from another, or (2) that living things change by adapting to their environment. The *Zhuangzi* chapter titled "Ultimate Felicity" (*Zhuangzi* 18) ends with an elaborate account of how species transform into one another under the influences of different environments:

> Species have minute beginnings. When they reach water they become minute organisms. When they reach the border of water and land they become algae. When they germinate in elevated places they become *lingxi* 陵舄. When it reaches ferti-lized soil it becomes crowsfoot; its roots become grubs; its leaves become butterflies. The butterflies transform into insects that live under the kitchen stove; they look like new-grown skin and are called *qutuo* 鴝掇. After a thousand days these insects become birds called *ganyugu* 乾餘骨; their saliva becomes the *simi* 斯彌 insect. It becomes a *shixi* 食醯 wine fly, which gives birth to the *yilu* 頤輅. *Huangguang* 黃軦 are produced from the *jiuyou* 九猷; gnats are born from putrid *huan* 腐蠸 bugs. The *yangxi* 羊奚 plant couples with bamboo that has not shooted for a long time and the bamboo produces the green *ning* 寧 plant. It produces panthers; pan-thers produce horses; horses produce humans. Humans return to minute begin-nings. All living things come from minute beginnings and return to minute begin-nings.[36]

It is very obscure, and impossible to translate with certainty. It describes repeating cycles of transformation (not evolution), and depicts living things evolving from minute creatures, to plants, insects, birds, animals, and humans. These transformations occur in response to different physical envi-ronments: water, land, altitude, fertilized soil, etc.

This passage was noticed by Hu Shih 胡適 (1891–1962) as an example of a possible early theory of biological evolution, and was part of a debate on "spontaneous generation" in early twentieth-century China. (Hu, one of the great scholar-diplomats of twentieth-century China, was a student of John Dewey at Columbia University.) Hu argued that theories of *qi* introduce issues of potentiality and actuality: if all organisms arise from some kind of pri-mordial, generative *qi*, it must contain the potential for all later forms, pro-viding the conceptual groundwork for a theory of evolution. He used this *Zhuangzi* passage to argue that Warring States thinkers recognized organic continuity throughout the gradations of the animate world, beginning with undifferentiated *qi* and culminating in humanity.[37]

The Genre of Zhiguai 志怪

Another type of transformation story appears in the indigenous Chinese genre of *zhiguai*. This term has no English equivalent, but can be translated as "tales of the strange" or "records of anomalies." The first reference to them is in the *Zhuangzi*, but they became prominent toward the end of the Han, Six Dynasties and Tang periods. Chinese sources classify them as history, not fiction. They contain brief descriptions of anomalous events, including reincarnation and human interactions with gods, ghosts, and spirits.[38] *Zhiguai* stories extend the boundaries of the human by portraying both humans and animals as part of a continuous moral community.[39] They contain chapters on the transformation of humans into plants and animals, animals spirits, and rewards and retribution by animals.

Many *zhiguai* stories involve crossing the animal-human boundary. These include human-animal hybrids and transformations between species.[40] Some describe partial transformations where an animal grows extra or inappropriate body parts; others describe transformations between species. Others recount cross-species matings and anomalous births, such as one species giving birth to another, or babies born with multiple heads or feet. Some transformations involve gender.[41] Especially interesting are highly normative accounts of reward and retribution between humans and animals. Animals typically exhibit human morality, sometimes in response to virtuous humans and other times in contrast to human misbehavior.

Zhiguai was one of several genres concerned with the supernatural in late imperial China. The Ming dynasty bibliographer Hu Yinglin 胡應麟 (1551–1602) reconsidered the traditional genre of "fiction," literally "small talk" (*xiaoshuo* 小說), which he considered too vague, and reworked it into six distinct genres. The first two dealt with the supernatural: anomaly accounts (*zhiguai*) and "prose romances of the marvellous" (*chuanqi* 傳奇), a genre that dates from the Tang dynasty.[42] Several influential figures linked martial arts fiction (*wuxia xiaoshuo* 武俠小說), with *chuanqi*. The most important is Jin Yong 金庸 (Louis Cha), author of many of the most influential contemporary martial arts novels, which form the basis of numerous martial arts films.[43]

What is important for the present discussion is the clear distinction between anomaly accounts and prose romances. It occurs in several ways. First, contemporary martial arts fiction privileges realism and has tended to eclipse nonrealist narratives derived from the traditional genres of *zhiguai* and *chuanqi*. Contemporary martial arts fiction also uses vernacular language (*bai hua* 百花), which further distances it from the literary language of the older genres. Li Tuo argues that these two phenomena are related. He suggests that non-realist genres dominated Chinese premodern literary history in *zhiguai, chuanqi,* Yuan drama, and Ming novels; and asks whether the Europeanization of the modern Chinese language has inexorably connected modern Chinese narratives and Western models of representation.[44] The point is that modern Chinese narratives conspicuously include science fiction, and Chinese sf inherently includes the non-realism of *zhiguai* and *chuanqi.* We can press this distinction further by arguing that realist martial arts fiction draws on *chuanqi,* and sf draws on *zhiguai.*

Both late Qing dynasty and contemporary new-wave science fiction draw on *zhiguai.* Human-animal hybrids reappear in the cat-headed citizens of Lao She's *Cat Country* (*Mao cheng ji* 貓城記, 1932).[45] Another important sf element that first appears in *zhiguai* is also a seed of utopian literature in China, since several *zhiguai* stories imagine nonexistent "utopias" or dystopias. For example, a story in Pu Songling's 蒲松齡 (1640–1715) *Strange Tales from a Chinese Studio* (*Liaozhai zhiyi* 聊齋誌異, 1880) opposes a dystopian "City of Ogres" to an idealized "City under the Ocean."[46] Another examples is Wu Jianren's (吳趼人, 1866–1910) *New Story of the Stone* (*Xin shitou ji* 新石頭記, 1908), one of the great novels of late Qing China, a utopian account of the travels of Jia Baoyu, the main character of the original *Story of the Stone* (*Shitou ji* 石頭記), after the end of the original novel.[47] Baoyu encounters a "Civilized Realm" (*wenming jingjie* 文明境界) with futuristic technology, including medical lenses that image bone and soft tissue, underground trains, underwater telephones, and submarines that fire "silent electric cannons" (*wusheng dianpao* 無聲電炮). Yet its vision of moral governance is Confucian; it is ruled by a benevolent monarch, Dongfang Qiang 東方強 (Strength of the East). Its districts are named for traditional Confucian virtues: compassion (*ci* 慈), filiality (*xiao* 孝), loyalty (*zhong* 忠), benevolence (*ren* 仁), and trustworthiness (*xin* 信).[48]

Modes of Immortality

Extreme longevity and immortality are staples of Western sf, for example Aldous Huxley's classic *After Many a Summer Dies The Swan* (1939). The *Encyclopedia of Science Fiction* describes immortality as one of the basic motifs of speculative thought; "the elixir of life and the fountain of youth are hypothetical goals of classic intellectual and exploratory quests," including extreme longevity, eternal youth, and rejuvenation.[49]

Chinese medical and scientific traditions have been concerned with immortality in a spectrum ranging from health to longevity and—in some cases attempts at literal, physical immortality, for some two millennia.

Nurturing Life

Several Warring States texts express the need to preserve one's person, self, or essential nature by "nurturing life" (*yang sheng* 養生), an area of common ground for philosophers and practitioners of medical arts. The term *yang sheng* first appears in the *Zhuangzi*, which makes fun of *daoyin* 導引 (pulling and guiding), a tradition of exercise for therapy and health. The *Zhuangzi* contrasts real sages to *yang sheng* practitioners who "blow out, breathe in, old out, new in, dormant like the bear, neck-stretched like the bird, their only care for longevity"; these are the practitioners of "guide-and-pull" (*daoyin*) and "nourishing the body" (*yang xing* 養形).[50]

In the Han dynasty, "nurturing life" techniques became a major concern of the Recipe Masters (*fang shi* 方士) of the Han court. *Fang* texts on nurturing life include methods for absorbing and circulating *qi* in the body, breathing and meditation exercises, diet, drugs, and sexual techniques. Medical texts excavated from Han dynasty tombs also document these practices, especially the medical manuscript excavated at Mawangdui 馬王堆 (Changsha, Hubei, 169 BCE) entitled "Drawings of Guiding and Pulling" (*Daoyin tu* 導引圖), a series of forty-four drawings of human figures performing exercises.[51] Some are described in another excavated text, the *Pulling Book* (*Yin shu* 引書), excavated from a tomb at Zhangjiashan 張家山 (Jiangling, Hubei, tomb no. 247), which describes exercises based on the movements of animals. The "*yang sheng* culture" of these texts emphasized control over physiological and mental processes, both understood as self-cultivation, through the transformation of *qi*.

We also find evidence on *yang sheng* from lists of titles of now lost books on these topics in the *Hanshu* Bibliographic Treatise. It includes intriguing (but lost) titles such as "Food Prohibitions of [the legendary sages] Shen Nong and Huangdi" (*Shen Nong Huangdi shi jin* 神農黃帝食禁) and "Recipes of Huangdi and the Three Sage-Kings for Nurturing Yang" (*Huangdi sanwang yangyang fang* 黃帝三王養陽方).[52]

In summary, most of these texts can be described as part of a *yang sheng* culture, which offered and emphasized control over physiological processes of the body and mind that were understood as transformations of *qi*. What is the relation of these detailed technical texts to philosophy? These technical arts form a continuum with philosophy because their transformations were understood as self-cultivation in the coterminous senses of moral excellence, health, longevity, and physiological transformation through the manipulation of *qi*. These views informed Warring States accounts of dietary practices, exercise regimens, breath meditation, sexual cultivation techniques, and other technical traditions associated with *fang shi*.[53]

Daoist Medical Traditions

Finally, longevity practices were closely linked with traditional Chinese medicine. Three of the most important physicians were also Daoist scholars, and were concerned with longevity practices.

Ge Hong 葛洪 (283–343 or 363 CE) was the first of several explicitly Daoist physicians who wrote about the practice of alchemy. He initially studied the Confucian classics, but eventually became interested in immortality techniques. He gave up a military career and political life in order to devote himself to immortality practices, and eventually settled at Mt. Luofu 羅浮 in Guangxi where he studied alchemy until his death. Ge Hong was the first to systematically describe the history and theory of Daoist immortality techniques such as "preserving unity" (*shou yi* 守一), circulating energy (*xing qi* 行氣), "guiding and pulling" (*dao yin*), and sexual longevity techniques (*fang zhong* 房中). As an alchemist, he experimented with drugs and minerals.[54]

Tao Hongjing 陶弘景 (456–536) was the effective founder of Shangqing 上清 (Highest Clarity) Daoism. He held several court positions under the Liu Song and Qi dynasties. Tao was educated in Daoist traditions associated with the *Daode jing, Zhuangzi,* and the works of Ge Hong. He was also actively engaged in mostly unsuccessful attempts to produce alchemical elixirs.[55]

Sun Simiao 孫思邈 (581–682) was the author of two major works on medical practice and a work on Daoist longevity prescriptions. He is still worshipped as the "Medicine Buddha," and as the "King of Medicine" (*yao wang* 藥王). He was the author of two major medical works that are still consulted.[56] Sun was also the author of several works on Daoist alchemy, which he is believed to have practiced (he died at the age of 101). His "Essay on Preserving and Nourishing Life" (*Sheyang lun* 攝養論) gives monthly advice on food, sleeping habits and action of good and ill auspice.[57]

In summary, Sun Simiao, Ge Hong and Tao Hongjing all combined explicit interests in Daoist philosophy, medicine, materia medica and alchemy. All these focused, to varying degrees, on longevity and immortality.

Despite its importance in philosophy and medicine, immortality is not a major trope in Chinese sf. The single exception is Xu Nianci's 徐念慈 (1875–1908) *New Tales of Mr. Braggadocio* (*Xin Faluo xiansheng tan* 新法螺先生譚).[58] It describes a man whose body and soul are separated in a typhoon.[59] His body sinks toward the center of the earth, but his soul travels to Mercury and Venus. On Mercury, his soul watches the transplantation of brains as a method of rejuvenation. (On Venus it discovers that rudimentary plants and animals appear at the same time, refuting biologists' claims that plants preceded animals in evolution.) Immortality appears again when his body, having arrived at the center of the earth, encounters a quasi-immortal man.[60]

The story imitates—and directly quotes—the *Zhuangzi*, a key early source for speculative writing in the Chinese philosophical tradition. But immortality and rejuvenation are passing plot elements, and not the central concern of the text.

Immortality themes also appear in new wave writing, but in new guises that are still closely linked to science. For example, in Fei Dao's "The Demon's Head" (2007), a scientist preserves the brain of a general whose brain somehow survived when he and his retinue were assassinated, conveniently close to a neurological research institute. Here, his "immortality" arises from neuroscience, not immortality practices.

Conclusion

It is striking that themes of time travel, transformation, and longevity have longstanding roots in Chinese philosophy, literature and some indigenous sciences, but are almost completely absent from Chinese sf. Although their after-images may briefly appear in new wave writing, they are not pursued, or are re-imagined in scientific or technological contexts. Why is this so?

The simplest explanation is genre. On a genre account, all these themes belong to the Chinese genre of *xuan huan*, fantastic fiction with Chinese supernatural elements. But that explanation fails because Chinese fantasy literature typically excludes the themes of time travel (*chuan yue* 穿越) and Daoist immortality stories (*xiu zhen* 修真). A different and perhaps better explanation is that Chinese sf is, at least up until now, inextricably linked to modern science in ways that largely preclude the indigenous sciences. This approach harks back to the late nineteenth-century history of Chinese sf and its close relation to Western science, evolution, and technology.

This approach raises another question: what will happen as new wave authors reject the premises of early Chinese sf and increasingly extend their reach beyond its concerns? Here an interesting divide arises between the very different training of contemporary Chinese "hard sf" and new wave writers. The most prominent hard sf writers, Liu Cixin and Wang Jinkang, were trained as engineers, hydroelectric and civil, respectively. By contrast, several new wave writers hold advanced degrees and university positions, primarily in literature, which would provide familiarity with themes drawn from philosophical writing: time travel, transformation, and Daoist immortality motifs.

But neither group has obvious exposure to themes in the indigenous Chinese sciences, so it is perhaps not surprising that explicit themes from these areas do not appear. Nor do debates about what counts as Chinese sf help to clarify the absence of the indigenous Chinese sciences. Some scholars try to trace Chinese sf back to *zhiguai*, while others date it to the 1930s, 1950s, or even the post–Mao period. An interesting middle ground is offered by Isaacson, who dates it to the late Qing dynasty. He argues that it arose as a response to two factors: an epistemological crisis due to subjugation to European powers and the translation into Chinese of newly emergent Western science fiction. He also argues that an adequate account of the history of sf in China requires an understanding of its relationship to earlier genres.[61] His approach helps explain the absence of the indigenous sciences, which could have been lost under the pressure of two developments that were fundamentally responses to the West. But that situation may change as the agenda of Chinese sf changes.

My goal here is not to argue for *zhiguai* or *chuanqi* as the origins of Chinese science fiction, nor is it to claim that the indigenous sciences inform Chinese sf, which they largely do not, for clear reasons. But there are good reasons that we do not find it in Chinese sf, because of the latter's close links with both modernity and empire. Instead, this brief overview of three distinct Chinese indigenous literary, religious, and scientific traditions provide an alternative literary path, and one that could happen. In conclusion, relations between Chinese literary genres, its indigenous scientific traditions, the introduction of Western science, and the introduction and development of science fiction all form a complex network that warrants further study and should not be over-simplified.

A Bibliography of Chinese Science Fiction

Bao Shu 宝树. "Preserve Her Memory" (*Liuxia ta de jiyi* 留下她的記憶). Translated by Ken Liu. *Clarkesworld*, No. 108 (September 2015), at http://clarkesworldmagazine.com/bao_09_15/.

_____. "Everybody Loves Charles" (*Renren dou ai Chaersi* 人人都爱查尔斯). Translated by Ken Liu. *Clarkesworld*, No. 112 (January 2016), at http://clarkesworldmagazine.com/bao_01_16/.

Bi Heguan zhuren 碧荷馆主人. See Yang Ziyuan 楊致遠.

Chan, Stanley. See Chen Qiufan 陈楸帆.

Chen Qiufan 陈楸帆 [Stanley Chan]. "The Fish of Lijiang" (*Lijiang de yu'er men* 丽江的鱼儿们] Translated by Ken Liu, *Clarkesworld*, No. 59 (August 2011), at http://clarkesworldmagazine.com/chen_08_11/ ; republished in Liu, *Invisible Planets*, 51–68.

_____. "The Flower of Shazui" (*Shazui zhi hua* 沙嘴之花). *Interzone*, No. 243 (November-December 2012), 20–29; republished in Liu, *Invisible Planets*, 69–87.

_____. "The Year of the Rat" (*Shu nian* 鼠年). *The Magazine of Fantasy & Science Fiction*, 125:1/2 (July-August 2013), 68–92; republished in Liu, *Invisible Planets*, 21–49.

_____. "The Mao Ghost" (*Mao de guihun* 猫的鬼魂). Translated by Ken Liu. *Lightspeed*, No. 46 (March 2014), at http://www.lightspeedmagazine.com/fiction/the-mao-ghost/.

_____. "The Smog Society" (*Mai* 霾). Translated by Carmen Yiling Yan and Ken Liu. *Lightspeed*, No.63 (August 2015), at http://www.lightspeedmagazine.com/fiction/the-smog-society/.

_____. "A Man out of Fashion" (*Guoshi de ren* 过时的人). Translated by Ken Liu. *Clarkesworld*, No. 131 (August 2017), at http://clarkesworldmagazine.com/chen_08_17/.

_____. *The Waste Tide.* Translated by Ken Liu. London: Head of Zeus Press, 2019.

Fei Dao 飞氘. "The Demon's Head" (*Mogui de toulu* 魔鬼的头颅). Translated by David Hull. *Renditions,*77/78 (2012), 263–271.

Han Song 韩松. *Yuzhou mubei* 宇宙墓碑 (Cosmic tombstones). Beijing: Xinya chubanshe, 1991.

_____. *Renzao ren* 人造人 (Artificial people). Beijing: Zhongguo renshi chubanshe, 1997.

_____. *Wo de zuguo bu zuomeng* 我的祖国不做梦 (My homeland never dreams). 2007, at https://journals.openedition.org/ideo/471?file=1. (This novella never appeared in print in China.)

_____. "The Passengers and the Creator" (Chengke yu chuangzaozhe 乘客与创造者). Translated by Nathaniel Issacson. *Renditions,* 77/78 (2012), 144–172.

_____. "Chinese Science Fiction: A Response to Modernization." *Science Fiction Studies,* 40:1 (2013), 15–21.

He Xi 何夕. "Ban Gu." *Kehuan Shijie* 科幻世界 (Science Fiction World), 1996.

_____. *Yiyu* 異域 (Foreign land). *Kehuan Shijie* 科幻世界 (Science Fiction World), 1999.

_____. *Liudao Zhongsheng* 六道眾生 (Six Lines from Samasara). 2002. Wuhan: Changsha Wenyi chubanshe 长江文艺出版社, 2012.

Huss, Mikael. "Hesitant Journey to the West: SF's Changing Fortunes in Mainland China." *Science Fiction Studies,* 27:1 (March 2000), 92–104.

Isaacson, Nathaniel, translator. "New Tales of Mr. Braggadocio." By Xu Nianci. *Renditions,* 77/78 (2012), 15–38.

_____. *Celestial Empire: The Emergence of Chinese Science Fiction.* Middleton, Connecticut: Wesleyan University Press, 2017.

Jia Liyuan 賈立元. See Fei Dao 飞氘.

Jiang, Qian. "Translation and the Development of Science Fiction in Twentieth-Century China." *Science Fiction Studies,* 40:1 (March 2013), 116–132.

Jiang Yunsheng 姜云生. "Boundless Love" (*Wubian de juanlian* 无边的眷恋). In Murphy and Wu 1989, 157–164.

La La 拉拉. "The Radio Waves That Never Die" (*Yongbu xiaoshi de dianbo* 永不消逝的电波). Translated by Petula Parris-Huang. *Renditions,* 77/78 (2012), 210–238.

Li Boyuan 李伯元. "Manifesto." *Xiuxiang xiaoshuo* 繡像小説 (Illustrated Fiction), 1:1 (1903).

Li Jun 李峻. See Bao Shu 宝树.

Ling Chen 凌晨. "A Story of Titan" (*Taitan de gushi* 泰坦的故事). Translated by Joel Martinsen. *Pathlight: New Chinese Writing.* Seattle: Paper Republic, 2013. At http://paper-republic.org/ (eBook, no pagination).

Liu Cixin 劉慈欣. *Santi* 三体 (The Three-Body Problem). Chongqing: Chongqing chubanshe, 2007. Translated by Ken Liu, 2014.

_____. *Heian sanlin: Santi di er bu* 黑暗森林: 三體第二部 (The Dark Forest: Three Body Problem Part 2). Chongqing: Chongqing chubanshe and Taiwan: Taipei, Maotouying chubanshe, 2008. Translated by Joel Martinsen, 2015.

_____. *Wei ji yuan* 微纪元 (The Micro-Age). 1998; Shenyang: Shenyang chubanshe, 2010.

_____. *Santi. Di III bu, Si shen yong sheng* 三體第三部, 死神永生 (Santi Part 3: Death's End). Taiwan: Taipei, Maotouying chubanshe 貓頭鷹出版社, 2011. Translated by Ken Liu, 2016.

Liu, Ken. "China Dreams: Contemporary Chinese Science Fiction." *Clarkesworld,* No. 88 (December 2014), at http://clarkesworldmagazine.com/liu_12_14/.

_____, translator. *The Three-Body Problem.* By Cixin Liu. New York: Tor Books, 2014.

_____, translator. *Death's End.* By Cixin Liu. New York: Tor Books, 2016.

_____, translator and editor. *Invisible Planets.* London: Head of Zeus Press, 2016.

Mao Boyong 马伯庸. "The City of Silence" (*Jijing zhi cheng* 寂静之城). Translated by Ken Liu. *Invisible Planets,* 153–196.

Martinsen, Joel, translator. *The Dark Forest.* By Cixin Liu. New York: Tor Books, 2015.

Murphy, Patrick D. and Wu Dingbo, editors. *Science Fiction from China.* New York: Praeger Publishers, 1989.

Price, Robert G. *Space to Create in Chinese Science Fiction.* Kaarst: Ffoniwch y Meddyg, 2017.

Qian Lifang 钱莉芳. *Tian yi* 天意 (The will of Heaven). Chengdu: Sichuan Keji chubanshe, 2004.

Qian, Lifang 钱莉芳. *Tian ming* 天命 (The command of Heaven). Changchun: Shidai wenyi chubanshe, 2011.

Rao Zhonghua 饶忠华. *Zhongguo Kexue Xiaoshuo Daquan* 中国科幻小说大全 (Compendium of Chinese Science Fiction). 3 volumes. Beijing: Haiyang chubanshe, 1982.

Raphals, Lisa. "Alterity and Alien Contact in Lao She's Martian Dystopia, Cat Country." *Science Fiction Studies*, 40:1 (March 2013), 73–85.

Song Mingwei 宋明炜. "After 1989: The New Wave of Chinese Science Fiction." *China Perspectives*, 1:101 (2015), 7–13.

_____, editor. "Chinese Science Fiction: Late Qing and the Contemporary." *Renditions*, 77/78 (2012).

Takeda Masaya 武田昌也 and Hayashi Hiskayuki 林久之. *Chūgoku kagaku gensō bungakukan* 中国科学幻想文学館 (Compendium of Chinese science fantasy literature). 2 volumes. Tokyo: Taishūkan Shoten, 2001.

Tong Enzheng 童恩正. *Shanhu Dao Shang de Siguang* 珊瑚岛上的死光 (Death Ray on a Coral Island). *Renmin wenxue* 人民文学, 8 (1978), 41–58.

Wang Jinkang 王晋康. *Yu Wu Tong Zai* 與吾同在 (Being with me). Chongqing: Chongqing chubanshe, 2011.

_____. "The Reincarnated Giant" (*Zhuansheng de juren* 转生的巨人). Translated by Carlos Rojas. *Renditions*, 77/78 (2012), 173–209.

Wang Xiaoda 王晓达. *Wang Xiaoda juan: Bing xia de meng* 王晓达卷: 冰下的梦 (Collected short stories of Wang Xiaoda: Dream under the ice). Edited by Dong Renwei 董仁威 and Yao Haijun 姚海军. *Shijie huaren ke huan xie huizu bian* 世界华人科幻协会组编 (World Chinese Science Fiction Association). Beijing: Renmin youdian chubanshe, 2012.

Wei Yahua 魏雅华. "Conjugal Happiness in the Arms of Morpheus" (*Wenrou zhi xiang de meng* 温柔之乡的梦). 1982. Translated in Murphy and Wu, 9–52.

Wang Yao 王瑶. See Xia Jia 夏笳.

Wu Jianren 吳趼人. *Xin shitou ji* 新石頭記 (New Story of the Stone). 1908. Guangzhou: Huacheng chubanshe, 1987.

Wu Yan 吳岩 (ed.). *Jia Baoyu zuo qianshuiting: Zhongguo zaoqi kehuan yanjiu jingxuan* 賈寶玉坐潛水艇: 中國早期科幻研究精選 (Jia Baoyu by submarine: Selected research on China's early science fiction). Fuzhou: Fujian shaonian ertong chubanshe, 2006.

_____. *Kehuan wenxue lungang* 科幻文學論鋼 (Science Fiction literature). Chongqing: Chongqing chubanshe, 2011.

_____. "'Great Wall Planet': Introducing Chinese Science Fiction." Translated by Wang Pengfei and Ryan Nichols. *Science Fiction Studies*, 40:1 (March 2013), 1–14.

Xia Jia 夏笳. *Kamen* 卡门 (Carmen). *Kehuan Shijie* 科幻世界 (Science Fiction World), 8 (2005).

_____. *Yong xia zhi meng* 永夏之梦 (Dream of eternal being). *Kehuan Shijie* 科幻世界 (Science Fiction World), 9 (2008).

_____. "The Demon-Enslaving Flask" (*Guan yaojing de pingzi* 關妖精的瓶子). Translated by Linda Rui Feng. *Renditions*, 77/78 (2012), 272–282.

_____. "A Hundred Ghosts Parade Tonight" (*Bai gui yexing jie* 百鬼夜行街). Translated by Ken Liu. *Invisible Planets*, 91–109.

_____. "Night Journey of the Dragon-Horse" (*Long ma yexing* 龙马夜行). Translated by Ken Liu. *Invisible Planets*, 131–149.

Xu Nianci 徐念慈. *Xin Faluo xiansheng tan* 新法螺先生譚 (New Tales of Mr. Braggadocio). Shanghai: Xiaoshuo lin 小混林 Fiction Forest Press, 1905. Republished in. *Zhongguo jindai wenxue daxi 1840–1929: xiaoshuoji* 中國近代文學大系 1840–1919: 小說集 (A treasury of modern Chinese literature 1840–1929: fiction collection). Volume 6. Edited by Wu Zuxiang 吳組緗, Duanmu Hongliang 端木蕻良, and Shi Meng Zhu Bian 时萌主编. Shanghai: Shanghai shudian, 1991, 323–343.

Yang Ziyuan 楊致遠 (Bi heguan zhuren 碧荷館主人, "Master of the sapphire lotus house"). *Xin jiyuan* 新纪元 (New Era), 1908. Nanning: Guangxi shifan daxue chubanshe, 2008.

Zhao Haihong 赵海虹. *Shijian de bifang* 时间的彼方 (*The Other Side of Time*), 1998. Wuhan: Hubei shaonian ertong chubanshe 湖北少年儿童出版社, 2006.

_____. *Yiekasida* 伊俄卡斯达 (*Jocasta*). *Kehuan Shijie* 科幻世界 (Science Fiction World), 3 (1999).

_____. "1923—a Fantasy" (*Yijiuersan nian kehuan gushi* 一九二三年科幻故事). Translated by Nicky Harman and Pang Zhaoxia. *Renditions*, 77/78 (2012), 239–254.

Zheng Wenguang 鄭文光. *Feixiang Renmazuo* 飞向人马座 (Flying to Sagittarius). 1979.

Shijie kehuan bolan 世界科幻博览 (World Scifi Expo), 5 (2005).

NOTES

1. This essay is derived in substantial part from the article "Chinese SF: Imported and Indigenous," *Osiris* 34 (2019), "Presenting Past Futures: Science Fiction and the History of Science," edited by Amanda Rees and Iwan Rhys Morus, 186–207.

2. Pinyin transliteration of Chinese words is used throughout, except for personal names, where I follow authors' own usages. For consistency, all Chinese references are in traditional characters (*fanti*), including contemporary pieces originally published in simplified (*jianti*) characters. Chinese names are cited surname first in accordance with Chinese name conventions. Chinese characters are included because Chinese sf Anglophone literature often omits them, making names and titles harder to find in Chinese sources.

3. See in particular David D. Wang, *Fin-de-siècle Splendor: Repressed Modernities of Late Qing Fiction, 1849–1911* (Stanford, CA: Stanford University Press, 1997). See also Nathaniel Isaacson, *Celestial Empire: The Emergence of Chinese Science Fiction* (Middletown, CT: Wesleyan University Press, 2017); Song Mingwei 宋明煒, editor, "Chinese Science Fiction: Late Qing and the Contemporary," special issue of *Renditions: A Chinese-English Translation Magazine*, 77/78 (Spring/Autumn, 2012); Wang Dun, "The Late Qing's Other Utopias: China's Science-Fictional Imagination, 1900–1910," *Concentric: Literary and Cultural Studies* 34:2 (September 2008), 37–61; Wu Xianya 吳獻雅, "Kexue huanxiang yu kexue qimeng: Wan Qing, 'kexue xiaoshuo' yanjiu" 科學幻想與科學啟蒙: 晚清科學小說"研究 [Science Fiction and the Scientific Enlightenment: A Study of "Science Fiction" in the Late Qing Dynasty], in *Jia Baoyu zuo qianshuiting: Zhongguo zaoqi kehuan yanjiu jingxuan* 賈寶玉坐潛水艇: 中國早期科幻研究精選 [Jia Baoyu by Submarine: Selected Research on China's Early Science Fiction], edited by Wu Yan 吳岩 (Fuzhou: Fujian shaonian ertong chubanshe, 2006), 37–91; and Zhang Zhi 張治, "Wanqing kexue xiaoshuo chuyi: dui wenxue zuopin ji qi sixiang beijing yu zhishiye de kaocha" 晚清科學小說芻議: 對文學作品及其思想背景與知識野的考察 [On Science Fiction in the Late Qing Dynasty: A Study of Literary Works and their Ideological Background and Field of Knowledge], *Kexue wenhua pinglun* 科學文化評論 (Scientific and Cultural Commentary), 6:5 (2009), 69–96.

4. Jiang Jing, "From the Technique for Creating Humans to the Art of Reprogramming Hearts: Scientists, Writers, and the Genesis of China's Modern Literary Vision," *Cultural Critique*, 80 (Winter, 2012), 131.

5. Han Song, "Chinese Science Fiction: A Response to Modernization," *Science Fiction Studies*, 40:1 (March 2013), 15–21.

6. This term first appeared in the table of contents of Liang Qichao's literary magazine *New Fiction* (*Xin Xiaoshuo* 新小說), first published in Japan in 1902. See Isaacson, *Celestial Empire*, 7–8.

7. Quoted from Wang, *Splendor*, 256.

8. Translation of sf into Chinese declined, but renewed after 1949, with yet more translations of Jules Verne and a substantial amount of Russian works. It was only in the early 1980s that a wider range of sf was translated into Chinese, including works by Ray Bradbury, Arthur C. Clarke, and Isaac Asimov. See Jiang Qian, "Translation and the Development of Science Fiction in Twentieth-Century China," *Science Fiction Studies*, 40:1 (March 2013), 116–132, especially 120–121.

9. See Song Mingwei, "After 1989: The New Wave of Chinese Science Fiction," *China Perspectives*, 1:101 (2015), 7–13.

10. Wu Jianren's 吳趼人 (1866–1910) *New Story of the Stone* (*Xin shitou ji* 新石頭記) was published in 1908, as was Yang Ziyuan's 楊致遠 (1871–1919) *New Era* (*Xin jiyuan* 新纪元), written under the pseudonym "Master of the Sapphire Lotus House" (Bi heguan zhuren

碧荷馆主人). Lu Shi's 陸士諤 (1878–1944) *New China* (*Xin Zhongguo* 新中國) was published in 1910. For further details see Lorenzo Andolfatto, Paper Worlds: The Chinese Utopian Novel at the Beginning of the Twentieth Century, 1902–1910, Ph.D. Dissertation, Università Ca' Foscari Venezia, 2015; Douwe Fokkema, *Perfect Worlds: Utopian Fiction in China and the West* (Amsterdam: Amsterdam University Press, 2011); Mikael Huss, "Hesitant Journey to the West: SF's Changing Fortunes in Mainland China," *Science Fiction Studies* 27:1 (March 2000), 92–104; Song Mingwei, "After 1989"; Wang, *Splendor*; and Wang Dun, "The Late Qing's Other Utopias."

   11. Li Boyuan, "Manifesto," *Xiuxiang xiaoshuo* 繡像小説 (Illustrated Fiction), 1:1 (1903), cited in Wang Xiaoming, "From Petitions to Fiction: Visions of the Future Propagated in Early Modern China," *Translation and Creation: Readings of Western Literature in Early Modern China, 1840–1918,* edited by David E. Pollard (Amsterdam and Philadelphia: John Benjamins, 1998), 50.

   12. Rudolf G. Wagner, "Lobby Literature: The Archaeology and Present Functions of Science Fiction in the People's Republic of China," *After Mao: Chinese Literature and Society 1978–1981,* edited by Jeffrey C. Kinkley (Cambridge: Harvard University Press, 1985), 17–62.

   13. See Liuluepu Luofu (B. Liupulov), 1959, as summarized in Wu Yan, "'Great Wall Planet': Introducing Chinese Science Fiction," translated by Wang Pengfei and Ryan Nichols, *Science Fiction Studies,* 40:1 (March 2013), 1–14.

   14. For accounts of this situation see Wu, "Great Wall Planet," and Rui Kunze [Wang Rui 王瑞], "Displaced Fantasy: Pulp Science Fiction in the Early Reform Era of the People's republic Of China," *East Asian History,* No.41 (August 2017), 25–40.

   15. Wagner, "Lobby Literature," 19–23.

   16. Wu Dingbo and Patrick D. Murphy, *Science Fiction from China* (New York: Praeger, 1989), xxxvi.

   17. Examples include Tong Enzheng's 童恩正 (1978) "Death Ray on a Coral Island" (Shanhu Dao Shang de Siguang 珊瑚岛上的死光), *Renmin wenxue* 人民文学, 8 (1978), 41–58; Zheng Wenguang's "Flying to Sagittarius" (Feixiang Renmazuo 飞向人马座), *Shijie kehuan bolan* 世界科幻博览 (World Scifi Expo), 5 (2005); Wang Xiaoda's 王晓达 "Dream Under the Ice" (*Bing xia de meng* 冰下的梦), in *Wang Xiaoda juan: Bing xia de meng* 王晓达卷: 冰下的梦 (Collected Short Stories of Wang Xiaoda: Dream Under the Ice), edited by Dong Renwei 董仁威 and Yao Haijun 姚海军, *Shijie huaren ke huan xie huizu bian* 世界华人科幻协会组编 (World Chinese Science Fiction Association) (Beijing: Renmin youdian chubanshe, 2012); Wei Yahua's 魏雅华 (1982) " Conjugal Happiness in the Arms of Morpheus" (*Wenrou zhixiang de meng* 温柔之乡的梦), in Wu and Murphy, *Science Fiction from China,* 9–52; and Jiang Yunsheng's 姜云生 (1978) "Boundless Love" (*Wubian de jianlian* 无边的眷恋), in Wu and Murphy, *Science Fiction from China,* 157–164.

   18. Rao Zhonghua 饶忠华, *Zhongguo Kexue Xiaoshuo Daquan* 中国科幻小说大全 (Compendium of Chinese Science Fiction), 3 volumes (Beijing: Haiyang chubanshe, 1982).

   19. For surveys of "new wave" sf see Han Song, "Chinese Science Fiction"; Isaacson, *Celestial Empire;* and Song Mingwei, "After 1989." Several websites also provide useful information. The Francophone website Sinosf provides a useful inventory of translations of Chinese sf into English, French, German, and Italian (at https://sinosf.hypotheses.org/146), to which the following discussion is indebted.

   20. See Liu Cixin 劉慈欣, *Santi* 三体 (Chongqing: Chongqing chubanshe, 2007), translated by Ken Liu, *The Three-Body Problem* (New York: Tor Books, 2014). The next two volumes of the trilogy were *Heian sanlin: Santi di er bu* 黑暗森林: 三體第二部 (The Dark Forest: Three Body Problem Part 2). (Chongqing: Chongqing chubanshe, 2008) and *Santi. Di III bu, Si shen yong sheng* 三體第三部, 死神永生 (Santi Part 3: Death's End) (Taiwan: Taipei, Maotouying chubanshe, 2011). Joel Martinsen and Ken Liu respectively translated the next two books of the series as *The Dark Forest* (New York: Tor Books, 2015) and *Death's End* (New York: Tor Books, 2016). For an excellent review of the trilogy see Nick Richardson, "Even What Doesn't Happen Is Epic," *London Review of Books,* 40:3 (February 8, 2018), 34–36.

   21. This point is indebted to Ken Liu, "China Dreams: Contemporary Chinese Science Fiction," *Clarkesworld,* No. 99 (December 2014), at http://clarkesworldmagazine.com/liu_12_14/.

22. Zhao Haihong is a professor at the Institution of Foreign Languages of Zhejiang Gongshang University. Jia Liyuan (Fei Dao) holds a Ph.D. in Comparative Literature from Tsinghua University. Wang Yao (Xia Jia) holds a Ph.D. in comparative literature and world literature from the Department of Chinese, Peking University (2014), and is currently a lecturer of Chinese literature at Xi'an Jiaotong University.

23. Fan Fa-ti, "Redrawing the Map: Science in Twentieth-Century China," *Isis*, 98:3 (September 2007), 526.

24. Much of his early work focused questions of why the European Scientific Revolution did not take place in China. See Joseph Needham with Wang Ling, *Science and Civilisation in China, Volume 1: Introductory Orientations* (Cambridge: Cambridge University Press, 1956); *Science and Civilisation in China, Volume 2: History of Scientific Thought* (Cambridge: Cambridge University Press, 1956); and *Science and Civilisation in China, Volume 3: Mathematics and the Sciences of the Heavens and Earth* (Cambridge: Cambridge University Press, 1959). See also Needham and Donald Leslie, "Ancient and Mediaeval Chinese Thought on Evolution," *Bulletin of the National Institute of Science of India*, 7 (1955), 1–18; Needham, Ho Ping-Yu, and Lu Gwei-djen, *Science and Civilisation in China, Volume 5: Chemistry and Chemical Technology, Part 3: Spagyrical Discovery and Invention: Historical Survey, from Cinnabar Elixirs to Synthetic Insulin* (Cambridge: Cambridge University Press, 1976); and Needham, *The Grand Titration: Science and Society in East and West* (Boston: G. Allen & Unwin, 1979).

25. See Nathan Sivin, "Why the Scientific Revolution Did Not Take Place in China— Or Didn't It?," *Chinese Science*, 5 (1982), 45–66.

26. See Nathan Sivin, "Science and Medicine in Imperial China—The State of the Field," *Journal of Asian Studies*, 47 (1988), 41–90; "Science and Medicine in Chinese History," *Heritage of China: Contemporary Perspectives on Chinese Civilization*, edited by Paul S. Ropp (Berkeley: University of California Press, 1990), 164–196; and "State Cosmos and Body in the Last Three Centuries B.C.E.," *Harvard Journal of Asiatic Studies*, 55:1 (1995), 5–37. For further discussion see Lisa Raphals, "Science and Chinese Philosophy," *The Stanford Encyclopedia of Philosophy*, Spring 2017 Edition, edited by Edward N. Zalta, at https://plato.stanford.edu/archives/spr 2017/entries/chinese-phil-science/.

27. For more information on Chinese science and medicine, see Christopher Cullen, *Astronomy and Mathematics in Ancient China: the Zhou bi suan jing* (Cambridge: Cambridge University Press, 1996); Benjamin Elman, *On Their Own Terms: Science in China, 1550–1900* (Cambridge: Harvard University Press, 2005); Donald Harper, *Early Chinese Medical Literature* (London and New York: Kegan Paul International, 1998); Vivienne Lo and Cullen, *Medieval Chinese Medicine: The Dunhuang Medical Manuscripts* (London: Routledge, 2005); Georges Métaillié, *Science and Civilisation in China: Volume 6: 4, Traditional Botany: An Ethnobotanical Approach* (Cambridge: Cambridge University Press, 2015); David Pankenier, *Astrology and Cosmology in Early China: Conforming Earth to Heaven* (Cambridge: Cambridge University Press, 2013); Raphals, "Science and Chinese Philosophy"; Raphals, "Chinese Philosophy and Chinese Medicine," *The Stanford Encyclopedia of Philosophy*, at https://plato. stanford.edu/archives/spr2017/entries/chinese-phil-medicine/ ; Michael Strickman, *Chinese Magical Medicine*, edited by Bernard Faure (Palo Alto: Stanford University Press, 2002); Paul U. Unschuld, *Medicine in China: A History of Pharmaceutics* (Berkeley: University of California Press, 1986); and *Alchemy, Medicine & Religion in the China of A.D. 320: The Nei P'ien of Ko Hung (Pao-p'u tzŭ)*, edited by James Roland Ware, 1966 (New York: Dover Publications, 1981).

28. *Zhuangzi jishi* 莊子集釋 (Collected Explanations of the Zhuangzi), edited by Guo Qingfan MingLiU (Beijing: Zhonghua shuju, 1961), 1:28. Translations from the *Zhuangzi* are my own, but are indebted to Angus Graham (translator), *Chuang tzu: The Inner Chapters* (Indianapolis: Hackett, 1981), 46. Subsequent quotations and translations of the *Zhuangzi* refer to these editions.

29. 未成乎心而有是非，是今日適越而昔至也。是以無有為有. *Zhuangzi* 2:56, cf. Graham, *Inner Chapters*, 51.

30. Attributed to Arthur Henry Reginald Buller (1974–1944). See Arthur Buller, "Relativity," 1923, cited in Elizabeth Knowles, editor, *Oxford Dictionary of Modern Quotations*, Third Edition (Oxford: Oxford University Press, 2007), 47.

31. 今日適越而昔來. *Zhuangzi* 33:1102, cf. Graham, *Inner Chapters*, 283.

32. *The Myth* was produced in Hong Kong, directed by Stanley Tong, and starred Jackie Chan, Tony Leung Ka-fai, Kim Hee-sun and Mallika Sherawat.

33. Cited in Robert G. Price, *Space to Create in Chinese Science Fiction* (Kaarst, Germany: Ffoniwch y Meddyg, 2017), 70.

34. Richard Brody, "China Bans Time Travel," *The New Yorker*, 87:9 (April 8, 2011), at http://www.newyorker.com/culture/richard-brody/china-bans-time-travel.

35. Qian Lifang 钱莉芳, *Tian yi* 天意 (The Will of Heaven) (Chengdu: Sichuan Keji chubanshe, 2004) and *Tian ming* 天命 (The Command of Heaven) (Changchun: Shidai wenyi chubanshe, 2011). I am grateful to my Ph.D. student Fan Yilun for calling these works to my attention.

36. *Zhuangzi* 18: 624–625; cf. Graham, *Inner Chapters*, 21–22.

37. Hu Shih 胡適, The Development of the Logical Method in Ancient China, Ph.D. Dissertation, Columbia University (Shanghai: Shanghai Oriental Publishing Company. 1922), 121–122 and 135–136. This point is explicitly echoed by Joseph Needham and Donald Leslie, who quote Hu in "Ancient and Mediaeval Chinese Thought on Evolution." For discussion of debates on "spontaneous generation" in early twentieth-century China see Fan Fa-ti, "The Controversy over Spontaneous Generation in Republican China: Science, Culture, and Politics," *Routes of Culture and Science in Modern China*, edited by Benjamin Elman and Jing Tsu (Leiden: Brill, 2014), 209–244.

38. For introductions to *zhiguai and* anomaly literature see Robert Ford Campany, *Strange Writing: Anomaly Accounts in Early Medieval China* (Albany: State University of New York Press, 1996), and Hu Ying, "Records of Anomalies," *The Columbia History of Chinese Literature*, edited by Victor H. Mair (New York: Columbia University Press, 2001), 542–554. For comparison with science fiction see Liu Mingming, Theory of the Strange towards the Establishment of Zhiguai as a Genre, Ph.D. dissertation, University of California, Riverside, 2015, and Raphals, "The Limits of 'Humanity' in Comparative Perspective: *Cordwainer Smith* and the *Soushenji*," *World Weavers: Globalization, Science Fiction, and the Cybernetic Revolution*, edited by Wong Kin Yuen, Gary Westfahl, and Amy Kit-sze Chan (Hong Kong: Hong Kong University Press, 2005), 143–156.

39. Most important is the fourth century "Records of an Inquest into the Spirit Realm" (*Soushen ji* 搜神記) of Gan Bao 干寶 (335–49 CE).

40. See Campany, *Strange Writing*, 52–79, especially 52, 58–59, and 79.

41. Gan Bao, "Records of an Inquest into the Spirit Realm," *Congshu jicheng chubian* 叢書集成初編 (Complete collection of books from various collectanea), edited by Wang Yunwu 王雲五 (Shanghai: Shangwu yinshuguan, 1935–1940), vols. 2692–2694. For examples, see chapter 6, 38–46.

42. The other four are anecdotes (*za lü* 雜錄), miscellaneous notes (*cong tan* 叢談), researches (*bian ding* 辯訂), and moral admonitions (*zhen gui* 箴規). See Lu Xun, A *Brief History of Chinese Fiction*, translated by Gladys Yang and Yang Xianyi (Beijing: Foreign Languages Press, 1959), 5.

43. See Cao Zhengwen 曹正文, *Zhongguo xia wenhua shi* 中國俠文化史 (History of Chinese Martial Arts Culture) (Shanghai: Shanghai wenyi chubanshe, 1994) and *Xia ke xing: Zong tan Zhongguo wuxia* 俠客行: 縱談中國武俠 (Chivalry: On the Chinese Knight-Errant) (Taipei: Yunlong, 1998) and Fei Yong 费勇, Zhong Xiaoyi 钟晓毅, and Bian Zhu 編珠, *Jin Yong chuanqi* 金庸传奇 (Chuanqi in Jin Yong's stories) (Guangzhou: Guangdong renmin chubanshe, 1995). Jin Yong includes four heroes from Tang *chuanqi* in his "Illustrations of the Thirty-Three Swordsmen." The four Tang romances are "The Romance of the Curly-Bearded Stranger" (Qiuran Ke Zhuan 虬髯客傳), "Nie Yinniang"(聶隱娘), "The Red-Thread Maid" (Hong Xian 紅線), and "The Servant from Qunlun" (Qunlun Nu 崑崙奴).

44. See Li Tuo, "The Language of Jin Yong's Writing: A New Direction in the Development of Modern Chinese," *The Jin Yong Phenomenon: Chinese Martial Arts Fiction and Modern Chinese Literary History*, edited by Ann Huss and Jianmei Liu (Youngstown, New York: Cambria Press, 2007), 42 and 45; and in the same volume, Huss and Liu, "Introduction: Jin Yong and Martial Arts Fiction," 15.

45. For discussion see Raphals, "Alterity and Alien Contact in Lao She's Martian

Dystopia, *Cat Country*," *Science Fiction Studies*, 40:1 (March 2013), 73–85. Anomaly accounts also inform martial arts fiction which has also retained ongoing popularity in both text and film.

46. Pu Songling, "City of Ogres and the City Under the Ocean" (*Luosha hai shi* 羅剎海市), *Strange Tales from a Chinese Studio* (*Liaozhai zhiyi* 聊齋誌異), Volume 2, translated by Herbert Allen Giles (London: T. De la Rue, 1880), 1–16. Giles translates the title as "The Lo-cha Country and the Sea Market."

47. Also known as the *Dream of the Red Chamber* (Honglou meng 紅樓夢), the *Story of the Stone*, by Cao Xueqin 曹雪芹 (1715 or 1724–1763 or 1764) is considered one of the four classic novels of China.

48. See Wang Dun, "The Late Qing's Other Utopias," 38. *The New Story of the Stone* was initially serialized under the pen name "Old Youth" (Lao Shaonian 老少年) in the newspaper (*Nanfang Bao* 南方報) in 1905 (8/21–11/29) as "social fiction" (*shehui xiaoshuo* 社會小說). It was published as an illustrated book in 1908 by Shanghai Reform Fiction Press (Shanghai gailiang xiaoshuo she 上海改良小說社) under the pen name Wofo Shanren 我佛山人, and labeled as "fiction of ideals" (*lixiang xiaoshuo* 理想小說).

49. See Brian M. Stableford and David Langford, "Immortality," *The Encyclopedia of Science Fiction*, edited by John Clute, David Langford, Peter Nicholls, and Graham Sleight (Gollancz, August 12, 2018), at http://www.sf-encyclopedia.com/entry/immortality. For the immortality theme in sf see George Slusser, Gary Westfahl, and Eric S. Rabkin, editors, *Immortal Engines: Life Extension and Immortality in Science Fiction and Fantasy* (Athens: University of Georgia Press, 1996).

50. *Zhuangzi* 15:535.

51. For a translation see Harper, *Early Chinese Medical Literature*.

52. *Hanshu* 漢書 (Standard History of the Han Dynasty) (Beijing: Zhonghua shuju, 1962), 30, 1778–1779.

53. For further information on this material see Raphals, "Chinese Philosophy and Chinese Medicine."

54. *Baopuzi waipian*, chapters 2 and 50. For translation of chapter 2 see Lai Chi-Tim, "Ko Hung's Discourse of Hsien-Immortality: A Taoist Configuration of an Alternate Ideal Self-Identity," *Numen*, 45:2 (1998), 183–220, especially 203–204. For chapter 5 see J. Sailey, *The Master Who Embraces Simplicity: A Study of the Philosopher Ko Hung, A.D. 283–343* (San Francisco: Chinese Materials Center, 1978), 242–272 and 277–278 and J.R. Ware, *Alchemy, Medicine and Religion in the China of A.D. 320: The Nei P'ien of Ko Hung* (New York: Dover Publications, 1966), 6–21. The "Gold Elixir" (*Jin dan* 金丹) and "Yellow and White" (*Huang bai* 黃白) chapters of the *Baopuzineipian* survey the history of alchemy and describe in detail a method for "alloying cinnabar," quoting from ancient recipes and "cinnabar methods." The "Immortal Herbs" (*Xian yao* 仙藥) chapter gives information on medical herbs. See Gao Riguang 高日光, "Ge Hong 葛洪," in *Zhuzi baijia da cidian* 諸子百家大辭典 (Dictionary of Philosophers), edited by Feng Kezheng 馮克正 and Fu Qingsheng 傅慶升 (Shenyang: Liaoning renmin chubanshe, 1996), 87; and Qing Xitai 卿希泰, *Zhongguo daojiao* 中國道教 (Chinese Daoism) (Shanghai: Zhishi chubanshe, 1994), Volume 1, 236–238. Michel Strickman, "On the Alchemy of T'ao Hung-ching," in *Facets of Taoism: Essays in Chinese Religion*, edited by Holmes Welch and Anna Seidel (New Haven: Yale University Press, 1979), 152.

55. Michel Strickman, "On the Alchemy of T'ao Hung-ching," *Facets of Taoism: Essays in Chinese Religion*, edited by Holmes Welch and Anna Seidel (New Haven: Yale University Press, 1979), 152.

56. *Prescriptions Worth a Thousand Gold* (*Qian jin fang* 千金方, printed in 652 CE) was a comprehensive treatise on the practice of medicine. It contained herbal remedies and reviewed the history of medicine since the Han Dynasty. It also includes the first Chinese treatise on medical ethics. The second book is a supplement to the first. The supplement (*Qian jinyi fang* 千金翼方, printed in 682) records some thirty years of Sun's own experience with special attention to folk remedies.

57. Fabrizio Predagio, editor, *The Encyclopedia of Taoism*, Volume 2 (London: Routledge. 2013), 928.

58. It was published under the pseudonym Donghai Juewo 東海覺我 (The Awakened

One from Eastern Sea), and included in *The New Braggadocio* (Xin Faluo 新法螺), published by Fiction Forest Press (Xiaoshuo lin she 小說林社). A founder of the press, Xu Nianci, was one of the editors of the journal *Forest of Novels* (Xiaoshuolin 小說林). The novel is a sequel to Iwaya Sazanami's 岩谷小波 (1870–1933) "Tales of Mr. Braggadocio" (Hora Sensei 法螺先生), published by Forest of Fiction (小說林). For a translation see Isaacson, "New Tales of Mr. Braggadocio," *Renditions*, 77/78 (2012), 15–38. For further discussion see Isaacson, "Orientalism, Scientific Practice, and Popular Culture in Late Qing China," *The Oxford Handbook of Modern Chinese Literatures*, edited by Carlos Rojas and Andrea Bachner (Oxford: Oxford University Press, 2016), Oxford Handbooks online, at http://ebook-dl.com/md5/ee0eb3cef95944db833888dbafe564cd.pdf.

59. Xu Nianci 徐念慈, *Xin Faluo xiansheng tan* 新法螺先生譚 (New Tales of Mr. Braggadocio) (Shanghai: Xiaoshuo lin 小混林 Fiction Forest Press, 1905), reprinted in *Zhongguo jindai wenxue daxi 1840–1929: xiaoshuoji* 中國近代文學大系 1840–1919 小說集 (A Treasury of Modern Chinese Literature 1840–1929: Fiction Collection), Volume 6, edited by Wu Zuxiang 吳組緗, Duanmu Hongliang 端木蕻良, and Shi Meng Zhu Bian 时萌主编 (Shanghai: Shanghai shudian, 1991), 323–343, especially 325, translated in Isaacson, "New Tales." Chinese has no word that is equivalent to English "soul." Two terms in use in popular religion and medicine refer to a "cloud soul" (*hun* 魂) and a "white soul" (*po* 魄). For "soul" Xu uses the unusual term *linghun* (靈魂), which he explains thus: "I have no word for it, but it would be referred to in the common language of religion as the 'soul.'" Xu uses the terms "soul-body" (*linghun zhi shen* 靈魂之身) and "corporeal-body" (*quqiao zhi shen* 余軀殼之身). He avoids the strong mind-body dualism of some Western traditions and apparent mind-body holism of traditional China by clearly referring to the *linghun* soul as a kind of body (*shen* 身). For the semantic field of Chinese words for mind, soul, and spirit and for discussion of issues of mind-body dualism in China see Raphals, "Body and Mind in Early China and Greece," *Journal of Cognitive Historiography*, 2:2 (2015), 132–182.

60. See Wu Dingbo, "Chinese Science Fiction," *Handbook of Chinese Popular Culture*, edited by Patrick Murphy and Wu Dingbo (Westport, Connecticut: Greenwood Press, 1994), 260.

61. See Isaacson, *Celestial Empire*, 2, 26, and chapter 7, 146–180; Huss, "Hesitant Journey"; Takeda Masaya 武田昌也 and Hayashi Hiskayuki 林久之, *Chūgoku kagaku gensō bungakukan* 中国科学幻想文学館 (Compendium of Chinese Science Fantasy Literature), 2 volumes (Tokyo: Taishūkan Shoten, 2001); Wu Xianya, "Kexue huanxiang"; Wu Yan, *Kehuan wenxue lungang* 科幻文學論鋼 (Science Fiction Literature) (Chongqing: Chongqing chubanshe, 2011); and Zhang Zhi, "Wanqing kexue xiaoshuo."

PART THREE

The Business of Science Fiction Scholarship

The Slusser Test
for Generic Identity

Reflections on George Slusser's
"Reflections on Style in Science Fiction"

Alvaro Zinos-Amaro

In his essay "Reflections on Style in Science Fiction," George Slusser performs a vigorous theoretical analysis of how style relates to science fiction and how style may in fact be argued to be one of science fiction's defining features.[1] My intent here is to both pay homage to Slusser's fine line of reasoning and to investigate whether we can build on it, namely by invoking ideas from stylometry and data analysis.

Let us begin at the end, with a summary of Slusser's essential conclusion. The fields of human endeavor which we may loosely term "sciences," Slusser observes, proceed by means of a process of "scientific analogy" (18). In contrast, the areas of human study which with comparable looseness we may term "humanities" instead rely for their development on "traditional figuration" (22). A priori, these two ways of investigating reality, and our human existence within that reality, may appear discontinuous. Style, however, Slusser argues, can be interpreted as a bridging element between them, an agent of ontological mediation between scientific analogizing and traditional figuration. Even more significantly, we may think of science fiction (henceforth abbreviated to "sf") as a kind of literature comprised of stylistic statements specializing in these types of strong ontological claims, which through its reading makes possible "communal acts of discovery." This, in grossly abbreviated terms, is Slusser's central thesis.

Before focusing on the specifics of the argument most germane to us, I'm going to offer an incredibly compact synopsis of how Slusser arrives at his conclusion. Understanding each of these steps, and the reasoning linking them, is not necessary to what follows; instead, I offer the synopsis as evidence of Slusser's incredible mental nimbleness and extremely broad-ranging theoretical apparatus. In summary, then, Slusser proceeds more or less as follows:

1. Contemporary theory favors Saussurean "langue" over "parole."
2. Classical treatises on poetics by Aristotle and Plato set a baseline precedent for the secondary role of style.
3. Structuralists tend to reduce sf to either stylistic idioms or stylistic anarchy.
4. Richard M. Ohmann is one notable figure—perhaps the first of prominence?—to contravene the general trend pointed out in (1) and suggest an expanded role for style.
5. Language creates impositions upon the world not through syntax but through Whorfian metalinguistics.
6. Nietzsche views epistemology as intransitive and science as tautological; self-referentiality dominates.
7. There is therefore a clear conflict between Ohmann's notion of metaphorical discovery and the process of Nietzschean metaphorical closure.
8. The perceived divide between sf and so-called experimental mainstream literature neatly parallels the divided between Ohmann and Nietzsche in (7).
9. Paul de Man's epistemology of metaphor exemplifies the modern rhetoric of ontological impossibility.
10. Sf stories are unique when viewed as stylistic statements makings strong ontological claims; they entail communal acts of discovery.

Time to take a deep breath. Each of these observations contains multitudes; for the full details and beauty of Slusser's elaboration thereof, I encourage readers to seek out his essay (and to be prepared for a mental workout). Perhaps unsurprisingly, but nevertheless amusingly, Slusser himself reports "a sense of dismay" (22) at how much theorizing has been required to reach his conclusion that style in sf is what enables a stimulating intellectual experience of heuristic judgment. If style, as Slusser compellingly argues, is what sets sf apart from other types of literature, a straightforward question is whether such style may be amenable to measurement or approximate quantification, even in theory. In order to tackle this question, let's now zoom in on the three key stylistic elements highlighted by Slusser (following work done by Richard Ohmann).[2]

These three elements of style, according to Ohmann, are neologisms, metaphors, and the uprooting of ordinary syntax. In this context, style is an expression of our "hidden thoughts" (cited in Slusser 6). Neologisms, we note, may refer to absolutely new words, or to new uses of existing words, or to newly created words derived from the combination of existing words. Scientific neologisms, in the framework of this discussion, become attempts at knowing, extrapolations which Dedre Gentner calls structure mappings.[3] The word "metaphor" is here intended in its conventional sense. Lastly, for examples of syntactical innovation that can be found outside sf, we can look to works by James Joyce and William Faulkner, with the caveat that these are approximations of what Slusser has in mind, not explicit instances per se.

Before proceeding to a discussion of whether, or to what extent, these three elements may be measureable, I'd like to reference the work of another brilliant theoretician of sf, Istvan Csicsery-Ronay, Jr. In an extremely dense, book-length study, this critic lays out seven significant characteristics of sf.[4] I will not attempt to define them all here, as that would exceed the purview of our investigation, but will nevertheless list them: fictive neology, fictive novum (or nova), future history, imaginary science, the science-fictional sublime, the science-fictional grotesque, and lastly, the technologiade. If I understand Csicsery-Ronay, Jr., correctly, we can think of these seven "beauties" of sf as comprising a kind of working *quorum* definition of sf. Therefore, a text lacking all seven "beauties" is unlikely to be sf by any stretch of the imagination; conversely, a text exhibiting any given subset of them will likely be sf by conventional standards. I find it of note that the first of these seven proposed notions, the fictive neology, coincides to some degree with the first of the three stylistic elements with which we are concerned, the neologism. Here is how Csicsery-Ronay Jr., describes the fictive neology:

> Readers of sf expect to encounter new words and other signs that indicate worlds changed from their own, just as viewers of visual sf expect special visual effects, and listeners expect special sonic effects representing new sense-perceptions and aesthetic designs. Our culture treats sf as the primary source for such symbolic indications of radical newness. The fictive neologies of sf are variations and combinations based on the actual process of lexicogenesis experienced in social life. They can appear in a great variety of forms, in diverse registers, from the prophetic to the comic. In every case, they imply linguistic-symbolic models of technological transformation, playfully suspended and seriously displaced. They engage audiences to use them as clues and triggers to construct the logic of science-fictional worlds [5].

In order to shed some light on my interpretation of Csicsery-Ronay, Jr.'s work, and how it may be applied practically, I'd like to spend a few moments discussing a specific novel which makes for a fascinating test case, Robert Silverberg's *The Book of Skulls* (1972).

In this novel four college students search after eternal life. Using Csicsery-Ronay Jr.'s scheme, we might be tempted to say that since immortality fits under the framework of conceptual prosthesis, in turn a subcategory of imaginary science, the book is clearly sf. This seems straightforward enough—case closed. But there arise several complications. First, we may think of other narratives preoccupied with immortality, such as the *Epic of Gilgamesh*, which would seem ill-at-ease in the grouping of "imaginary science," and which are unlikely to be considered sf by a majority of modern readers. Second, *The Book of Skulls* provides no definitive proof that immortality actually exists within its narrative framework; it deals only, to be strict, in potential immortality. As a result, if we are to find its sf-nal core, we may need to look outside of the "imaginary science" category. The idea of the sublime, if we recall the works of philosophers like Immanuel Kant and Edmund Burke, historically entails an internalization of the smallness of humankind juxtaposed with the immensity of nature. Csicsery-Ronay, Jr., builds on this notion to develop the specifically sf-nal sublime, which he describes as often being achieved by space operatic means. Immortality—even *in potentia*—lends itself well to intimations of sublimity: consider, for instance, the psychological exploration of the fleetingness of ordinary human life contrasted with the immensity of time, and how such an awareness may impel individuals to crave immortality, and to contemplate how far, morally, they'd be willing to go to achieve it. It is this latter component that takes Silverberg's book into the grotesque. On the whole, then, *The Book of Skulls* derives much of its thematic power from its conflation of the sublime and the grotesque, both as applied to the imaginary science of immortality. The book's theme is wonderfully evoked through a narrative quartet of individualized voices, which root the imaginary science in a contemporary (at the time of publication) and therefore plausible reality. The *Epic of Gilgamesh*, while preoccupied with immortality, differs in that it is fundamentally a mythological quest/travelogue, unfolding in a supernatural world and featuring magic and divinity rather than imaginary science as meant by Csicsery-Ronay, Jr.

Let us return now to the question of style as a defining trademark of sf, and Ohmann's three key stylistic elements. In order to ascertain what modern stylometry and data analysis may have to say about these elements, a short review of some impressive stylometric accomplishments is in order.

One dramatic example of the application of stylometry involves an analysis of twelve essays published as part of *The Federalist Papers* in 1787 under the pseudonym "Publius." While the authorship of the majority of the eighty-five texts comprising *The Federalist Papers* was known, that of the twelve pieces in question was not. The three candidates suspected of authorship were Alexander Hamilton, James Madison, and John Jay, but both contextual clues and inferences based on the essays' contents proved insufficient for a consensus view regarding their author. Complicating matters, in 1804, Hamilton, preparing to duel Aaron Burr, wrote a letter to a friend and claimed authorship of the essays, but thirteen years later Madison put out his own authorship claim. Enter, in 1890, the work of Polish philosopher Wincenty Lutoslawski, whose *Principes de Stylométrie* presented a formalized attempt to define measurable elements of style, as for example counting certain word frequencies. A modernized implementation of these notions, amplified by statistical methods, was derived by Frederick Mosteller of Harvard University and David Wallace of the University of Chicago, who set out to definitively solve *The Federalist Papers* authorship mystery. In their study, they applied stylometric tests to essays whose authorship by Madison and Hamilton was known, and correctly predicted the author in each instance. Then, using the same criteria for the twelve articles in question, they concluded that Madison was their author, a view that holds to this day.[5]

Another thought-provoking example of stylometric analysis involves the 18th-century play *Double Falshood; or, The Distrest Lovers* by Lewis Theobald (1727). The play is constructed around the so-called "Cardenio" episode of Miguel de Cervantes's *Don Quixote* (1605, 1615), and Theobald himself claimed it was based on an unnamed lost play by William Shakespeare. In 2015 a detailed stylometric study was performed and found that *Double Falshood*'s main text was indeed a collaboration between Shakespeare and John Fletcher, essentially their lost play *The History of Cardenio*, with minor contributions by Theobald.[6]

In another recent example of author identification, 2017 stylometric research was conducted on the works of "Elena Ferrante," the known pseudonym of an Italian writer who has won the Man Booker International Prize and received many other accolades. This investigation, which analyzed over a hundred novels by forty authors, concluded that Ferrante was in fact the writer Domenico Starnone.[7]

An early application of stylometry in sf explores the works of Isaac Asimov. This book-length study (Goble), performed without the benefit of modern text digitization and analytical software, was based on samples of each work by Asimov rather than their every word. Nevertheless, the study was comprehensive in its scope, covering both Asimov's fiction and nonfiction. Documented measures, focusing on Asimov's non-dialogue fiction prose, included average sentence and paragraph lengths, characteristics of his "personal" sentences (questions, commands, exclamations, and stopping short), his use of first person and second person, ratios of active versus passive sentences, his diction (for example, preferred ways of opening paragraphs), his modulation (i.e., his use of quotes, italics, parentheses, dashes and semicolons), and the variability of such metrics based on the age of his target readers.[8]

A contemporary example, accessible for lay readers, of wide-ranging stylometric work that fully deploys modern statistical techniques and utilizes vast repositories of digitized texts and tables of specific word types, may be found in Ben Blatt's *Nabokov's Favorite Word Is Mauve: What the Numbers Reveal About the Classics, Bestsellers, and Our Own Writing* (2017).[9] This survey examines adverb usage, how word choices relate to gender, the changes in grade levels of bestsellers over time, U.K. versus U.S. usage, the percent of clichés in modern popular fiction, how much space author names occupy on book covers, line openings and opening lines, the use of anaphora (the repetition of a word or phrase at the start of consecutive sentences), and author's most oft-repeated words. To convey the kinds of insights gleaned through these studies, I'd like to cite some specific findings.

In his book *On Writing: A Memoir of the Craft* (2000), Stephen King suggests that writers should use adverbs (meaning specifically adverbs ending in "-ly") sparingly. Blatt calculates that, from his pool of authors, Ernest Hemingway uses "-ly" adverbs least, at a rate of only 81 per 10,000 words throughout ten major works. Stephen King, meanwhile, is roughly in the middle of the list, with a usage of 105 "-ly" adverbs per 10,000 words over the course of 51 novels. J.K. Rowling, for another genre comparison, is much higher, at 140 per 10,000 words. In terms of anaphora, Blatt finds that Virginia Woolf's *The Waves* (1931) contains a whopping 16 percent. When considering clichés, his analysis relies on Christine Ammer's *The Dictionary of Clichés: A Word Lover's Guide to 4,000 Overused Phrases and Almost-Pleasing Platitudes* (2013), which compiles some 4,000 clichés. Examining hundreds of novels by fifty authors, Blatt places James Patterson at the top of the list, with 160 per 100,000 words, while Jane Austen, with only 45 per 100,000 words, is at the lower extreme. Stephen King, like Patterson, is on the high end, with 125, while J.K. Rowling, with 92, is roughly at the same level as Dan Brown, with 93. Examples of clichés favored by famous sf/f writers include Ray Bradbury's use of "at long last," George R.R. Martin's use of "black as pitch," Rick Riordan's repetition of "from head to toe," and Tolkien's reliance on the phrase "nick of time."

"Nod" words Blatt describes as non-proper-nouns appearing at the rate of at least 100 per 100,000 and occurring in all of an author's works. These may be considered tantamount to stylistic tics or affectations. Ray Bradbury's top nod words are "someone, cried, boys"; Cassandra Clare's are "blood, hair, looked"; George R.R. Martin's are "lady, red, black"; and Lemony Snicket's are "siblings, orphans, children." Blatt denotes as "cinnamon words" specific words used by an author much more frequently than other authors. Bradbury uses spice-related terminology quite often: "spearmint," for instance, appears in his work fifty times more frequently than it does in the Corpus of Historical American English.[10] "Mauve," meanwhile, is Vladimir Nabokov's top cinnamon word, thus inspiring the title of Blatt's book, and is followed by "banal" and "pun."

Having expounded on these already-proven applications of stylometry, we can now return to Slusser's contention and attempt to conceive an extension of today's methods that might prove or disprove Slusser's idea about the centrality of style to sf. Besides the three elements of style remarked upon earlier, Slusser's essay emphasizes the importance of ontologico-stylistic content in sf, and the particular ways in which first lines are different from those in other texts. These two categories, then, may tentatively define the parameter space for our thought experiment. Next we need sample data.

Locus, the trade journal of sf, tallies yearly totals of new, original books (not reprints) that are considered sf. From 2008 through 2017 this total comes to 19,089 volumes that might make for a suitable, statistically meaningful data set. If we wish to proceed with a less ambitious body of work, we might limit ourselves to *Locus*'s recommended sf novels; in 2017 there were twenty-eight such titles, or approximately 1.5 percent of new books published. Assuming a comparable recommended-to-published ratio for our 2008–2017 total, we might reasonably confine our study to some 294 sample texts. We should note that these books don't include collections, which *Locus* lists separately, or first novels, which are also awarded their own category. In order to prevent our survey from becoming recursive (limiting our sample data to agreed-upon sf texts we find that they are, stylistically speaking, sf) we would need to complement our approximately 300 volumes with other texts, for example novels having won the Arthur C. Clarke Award or Nebula Award, or perhaps books covered by *Locus* reviewers but not included in the recommended lists. Alternatively, one might follow any number of historical approaches, or deliberately select for inclusion non-genre books published by mainstream publishers but nevertheless containing known sf tropes.

Having defined our sample data, we might then begin by using software to count the number of neologisms in said texts. Comparing these frequencies with those found in non-genre-specific data sets, such as the aforementioned Corpus of Historical American English, might establish neologism-related thresholds related to generic identity.

Beyond this element, we might inquire as to how precisely we should measure our data's ontologico-stylistic content, the particularities of its first lines, its use of metaphors, and its uprooting of ordinary syntax. Clearly such evaluations are much more complex than counting neologisms. Currently available language software does not appear to be up to these tasks. However, future natural language processing (NLP) techniques, harnessing the power of artificial intelligence and vast quantities of natural language data, may come to the rescue. In this scenario, we can envision a "Slusser test" for generic identity. In the same way that an unknown entity answering carefully selected questions in a way indistinguishable from humans may be thought of, per the Turing test, as human, a text exhibiting certain quantities of stylistic distinction in a way indistinguishable from those of known sf texts would, per the Slusser test, perforce be considered sf.

We could apply this Slusser test to increasingly borderline cases in an attempt to find the borders of genre. Naturally this raises the questions of genre hybridization and porousness. These subjects have been studied, and at least semi-formally documented, in Gary K. Wolfe's *Evaporating Genres: Essays on Fantastic Literature* (2011) and elsewhere.[11] Key notions in this survey relate to the escaping into general culture of sf tropes, and to artists breaking categories rather than helping to build them, a process which often occurs retrospectively. More specifically, we can use this survey to propose a starter list of authors that might yield intriguing results when Slusser-tested: Peter Straub, Jonathan Carroll, Jonathan Lethem, M. John Harrison, China Miéville, Kelly Link, Elizabeth Hand, and Jeffrey Ford. Further author suggestions may be located in recommended bibliographies of various literary movements at least tangentially connected with sf, such as "slipstream," "New Wave fabulism," "Weird," and the "New Weird."

Pursuing such studies, we may well find that the Slusser test may be, in light of the inherent limits of genre categorization, of limited use for a binary yes/no identification of a given text as sf. However, given certain trends in genre over the last fifteen or so years, we may envision a slightly more subtle application of the test. Prose sf and fantasy have spawned a multitude of sf subgenres, such as alternate history, military action, and paranormal romance. Further, within such subgenres, readers tend to gravitate to particular author cohorts. Further still, many contemporary readers, while enmeshed in overlapping cohorts, exhibit particular loyalty to specific authors, regardless of those authors' movements between cohorts, sf subgenres, or even out of sf and into other arenas. The concept of author branding is prevalent in modern-day marketing and recommendation algorithms. The Slusser test might then be used to determine whether a particular text resides inside a given subgenre or cohort, or whether it can be associated with a particular author brand, regardless of its sf-ness.

Following this train of thought, let us consider recent work done on what we might term the topology of literature. Franco Moretti's theory of "distant reading" emphasizes measureable aspects of texts not contingent on traditional techniques of subjective literary criticism.[12] Moretti, together with Matthew Jockers, founded the Stanford Literary Lab, some of whose areas of statistical inquiry include: the "loudness" of novels, geographic distributions of emotions, the evolution of bureaucratic doublespeak, distinguishing aspects of the Gothic novel (which turn out to be not just castles and ghosts, but more frequent use of certain verb tenses and prepositions), and the curious finding that from 1785 to 1900 the language of the British novel steadily shifted away from words relating to moral judgment to words associated with concrete description.[13] Following this and related examples that emphasize visual depictions of literary features and textual relationships,[14] we might imagine using the Slusser test in combination with data generated through reader surveys to construct a genre map.

Such a map might take the form of a proximity graph whose constituent elements would be either individual authors, pre-defined author cohorts, or approximately defined subgenres. In order to assemble this proximity graph we would rely principally on circles, or nodes, and connecting lines. First, the size of a given node would be directly proportional to how many readers of a given survey indicated that the element represented by the node—author, cohort, subgenre—was one of his or her favorites. Second, the proximity of nodes on the map would indicate how much their respective fanbases overlap: the closer two nodes, the more similar their fanbases. After constructing the proximity graph based purely on reader survey responses, we could then interpret clusters of nodes in a particular way. For instance, if we take nodes to represent authors, then node clusters might indicate subgenres, and the emerging concentration of a given super-cluster might represent sf as a genre itself. The Slusser test, aided with other emerging forms of textual data analysis, might then be used as a predictor of that text's nodality. Examining the node network would likely suggest further testable hypotheses, for example relating to the traditional "commerce versus craft" debate. One such hypothesis might entail positing that certain authors or cohorts have larger nodes because of the commercial efforts to promote their works rather than due to their stylistic genre markers or distinctiveness. It may indeed be found that for an author's work to live inside a given cluster of nodes, such work may not surpass critical values of ontologico-stylistic density. Relationships between the economics of publishing and book distribution and the content of texts could thus be at least partially quantified.

Interesting test cases that might push against the limits of these techniques would likely include book series taken over by one author from another, satires, or genre meta-commentaries.

At any rate, we can imagine a host of provocative—and perhaps amusing—results deriving from this dual line of attack involving survey-based proximity mapping and data analysis-driven variants of our proposed Slusser test. Such results, if ever pursued by future scholars, would naturally be of intrinsic interest to genre students and critics. Not only would this approach directly extend George Slusser's own work, by manifestly bridging the divide between the sciences and humanities, but it would also echo the unique function of sf itself, leading to what Slusser would term "a communal act of discovery" (21).

NOTES

1. George Slusser, "Reflections on Style in Science Fiction," *Styles of Creation: Aesthetic Technique and the Creation of Fictional Worlds*, edited by Slusser and Eric S. Rabkin (Athens: University of Georgia Press, 1992), 3–23. Page references are to this edition.

2. See Richard M. Ohmann, *Prolegomena to the Analysis of Prose Style* (Indianapolis: Bobbs-Merrill, 1966).

3. See Dedre Gentner, "Structure-Mapping: A Theoretical Framework for Analogy," *Cognitive Science*, 7:2 (April/June 1983), 155–170.

4. Istvan Csicsery-Ronay, Jr., *The Seven Beauties of Science Fiction* (Middletown, CT: Wesleyan University Press, 2011). Page references are to this edition.

5. Frederick Mosteller and David L. Wallace, *Inference and Disputed Authorship: The Federalist* (Reading, MA: Addison-Wesley, 1964).

6. Ryan L. Boyd and James W, Pennebaker, "Did Shakespeare Write *Double Falsehood*? Identifying Individuals by Creating Psychological Signatures with Text Analysis," *Psychological Science*, 26:5 (May 2015), 570–582.

7. Jacques Savoy, "Elena Ferrante Unmasked: Is Starnone Really the Author behind Ferrante?," https://www.researchgate.net/publication/320131096_Elena_Ferrante_Unmasked (September 2017).

8. Neil Goble, *Asimov Analyzed* (Baltimore: Mirage Press, 1972).

9. Ben Blatt, *Nabokov's Favorite Word Is Mauve: What the Numbers Reveal About the Classics, Bestsellers, and Our Own Writing* (New York: Simon & Schuster, 2017).

10. Corpus of Historical American English, Brigham Young University, at https://corpus.byu.edu/coca/.

11. Gary K. Wolfe, *Evaporating Genres: Essays on Fantastic Literature* (Middletown, CT: Wesleyan University Press, 2011).

12. See Franco Moretti, *Distant Reading* (London: Verso, 2013).

13. See Moretti, *Canon/Archive: Studies in Quantitative Formalism from the Stanford Literary Lab* (New York: n+1 Foundation, 2017).

14. See Moretti, *Graphs, Maps, Trees: Abstract Models for Literary History* (London: Verso, 2007).

The Early Life
of the Eaton Collection
and Dr. George Slusser's
Invaluable Contributions

Julia D. Ree

Librarians know how to research. We revel in the literature search and in the gathering of data. This essay, however, is more anecdotal and observational than heavily researched. I joined the University of California, Riverside (UCR) Library staff in 1979 and, throughout my career there, was involved in almost every aspect of collecting, acquiring, processing, preserving, and relationship-building for the J. Lloyd Eaton Collection of Science Fiction, Fantasy, Horror, and Utopian Literature. While I was not present at the very start of this remarkable collection, I had the good fortune to be associated with the Eaton Collection and its ancillary activities in one form or another since the mid–1980s. I can attest that it was a long and difficult road to making the Eaton Collection a world-class science fiction repository and that Dr. George Slusser was at the apex of giving that collection its fine reputation. For information on the collection's nascent beginnings, I have relied on the memories of Mary Burgess and Leslie K. Swigart. In fact, it is Swigart's unflinchingly generous provision of her dissertation draft on the History of the Eaton Collection and her studies of Eaton that I have consulted in order to fill in some of the blanks to this narrative.[1] I am indebted to both of these women for their support. They prove above all else that library people are truly collaborative.

This exploration is decidedly library-centric. And so, a little background information is in order to set the stage. There are thousands of libraries, big, small, local, global. We depend on many of them to satisfy the general needs of their community, but, what is it that makes a library truly special, truly great? The Hemet Public Library, for example, is a small, city-run, typical small-town public library. It makes every effort, budget willing, to accommodate the local community by making available the current best sellers and volumes for the DIY project-minded. It also has the single, most comprehensive special collection of books and articles on the Ramona Pageant, which is based on Helen Hunt Jackson's novel *Ramona* (1884). The outdoor play that is based on that novel is a mainstay for the community and an annual event for the whole city. No other library in the area, or indeed the world, has the depth and breadth of coverage for that one event. So, whether it is a room, a closet, a whole floor, or an entire building, what distinguishes a library ultimately is its Special Collections.

Now, not every great library has the resources or longevity to have a spectacular collection. Not every library can achieve the status of a "Harvard" or a "Yale." So, without that sense of prominence, how does any library even hope to achieve that designation of being a destination for scholars and researchers? If the management of a library has some measure of forward thinking, they can begin to collect in areas that might seem newer or perhaps unusual. If a library is attached to a university, they may wish to acquire more heavily toward the subject areas covered by the curriculum. Or they may want to move toward a specific subject area, with the clear understanding that the subject might be taught sometime in the future. A special collection can develop if what is being collected is something unique. It can grow, if the items are relatively inexpensive. It can set itself apart by striving for comprehensive coverage. It can entice researchers if there is educational and research value, and ultimately, if it builds a reputation, it can perpetuate itself in crazy good ways. A good collection will incorporate one or two of these points. A truly great collection will effectively use all of them. Of course, when speaking of great collections, what we are really talking about are great public collections. These are the institutions and businesses that take the initiative to be a public resource. There are untold private collections out there and only a relative few of us have a notion of the depth of what those private collections might hold.

So let's talk specifically about the Eaton Collection. J. Lloyd Eaton was a Bay-area physician with a fan boy's heart. An avid collector of first editions from the late 19th and early 20th centuries, Eaton was a frequent attendee of science fiction conventions and firmly a part of the science fiction fandom community. His death, in 1968, opened up the possibility that his 7500 volumes of science fiction, fantasy, and adventure stories might be made available. In fact, the collection was in danger of being broken up by booksellers and sold piecemeal. The family wanted the collection sold. The University Librarian for UC Riverside at that time, Mr. Donald Wilson, recognized that this collection might just satisfy some of those traits that make a special collection shine. It was certainly unique. There was virtually no scholarship in science fiction at the time and certainly not at UCR. In 1969, the cost for the 7500 volumes was within the purchasing parameters of the library's budget; otherwise, the purchase would not have received the green light. The value to future research, especially in 1969, could be considered exceptional, and ultimately it would give UCR Library the means to build a reputation.

Unfortunately, campus leadership at that time was not as forward-thinking as Mr. Wilson. So, that initial collection, named after the man who painstakingly collected those volumes, sat in a closet dubbed "The Freezer" until the middle of the following decade. According to Mary Burgess, she and her husband Mike Burgess (who published as Robert Reginald) were allowed to look over the items in the collection, sometime during the mid–1970s, to come up with ideas about fully processing the pieces. When the UCR Library cataloging department finally began their work of processing the materials, only one person was initially assigned to the task of adding records to the library catalog. The Burgesses were friends with and supportive of Dr. George Slusser in those early days. Slusser had been a member of the staff at California State University, San Bernardino, as had Mike. The Burgesses, as the publishers for Borgo Press, would come to publish several of Slusser's works and were instrumental in recommending that Slusser be named curator of the Eaton Collection. The Special Collections librarian at the time, Clifford Wurfel, was able to advocate for the position of curator, and so Slusser began his relationship with the Eaton collection and the UCR Library.

Slusser was an academic, first and foremost. In the policies he put forward and the measures he took to ensure the health of the collection, he showed himself to be more a raconteur than a librarian. He established relationships. He hated the day-to-day mundane tasks that librarians endure and only sometimes enjoy. Collection Development departments determine the needs of the community they serve. They have the responsibility to work with a sometimes meager budget to supply research materials for students, scholars, and the community. A Collection Development librarian should strive to fill in gaps with a careful and vigilant eye. They watch their budget and adhere to the bottom line. Slusser, however, wanted it all! And as a person willing to develop relationships, he was responsible for allowing the growth that would ensure a richness and reputation that made the Eaton Collection, at least for a time, the single finest publicly accessible science fiction collection in the world.

Slusser contributed heavily to the establishment of policy statements on collecting science fiction for the UCR Library. One such document, dated 2002, shows that the intent of the collection was to be comprehensive. Any worthy collection development policy should be a living, fluid document and should be nurtured and changed to fit the needs of evolving scholarship. I remember the day that Slusser rather emphatically stated: we will never collect comic books! It was a sound decision at the time. It is prohibitively expensive to keep current in comic book collecting and as a current collector I can attest to this. To comprehensively gather back issues is simply too costly for any library's budget without some specific and extensive financial support. It would have been a poor decision to collect any comic books at that time. And then, the Edwin Casebeer donation came in. Suddenly, the UCR library was in the business of collecting comic books. One collection begets another and another and now the UCR Library has a fairly substantial comic book collection. They still do not use the purchasing budget to fill in gaps and there is no systematic effort to purchase new titles. The comic book collection will never be on par with that of Michigan State University, but it is certainly one of the top 10 libraries that offer comics as a part of their research collection.

In the 1980s, few outside of science fiction fandom had heard of fanzines until Slusser brokered the purchase of 71 linear feet of Terry Carr's fanzine collection. The UCR library is now one of the preeminent gatekeepers of fanzines, and the library is currently in the process of more fully cataloging those issues. Having the Carr fanzines prompted others to donate their sizable fanzine collections and thanks to that initial foresight on Slusser's part, the UCR Library is one of the preeminent repositories for fanzines published in the United States.

Also during the 1980s, three grants were filed and awarded to UCR Library. These National Endowment for the Humanities grants provided for the purchase of materials for the purpose of filling in gaps and the processing of those materials. Slusser would have provided expert justification for these lucrative opportunities to augment the Eaton Collection which, at the time, was still struggling to be comprehensive. The three grants added thousands of titles to the existing collection. Although I had been a member of the UCR Library staff before, I came on board as a cataloger for the third of these grants and stayed more closely connected to Eaton from that point forward.

Slusser created relationships with book vendors in other countries and would often go outside the normal channels of the library to establish approval plans: the kind of collecting where the vendor chooses what titles a library must have, based on a profile established with those vendors. That is how the UCR library's French and Russian science fiction titles became prominent within the collection.

Slusser also brokered the acquisition of Ace Science Fiction paperback books and the genre of proto science fiction, known as boys' books. But he did not stop there. Slusser was tasked to build the collection, to make it sustainable, and to make it thrive. He accomplished these tasks in a variety of ways.

In terms of acquiring new materials, that raconteur Slusser engaged the services of two different and unconventional vendors. For paperback books, Slusser sought out a local distribution company, Arrowhead Paperbacks. This warehouse, located in San Bernardino, California, distributed to local supermarkets and stores like 7-Eleven but not to places like the University of California. Slusser asked the employees to pull one copy of anything that had sf, F, or H on the spine. Then, once a month, he would go to the warehouse, pick up the books collected, and deliver the month's acquisition to the library himself. This was hardly collection development in the librarian sense, but very much in keeping with Slusser's style. The other vendor was a former librarian with UCLA who had gone into the book-selling business after retirement. Slusser's only instructions to him were, you guessed it, to deliver everything that was science fiction, fantasy, or horror in nature. Establishing a relationship with this particular vendor would prove to be a fortuitous act.

Remembering that one donation helps to build the reputation of a special collection and that one donation begets another, Slusser established relationships with key members of the Los Angeles area science fiction fandom. In the years leading up to his retirement and due solely to Slusser's relationship-building, the Eaton Collection was the recipient of the collection of that retired UCLA librarian, Bruce Pelz. Pelz's collection of science fiction was enormous, but his collection of fanzines was priceless in terms of the richness of potential scholarship. Once the UCR Library had the Pelz collection, the Rick Sneary collection soon followed. Not only did Sneary have thousands of fanzines, but he also kept a treasure trove of correspondence between himself and hundreds of fans and authors and fans who would become authors. This archive of correspondence shows great promise for researchers as a potential for providing deeper understanding of science fiction fandom culture as it was developing in the 1940s, 1950s, and 1960s.

The ultimate donation came to the UCR Library, however, with the Fred Patton collection. When Fred suffered a massive and debilitating stroke, his 40 years of collecting in the areas of furry fiction, Japanese anime and manga, and general science fiction had to leave his tiny apartment. He wanted his collection to go to the one place he knew it would be appreciated and used: the Eaton Collection. The collection had a new home 820 moving-sized boxes later. The process to create discoverability for this massive donation still continues. Others in the Los Angeles science fiction fandom community know and appreciate the reputation of Eaton and have plans in place to contribute to the collection in the future. Thanks to the early reputation building that was Slusser's forte, the Eaton Collection has the potential to be first in line for critical one-of-a-kind donations.

As a scholar and as the co-founder of the Eaton Conference with Mike Burgess, many will argue rightly that Slusser's legacy is firmly established and forever intertwined with the Eaton Conference. These boutique-style, one-track, three-day annual events allowed future scholars the opportunity to present papers alongside noted academics in the genre and renowned authors of science fiction, fantasy, mystery, and horror. Thanks in large part to Slusser's relationship-building with those scholars and writers during those 20 plus conferences, the UCR Library was able to establish amazing archives for the Eaton Collection. Gregory Benford continues to be a major donor. David Brin, Sheila Finch, Paul Alkon, Robert L. Forward, and Anne McCaffrey are but a few of the authors who have donated their archives to the UCR Library. These are one-of-a-kind treasures and priceless to the study of science fiction and fantasy. They would not be an integral part of the collection had Slusser not urged and influenced these writers and scholars to donate to the Eaton Collection.

It is a rare thing to have a complete history of any collection, and institutions in general are terrible about preserving their own history. There are many gaps in the telling of this tale of the Eaton Collection. We sometimes overlook what may be a key area in some future historian's footnote. But an affirmation of Slusser's influential status of building the Eaton Collection came in January of 2006 when the journal *College and Research Libraries* published the article entitled "Science Fiction Collections in ARL Academic Libraries," written by Kevin P. Mulcahy.[2] Mulcahy wanted to know to what extent science fiction was being actively collected in academic settings. He tailored his survey to include award winners and/or "Best of" materials from the time period from 1950 to 2000. Out of 112 academic research libraries listed, the Eaton Collection was number one by a huge margin. This distinction was made possible, thanks in large part, to George Slusser.

The Eaton Collection has had its share of nurturers and detractors. It really does take a village to make sure that what is considered excellent stays that way, no matter how much your definition of excellence changes. The signs may be pointing to a determined change in the collecting trends for the Eaton Collection and some very vocal and perhaps former champions of the collection are already envisioning its demise. To them and to you I would ask you to remember this: the Eaton Collection began slowly and with many fragile steps. It took pioneers, like Slusser, willing to take chances to ensure that the collection was purchased, augmented, processed, and celebrated. It took decades to be the best and it might very well take far less time to fall from that high perch. If what is happening to the Eaton Collection today is a natural progression, it may be that it no longer serves scholars and researchers the way it once did. But if there are still vibrant aspects to the collection, it is up to those same scholars and researchers to take a stand and make their voices heard. Staffing comes and goes. The collection endures. But it endures only if those stakeholders demand the kind of excellence that they need. We still face struggles with administrations that don't understand the value of science fiction as a legitimate course of study. This roadblock that many of us face must be challenged. It is up to all of the scholars, the experts in the field, to advocate on behalf of the Eaton Collection, to explain why this comprehensive collection is so important to the study of the genre and that it has lasting value. If the questions of space and money come up, it is up to us to counter with solutions that involve acquiring that space and having that money provided. Whether the Eaton Collection is number one right now is not as important as finding the champions who will insure the future of the collection as a comprehensive research center. It is up to all of us to take a page from Slusser's philosophy to establish relationships and create lasting connections for the sake of future scholarship. In this way, the Eaton Collection will continue to thrive and Slusser's legacy will be secured.

NOTES

1. Leslie K. Swigart, The J. Lloyd Eaton Collection of Science Fiction, Fantasy, Horror, and Utopian Literature: A History and Description (unpublished dissertation, University of California, Riverside, 2005). Other sources consulted include the three issues of *The J. Lloyd Eaton Collection Newsletter*, 1:1, 1:2, 1:3 (1988–1990) and the J. Lloyd Eaton Papers (archival material, Tomás Rivera Library, University of California, Riverside).

2. Kevin P. Mulcahy, "Science Fiction Collections in ARL Academic Libraries," *College & Research Libraries*, 67:1 (January 2006), 15–34.

The Odd Couple

*Blending Disciplines of Science
and Humanities Through Teaching*

ROBERT L. HEATH

Neil Simon wrote *The Odd Couple* (1965), where he paired a "neat freak" with an "untidy slob." Although very different, they found a strong and lasting friendship. That "odd couple" relationship was repeated at the University of California, Riverside, where two of us with very distinct backgrounds found a common goal of teaching sf. I (a professor of Plant Physiology and Biophysics in the College of Natural and Agricultural Sciences) and George Slusser (a professor of French Literature and Science Fiction Studies in the College of Humanities, Fine Arts, and Social Science) joined together to attempt a fusion of the disciplines of science and humanities. Which is the "neat freak" or "untidy slob" will remain unsaid, but the UCR couple managed to survive over 15 years of working together, writing proposals and even publishing a paper as a team.

The story started in 1990 when I was invited to lunch to meet George at the faculty club by Jean-Pierre Barricelli, a Classics professor of George's department. Jean-Pierre and I served on several Academic Senate committees and he must have felt that I could be in some way a fit with George. George at that time was under a fair amount of stress because he had two very different positions: professor in Literature and Languages and the Curator of the Eaton Science Fiction Collection in UCR's Tomás Rivera Library. Both groups wanted him to perform solely for them, of course at full time. What Jean-Pierre wanted was never really stated, but he did want two people who loved sf to meet and that must have meant something to him.

Varied Teaching Courses

The first few years I was a "tag along" in George's courses, listening and adding some small notes, but I loved what I was hearing. I had been to a few Eaton Conferences, but I could not understand nor appreciate how people in the humanities approached sf. I learned that I was a "hard sf" person and worried more about the science that was the hub of the story. Over time, I saw what George was saying: it is the humanity of us in the stories and how the stories were constructed that are important. The science is and should be the bedrock of the story and must be maintained as honest as possible. As Gregory Benford has said, writers must "play[ ] tennis with the net up."[1] Scientific rules and laws must be followed throughout the story. But the characters, plot, and meaning of the story must also come through. It is the blending of science and humanity that is critical; sf came into its own when science and engineering were creating a new world for humanity. The question then and now remains: will science retain its humanity or overwhelm it? As a scientist you can discover the world and make it different, but must be careful of what is done to us humans.

What this also means is that stories that were somewhat correct science in the 1920s can still serve a function of describing human actions, even after the science was shown to be "incorrect." George used two stories somewhat constantly in his courses: "The Cold Equations" (1954) by Tom Godwin and *Frankenstein; or, The Modern Prometheus* (1818, 1831) by Mary Shelley. His concept was there was an element of horror in all sf stories. Science in itself can lead to horror if it is not controlled. Something happens in the flow of the story that will shock you; "the horror of it all" was a common phrase of his. Of special note was C.L. Moore and Henry Kuttner's "Vintage Season" (1946), which showed how easily people could disconnect themselves from horrors happening to others—the rich ignore the poor, especially with differences of when they existed in time.

Interestingly, students reacted to "The Cold Equations" illogically. They did not wish to see a young girl seemingly kill herself needlessly when clearly one should be able to find a technological solution. They argued that this waste of a good life should not be; "technology should be able to solve such a simple problem," they shouted. Even when it was pointed out that this was "just a story," they continued to argue. Technology should not and cannot let this happen! Yet as George continued to state, "technology can have some very bad side effects."

Other old faithfuls of his, such as *The Time Machine* by H.G. Wells (1895) and *Journey to the Center of the Earth* by Jules Verne (1864), were often used to show the concept that even if the sciences wasn't quite correct, it still could be used to show that the story was the master driver as long as the science was nearly correct and good for the time. Those stories could also be used to give a sense of history of both civilization and science.

Of course George could never let his early hero rest and used him in nearly every course, especially Robert A. Heinlein's "By His Bootstraps" (1941). But we together did progress to current literature. We found and used Ted Chiang's "Story of Your Life" (1998) in 2000. It gave the students trouble in terms of how we, as humans, look at how our lives move forward in time, while aliens may have very different ways of thinking about a life. Unfortunately George did not live to see that story as a film (*Arrival*, 2016); yet I am sure he would complain that it lost much of its meaning with all of the Hollywood special effects.

As time went on, George brought me more into the discussion. I described how orbital mechanics worked, what are truly alien-like biological organisms here on Earth, and that we know only of the $N = 1$ case of biology on Earth. I could easily lead the discussion of how computers worked and were different from our brain, and what "time" is. These courses led us into a real cooperation that was finalized by the Hewlett Course of Sf in the very early 2000s.

Part of the concept of our joint work was my understanding of the student psyche from my years as an Associate Dean of Student Affairs. One way of dividing students is: those students who only wish to major in science (and engineering), those who only wish to major in humanities (and the subjects linked to them at UCR), and those who do not know what they wanted. Hard science students did not want to take English or history, as those courses were a waste of time. Hard humanists did not want to take science as it was boring, hard, and worthless. The "lost ones" needed to see a range in order to find their "love." Both George and I saw that and tried to change it. Since sf consists of both science and humanities, and requires discussions of both disciplines, it can help some make a decision about what major they actually would love.

Our real concept was a course that incorporated a bit of all of human endeavors, which would allow students in the two areas to communicate with each other, including arguments as to what is important. To George and me, it was obvious that such a course was the way to go. Perhaps we were just a bit naïve, as it turned out.

The Two Cultures Problem

In 1959, C.P. Snow articulated a major problem of twentieth-century education in his Rede Lecture in the Senate House of the University of Cambridge ("The Two Cultures and the Scientific Revolution," May 7, 1959). He saw two cultures in the intellectual world (the sciences and the humanities) separated by fundamentally different methodologies and world views. As Snow said,

> I believe the intellectual life of the whole of the Western society is increasingly being split into two polar groups ... at one pole we have the literary intellectuals ... at the other scientists, and as the most representative, the physical scientists. Between the two a gulf of mutual incomprehension—sometimes (particularly among the young) hostility and dislike, but most of all lack of understanding....
>
> The non-scientists have a rooted impression that the scientists are shallowly optimistic, unaware of man's condition ... the scientists believe that the literary intellectuals are totally lacking in foresight ... the scientific culture really is a culture, not only in an intellectual but also in an anthropological sense. That is, its members need not ... always completely understand each other ... but there are common attitudes, common standards and patterns of behaviour, common approaches and assumptions ... the pole of total incomprehension of science radiates its influence on all the rest [of society and culture and] gives an unscientific flavour to the whole "traditional" culture, and that unscientific flavour is often, much more than we admit, on the point of turning anti-scientific.[2]

Snow's lecture set out to show that this gulf between two cultures was not merely an obstacle to scientific progress but even represented a threat to the survival of western civilization.

Snow argued that, though bringing these two cultures together seemed an impossible task, the attempt should still be made. Today it seems that little progress—and sometimes even less effort—has been made in uniting these cultures. Human thought and experience are increasingly fragmented; and the humanities and the sciences are separated by a large gulf—a gulf of vocabulary, methods, and values. George and I made it our goal to bring these cultures together at the undergraduate level through courses that not only educate participants of each culture in the other's concepts, but also through a literature or a process which can be appreciated by both, even if on different levels and addressing different needs.

It is difficult for faculty to cross it, but some do in their later years as they finally see the unity of humankind. It is more important, indeed critical, that that gulf be made small in the younger minds. A small opening can be easily leaped across, while a large gulf, widened over many years, is often impossible to span. Certainly communication is part of the answer—discussions on what are the common denominators of humanity are useful.

Unfortunately the problem elucidated by Snow is still with us. In 2009, the 50th anniversary of Snow's talk, Lawrence M. Krauss, writing in *Scientific American*, reviewed what had been done to bring both cultures together, found that actually nothing had been done and, if anything, the divide still existed and was widening.[3]

George and I worked to bring the two cultures together via sf. First we tried to obtain a grant from UCR's Center for Ideas. Our idea was to run a year-long endeavor with invited speakers, symposiums, local meetings, and mini-courses. We requested the funding of this proposal in order to establish a multi-year project for understanding and addressing the differences between scientific and humanistic views. The primary purpose of this project was to be to bring together a diverse group of people and disciplines in order to formulate a basic set of questions concerning various ways the sciences and humanities perceive and conceive the world. The result of formulating questions and setting forth tentative answers to these questions would be the beginning of a formal dialogue between the sciences and humanities. It was a failure because evidently ideas could only come from those in humanities, since that was where the Center was housed. Proving Snow and us correct but doing little to bridge the gap, they maintained their "purity of humanities."

However, as we said in our grant, "It [a series of discussions between scientists and humanists] cannot stop with only faculty. The students must be brought into the discussions. The young must be exposed to the problem of the two cultures and understand why it exists. Then the young can be shown that we all are part of the same society. Ideas and problems come from both cultures and both cultures must be part of the solutions of those problems. An educated person cannot be only one cultured. Thus, both the scientist must appreciate all of the humanist portion of society and the humanist must appreciate all of the scientific portion of society. We cannot have half trained students, no matter what their culture may be."

Hewlett Grant in the College of Humanities, Social Sciences, and Arts

Refusing to give in, we then put a successful proposal for the Hewlett Grant, run by same College of Humanities. But here our proposal was for a course, not a mixed approach.

In 2001–2002, George and I ran a new course (HASS 23 at UCR) that combined science fiction and hard science, which was a segment of the year-long multidisciplinary Hewlett Cluster sequence "Bridging the Two Cultures: Science and the Humanities through Speculative Fiction." Two segments on the physical and biological sciences would have been of interest to a large body of students on campus, including those in premed, physical science, philosophy, English, and history. Participating faculty and teaching assistants would be involved in all three segments of this year-long course, and hence could encourage students to make connections with material introduced in earlier courses. This in turn would link parallel issues in the physical and biological sciences, and further connect those issues with the history of science in its broader cultural contexts.

It was to be an exploration of the concepts and development of the physical and biological science through the medium of science fiction stories. Sf stories introduce themes or problems which can only be understood in light of the fundamental concepts of physics, chemistry, and their technological extensions in engineering, medicine and other "applied sciences." The course would explore ways in which new scientific concepts and inventions interact with fundamental areas of human inquiry, such as ethics, religion, philosophy, and the arts. Science fiction was to be the "workshop" in which new ways of seeing the physical world were studied in terms of their impact on human beings and institutions, in their historical and mythical sense.

The course was to have been a full-year sequence of three quarters, each somewhat self-contained. Of course this would have been impossible since it would force redundancies. Yet a full year of sequenced sf, while good, would have been impossible for most students to take, due to limits upon total units for graduation and major requirements. We found that we had to have redundancy so that different students could take any quarter course.

The original concept was to be:

1. Historical linkage to sf. This was to be led by an engineer and a historian, with some lectures from a political scientist, an economist, or a pure scientist. It would combine the development of technology with the development of political and economic forces during the 19th century and the 20th century, concentrating on the flow of history and the topics of science fiction. Older science fiction stories would be linked to what was occurring during that particular time period. Alternate histories were to be used to explore early historical developments and how they could be changed by some alteration of technology and/or political thought.

2. Physical sciences in sf. This was to be led by a philosopher and physicist, with some lectures from a geophysicist, an astronomer, and a professor of comparative literature. The role of hard science fiction was to be investigated for understanding both philosophical and scientific thought, especially during the end of 19th century and the beginning of the 20th century. Concepts of the universe were to be described in terms of how humankind thought of them with respect to time travel (forward and reverse) and space travel (faster-than-light drive). Topics would include the types of worlds which may exist within the universe, how generation starships travel through space at near-light speeds, and how the terraforming of planets interrelates with ecology.

3. Biological sciences in sf. This was to be led by a biologist and a

professor of literature with some lectures from an engineer, a computer scientist, and/or professors of religion and philosophy. The discussions would center on the fundamental questions of what is alive and how is sentience measured and formed. Of special concern would be the mind and soul interaction from a religious point of view and how evolution aided the shape of their current interaction. Robots and artificial intelligence would be examined to understand human existence and the role that they may play in human civilization. The stories would center upon computers versus intelligent beings and nanomachines versus biological organisms for control of human diseases and evolution itself.

The course did not turn out to be exactly what we hoped. We could not find enough professors with free time to teach to be involved with the courses. The syllabus of the course in the original concept was too excessive to be fit into a single series of courses. Cuts were made and a three-quarter sequence was planned.

The first quarter was the physical sciences and sf run by George and me. It did center upon the universe as written in literature following Concept 2 above. The third quarter was the biological sciences, run again by George and me and followed Concept 3 above. Both Concept 2 and 3 were substantially cut because our choices of literature were too vast and we could not cover all of the proposed topics. The second quarter was turned over to another professor of languages and literature who gave a normal sf course reading classic literature.

Improving the Hewlett Course Concept

Unfortunately, the course did not work well, though not because of the topics or sequence. The students taking the course found it exciting and interesting. Several took both quarters and wanted more. However, the Hewlett concept demanded that we offer the course to only freshmen, some of whom did not have enough background to probe deeply into the segments. Students beginning college have a background of schooling, yet many have not been able to, or have not had the time, to develop critical analytical skills, even though high schools proclaim that they are now doing just that. Furthermore, most freshmen have not yet settled into a major. They say what they are majoring in but they have not yet really tried it. Many students have told me as a counselor or a Dean that "my mother wants me to be a doctor," or some variation on that statement. They are young. After several years they settle into a field in which they are comfortable. That is the time to branch out with thoughtful and logical discussions of other diverse fields.

More problematically, the course was made up of two major disciplines (corresponding to two major and competitive colleges); thus, the course had no focus according the campus reviewing agents. Therefore, no credit could be given for either discipline and so the course did not count towards graduation credit. The bridging of the "Two Cultures" was not very important compared with what course requirements had to be met. The solution to this problem seemed to demand rational and probably lengthy discussions with all campus agents to show them that it is important to bridge cultures, so such courses could be allowed as "countable" courses. It could be that for science students the course would count as a humanities course, and for humanities students it would count as a science course. In addition, the age-old university battles over who gets credit for student head count would have to be worked out, perhaps determined by the professor or professors who teach the course. Nonetheless, this is not a trivial problem, as George and I found out.

The Hewlett Course was also supposed to be an integrative and sequential series of courses. Based upon the above problems and the course loads of students, it would be impossible to offer a year-long sequence that the students must take. It would have been better to have a series of independent courses, a mix-and-match group, that could be taken in any order. This could allow a student to fill in with one course when they had time in their schedule. One course would give the "Hewlett Experience" to more students and would be better than nothing towards solving the "Two Cultures" problem.

Of course, as is usually the case when launching the "beta version" of any course, mistakes were made in terms of the speed of topics covered and how each lecture was run by two faculties from different disciplines. These errors could have easily been corrected. Yet the competitive nature of faculty on campus regarding courses could not allow corrections to be made.

Also the discussion and/or lectures should have been more strongly based upon reading, with fewer short stories and several novels. The fundamental discussion should have focused upon why it is a good story, how does it hold your attention, and how do the characters evolve with the plot. A counter-discussion of what is wrong with the story with regards to writing style, the philosophy expressed, fundamental scientific theories, and the future direction of science should also occur. In essence, we should have broached the concept of how the story could have been improved more rigorously. Other areas, from specific areas of science to history and creative writing, could have been solved by involving guest lecturers to explain their approach to the story. Such an approach was done, back in the late 1970s with Richard Wing (a chemist) and me (a biologist) jointly leading a discussion of Michael Crichton's *The Andromeda Strain* (1969).

Finally, technology has changed and improved greatly since we formulated our course in 1999. We xeroxed our stories and articles and had them bound into a hard-copy by the bookstore, which took care of the possible copyright problems. The book was large, expensive, and quite variable with regards to the presentation of each story. New technology would allow stories online (from the internet or previously scanned and stored) and movies could be streamed over the internet with the establishment of chat-rooms for students. This would also allow a better monitoring of who actually read the stories and what they really thought of them.

After the Hewlett Course

Before the retirement of both of us (in 2007 and 2008), we worked together on graduate courses, run out of the Department of Languages and Literature. Those courses, by nature, are more casual and more fun. As they were populated by graduate students of the humanities, not merely those of Languages and Literature, with little background in sciences, I became more active with discussions of basic science and current scientific investigations and thoughts. We used many of the short stories that we found during the Hewlett Course but did not follow the Hewlett Course outline. George became more interested in historical and non–Anglophone sf stories such as "The Horla" (1887), a short horror story written in the style of a journal by the French writer Guy de Maupassant. He turned more to investigations of the French world of horror and sf in his writings at the same time. After the work and problems that were associated with the Hewlett Program, he seemed to be retreating into his own topics. Furthermore, this was the time of his battle with cancer and I was his fill-in from time to time in "our" Courses. As luck would have it, my long association with George made it easy to follow him. For me, it was a breather outside of my science investigations (of avocado growth and production).

Conclusion

We have spoken in the abstract of two cultures. But society does not continue and progress in the abstract. Society has problems which must be solved by both cultures. How should agriculture use plants and animals for food and fiber? To feed the world we must use recombinant DNA technology, breeding, and nutritional protocols which may be "unnatural." Humanists who see us as part of the whole of life on Earth may not understand why we must use those protocols, but they certainly do not wish to see Third World cultures collapse from the want of food. How do we eliminate pollution of our lands and waters, yet maintain normal productivity in economic work so that the arts and literature can be supported? What is the place of humankind in a universe which is stranger than Newton's clockwork system and even more fearful to the individual psyche?

There is no doubt that increasingly all students must understand the full aspects of our society and what forces mold it. We should not have gaps in education; the classical and narrowly focused education of the past and currently offered will not best serve the future of humankind. Further each small piece of education (the course) must not *de facto* eliminate knowledge from other segments of education. Integration must be the key word for education.

Modern economic and business needs require both a concept of humanities (what is good for humans in terms of support for humanities) and a blend of science and humanities (technology versus humanity). It is an age-old question; just because you can do something, should you do it? Net neutrality, new transportation units (self-driving cars), exploration of outer space, and modification of humans by our own science are all looming problems which have not been broadly discussed. The current interaction between internet communication and the alteration of our political institutions was not discussed until it become a really obvious problem that now seems impossible to solve. And even now, with the problem obvious, the discussions are mostly shouting matches between polarized groups—groups ignorant of each other's defining foundation, precisely what Snow decried long ago.

Sf writers have been asked to meet with governmental officials to give new approaches to problems confronting civilization (such as the storage of radioactive waste for thousands of centuries).[4] Certainly one can use sf stories of the past to help gain new insight into future directions. Perhaps the Hewlett concept can be relaunched.

In the end, the Odd Couple did work well together, just as in Simon's original play. Yet I believe it is mainly due to our personalities, and it would not do to place just any two professors, especially from such distinct professions, together. Both must understand and respect what each has to offer. Both have to work together to blend their disciplines, as each discipline has very different methods of education. In my opinion, I had worked well with many in my College to jointly teach courses that were in both our areas. Yet there are academics who are very self-centered, believed that what they work on is the only important area of research and therefore it should be what is taught.

One of the Deans in my college once said, as I was trying to form some sort of a long-lasting connection between us and the other college, "yes, I also liked science fiction … when I was 12." For him science fiction was much like comic books; something you read before you were an adult. He could not see how the connection of science with humanities could be made through sf. He lacked vision, I thought, and that failure went into other of his endeavors.

The "Two Cultures" are alive and well, and they absolutely require some sort of a solution because most of the world's problems will require people with scientific and engineering knowledge to work seamlessly with people who understand and can express the ethics of, and heart and soul of, humanity. One can argue, as Snow did, that this division of civilization into two seemingly distinct groups of people will ultimately lead to major problems in our economy. The human problems of intolerance, food supply, war, and happiness, then, can only be addressed with a true blend of science and humanities.

NOTES

1. Gregory Benford, "Journey to the Genre's Core," *Vector*, No. 121 (1984), 23.

2. C.P. Snow, "The Two Cultures and the Scientific Revolution," 1959, *The Two Cultures* (Cambridge: Cambridge University Press, 2012), 3–5, 9, 11.

3. Lawrence M. Krauss, "Critical Mass: C.P. Snow in New York," *Scientific American*, 301:3 (September 2009), 32.

4. As discussed by Gregory Benford in a personal conversation in 2006, and in his book *Deep Time: How Humanity Communicates across Millennia* (New York: Avon Books, 1999).

Profiting from Prophecies

Science Fiction Scholars and Their Textbooks

GARY WESTFAHL

It was once believed that literary scholars should have absolutely no need to make money. Like other tenured professors, they enjoyed generous salaries enabling them to easily maintain a comfortable lifestyle, and unlike experts in other fields, their research usually involved nothing more than the careful perusal of freely available materials, so they had no need to scramble for grants or other types of financial support—except, perhaps, an occasional travel grant to gain access to elusive documents.

Today, of course, everything has changed. Tenured positions may not seem as lucrative as they once were, and it is no secret that even people who are making enough money are often keenly interested in making more money. Furthermore, it has become increasingly difficult to garner a tenured position, so aspiring professors routinely choose areas of specialization that advertising universities most frequently mention, and even market-savvy scholars may never find a full-time position, requiring them to eke out a living by teaching at multiple universities as lecturers, or even by taking jobs outside of academia and occasionally contributing to the critical literature as "Independent Scholars." In other words, many contemporary literary scholars probably have an intense desire to increase their income.

There are many ways they might do. Some science fiction scholars, for example, have dabbled in writing science fiction, written book reviews for newspapers and magazines, or worked as editorial consultants for publishing companies. However, the scholar's most respectable and most reliable mechanism for generating additional income is to write or edit a textbook. A typical university press book will sell only a few hundred copies at best, providing only minimal royalties, but a textbook that students are required to purchase for college classes across the nation might sell thousands of copies, and it might do so for several years or even decades. In addition, while university presses are increasingly selective in the critical studies that they choose to publish, a book that seems likely to become a widely adopted textbook will always be an attractive proposition; indeed, whenever I submit a book proposal to such a press, I am always asked to address the subject of whether the book might be employed as a textbook.

To be sure, professors can make eccentric choices when deciding which books to assign as textbooks, and virtually any sort of scholarly book about science fiction might occasionally appear on a course syllabus; thus, when I recently observed a huge and anomalous increase in sales for one critical anthology I had long ago edited with George Slusser, *Nursery Realms: Children in the Worlds of Science Fiction, Fantasy, and Horror* (1999), it was evident that some professor was employing it as a textbook. But there are two types of books that numerous professors might regularly assign to students in their science fiction classes, books that are clearly designed primarily to be textbooks: comprehensive anthologies of science fiction stories, and "handbooks" or "companions" consisting of scholarly essays on various aspects of science fiction. One does not need to survey thousands of college campuses to determine that, in contrast to earlier decades, there are now innumerable science fiction classes being offered; rather, one only has to look at the modern proliferation of such books prepared for classrooms to prove that there must be a significant market for such publications.

Without personally interviewing all of the editors who have worked on these books, one cannot say anything definitive about their motives, and one can charitably imagine an idealistic professor, dissatisfied with the quality of the available textbooks, altruistically resolving to develop her own textbook in order to offer her and others' students the best possible resource in coming to understand science fiction. However, there are reasons to believe that filthy lucre might also be a factor in their decisions. For one thing, some universities—like those that are part of the University of California—discourage professors from writing or editing textbooks, and refuse to count them as publications when making decisions about tenure and promotions. Thus, the royalties represent the only way that these sorts of books might benefit professors working for such institutions. Some of the books also include language aggressively promoting their contents as ideal for classroom use, suggesting the editors' desire to increase sales. In any event, while the individuals responsible for these anthologies and handbooks may or may not be interested in making money, the fact remains that in some cases their books have clearly generated significant profits for their editors, though in other cases they apparently have not, for reasons to be discussed.

Excluding anthologies devoted to particular topics, authors, or periods, science fiction anthologies might be generally divided into two categories: descriptive—endeavoring to portray the nature of the genre as it has been and is today—and prescriptive—aimed at promoting particular sorts of science fiction that the editors wish to identify as representing the direction science fiction should take in the future. For the purpose of teaching a science fiction class, one would imagine that descriptive anthologies would be most desirable, and surveying the history of these classroom anthologies does indicate that, as a rule, descriptive anthologies are likely to enjoy the most success.

As it happens, the first anthology to be widely used in science fiction classes—Robert Silverberg's *The Science Fiction Hall of Fame, Volume I* (1970)—could be accurately described as descriptive, though it was not primarily created to represent the genre and was not designed to be employed as a textbook. Rather, after establishing their Nebula Awards in 1965 to honor each year's best novel and short fiction, the members of the Science Fiction Writers of America (SFWA), who had not yet added "and Fantasy" to their name, decided that it would be fitting to recognize the most meritorious stories published before the Nebula Awards existed by compiling an anthology that would informally grant them retrospective Nebula Awards. Accordingly, the current members voted to select the best short stories and best novellas from those earlier times, and editors were assigned to compile anthologies of the highest ranking titles, though they were given the right to make minor adjustments and include a few stories that received fewer votes than other stories that were excluded. Only these decisions reflected specific concerns that the volume include all of the genre's major writers and thus best encapsulate the genre.[1] While Ben Bova's compilations of the most popular novellas—*The Science Fiction Hall of Fame, Volume IIA* and *Volume IIB* (both 1973)—never garnered much popularity, Silverberg's collection of short stories struck a number of pioneering instructors as the best available anthology for their classes, and at late as 1996, when the journal *Science Fiction Studies* conducted a survey of textbooks used in science fiction classes, it was the anthology most frequently assigned in those classes.[2]

It is easy to see why *The Science Fiction Hall of Fame, Volume I* proved so appealing to college professors like myself, who used the book as a required textbook in the occasional science fiction classes that I taught during the 1990s. Virtually all of the major science fiction writers active before 1960 were represented, and most of the included stories were widely acknowledged classics that had already been anthologized on numerous occasions. However, its limitations were obvious: writers who had almost universally written stories for American science fiction magazines had almost universally chosen stories that had originally appeared in American science fiction magazines, so there were no stories published before 1926—the year when the first science fiction magazine, *Amazing Stories*, appeared—and no stories by foreign-language writers; indeed, except for the British Arthur C. Clarke and Canadian A.E. van Vogt, all of the represented writers were American. The absence of any stories by H.G. Wells—who produced many memorable short stories during his first decade of work—is particularly striking (although Wells's *The Time Machine* [1895] was included—along with another venerable story from a British author, E.M. Forster's "The Machine Stops" [1909]—in Bova's anthologies of novellas). Further, since writers in the milieu of pulp magazines had been predominantly white and male, there were no stories by minority writers, and only two stories by women. Still, instructors could always add more diversity to their syllabuses in the novels they chose for their classes, and the anthology usefully provided a capsule history of the American tradition of magazine science fiction that virtually everyone would agree merited close attention; in fact, to analyze that tradition, John Huntington's critical study *Rationalizing Genius: Ideological Strategies in the Classic American Science Fiction Short Story* (1989) chose to focus exclusively on the stories in Silverberg's anthology.

Despite its virtues, however, it may have rankled professors in the 1970s that the book had not been edited by one of their own; Silverberg's anthology lacked the sorts of added pedagogical material—such as questions for discussion, possible topics for research papers, and a bibliography of useful resources—that anthologies designed for students typically include; and of course, there had been many fine stories published after 1964 that professors might want their students to read. So it was only to be expected that there would emerge anthologies edited by academics that were specifically designed for use in the classroom. The surprising thing is that the first book of this kind—Sylvia Z. Brodkin and Elizabeth J. Pearson's *Science Fiction* (1973)—was aimed exclusively at high school English classes, and it was edited by two high school teachers who had assembled similar high school anthologies of plays and essays but had no background in science fiction. Online commentators have recalled using the book in their high school classes, and the appearance of a second edition in 1979 also indicates that it had been employed in numerous classrooms; but the book remained entirely unknown to the larger science fiction community. (I recently became aware of it solely because, while researching the bibliography of my book *Arthur C. Clarke* [2018], I found a reference to a Clarke interview that the editors had republished in the revised edition.)

Considered as an introduction to science fiction, the book is not impressive; about half of the stories are defensible but not ideal choices to represent the genre and its major authors, such as Stephen Vincent Benét's "By the Waters of Babylon" (1937), Robert A. Heinlein's "'—And He Built a Crooked

House'" (1941), A.E. van Vogt's "The Enchanted Village" (1950), Isaac Asimov's "Green Patches" (1950), and two of Ray Bradbury's and Clarke's better stories. But the rest of the book is filled with forgettable stories from minor authors and, oddly, 15 science fiction poems and an Asimov essay; the revised version adds a second essay and the aforementioned Clarke interview. Even if college instructors had been aware of the book, it seems unlikely that any of them would have preferred this spotty collection to Silverberg's anthology. But high school textbooks are selected not by individual instructors but by senior administrators, who in the 1970s almost surely knew nothing about science fiction but were willing to adopt the book because it came from a well-known publisher and experienced editors who could be trusted to include no stories that some parents might find objectionable.

One year later, as it happens, three academics who were far more knowledgeable about science fiction—two college professors in Wisconsin, Martin Harry Greenberg and Patricia S. Warrick, and a college administrator in Florida, Joseph D. Olander—decided to team up to edit a series of anthologies that would be suitable for use in college classrooms. Collectively, these editors and additional collaborators produced fifteen volumes in what is described by the online Encyclopedia of Science Fiction as the "Through Science Fiction" series. It may surprise some contemporary science fiction scholars, accustomed to the now-supportive attitudes they encounter regarding their field of study, that their anthologies were not designed for classes in literature departments, but rather for classes in other disciplines of the humanities and social sciences. Their plan reflected the simple fact that at the time, with rare exceptions, departments of literature simply did not want to offer classes in science fiction, believing that the genre did not merit their students' attention. Beleaguered science fiction scholars then developed a strategy that I heard articulated by legendary scholar Thomas D. Clareson when I served with him on a panel at the 1990 Science Fiction Research Association (SFRA) Conference about "The Future of Science Fiction in Academia": since there were few classes explicitly devoted to science fiction, he explained, works in the genre must be "smuggled in" to other sorts of classes where they ostensibly did not belong.[3] So, if English and foreign language professors were not being permitted to teach science fiction, the reasoning of these editors went, it might be possible to persuade professors in other fields like psychology and sociology, seeking some new way to interest students in their subjects, to assign an anthology of science fiction stories that were relevant to their discipline.

The first anthology that Greenberg and Warrick edited, *Political Science Fiction: An Introductory Reader* (1974), was perhaps most explicit in articulating its pedagogical agenda. Its "Preface" explains that

> The student who encounters political theory only in a textbook tends to see it as already determined, fixed, and static.... This book offers an additional approach.... The student is asked to participate in the inductive thinking that yields generalizations by examining these particulars and abstracting the elements that will allow him to formulate the concepts functioning in the story. He is asked to become an active learner rather than a passive learner.[4]

Language clearly designed to persuade government professors to employ the anthology as a textbook also dominates their "Introduction":

> The ways in which science fiction can be effective as a device for studying the concepts of political science become immediately apparent ... when the resultant theories are studied, it is not always easy for the student to relate them back to his world and see them functioning. Here the science fiction story, because it usually isolates and handles only one theme, functions well as a means of illustrating concepts not readily discernible in society.... Science fiction can focus the attention of the student and teacher of political science on the future course of political life, enriching our awareness of the alternatives that may be available [4, 5, 8].

To further emphasize the educational value of the included stories, each of the anthology's six sections concludes with a bibliography of nonfictional studies of political science, entitled "For Further Reading"; bibliographies of this kind are also found in several of their later titles.

Similar arguments about the pedagogical effectiveness of science fiction appear in other books in the series. The dust jacket of Greenberg, Joseph D. Olander, Warrick, and John W. Milstead's *Sociology Through Science Fiction* (1974) announces that "This exciting new anthology uses contemporary science fiction to add a fresh new dimension to the study of sociology," and the editors' "Introduction" notes that "To the development of sociological consciousness, or sociological imagination, science fiction is particularly well suited."[5] The "Introduction" to Greenberg, Olander, and Warrick's *School and Society Through Science Fiction* (1974) maintains that "Science fiction can contribute to this study [of school and society] in several distinct ways.... By depicting the potential development of trends in society today and by conceptualizing alternatives to those trends, science fiction offers the student of school and society a methodological tool by which man and his relationships—actual and possible—can be studied."[6] The "Preface" to Greenberg, Olander, and Warrick's *American Government Through Science Fiction* (1974) improbably asserts that the "purposes" of the book include

> 1. enabling the student to describe, explain, and evaluate American government and politics on the basis of fiction;
> 2. familiarizing the student with a selected number of science fiction writers whose work contains rich insight into political processes;
> 3. encouraging the student to exercise the powers of his imagination in relation to a serious analysis of American government.[7]

The "Introduction" to Val Clear, Greenberg, Olander, and Warrick's *Marriage and the Family Through Science Fiction* (1976) states that "There are several ways in which science fiction effectively augments conventional marriage and family textbooks…. Since the student generation of today will be making decisions and setting patterns a few years hence, it is appropriate to encourage students to use their imaginations as experimental laboratories in which to create new alternatives and weigh suggestions."[8] And the "Introduction" to Greenberg and Olander's *Criminal Justice Through Science Fiction* (1977) claims that "Since criminal justice is an important human activity involving socially significant institutions, is an increasingly serious public policy area in need of continuing analysis and criticism, and is an integral part of our civilization that is undergoing rapid change, the appropriateness of science fiction for the study of criminal justice becomes evident"; speaks enthusiastically about "the conceptual richness and the theoretical insights that can be developed about criminal justice from the literature of science fiction"; and goes to describe five "specific reasons for the use of science fiction in the study and teaching of criminal justice."[9]

Another of the early anthologies in the series, *Anthropology Through Science Fiction* (1974, edited by Greenberg, Warrick, and Carol Mason), also asserts the educational values of its contents in its "Introduction": "It is only natural that science fiction should be used as a vehicle to explore some of the ideas of anthropology."[10] Yet its "Preface" includes what amounts to an apology for its inclusion of section introductions and suggestions for further reading: "Such pedagogical apparatus, however, is meant merely to point in useful directions; it should never stand between the reader and the stories themselves. For we believe that, more often than not, it is a genuine impulse to exploration and discovery that motivates students to choose courses in anthropology, and we very much hope that students will find their experience with the imagined cultures presented here just as fascinating, challenging, and stimulating as we have" (v). It is possible to read this passage as a suggestion that students ignore all the ancillary material and simply focus on enjoying the stories; perhaps one or more of the editors were already having second thoughts about the wisdom of burdening science fiction stories with introductory language and bibliographies endeavoring to recast them as lessons.

In any event, despite such strenuous efforts to promote these books as essential additions to the college classroom, there are excellent reasons to suspect that they were only rarely employed as textbooks—with one exception. One first notes the way that the series kept moving from publisher to publisher, most probably because disappointing sales kept causing publishers to lose interest in these volumes. Second, whenever a textbook is successful, publishers usually rush to produce a second edition, so that students are obliged to purchase expensive new books instead of acquiring the less expensive used books that become widely available; yet only one book in this series—Greenberg, Warrick, and Harvey Katz's *Introductory Psychology Through Science Fiction* (1974)—generated a second edition (in 1977), with a new "Preface" indicating that it had indeed been employed by a number of psychology professors:

> We are gratified that professors in many excellent schools saw the expansive vistas that the use of science fiction for introductory psychology promised. We are happy that a whole new audience could experience the imagination and human understanding with which our authors fill their stories. We are pleased that our introductions and other editing contributions has [sic] enabled students to learn introductory psychology in a new and interesting way. Hopefully, students have been able to take with them a feel for the psychological problems of modern man today and tomorrow. Finally, we are excited over the fact that the level of acceptance of our first edition has warranted a second one.[11]

As to why this particular book sold so well in the academic market, a passage explaining the changes made in the Second Edition offers interesting clues: "We have had the benefit of using the book in introductory psychology classes, intuiting which stories worked better than others by student reactions as well as the constructive comments of our own critics and friends like Professor Charles Waugh" (vi). The editorial "we" in this sentence surely cannot be trusted; since they respectively taught in government and English departments, Greenberg and Warrick would not have been able to teach any "introductory psychology classes." Yet Katz was indeed a professor of psychology at Suffolk University, and he undoubtedly assigned his own textbook as frequently as possible. And Waugh was another psychology professor with an interest in science fiction who had met Greenberg in 1974 at a Boston science fiction convention, probably heard about the book from him, and needed no further encouragement to use the book in his own classes. And if they were each teaching hundreds of students each year, these two professors might have been able to generate enough sales to justify a new edition all by themselves.

Still, even if their other books were not becoming popular textbooks, the fact that Greenberg and various colleagues persisted in editing these volumes indicates that they were generating income for their editors, though they must have been purchased by general readers, not students mandated to purchase them for their classes. Indeed, there are indications that the editors were gradually shifting their focus to this other market, as the references to pedagogical goals in Greenberg, Olander, Warrick, and Milstead's *Social Problems Through Science Fiction* (1975) and Greenberg and Olander's *International Relations Through Science Fiction* (1978) are few and understated, and five of the later books in the series that I examined—Greenberg and Warrick's *The New Awareness: Religion Through Science Fiction* (1975), Greenberg, Olander, and Warrick's *Run to Starlight: Sports Through Science Fiction* (1975), Greenberg, Olander, and Ralph S. Clem's *The City: 2000 A.D.: Urban Life Through Science Fiction* (1976), Greenberg, Olander, and Clem's *No Room for Man: Population and the Future Through Science Fiction* (1979), and Greenberg, Olander, and Robert Silverberg's *Dawn of Time: Prehistory Through Science Fiction* (1980)—contain absolutely no language or extra features suggesting any use as a textbook. In fact, *The City: 2000 A.D.* was even published as a mass market paperback, virtually defining its intended audience as general readers.[12]

In the 1980s, Warrick only edited anthologies on a few occasions, focusing on a scholarly career that produced two books; but Greenberg and Olander must have reached two conclusions: they had a genuine talent for editing science fiction anthologies, and such volumes could provide them with significant profits by targeting science fiction readers, not instructors and students. Accordingly, the two men abandoned any interest in scholarly writing, made connections to major writers and publishers, and launched a career of editing innumerable science fiction anthologies for general readers, usually in collaboration with a major writer like Isaac Asimov, their old academic colleague Waugh, and/or various others. They thus lost interest in editing textbooks for college classes, having broken into a much more lucrative market.

Still, during the 1970s and 1980s, Greenberg and Olander would occasionally return to their roots by working on anthologies aimed at academia. One of these projects, edited by Greenberg, Olander, and Warrick, was interestingly the first anthology designed specifically for college classes in science fiction, co-sponsored by the SFWA and the SFRA: *Science Fiction: Contemporary Mythology: The SFWA-SFRA Anthology* (1978). However, despite the impressive endorsement of those two organizations and the knowledge and experience of its editors, the book proved to be very disappointing, largely because of the unwise decisions that governed how it was assembled.

In the first place, instead of merely endeavoring to select the very best science fiction stories available, the editors resolved to devote their anthology to illustrating what they termed ten "mythic patterns" in science fiction— Science Fiction Myths and Their Ambiguity, The Remarkable Adventure, Beyond Reality's Barriers: New Dimensions, Aliens, The Scientist, The Machine and the Robot, More Than Human: Androids, Cyborgs, and Others, The City, Utopias and Dystopias, and Apocalypse. A critical observer might immediately note that their list of "mythic patterns" was actually a strange and incomplete mixture of science fiction subgenres, characters, and settings, but the editors themselves were so thrilled by their taxonomy of science fiction that they blithely recommended in their "Introduction: Mythic Patterns" that instructors using the anthology "might in addition select a novel from each category. The reading of the essay, the short stories, and novel in each mythic pattern would give the student a good overall view of the ideas and literature of the science fiction genre."[13] Surely, one reason that the anthology failed was the indefensibility of the structure they were attempting to impose on both the genre and its classes, making it a peculiar but clear example of the prescriptive anthology.

Yet the larger problem was that, in the process of choosing a few stories that would best illustrate these "mythic patterns," editors might prefer inferior stories that best matched those "patterns" instead of superior stories that did not fit neatly into their categories. The most egregious example of this problem, perhaps, was that one "story" chosen to exemplify science fiction's "Utopias and Dystopias" was actually an excerpt from Hugo Gernsback's novel *Ralph 124C 41+: A Romance of the Year 2660* (1911–1912, 1925)—and even his most enthusiastic admirers would agree that this terrible writer had no business appearing in an anthology purportedly devoted to the very best that science fiction could offer. And many of the acknowledged classics that had appeared in Silverberg's anthology, like Isaac Asimov's "Nightfall" (1941) and Robert A. Heinlein's "The Roads Must Roll" (1940), could not be included because they were square pegs that could not be fit into the round holes that the editors had devised.

Next, for each of the ten sections, the editors recruited one science fiction author and one science fiction critic to write an introduction (though the introductions to two sections only had one author, and one introduction had three authors); the policy was reasonable, but the editors then proceeded to allow each team to actually select the stories that would appear in their section. The result was an anthology that effectively had nineteen different editors with highly varying degrees of expertise and experience in editing anthologies.

Finally, after the editors chose authors who seemed especially qualified to discuss each of their "mythic patterns"—presumably because they had characteristically addressed them in their own stories—the authors were advised that they were not allowed to select any of their own works. Thus, despite the fact that Isaac Asimov had undoubtedly written more admirable stories about robots than any other author, one of them could not be presented in the section he introduced on "The Machine and the Robot." And Frederik Pohl's "The Midas Plague" (1954), selected to appear in one of Bova's anthologies, might have been one good choice for the "Utopias and Dystopias" section—certainly, it was far superior to Gernsback's work—but Pohl was assigned to co-introduce that section so none of his stories could be included.

Thus, even though in their "Prefatory Comments" Pohl called the book "a useful teaching guide for any science fiction course, anywhere" (xi) and

Thomas D. Clareson said that it would "provide readers with a selection of some of the best science fiction written" (xiii), the overall quality of the anthology, compared to Silverberg's, seems very poor; indeed, the editors only chose two stories—John W. Campbell, Jr.'s "Twilight" (1934) and Fritz Leiber's "Coming Attraction" (1950)—that the science fiction writers had voted for. Of their other selections, in my view, only two of them, Robert Sheckley's "Specialist" (1953) and J.G. Ballard's "Billennium" (1961), might be credibly advanced as stories that members of the SFWA should have chosen. There are also a disproportionate number of stories from 1965 and thereafter, though only three of those stories—Ursula K. Le Guin's "Nine Lives" (1969), Poul Anderson's "Goat Song" (1972), and Larry Niven's "The Hole Man" (1974)—had won Hugo or Nebula Awards, further contributing to the sense that the genre's finest stories were not being presented in the collection.

One has to suspect that this anthology was not particularly popular among science fiction instructors because one decade later, instead of producing a second edition, Warrick, Greenberg, and Waugh assembled an entirely new anthology, *Science Fiction: The Science Fiction Research Association Anthology* (1988). This time, as announced in their "Preface," they decided to emulate the SFWA by asking their members "to nominate and select novelettes and short stories they wanted to appear in a definitive anthology. The 26 stories in this book are the result."[14] Still, instead of simply asking those members to choose their favorites, the editors put their thumbs on the scales "for the purpose of historical perspective" (ix). After compiling a list of "the 75 stories most frequently mentioned" in the original survey, "for the final ballot" they divided them into three categories—before 1926, 1926–1970, and 1971–1979—and the members were told to "vote[ ] for 3 of the 10 stories in the first era, for 20 of 55 stories in the second era, and for 3 of 10 stories in the third era" (ix). They also exercised some "editorial discretion" (x): since "Many respondents suggested reducing potential overlap with the first three *Science Fiction Hall of Fame* anthologies ... we decided to limit ourselves to no more than four stories from the first volume (of a total of 26 stories) and no more than one from each of the other anthologies (containing eleven stories each)"; the editors also did some additional "fiddling" with the results (x). Imposing such arbitrary chronological restrictions undoubtedly distorted some of the results; perhaps, for example, six of the earlier stories actually merited inclusion, and their inclusion would have made the book a stimulating alternative to Silverberg's anthology, which had no stories from that era, but only three were allowed to appear in the anthology.

Still, one has to acknowledge that the overall result was an anthology that did a better job of representing science fiction, and it also offered some retrospective criticism of the earlier, more idiosyncratic 1978 anthology because the members' choices included only two stories—Cordwainer Smith's

"The Game of Rat and Dragon" (1955) and Le Guin's "Nine Lives"—that had appeared there. The editors also hit upon what might be regarded as an ingenious marketing device, as they recruited some noted science fiction scholars to write afterwords to each story, increasing the chances that those scholars would employ the book in their own science fiction classes. It is not surprising, then, that the 1988 anthology finished second to *The Science Fiction Hall of Fame, Volume I* in the 1996 survey, assigned in 36 classes, while Silverberg's anthology had been assigned in 42 classes.

Still, suggesting some lingering dissatisfaction with their 1978 and 1988 anthologies, the Science Fiction Research Association did try one more time to assemble a definitive anthology of science fiction, recruiting noted editor David G. Hartwell to team up with scholar Milton T. Wolf to edit *Visions of Wonder: The Science Fiction Research Association Anthology* (1996). To justify its existence, the editors' "Introduction" recast its predecessors—both designed to be comprehensive surveys of the genre's history—as volumes solely focused on their own decades: "The first two, in the 1970s and 1980s, each used by a generation of teachers, reflected the current concerns of SF and the SF field in those decades"; for that reason, as the book's dust jacket claimed, this anthology "was created to fill an urgent need for a thoughtful, readable classroom anthology that focuses on science fiction as it is today, in the 1990s."[15]

Surveying its contents, all one can say is that the book is bizarre: limiting itself to stories published after 1960 and emphasizing recent works, it intermingles acknowledged classics, obscure and sometimes forgettable stories from the previous decade, and random essays from several editors and critics that only imperfectly relate to the volume's other contents. As if to defend its peculiar contents, the "Introduction" acknowledges that "*Visions of Wonder* is, then, an unusual anthology of SF, a bit quirky, full of juxtapositions, intentionally off-center" (12). Bluntly, however, it is impossible to imagine that any knowledgeable instructor would consider such an inchoate anthology to represent a proper introduction to the genre, which would explain why it quickly vanished from sight, and probably why the SFRA collectively resolved to permanently remove itself from the business of overseeing and endorsing science fiction anthologies for the college classroom.

Prior to Greenberg, Warrick, and Olander's 1978 anthology, another college professor who was also a noted science fiction writer, James Gunn, had launched his own series of anthologies aimed at classrooms with *The Road to Science Fiction: From Gilgamesh to Wells* (1977), soon followed by *The Road to Science Fiction #2: From Wells to Heinlein* (1979), *The Road to Science Fiction #3: From Heinlein to Here* (1979), and *From Here to Forever* (1982). With his experience in both teaching and writing science fiction, Gunn seemed unusually well qualified to select material for students; his choices were consistently judicious, reflecting consensus opinions; he made an effort to include one work by every major science fiction writer, either a short story or an excerpt from a novel; and he preceded each selection with a brief and intelligent essay about the author. The problem with this effort to be comprehensive, of course, was that he could not offer professors what they would normally prefer for their classes, a single volume of stories, which would explain why none of these books appear in the *Science Fiction Studies* list of most frequently assigned anthologies. Still, suggesting that they had found favor in some circles, all four anthologies were republished at least once in the 1990s and 2000s, and while the book in the series that I reviewed, the 1996 republication of *The Road to Science Fiction #3: From Heinlein to Here*, contained no language regarding its use in classrooms, its back cover does present a telling quotation from *The Science Fiction & Fantasy Book Review*: "[T]he most valuable text/anthology for the instructor, regardless of the level."[16] Even as they remained in print, Gunn must have heard complaints that he had been insufficiently attentive to science fiction not originally published in America, because he added two additional volumes to the series, *The Road to Science Fiction Volume 5: The British Way* (1998) and *The Road to Science Fiction 6: Around the World* (1998).

Thus, by the early 1990s, college instructors teaching science fiction classes did have a few credible options in choosing anthologies of science fiction stories for their classrooms; yet one major publisher that specialized in publishing literary anthologies for college students—W.W. Norton—had not yet entered this market. It is at this time that George Slusser and I, very tangentially, become a part of this story, because at the time I vividly remembered all of the massive Norton anthologies I had purchased for my own literature classes and decided it was high time for that venerable company to add a science fiction anthology to its offerings. I accordingly prepared a detailed proposal for *The Norton Anthology of Science Fiction*; while I have not been able to locate a copy of this typewritten document, I recall that I strived to compile a proposed table of contents that was lengthy and comprehensive. Since I was virtually unknown in the early 1990s, I recruited Slusser, a colleague who was already renowned in the field, to serve as its ostensible lead editor, though he probably suspected (correctly) that it had little chance of success. As best I can recall, I was not primarily interested in the royalties that the book might provide, hoping instead that such a publication might finally inspire some university to hire me as a full-time, tenure-track professor, so I could be financially rewarded in another way; Slusser, who would be the beneficiary of a generous inheritance, was surely only motivated by his recurring desire to support the efforts of aspiring science fiction scholars. Thus, I can provide personal testimony that these projects are not always directly driven by a desire to make money, even if that is one easily anticipated result of their publication.

In response to our proposal, a Norton editor sent us a long and friendly letter praising the quality of our proposal but blandly stating that the project did not accord with their current plans. At the time, I suspect, they were already working with a more renowned editor—veteran author Ursula K. Le Guin—on the compilation that she and Brian Attebery would publish in 1993 as *The Norton Book of Science Fiction: North American Science Fiction, 1960–1990*. In fact, the first line of Le Guin's "Introduction" to that volume—"When the publisher invited me to edit this book…"—indicates that Norton specifically sought her out to perform the task of preparing their groundbreaking science fiction anthology.[17] More so than any other anthology yet published, this was clearly designed to become the definitive anthology for college science fiction classes; for as someone who sometimes taught such classes, I was one of undoubtedly innumerable scholars who received a mailed message offering to provide me with a complementary copy of the book for consideration as a possible textbook for my science fiction classes. (I declined the offer as a matter of principle, and still do not possess a copy of the book, because I knew from published descriptions that I would never assign it as a textbook in any of my classes.) Still, the book as published contained only one specific reference to that intended purpose—Le Guin's recommendation that readers concerned about defining science fiction "should obtain Brian Attebery's Teaching Guide to this volume" (21).

Based on any examination of its contents, there were two obvious problems with *The Norton Book of Science Fiction* as a textbook for science fiction classes. In the first place, its announced inclusion of only works published after 1960—on the grounds stated in Le Guin's introduction that this represented the era of the field's "maturity"—dubiously excluded any number of authors, ranging from icons like Edgar Allan Poe, Jules Verne, and H.G. Wells to science fiction's "Big Three" of Isaac Asimov, Arthur C. Clarke, and Robert A. Heinlein, whose classic short fiction mostly predated 1960, though Le Guin took pains to carefully defend that decision on these grounds:

> Without in the least dismissing or belittling earlier writers and work, I think it is fair to say that science fiction changed around 1960, and that the change tended towards an increase in the number of writers and readers, the breadth of subject, the depth of treatment, the sophistication of language and technique, and the political and literary consciousness of the writing [18].

Second, even within the time frame defined in the volume's subtitle, it was painfully evident that the editors were endeavoring to disproportionately represent female and minority writers and to deemphasize authors who were unfortunate enough to be white males, as persuasively demonstrated by a statistical analysis in one essay that criticized the anthology, Joseph D. Miller's "Popes or Tropes: Defining the Grails of Science Fiction" (2002).[18] As one egregious sign of editorial bias, the editors chose to ignore any number of award-winning stories by Harlan Ellison and instead represented his work with a story that had never been nominated for any awards—"Strange Wine" (1976)—presumably so that his superior stories would not outshine the female and minority writers that were included. Another prominent scholar, Slusser, attacked the anthology on similar grounds in "The Politically Correct Book of Science Fiction: Le Guin's Norton Collection" (1994), and he was surely not driven by any bitterness over the rejection of a competing proposal that he was only minimally involved in.[19] In sum, unusually for a volume aimed at a broad range of college professors, *The Norton Book of Science Fiction* was clearly a prescriptive anthology, not a descriptive anthology, as Le Guin effectively attempted to enlist college professors and students in a campaign to reshape the genre more to her liking; her introduction explicitly announced such a goal when she declared that "I wish science fiction were not as white as it is.... I wish science fiction were not as male as it is" (17). It was therefore unsurprising that the book met with harsh criticism, and that it ultimately failed in its obvious aim to become the default textbook for science fiction classes.

To be sure, one cannot say that Le Guin and Attebery's volume was a complete failure, since the aforementioned survey listed it as the third-most frequently assigned anthology in college classes—yet with 25 mentions, it fell significantly behind two other, more comprehensive anthologies that had been published earlier. Another sign of its relative unpopularity is that, in contrast to other Norton anthologies, there was never a second edition of *The Norton Book of Science Fiction*. I vaguely recall reading a Le Guin interview in which she attributed this to the fact that Attebery had conveyed his interest in preparing such a second edition while she had declined to participate; yet surely, if Norton had expressed a keen desire for a second edition, Attebery could have done the necessary work of updating and expanding the volume without Le Guin's active participation. One has to conclude that the executives at Norton were disappointed by the volume's sales and therefore had no incentive to produce a new version of the anthology. The lesson to be learned for subsequent anthologists aiming at the college classroom, then, is that they should respect consensus opinions about the genre's nature and classic stories, rather than being governed by the personal opinions of one famous editor.

Around the time that *The Norton Book of Science Fiction* was making a conspicuous effort to establish itself as a textbook, another major publisher, Oxford University Press, offered its own anthologies as additional alternatives: *The Oxford Book of Science Fiction Stories* (1992) and *The Oxford Book of Fantasy Stories* (1994), both edited by Tom Shippey. The first volume contains only two muted references to its possible use as a textbook: the dust jacket statement that it is an "outstanding anthology that will appeal to established science fiction readers as well as to students and other readers coming to the form for the first time," and a concluding comment in Shippey's "Introduction" that "Over the years, and entirely by their own efforts, its authors have created the devoted and participatory readership which, collectively, they deserve. I hope this anthology may help to make that achievement more widely recognized and, in institutions of literary education, more sympathetically, but more analytically, understood."[20] Shippey's science fiction anthology was also a prescriptive anthology, although of a more idiosyncratic nature than Le Guin and Attebery's espousal of a more diverse genre. For as he explained at length in a paper first presented in 1994 that discussed that anthology, Shippey had developed the theory that science fiction, in contrast to pastoral literature that celebrated the simple pleasures of rustic living, was a form of what he termed *fabril literature*, dedicated to "makers" who constructed artifacts and machines, and he freely admitted that he had chosen some stories because they best illustrated that thesis.[21] The result was yet another anthology that did not seem to be presenting the very best that the genre had to offer. Though Shippey did include some acknowledged classics, like Stanley G. Weinbaum's "A Martian Odyssey" (1933), Ballard's "Billennium," Cordwainer Smith's "The Ballad of Lost C'Mell" (1962), James Tiptree, Jr.'s "The Screwfly Solution" (1977), and William Gibson's "Burning Chrome" (1982), his other choices were generally less defensible. Few would argue, for example, that "The Land Ironclads" (1903) was Wells's best story; instead of Campbell's renowned "Twilight" (1934), Shippey included its less esteemed sequel "Night" (1935); and Le Guin was strangely represented by one of her obscure early stories, "Semley's Necklace" (1964). Shippey also excluded a number of major authors ranging from Robert A. Heinlein and Isaac Asimov to Harlan Ellison and Octavia E. Butler. All things considered, it is not surprising that by 1996, the book only ranked seventh in the *Science Fiction Studies* survey, chosen by only eight instructors, and as was the case with *The Norton Book of Science Fiction*, there never appeared a second edition, further evidence of its relative unpopularity.

Norton's and Oxford's apparent lack of success in conquering this market may have made competing publishers reluctant to offer their own entries in the competition, fearing that their sales would also fall short of expectations. But in the years after Le Guin and Attebery's anthology appeared, there had emerged an obvious need for new science fiction anthologies designed for the classroom. There were more science fiction classes than ever, as young scholars rushed into a field that was now emerging as a marketable specialty in seeking a tenure-track position, and their interests were different from those of their precursors: they were no longer impressed by long-admired stories like Lester del Rey's "Helen O'Loy" (1938) and Tom Godwin's "The

Cold Equations" (1954), both included in Silverberg's anthology, and they wanted to focus their attention on more recent science fiction from outside the magazine tradition, especially ethnically diverse and international writers. Signs of such a generational shift were evident even in 1996, as the less frequently assigned anthologies listed in *Science Fiction Studies*'s survey included Bruce Sterling's compilation of cyberpunk stories from the 1980s, *Mirrorshades: The Cyberpunk Anthology* (1986), chosen by 22 instructors; Pamela Sargent's collection of science fiction stories by women, *Women of Wonder* (1975), chosen by ten instructors; and what was at the time the most recent edition of Gardner Dozois's annual anthologies of the best science fiction stories of the year, *The Year's Best Science Fiction: Eleventh Annual Edition* (1994), chosen by ten instructors. Professors during the decade after the survey were undoubtedly making similar choices; in my own case, seeking to appeal to my young students with more recent material, I began in classes after 2000 to use Pat Cadigan's anthology *The Ultimate Cyberpunk* (2002), which I found appealing because, unlike *Mirrorshades*, it include some meritorious stories published before 1980 that were arguably precursors of cyberpunk as well as stories that had first appeared after Sterling's anthology.

The next science fiction anthology specifically designed for the classroom, Garyn G. Roberts's *The Prentice Hall Anthology of Science Fiction and Fantasy* (2000), came from a prestigious publisher, but it was burdened by one obvious liability: while its editor Roberts had some background in popular culture, he had mostly written about detective fiction, displaying a particular interest in Chester Gould's comic strip detective Dick Tracy; he thus had no demonstrable expertise in science fiction, and his name was entirely unknown to scholars in the field (like myself). Indeed, the online Science Fiction and Fantasy Research Database lists only three minor Roberts publications related to science fiction prior to the publication of his anthology. There are subtle indications of Roberts's lack of familiarity with science fiction: his "Preface" consistently capitalizes "Science Fiction" and "Fantasy," a practice found nowhere else in the critical literature; displaying a peculiar fastitiousness about rendering authors' names completely and correctly, the table of contents incorrectly renders the real name of Hal Clement—Harry Clement Stubbs (for that was literally his name, like Harry S Truman)—as "Henry Clement Stubbs"; and no one would with experience in the field would ever refer to William Gibson's groundbreaking story "Johnny Mnemonic" (1981) as "Johnny Neumonic."[22]

Suggesting that his research into the field's scholarship was incomplete, he provides these examples of "the best scholars of Fantasy and Science Fiction of all time": E.F. Bleiler, August Derleth, and Sam Moskowitz. Yet while all three men did make substantive contributions to science fiction research, anyone relying primarily on their work as sources would obtain a rather odd and incomplete picture of science fiction, and the absence of references to any more recent scholars with an academic background is striking.

As for the stories he chose for the anthology, there seemed to be an inordinate number of late nineteenth- and early twentieth-century stories (perhaps because they were in the public domain and hence required no expense to republish); reflecting his background, Roberts's historical surveys tend to emphasize the general history of popular literature more than the specific histories of science fiction and fantasy; many of the genre's classic stories were conspicuously absent; and the stories he chose to represent major authors sometimes were manifestly inferior to others they had written, such as Asimov's "Robbie" (1940) and Heinlein's "The Long Watch" (1949), which absolutely no one would consider their authors' best works. In its favor, the book did feature an introduction by veteran science fiction author Jack Williamson, who graciously opined that "This may be the best one-volume library of science fiction that I have seen" (xi); a republished Sam Moskowitz essay on "How Science Fiction Got Its Name" (1957); and reproductions of several pieces of artwork that had accompanied the original publication of some stories. Overall, though, pondering its erratic selections, I never would have considered this volume as a textbook for any of my classes, and all one can say in Roberts's defense is that he seemed to be working reasonably hard to properly epitomize a form of fiction that he was not particularly knowledgeable about. One's major complaint, then, is not that Roberts did an inadequate job, but rather that Prentice Hall hired him to do this job in the first place. In any event, as in other cases, the absence of a second edition suggests that Roberts's volume never became widely popular among college science fiction professors.

In stark contrast is another anthology intended for college classrooms, *The Wesleyan Anthology of Science Fiction* (2010). Its six editors—Arthur B. Evans, Istvan Csiscery-Ronay, Jr., Joan Gordon, Veronica Hollinger, Rob Latham, and Carol McGuirk, then the editors of the field's most prestigious journal, *Science Fiction Studies*—were undeniably qualified for this task, and I can personally testify that, as the "Introduction" states, lead editor Evans did solicit "many suggestions from our colleagues" (though my own recommendations were ignored, as perhaps is to be expected).[23] The book's pedagogical intention was explicitly announced: "It reflects … a consensus among us that a good anthology should … represent both the best and—not always the same thing—the most teachable stories in the field…. This anthology was created for the purpose of teaching sf at many levels" (xi, xviii). The stories the book included are generally exemplary, clearly representing widely shared opinions about the best that science fiction has to offer, and I was happy to assign the book as a required textbook in the classes I taught from 2012 to 2017. Further, while its stories are presented in chronological order, so as to provide a sort of historical survey, the book also has a thematic table of contents, and materials in its Teacher's Guide (available online) offered all the pedagogical support that an instructor might ask for. Granted, the suggested questions in its Guide were not always ideal, but I have never relied on such material in seeking student responses to stories, and I generally found that its stories both sufficiently represented the genre and provided solid bases for classroom discussions. To this day, although I am not currently teaching any science fiction classes, I consider *The Wesleyan Anthology* an excellent textbook for such classes, perhaps the best one ever assembled. My positive response to this anthology is not unique, since lead editor Evans has reported in a private message that its sales have been "averaging between 2500 and 3500 copies per year," and he guesses that it is being employed in "at least a couple of dozen universities in the U.S. and Canada, probably more."[24]

Given the proliferation of science fiction classes, it might seem surprising that there have not been greater numbers of recent anthologies aimed at that market. Before offering possible reasons why they have not been appearing, though, I first must briefly discuss the other type of book that scholars assemble as a potential textbook, the handbook or companion.

There is a long tradition of such books, devoted to various forms of literature and other topics, and they generally follow this format: an expert editor or editors recruit experienced scholars to write essays about various aspects of the subject to assist students in understanding primary texts. The first one devoted to science fiction, Edward James and Farah Mendlesohn's *The Cambridge Companion to Science Fiction*, was published in 2003; since then, several others focused on the genre have appeared or have been announced as future publications. I was asked to contribute to four of these volumes: *The Cambridge Companion to Science Fiction*, David Seed's *A Companion to Science Fiction* (2005), Rob Latham's *The Oxford Handbook of Science Fiction* (2014), and Eric Carl Link and Gerry Canavan's *The Cambridge Companion to American Science Fiction* (2015).[25] I was not asked to contribute to two others—Mark Bould, Andrew M. Butler, Adam Roberts, and Sherryl Vint's *The Routledge Companion to Science Fiction* (2009) and Nick Hubble and Aris Mousoutzanis's *The Science Fiction Handbook* (2014)—and I also did not contribute to two related volumes—James and Mendlesohn's *The Cambridge Companion to Fantasy Literature* (2012) and Mark J.P. Wolf's *The Routledge Companion to Imaginary Worlds* (2017). I have been privately informed about two other forthcoming volumes about science fiction that will also not include my work, and there may be others that have already been published or are now being prepared. The fact that publishers have kept producing these science fiction handbooks and companions suggests that they are proving profitable, and in a private message co-editor Mendlesohn reported that, as of 2019, *The Cambridge Companion to Science Fiction* had sold almost 9000 copies, making it one of Cambridge's top-selling companions.[26]

One obvious question to ask about these handbooks is why they are edited collections featuring numerous contributors instead of books entirely authored by one or a few respected scholars. After all, surveying the names of the editors of the listed handbooks, they have (with the exceptions of Hubble, Mousoutzanis, and Wolf, whom I had never heard of) published extensively about a wide variety of science fiction texts and subjects, and they seem capable of writing a textbook about science fiction entirely by themselves (a few of them, like Roberts and Vint, have actually done so); such an authored volume, planned and written entirely by one person or a small team, would further seem more likely to prove genuinely comprehensive, lacking the gaps or overlapping analyses that almost invariably appear in a book with multiple authors. Indeed, I deliberately neglected to mention another handbook, M. Keith Booker and Anne-Marie Thomas's *The Science Fiction Handbook* (2009), precisely because it broke the mold in being authored solely by one veteran scholar and a younger colleague, demonstrating that a credible handbook can be produced in this manner.

From one perspective, of course, recruiting a number of credible scholars is only sensible: different experts have different specialties, and one would presumably get the very best information and insights on a given topic from someone who has already researched and published in one particular area. In my own case, I had already written, sometimes at great length, on the four subjects that I was asked to address in handbooks (space opera, hard science fiction, the science fiction marketplace, and the development of American science fiction) and thus could properly be considered especially qualified to deal with them again. Yet this policy also creates problems: asked to write about something that they have already written about, scholars are necessarily tempted—perhaps even compelled—to simply repeat what they have said before, so that a considerable amount of authorial and editorial energy is being devoted to the task of simply presenting regurgitations of facts and ideas that are already available in print. In writing my own four essays, I always did some additional research and strived to come up with new things to say, but it remains true that some equally qualified scholar with less experience in those fields might have offered a fresher perspective and thus made a more substantive contribution to the scholarly literature on science fiction as a whole.

If enlisting dozens of experts to collectively address science fiction is not necessarily the best policy as a matter of principle, though, the practice can be defended on cynical grounds. When publishers market these books, it is helpful to emphasize that numerous renowned scholars are among its contributors, and listing their names might attract customers who are not familiar with the editors but recognize the names of some contributors. Yet there is an even more cynical reason why multiple contributors to such volumes may be preferred. After all, prominent science fiction scholars are likely to also teach science fiction classes on a regular basis, and they might be especially inclined to assign books that they have contributed to as textbooks. So, making conservative estimates, one might assume that a given handbook has ten contributors who each teach one science fiction class a year with about fifty students; further suppose that five of them decide to assign the handbook as a required text. The result would be 250 copies sold in a given year, a figure that would impress any scholarly press struggling to profit from dwindling sales to university libraries and general readers.

For the record, however, I myself never assigned any of the handbooks I contributed to as a course textbook, and the reason I did not is also the reason why both anthologies of science fiction and handbooks for college classes may be becoming less common: for I was able to assemble and employ my own textbook.

In the past, only a limited number of instructors had the ability to put together textbooks for their own classes, because getting published was difficult, and the process of obtaining permission to republish stories and essays was complex. Today, this is no longer the case. At most universities, instructors can assemble all of the stories and/or essays that they want their students to read and send them to their bookstores; usually working with an outside publisher, the bookstores then contact copyright holders to determine how much they will charge for limited republications of their works, add up the sums and the costs of publication to determine a price, and print the resulting collection as a required course "packet." Instructors can also charge their students a royalty for each packet sold, an amount which may be dictated by the bookstore or chosen by the instructor. What this means is that, as a matter of pedagogy, college instructors no longer have to depend on the judgments of the editors of particular books; instead, they can chose for themselves the stories and essays that they believe will best instruct their students about the nature of science fiction.[27] And, as a matter of income, they can consistently receive at least a few hundred dollars each semester by creating, and requiring their students to purchase, their own packets.

For my own classes at the University of La Verne, as noted, I relied upon *The Wesleyan Anthology* to provide my students with excellent science fiction stories to read, but recognizing that I had written a growing number of mostly unpublished essays aimed at general readers which addressed aspects of those stories, I assembled them into a packet, entitled Wonderful Worlds: Essays on the Tropes of Science Fiction, added some handouts on writing, and had it printed as a required textbook that students had to read and reference in their own essays. And yes, I did add a royalty to its purchase price, not feeling guilty at all because the resulting price was still far less than what students would have had to pay for a collection of essays in a handbook from a scholarly press.[28]

This practice, while in part diminishing the income of academic publishers who might otherwise sell their books to students, does at least occasionally compensate them for republications of excerpts from their works; yet a cursory survey of recent science fiction syllabuses indicates that some instructors are avoiding such expenses altogether by the strategy of posting texts on Blackboard and similar classroom websites, protected from paying for their use because only students in their classes can access these texts, and because policing such postings for copyright violations is virtually impossible. In the age of the internet, such postings will probably become the system preferred over the printing of packets, since it diminishes the money students must pay to attend classes even as it also diminishes the income that should properly be earned by authors and publishers. It also diminishes the income of instructors, who cannot profit from the materials that they post online, but some may prefer to make their classes as inexpensive as possible for students in an era when student debt represents an ever-increasing problem.

Overall, pondering the future of science fiction pedagogy and its practitioners, one can observe both positive and negative trends. On one hand, given all of the issues that they must deal with today, it is hard to object to any system that provides science fiction scholars with additional income, whether it comes from editing published anthologies and handbooks for broad audiences or assembling unique anthologies and handbooks for their own classes. One might also celebrate the democratization of this process: in the past, only a few prominent scholars could publish and profit from publications of such books, but today, virtually any college instructor can do so.

On the other hand, anthologies and handbooks edited by experts may have their deficiencies but they usually represent consensus opinions about science fiction that students should arguably be exposed to; yet contemporary students purchasing an instructor's packet or visiting a course website can be absorbing idiosyncratic viewpoints that may not benefit them if they pursue an interest in science fiction. Yet a variety of opinions is generally superior to a viewpoint imposed from above, so the genre may ultimately benefit from the diverse perspectives on the genre that are increasingly emerging from these college classes.

NOTES

1. After Robert Silverberg's "Introduction" to *The Science Fiction Hall of Fame* (later retitled *The Science Fiction Hall of Fame, Volume I* [1970; New York: Avon Books, 1971]), explained the voting process, he added this intriguing comment:

But there were some obvious injustices requiring remedies. One important and highly respected author had had four stories on the original ballot, including two from the same cycle. As a result of this competition with himself, no one of his stories finished within the top twenty, although the aggregate of his vote placed him well up among the leaders. Eliminating a man whose career had been so distinguished from a book of this nature seemed improper; and so I gave preference to one of his four stories over that of another writer whose only nominated piece had finished slightly higher on the list [xi].

As he confirmed in an email message sent to Gregory Benford on October 17, 2019, Silverberg was referring to Ray Bradbury, whose four stories on the ballot included two published in *The Martian Chronicles* (1950); the highest ranking of these, "Mars Is Heaven!" (1948), appeared in the anthology. Bradbury's novella "The Fireman" (1951) would have been included in Ben Bova's companion anthologies of outstanidng novellas but it was not available because Bradbury had expanded it as the novel *Fahrenheit 451* (1953).

2. Arthur B. Evans and R.D. Mullen, "North American College Courses in Science Fiction, Utopian Fiction, and Fantasy," *Science Fiction Studies*, 23:3 (November 1996), 437–528. The "Addenda" include a list of "The Books, Authors, and Films Most Frequently Assigned."

3. For a longer discussion of that panel, and my infuriated reaction to it, see Gary Westfahl, "A New Campaign for Science Fiction," *Extrapolation*, 33:1 (Spring, 1992), 6–23.

4. Martin Harry Greenberg and Patricia S. Warrick, editors, *Political Science Fiction: An Introductory Reader* (Englewood Cliffs, NJ: Prentice-Hall, 1974), ix–x. Page references are to this edition.

5. Greenberg, Joseph D. Olander, Warrick, and John W. Milstead, editors, *Sociology Through Science Fiction* (New York: St. Martin's Press, 1974), left dust jacket, xii.

6. Greenberg, Olander, and Warrick, editors, *School and Society Through Science Fiction* (Chicago: Rand-McNally, 1974), 3, 5.

7. Greenberg, Olander, and Warrick, editors *American Government Through Science Fiction* (Chicago: Rand-McNally, 1974), vii.

8. Val Clear, Greenberg, Olander, and Warrick, editors, *Marriage and the Family Through Science Fiction* (New York: St. Martin's Press, 1976), ix, xii–xiv.

9. Greenberg and Olander, editors, *Criminal Justice Through Science Fiction* (New York: Franklin Watts/New Viewpoints, 1977), xii, xiii, xiv.

10. Greenberg, Warrick, and Carol Mason, editors, *Anthropology Through Science Fiction* (New York: St. Martin's Press, 1974), ix. Page references are to this edition.

11. Greenberg, Warrick, and Harvey Katz, editors, *Introductory Psychology Through Science Fiction*, Second Edition (Chicago: Rand-McNally College Publishing, 1977), v. Page references are to this edition. The first edition was published by the same company in 1974.

12. Since these books came from different publishers, it is also possible that the editors adjusted the amount of emphasis on pedagogical goals to suit the different preferences of those publishers.

13. Greenberg, Olander, and Warrick, editors, *Science Fiction: Contemporary Mythology: The SFWA-SFRA Anthology* (New York: Harper & Row, 1978), xv. Page references are to this edition.

14. Warrick, Charles G. Waugh, and Greenberg, editors, *Science Fiction: The Science Fiction Research Association Anthology* (New York: Harper & Row, 1988), ix. Page references are to this edition.

15. David G. Hartwell and Milton T. Wolf, *Visions of Wonder: The Science Fiction Research Association Anthology* (New York: Tor Books, 1996), 11, left dust jacket. Page references are to this edition.

16. James Gunn, editor, *The Road to Science Fiction #3: From Heinlein to Here* (1979; Clarkston, Georgia: White Wolf Publishing, [1996]), back cover.

17. Ursula K. Le Guin, "Introduction," *The Norton Book of Science Fiction: North American Science Fiction, 1960–1990*, edited by Le Guin and Brian Attebery (New York: W.W. Norton, 1993), 15. Page references are to this edition.

18. Joseph D. Miller, "Popes or Tropes: Defining the Grails of Science Fiction," *Science*

252   Part Three: The Business of Science Fiction Scholarship

Fiction, Canonization, Marginalization, and the Academy, edited by Westfahl and George Slusser (Westport, CT: Greenwood Press, 2002), 79–87.

19. Slusser, "The Politically Correct Book of Science Fiction: Le Guin's Norton Collection," *Foundation: The Review of Science Fiction*, No. 60 (Spring, 1994), 67–84.

20. Tom Shippey, editor, *The Oxford Book of Science Fiction Stories* (Oxford: Oxford University Press, 1992), left dusk jacket, xxvi.

21. See Shippey, "Literary Gatekeepers and the Fabril Tradition," *Bridges to Science Fiction and Fantasy: Outstanding Essays from the J. Lloyd Eaton Conferences*, edited by Gregory Benford, Westfahl, Howard V. Hendrix, and Joseph D. Miller (Jefferson, NC: McFarland, 2018), 178–194. Originally presented at the 1994 Eaton Conference and originally published in 2002.

22. Garyn G. Roberts, editor, *The Prentice Hall Anthology of Science Fiction and Fantasy* (Upper Saddle River, NJ: Prentice Hall, 2003), xvi. Page references are to this edition.

23. Arthur B. Evans, Istvan Csicsery-Ronay, Jr., Joan Gordon, Veronica Hollinger, Rob Latham, and Carol McGuirk, editors, *The Wesleyan Anthology of Science Fiction* (Middletown, CT: Wesleyan University Press, 2010), xvii. Page references are to this edition.

24. Evans, email message to Gary Westfahl, January 31, 2019. As an aside, I should note Evans's comment that a second edition of his anthology is unlikely because of difficulties in obtaining rights to publishing its stories in an eBook, which evidently is increasingly the preferred format for college textbooks.

25. For the record, these are the chapters in question: "Space Opera," *The Cambridge Companion to Science Fiction*, edited by Edward James and Farah Mendlesohn (Cambridge: Cambridge University Press, 2003), 197–208; "Hard Science Fiction," *A Companion to Science Fiction*, edited by David Seed (Oxford: Blackwell Publishers, 2005), 187–201; "The Marketplace," *The Oxford Handbook of Science Fiction*, edited by Rob Latham (London: Oxford University Press, 2014), 81–92; and "The Mightiest Machine: The Development of American Science Fiction from the 1920s to the 1960s," *The Cambridge Companion to American Science Fiction*, edited by Eric Carl Link and Gerry Canavan (Cambridge: Cambridge University Press, 2015), 17–30.

26. Farah Mendlesohn, email message to Gary Westfahl, January 29, 2019.

27. To mention Slusser one more time, I can report that when I examined the uncatalogued George Slusser Papers in the Eaton Collection, I came across numerous copies of various stories and essays, indicating (like Robert L. Heath's essay above) that he also preferred to choose his own materials for his graduate classes in science fiction instead of relying upon published compilations.

28. I do hope to eventually publish this packet as a book, to perhaps be employed as a textbook by other instructors, though I will first have to write additional chapters that, distracted by other projects, I have not had the time to complete.

Bibliography of Primary
and Secondary Works
Related to Science Fiction
and Economics

The first two sections of this bibliography endeavor to provide comprehensive listings of science fiction novels and short stories, and science fiction films and television programs, that deal with economic matters in a creative fashion, including all relevant works identified by contributors to this volume and other commentators. In dealing with authors who repeatedly address economic issues, such as Poul Anderson and Mack Reynolds, we provide only a selected number of their works that particularly emphasize economics. We have generally avoided stories that merely portray conventional economic interactions in strange or futuristic settings. The third section lists nonfiction books and articles that in some way address the topic of economics and science fiction.

I. Novels and Short Stories

Allen, Henry Francis [as Pruning Knife]. *A Strange Voyage: A Revision of the Key of Industrial Cooperative Government: An Interesting and Instructive Description of Life on Planet Venus*. St. Louis, MO: Monitor Publishing Co., 1891.

Amadahy, Zainab. *The Moons of Palmares*. Toronto: Sister Vision, 1997.

Anderson, Poul. "The Helping Hand." 1950. *Possible Worlds of Science Fiction*. Edited by Groff Conklin. New York: Viking, 1951, 347–372.

_____. "Lodestar." *Astounding: John W. Campbell Memorial Anthology*. Edited by Harry Harrison. 1973. New York: Ballantine Books, 1974, 2–41.

_____. *The Man Who Counts*. New York: Ace Books, 1979. Shorter version originally published in 1958 as *War of the Wing-Men*.

_____. "Margin of Profit." 1956. *The Seven Deadly Sins of Science Fiction*. Edited by Isaac Asimov, Martin H. Greenberg, and Charles G. Waugh. New York: Fawcett Crest, 1980, 265–292.

_____. *Mirkheim*. New York: Berkley/Putnam, 1977.

_____. *Satan's World*. Garden City, NY: Doubleday, 1969.

_____. *Trader to the Stars*. Garden City, NY: Doubleday, 1964.

Ardrey, Robert. *World's Beginning*. New York: Duell, Sloan, and Pearce, [1944].

Asimov, Isaac. "Buy Jupiter." 1958. *Buy Jupiter and Other Stories*. New York: Fawcett Crest, 1975, 136–140.

_____. *The Caves of Steel*. 1953. Garden City, NY: Doubleday, 1954.

_____. "Dreaming Is a Private Thing." 1955. *Tomorrow, Inc.: SF Stories About Big Business*. Edited by Joseph D. Olander and Martin H. Greenberg. New York: Taplinger, 1976, 135–150.

_____. *Foundation*. New York: Gnome Press, 1951.

_____. *Foundation and Empire*. New York: Gnome Press, 1952.

_____. *Second Foundation*. New York: Gnome Press, 1953.

Atwood, Margaret. *The Year of the Flood: A Novel*. New York: Nan A. Talese/Doubleday, 2009.

Bacigalupi, Paolo. *Ship Breaker*. Boston: Little, Brown, 2017.

_____. *The Windup Girl*. San Francisco: Night Shade Books, 2009.

Ballard, J.G. "The Subliminal Man." 1963. *The Mirror of Infinity: A Critics' Anthology of Science Fiction*. Edited by Robert Silverberg. 1970. New York: Perennial Library/Harper & Row, 1973, 226–244.

Behr, Ira Steven, and Robert Hewitt Wolfe. *Legends of the Ferengi*. Star Trek: Deep Space Nine. New York: Pocket Books, 1997.

Bell, Hilari. *A Matter of Profit*. New York: HarperCollins, 2001.

Bellamy, Edward. *Equality*. New York: D. Appleton & Company, 1897.

_____. *Looking Backward: 2000–1887*. 1888. New York: New American Library, 1960.

Belloc, Hilaire. *But Soft—We Are Observed!* London: Arrowsmith, 1928.

Biggle, Lloyd, Jr. *Monument*. Garden City, NY: Doubleday, 1974.

Bova, Ben. *Privateers*. New York: Tor Books, 1985.

_____. *The Starcrossed*. 1976. New York: Ace Books, 1984.

Brant, John Ira. *The New Regime, A.D. 2022*. New York: Cochrane Publishing Co., 1909.

Brin, David. *Kiln People*. New York: Tor Books, 2002.

Brooks, Byron A. *Earth Revisited*. Boston: Arena Publishing Co., 1893.

Brown, Rosel George. "Signs of the Times." 1959. *A Handful of Time*. New York: Ballantine Books, 1963, 39–53.

Brunner, John. *Stand on Zanzibar*. 1968. New York: Ballantine Books, 1969.

Brunt, Captain Samuel [pseudonym]. *A Voyage to Cacklogallinia: with a Description of the Religion, Policy, Customs, and Manners of That Country*. 1727. New York: Columbia University Press, 1940.

Buchanan, Robert Williams. *The Rev. Annabel Lee: A Tale of To-Morrow*. London: C. Arthur Pearson, 1898.

Čapek, Karel. *R.U.R. (Rossum's Universal Robots): A Play in Three Acts and an Epilogue*. Play. Translated by Paul Selver. London: Oxford University Press, 1923.

Chavannes, Albert. *In Brighter Climes, or Life in Socioland: A Realistic Novel*. Knoxville, TN: Chavannes and Co., 1895.

Clarke, Arthur C. "I Remember Babylon." 1960. *The Collected Stories of Arthur C. Clarke*. New York: Tor Books, 2000, 702–710.

_____. *Imperial Earth: A Fantasy of Love and Discord*. London: Victor Gollancz, 1975.

_____. "Into the Past." *Satellite*, 3:1 (December 1939), 3–6.

_____. "Patent Pending." (As "The Invention") *Argosy*, 339:5 (November 1954), 34–37, 85–86.

_____. "Venture to the Moon." 1956. *The Collected Stories of Arthur C. Clarke*. New York: Tor Books, 2000, 530–549.

Clarke, Francis H. *Morgan Rockefeller's Will: A Romance of 1991–2*. Portland, OR: Clarke-Cree Publishing Co., 1909.

Cline, Ernest. *Armada*. New York: Broadway Books, 2015.

_____. *Ready Player One*. New York: Broadway Books, 2011.

Coblentz, Stanton A. *After 12,000 Years*. Amazing Stories Quarterly, 2:2 (Spring, 1929), 148–221.

_____. *The Blue Barbarians*. 1931. New York: Avalon Books, 1958.

_____. *In Caverns Below*. [Also published as *Hidden World*.] 1935. New York: Garland, 1975.

Collins, Suzanne. *Catching Fire*. New York: Scholastic, Inc., 2009.

_____. *The Hunger Games*. New York: Scholastic, Inc., 2008.

_____. *Mockingjay*. New York: Scholastic, Inc., 2010.

Conrad, Joseph, and Ford Madox Ford. *The Inheritors: An Extravagant Story*. London: Heinemann, 1901.

Cooper, James Finemore. *The Monikins: A Tale*. Philadelphia: Carey, Lea, and Blanchard, 1835.

Corey, James S.A. [Daniel Abraham and Ty Franck]. *Abaddon's Gate*. New York: Orbit, 2013.

_____. *Babylon's Ashes*. New York: Orbit, 2016.

_____. *The Butcher of Anderson Station*. Short story. New York: Orbit, 2011.

_____. *Caliban's War*. New York: Orbit, 2012.

_____. *The Chum*. Novella. New York: Orbit, 2014.

_____. *Cibola Burn*. New York: Orbit, 2014.

_____. "Drive." *Edge of Infinity*. EBook. Edited by Jonathan Strahan. Oxford: Solaris, 2012.

_____. *Gods of Risk*. Novella. New York: Orbit, 2012.

_____. *Leviathan Wakes*. New York: Orbit, 2011.

_____. *Nemesis Games*. New York: Orbit, 2015.

_____. *Persepolis Rising*. New York: Orbit, 2017.

_____. *Strange Dogs*. Novella. New York: Orbit, 2017.

_____. *Tiamat's Wrath*. New York: Orbit, 2018.

_____. *The Vital Abyss*. Novella. New York: Orbit, 2015.

Correy, Lee. [G. Harry Stine]. *Manna*. New York: DAW, 1983.

DeCandido, Keith. *Serenity*. New York: Pocket Books, 2005.

Del Rey, Lester, and Frederik Pohl [as Edson McCann]. *Preferred Risk*. New York: Simon & Schuster, 1955.

Delany, Samuel R. "Time Considered as a Helix of Semi-Precious Stones." 1968. *World's Best Science Fiction 1969*. Edited by Donald A. Wollheim and Terry Carr. New York: Ace Books, 1969, 87–126.

De Mille, James. *A Strange Manuscript Found in a Copper Cylinder*. New York: Harper, 1888.

De Mille, William. *"Food": A Tragedy of the Future in One Act*. New York: Samuel French, 1914.

Dick, Philip K. "Captive Market." 1955. *Tomorrow, Inc.: SF Stories About Big Business*. Edited by Joseph D. Olander and Martin H. Greenberg. New York: Taplinger, 1976, 227–244.

_____. *Galactic Pot-Healer*. 1969. Boston: Mariner Books/Houghton Mifflin Harcourt, 2013.

_____. "Paycheck." 1953. *The Best of Philip K. Dick*. New York: Del Rey/Ballantine, 1977, 67–108.

_____. *A Scanner Darkly*. Garden City, NY: Doubleday, 1977.

_____. *Solar Lottery*. New York: Ace Books, 1955.

_____. "War Game." 1959. *The Preserving Machine*. New York: Ace Books, 18–34.

Dickson, Gordon R. *Wolf and Iron*. New York: Tor Books, 1990.

Doctorow, Cory. *Down and Out in the Magic Kingdom*. New York: Tor Books, 2003.

_____. *Makers*. New York: HarperVoyager, 2009.

_____. *Walkaway*. New York: Tor Books, 2017.

Donnelly, Ignatius [as Edmund Boisgilbert]. *Caesar's Column: A Novel of the Twentieth Century*. Chicago: F.J. Schulte, 1890.

Edmondson, G.C. *The Man Who Corrupted Earth*. New York: Ace Books, 1980.

Effinger, George Alec. *The Exile Kiss*. Garden City, NY: Doubleday Foundation, 1991.

_____. *A Fire in the Sun*. Garden City, NY: Doubleday Foundation, 1989.

_____. *When Gravity Fails*. New York: Arbor House, 1987.

Egan, Greg. *Permutation City*. New York: HarperPrism, 1994.

Elder, Cyrus. "Dream of a Free-Trade Paradise." *Dream of a Free-Trade Paradise, and Other Sketches*. Philadelphia: Henry Carey Baird, 1872, 11–20.

Ellis, G.A. *New Britain: A Narrative of a Journey by Mr. Ellis to a Country So Called by Its Inhabitants, Discovered in the Vast Plain of Missouri, in North America, and Inhabited by a People of British Origin*. London: Simpkin and Marshall, 1820.

England, George Allan. "A Message from the Moon." 1907. *Worlds Apart: An Anthology of Interplanetary Fiction*. Edited by George Locke. London: Cornmarket Reprints, 1972, 96–101.

_____. *The Nebula of Death*. 1918. Normal, IL: Black Dog Books, 2011.

Farmer, Philip Jose. "Riders of the Purple Wage." 1967. *Dangerous Visions #1*. Edited by Harlan Ellison. New York: Berkley, 1969, 70–144.

Ford, John W. *How Much for Just the Planet? Star Trek #36*. New York: Pocket Books, 1987.

Fuller, Frederick T. *Beyond the Selvas: A Vision of a Republic That Might Have Been—and Still May Be*. Boston: publisher unidentified, 1929.

Galloway, James M. [as Anon Moore]. *John Harvey: A Tale of the Twentieth Century*. Chicago: Charles H. Kerr & Co., 1897.

Galouye, Daniel F. *Simulacron-3*. 1964. Rockville, MD: Phoenix Pick, 1999.

Geissler, Ludwig A. *Looking Beyond: A Sequel to "Looking Backward" by Edward Bellamy, and an Answer to "Looking Further Forward" by Richard Michaelis*. New Orleans: Graham and Sons Printers, 1891.

Gelula, Abner J. "Hibernation." *Amazing Stories*, 8:4 (July 1933), 302–315, 344. Available at https://archive.org/stream/Amazing_Stories_v08n04_1933–07#page/n57/mode/2up.

Gernsback, Hugo. *Ralph 124C 41+: A Romance of the Year 2660*. 1911–1912, 1925. Second Edition. New York: Frederick Fell, 1950.

Gibson, William. "Burning Chrome." 1982. *Burning Chrome*. New York: Arbor House, 1986, 168–191.

_____. "Johnny Mnemonic." 1981. *Burning Chrome*. New York: Arbor House, 1986, 1–22.

_____. *Johnny Mnemonic: The Screenplay and the Story*. New York: Berkley, 1995.

_____. "New Rose Hotel." 1984. *Burning Chrome*. New York: Arbor House, 1986, 103–116.

_____. *Pattern Recognition: A Novel*. New York: G.P. Putnam's Sons, 2003.

_____. *Spook Country*. New York: G.P. Putnam's Sons, 2007.

_____. "The Winter Market." 1985. *Burning Chrome*. New York: Arbor House, 1986, 117–141.

_____. *Zero History*. New York: G.P. Putnam's Sons, 2010.

_____, and Bruce Sterling. *The Difference Engine*. London: Gollancz, 1990.

Glynn, Alan. *Limitless*. New York: Picador, 2001.

Griffith, Ann Warren. "Captive Audience." 1953. *Tomorrow, Inc.: SF Stories About Big Business*. Edited by Joseph D. Olander and Martin H. Greenberg. New York: Taplinger, 1976, 67–79.

Griffith, Mary. *Three Hundred Years Hence*. 1826. Boston: Gregg Press, 1975.

Guthrie, Kenneth. *A Romance of Two Centuries: A Tale of the Year 2025*. Alpine, NJ: Platonist Press, 1919.

Hazlitt, Henry. *The Great Idea*. New York: Appleton-Century-Crofts, 1951.

Heinlein, Robert A. *Citizen of the Galaxy*. New York: Scribner's, 1957.

_____. *For Us the Living: A Comedy of Customs*. New York: Pocket Books, 2004.

_____. "'Let There Be Light...'" 1940. *The Man Who Sold the Moon*. 1950. New York: Signet Books, 1951, 11–25.

_____. "Logic of Empire." 1941. *The Green Hills of Earth*. 1951. New York: Signet Books, 1952, 135–176.

_____. "The Man Who Sold the Moon." *The Man Who Sold the Moon*. 1950. New York: Signet Books, 1951, 61–143.

_____. *The Moon Is a Harsh Mistress*. 1966. New York: Berkley Books, 1968.

_____. "The Roads Must Roll." 1940. *The Man Who Sold the Moon*. 1950. New York: Signet Books, 1953, 26–60.

_____. *The Rolling Stones*. New York: Scribner's, 1952.

_____. *Time Enough for Love: The Lives of Lazarus Long*. New York: G.P. Putnam's Sons, 1973.

Herbert, Frank. *Chapterhouse: Dune*. New York: Putnam, 1985.

_____. *Children of Dune*. New York: Berkley/Putnam, 1976.

_____. *Dune*. New York: Ace Books, 1965.

_____. *Dune Messiah*. New York: Putnam, 1969.

_____. *God Emperor of Dune*. New York: Ace Books, 1981.

_____. *Heretics of Dune*. New York: Putnam, 1984.

Hertzka, Theodor. *Freeland: A Social Anticipation*. 1890. Translated by Arthur Ransom. New York: D. Appleton & Co., 1891.

_____. *A Visit to Freeland, Or, the New Paradise Regained*. 1893. Translator unidentified. London: W. Reeves, 1894.

Holford, Castello N. *Aristopia: A Romance-History of the New World*. Boston: Arena Publishing Co., 1895.

House, Edward Mandell. *Philip Dru, Administrator: A Story of To-Morrow 1920–1935*. New York: B.W. Huebsch, 1912.

Howells, William Dean. *Through the Eye of a Needle: A Romance*. New York: Harper & Brothers, 1907.

_____. *A Traveler from Altruria: A Romance*. New York: Harper & Brothers, 1894.

Huxley, Aldous. *Brave New World*. 1932. New York: Harper Perennial, 1969.

_____. *Island*. New York: Bantam 1962.

"The Immortal Man." *Scoops*, 1:11 (April 21, 1934), 323–326. Author unknown.

Jakes, John. "The Sellers of the Dream." 1963. *Tomorrow, Inc.: SF Stories About Big Business*. Edited by Joseph D. Olander and Martin H. Greenberg. New York: Taplinger, 1976, 80–116.

Jameson, Malcolm. "Blind Alley." 1943. *Great Stories of Science Fiction*. Edited by Murray Leinster. New York: Random House, 1951, 88–120.

Jay, Peter, and Michael Stewart. *Apocalypse 2000: Economic Breakdown and the Suicide of Democracy*. London: Sidgwick & Jackson, 1987.

Jones, Alice Ilgenfritz, and Ella Marchant [as Two Women of the West]. *Unveiling a Parable: A Romance*. Boston: Arena Publishing Co., 1893.

Keeler, Harry Stephen. "John Jones's Dollar." 1915. *Amazing Stories*, 3:1 (April 1927), 25–29.

Keller, David H. "No More Tomorrows." 1932. *Life Everlasting and Other Tales of Science, Fantasy and Horror*. Newark, NJ: Avalon, 1947, 248–267.

Kessel, John. *The Moon and the Other*. New York: Saga Press, 2017.

Keyes, Greg. *Interstellar: The Official Movie Novelization*. London: Titan Books, 2014.

Kirwan, Thomas [as William Wonder]. *Reciprocity (Social and Economic) in the Thirtieth Century: The Coming Co-Operative Age: A Forecast of the World's Future*. New York: Cochrane Publishing Co., 1909.

Knapp, Adeline. "The Discontented Machine: An Economic Study." *One Thousand Dollars a Day: Studies in Practical Economics*. Boston: Arena Publishing, 1894, 73–100.

_____. "One Thousand Dollars a Day: A Financial Experiment." *One Thousand Dollars a Day*, 11–41.

_____. "The Sick Man: A Fable for Grown-Up Boys and Girls." *One Thousand Dollars a Day*, 42–72.

Knight, Ashley Leavitt. "The Millennium Engine." *Popular Magazine*, 35:6 (February 23, 1915), 87–96.

Knight, Damon. *A for Anything*. 1959. New York: Fawcett Gold Medal, 1972. Originally published as *The People Maker*.

_____. "The Big Pat Boom." 1963. *The Seventh Galaxy Reader*. Edited by Frederik Pohl. Garden City, NY: Doubleday, 1964, 240–247.

_____. *Hell's Pavement*. 1955. New York: Avon Books, 1980.

Koman, Victor. *Kings of the High Frontier*. Centreville, VA: Final Frontier Books, 1998. First published in 1996 as a downloadable HTML file.

Kornbluth, C.M. *The Syndic*. 1953. New York: Avon Books, 1974.

Kress, Nancy. *Beggars and Choosers*. New York: Tor Books, 1994.

_____. *Beggars in Spain*. New York: Avon Books, 1993.

_____. *Beggars Ride*. New York: Tor Books, 1996.

_____. "The Price of Oranges." 1989. *Paragons: Twelve Master Science Fiction Writers Ply Their Craft*. Edited by Robin Scott Wilson. New York: St. Martin's Press, 1996, 4–28.

Kuttner, Henry, and C.L. Moore. "The Iron Standard." 1943. *The Best of Henry Kuttner*. New York: Ballantine Books, 1975, 268–297.

Lafferty, R.A. "Slow Tuesday Night." 1965. *The Wesleyan Anthology of Science Fiction*. Edited by Arthur B. Evans, Istvan Csicsery-Ronay, Jr. Joan Gordon, Veronica Hollinger, Rob Latham, and Carol McGuirk. Middletown, CT: Wesleyan University Press, 2010, 359–366.

Laurie, André. *New York to Brest in Seven Hours*. London: Sampson, Low, Marston, Searle and Rivington, 1890.

Lawrence, J.A. *Mudd's Angels. Star Trek*. New York: Bantam Books, 1978.

Lawrence, Raymond Emery. "The Posterity Fund." *Amazing Stories*, 4:2 (May 1929), 162–171.

Le Guin, Ursula K. *Always Coming Home*. New York: Harper & Row, 1985.

_____. *The Dispossessed*. New York: Harper & Row, 1974.

Leacock, Stephen. "The Kidnapped Plumber: A Tale of the New Time." *Winsome Willie and Other New Nonsense Novels*. London: John Lane, 1920, 177–204.

Leckie, Ann. *Ancillary Justice*. New York: Orbit, 2013.

_____. *Ancillary Mercy*. New York: Orbit, 2015.

_____. *Ancillary Sword*. New York: Orbit, 2014.

_____. "Night's Slow Poison." *Electric Velocipede*, no. 24 (Summer, 2012). Emagazine.

_____. *Provenance*. New York: Orbit, 2017.

_____. "She Commands Me and I Obey." *Strange Horizons*, November 10, 2014, and November 17, 2014. Emagazine. Available at http://strangehorizons.com/fiction/she-commands-me-and-i-obey-part-1-of-2/ and http://strangehorizons.com/fiction/she-commands-me-and-i-obey-part-2-of-2/.

Leiber, Fritz. "A Bad Day for Sales." 1953. *Great Tales of Science Fiction*. Edited by Robert Silverberg and Martin H. Greenberg. New York: Galahad Books, 1983, 328–333.

Lester, Irwin, and Fletcher Pratt. *The Reign of the Ray. Science Wonder Stories*, 1:1 (June 1929), 6–33, 81; *Science Wonder Stories*, 1:2 (July 1929), 120–131.

Lewis, C.S. *That Hideous Strength*. 1946. New York: Macmillan Company, 1965.

Lewis, De Witt. *A Trip to the North Pole and Beyond to Civilization, Edited and Compiled by E.Z. Ernst*. Linwood, KS: The Industrial Exchange, 1912.

Liu, Cixin. *The Dark Forest*. 2008. Translated by Joel Martinsen. New York: Tor Books, 2015.

_____. *Death's End*. 2010. Translated by Ken Liu. New York: Tor Books, 2016.

_____. *The Three-Body Problem*. 2006, 2008. Translated by Ken Liu. New York: Tor Books, 2014.

Lockwood, Ingersoll. *1900: Or; the Last President*. New York: American News Company, 1896.

London, Jack. "The Dream of Debs." *The Strength of the Strong*. New York: Macmillan, 1914, 134–176.

_____. *The Iron Heel*. 1907. New York: Macmillan Company, 1908.

MacIsaac, Fred. *World Brigands. Argosy All-Story Weekly*, 196:1 (June 30, 1928), 2–18; *Argosy All-Story Weekly*, 196:3 (July 7, 1928), 217–236; *Argosy All-Story Weekly*, 196:3 (July 14, 1928), 347–366; *Argosy All-Story Weekly*, 196:4 (July 21, 1928), 553–573; *Argosy All-Story Weekly*, 196:5 (July 28, 1928), 658–678; *Argosy All-Story Weekly*, 196:6 (August 4, 1928), 821–831.

MacLeod, Ken. *The Cassini Division*. London: Orbit, 1998.

_____. *The Sky Road*. London: Orbit, 1999.

_____. *The Steel Fraction*. London: Legend, 1995.

_____. *The Stone Canal*. London: Legend, 1996.

Macnie, John [as Ismar Thiusen]. *The Diothas or a Far Look Ahead*. New York: Putnam, 1883.

Malzberg, Barry N. *Herovit's World*. New York: Random House, 1973.

Marshall, Archibald. *Upsidonia*. London: Stanley Paul, 1915.

McComas, J. Francis. "Brave New Word." 1954. *Tomorrow, Inc.: SF Stories About Big Business*. Edited by Joseph D. Olander and Martin H. Greenberg. New York: Taplinger, 1976, 23–35.

McCowan, Archibald. *The Billionaire: A Peep Into the Future*. New York: Jenkins and McCowan, 1900.

McCoy, John [as Lord High Commissioner]. *A Prophetic Romance: Mars to Earth*. Boston: Arena Publishing Co., 1896.

McDonald, Edward Richard [as Raymond McDonald], and Raymond Alfred Leger. *The Mad Scientist: A Tale of the Future*. New York: Cochrane Publishing Co., 1908.

McDonald, Ian. *Luna: New Moon.* New York: Tor Books, 2015.

_____. *Luna: Wolf Moon.* New York: Tor Books, 2017.

McGrady, Reverend Thomas. *Beyond the Black Ocean.* Terre Haute, IN: Standard Publishing, 1901.

Merrill, Albert Adams. *The Great Awakening: The Story of the Twenty-Second Century.* Boston: George Book Co., 1899.

Michaelis, Richard C. *Looking Further Forward: An Answer to* Looking Backward *by Edward Bellamy.* Chicago: Rand, McNally and Co., 1890.

Milne, Robert Duncan. "A Question of Reciprocity." 1891. *Into the Sun and Other Stories.* Edited by Sam Moskowitz. West Kingston, RI: Donald M. Grant Publishers, 1980, 217–253.

Moorcock, Michael. *The Steel Tsar.* New York: DAW Books, 1981.

More, Thomas. *Utopia.* 1516. Translated by Paul Turner. Middlesex, England: Penguin Books, 1965.

Morris, Alfred. *Looking Ahead: A Tale of Adventure (Not by the Author of "Looking Backward").* London: Henry & Co., 1892.

Morris, William. *News from Nowhere, or an Epoch of Rest, Being Some Chapters from a Utopian Romance.* Boston: Roberts Brothers, 1890.

Newitz, Annalee. *Autonomous.* New York: Tor Books, 2017.

Newte, Horace. *The Master Beast: Being a True Account of the Ruthless Tyranny Inflicted on the British People by Socialism A.D. 1888–2020.* London: Rebman, 1907.

Niven, Larry, and Jerry Pournelle. *Lucifer's Hammer.* Chicago: Playboy Press, 1977,

Older, Malka. *Infomocracy.* New York: Tor Books, 2017.

Oltion, Jerry. *Mudd in Your Eye. Star Trek* #81. New York: Pocket Books, 1997.

Orwell, George. *Nineteen Eighty-Four.* New York: Harcourt Brace, 1949.

Peck, Bradford. *The World a Department Store: A Story of Life Under the Cooperative System.* Lewiston, ME: Bradford Peck, 1900.

Phillifent, John T. "Owe Me." 1974. *Tomorrow, Inc.: SF Stories About Big Business.* Edited by Joseph D. Olander and Martin H. Greenberg. New York: Taplinger, 1976, 208–216.

Pohl, Frederik. *The Merchants' War.* New York: St. Martin's Press, 1984.

_____. "The Midas Plague." 1954. *The Best of Frederik Pohl.* New York: Ballantine Books, 1975, 128–187.

_____. "The Tunnel Under the World." 1955. *The Best of Frederik Pohl.* New York: Ballantine Books, 1975, 1–34.

_____, and C.M. Kornbluth. *Gladiator-at-Law.* New York: Ballantine Books, 1955.

_____, and C.M. Kornbluth. *The Space Merchants.* New York: Ballantine Books, 1953.

Pratchett, Terry. *Making Money.* Garden City, NY: Doubleday, 2007.

Proctor, Thomas H. *The Banker's Dream: A Fiction: An Argument for the Free Coinage of Silver.* Vineland, NJ: Progressive Book Publishing Co., 1895.

Rand, Ayn. *Atlas Shrugged.* 1957. New York: New American Library, 1959.

Reeve, Arthur. *Pandora.* New York: Harper, 1926.

The Reign of King George VI 1900–1925. 1763. London: Rivingtons, 1899. Author unknown.

Reynolds, Mack. "Adaptation." *Astounding/Analog: Science Fact and Fiction,* 65:6 (August 1960), 8–62.

_____. "The Business, as Usual." 1952. *The Best of Mack Reynolds.* New York: Pocket Books, 1976, 42–46.

_____. "Compounded Interest." 1956. *SF: The Best of the Best.* Edited by Judith Merril. 1967. New York: Dell, 1968, 199–212.

_____. "Criminal in Utopia." 1968. *Tomorrow, Inc.: SF Stories About Big Business.* Edited by Joseph D. Olander and Martin H. Greenberg. New York: Taplinger, 1976, 189–207.

_____. *The Earth War.* New York: Pyramid Books, 1963.

_____. *Equality: In the Year 2000.* New York: Ace Books, 1977.

_____. *Looking Backward, from the Year 2000.* New York: Ace Books, 1973.

_____. *Planetary Agent X.* New York: Ace Books, 1965. Published dos-à-dos with *Behold the Stars* by Kenneth Bulmer.

_____. "Radical Center." *Analog Science Fiction/Science Fact,* 79:1 (March 1967), 66–93.

_____. "Subversive." 1962. *The Best of Mack Reynolds.* New York: Pocket Books, 1976, 167–188.

_____. *Tomorrow Might Be Different.* New York: Ace Books, 1975.

Richter, Eugen. *Pictures of the Socialist Future (Freely Adapted from Bebel).* London: Swan Sonnenschein, 1893.

Roberts, J.W. *Looking Within: The Misleading Tendencies of "Looking Backward" Made Manifest.* New York: A.S. Barnes, 1893.

Robinson, Kim Stanley. *Aurora.* New York: Orbit, 2015.

_____. *Blue Mars.* London: Voyager/HarperCollins, 1996.

_____. *The Gold Coast.* New York: Tor Books, 1988.

_____. *Green Mars.* London: HarperCollins, 1993.

_____. *New York 2140.* New York: Orbit, 2017.

_____. *Pacific Edge.* New York: Tor Books, 1990.

_____. *Red Mars.* London: HarperCollins, 1992.

_____. *2312.* New York: Orbit, 2012.

_____. *The Wild Shore.* New York: Ace Books, 1984.

Rogers, Lebbeus Harding. *The Kite Trust (A Romance of Wealth).* New York: Kite Trust Publishing Company, 1900.

Rosewater, Frank [as Marian and Franklin Mayoe]. *Doomed: A Startling Message to the People of Our Day, Interwoven in an Antediluvian Romance of Two Old Worlds and Two Young Lovers by Queen Metel and Prince Loab, of Alto, Reincarnated in Its Editors, Marian and Franklin Mayoe, by the Atlon Calendar the Year 14,009, by Our Calendar the Year 1920.* New York: Frank Rosewater, 1920.

Rousseau, Victor. *The Messiah of the Cylinder.* Chicago: McClurg, 1917.

Russell, Eric Frank. "... And Then There Were None." 1951. *The Science Fiction Hall of Fame, Volume 2A.* Edited by Ben Bova. 1973. New York: Avon Books, 1974, 302–372.

Schindler, Solomon. *Young West: A Sequel to* Looking Backward. Boston: Arena Library Series, 1894.

Schulman, J. Neil. *Alongside Night.* New York: Crown Publishers, 1979.

Serviss, Garrett P. *The Moon Metal.* New York: Harper, 1900.

Sheckley, Robert. "Cost of Living." 1952. *Untouched by Human Hands.* New York: Ballantine Books, 1954, 12–23.

_____. "Something for Nothing." 1954. *Citizen in Space.* New York: Ballantine Books, 1955, 95–107.

Shelley, Mary. *Frankenstein: Annotated for Scientists, Engineers, and Creators of All Kinds.* 1818, 1831. Edited by David H. Guston, Ed Finn, and Jason Scott Robert. Cambridge: MIT Press, 2017.

Silverberg, Robert. "Company Store." 1959. *Tomorrow, Inc.: SF Stories About Big Business.* Edited by Joseph D. Olander and Martin H. Greenberg. New York: Taplinger, 1976, 151–165.

_____. *Regan's Planet.* New York: Pyramid, 1964.

_____. *World's Fair 1992.* 1970. New York: Ace Books, 1982.

Simak, Clifford D. *They Walked Like Men.* Garden City, NY: Doubleday, 1962.

_____. *The Visitors.* 1979. New York: Del Rey/Ballantine, 1980.

Sinclair, Upton. *The Millennium: A Comedy of the Year 2000.* Girard, KS: Haldeman-Julius Company, 1924.

Sladek, John. "The Hammer of Evil, or Career Opportunities at the Pascal Business School." 1975. *Keep the Giraffe Burning.* London: Panther/Granada, 1977, 79–88.

Smith, Cordwainer [Paul Linebarger]. *Norstrilia.* New York: Ballantine Books, 1975.

Smith, Garret. "On the Brink of 2000." 1910. *Famous Fantastic Mysteries*, 1:4 (January 1940), 6–36.

_____. *The Treasures of Tantalus.* 1920–1921. *Amazing Stories*, 2:7 (October 1927), 676–700; 2:8 (November 1927), 760–797.

Smith, George O. "Pandora's Millions." 1945. *The Complete Venus Equilateral.* New York: Del Rey/Ballantine, 1976, 317–346.

Smith, L. Neil. *The Probability Broach.* New York: Del Rey/Ballantine, 1980.

Smith, Titus K. *Altruria*. New York: Altruria Publishing Co., 1895.

Smith, William Hawley. *The Promoters: A Novel Without a Woman*. Chicago: Rand McNally, 1904.

Spinrad, Norman. "The Age of Invention." 1966. *Tomorrow, Inc.: SF Stories About Big Business*. Edited by Joseph D. Olander and Martin H. Greenberg. New York: Taplinger, 1976, 17–22.

Stephenson, Neal. *The Diamond Age: Or, a Young Lady's Illustrated Primer*. New York: Bantam Spectra, 1995.

_____. *Reamde*. New York: HarperCollins, 2011.

Sterling, Bruce. "The Beautiful and the Sublime." 1986. *The Ascent of Wonder: The Evolution of Hard SF*. Edited by David G. Hartwell and Kathryn Cramer. New York: Tor Books, 1994, 528–546.

_____. "Green Days in Brunei." 1985. *Crystal Express*. Sauk City, WI: Arkham House, 1989, 135–154.

_____. *Islands in the Net*. 1988. New York: Ace Books, 1989.

_____. *Schismatrix*. New York: Arbor House, 1985.

Stover, Leon E. *The Shaving of Karl Marx: An Instant Novel of Ideas, After the Manner of Thomas Love Peacock, in Which Lenin and H.G. Wells Talk About the Political Meaning of the Scientific Romances*. Lake Forest, IL: Chiron Press, 1982.

Stross, Charles. *Accelerando*. New York: Ace Books, 2005.

_____. *Neptune's Brood*. London: Orbit, 2013.

Thompson, W.R. *Debtors' Planet. Star Trek: The Next Generation* #30. New York: Pocket Books, 1994.

Thorne, Anthony. *Thirteen O'Clock: A Play in Three Acts*. London: Ernest Benn, 1929.

Tolstaya, Tatyana. *The Slynx*. 2000. Translated by Jamey Gambrell. Boston: Houghton Mifflin 2003.

Tucker, Louis D.D. "The Cubic City." *Science Wonder Stories*, 1:4 (September 1929), 316–325.

Turner, George. *Drowning Towers*. 1987. New York: Arbor House/William Morrow, 1988. Originally published as *The Sea and Summer*.

Vance, Jack. *The Many Worlds of Magnus Rudolph*. New York: Ace Books, 1966. Published dos-à-dos with *The Brains of Earth* by Vance.

_____. *Wyst: Alastor 1716*. New York: DAW Books, 1978.

Varley, John. *Steel Beach*. New York: Ace/Putnam, 1992.

Verne, Jules. *The Begum's Millions*. 1879. Translated by Stanford L. Luce. Edited by Arthur B. Evans. Middletown, CT: Wesleyan University Press, 2005.

_____. *The Earth Turned Upside Down*. 1889. Translated by Sophie Lewis. London: Hesperus Press, 2012. Also published as *The Purchase of the North Pole* and *Topsy-Turvy*.

Vincent, Harl. "Whisper of Death." *Amazing Stories*, 8:7 (November 1933), 11–49.

Vinge, Vernor. "The Blabber." 1988. *The Collected Stories of Vernor Vinge*. New York: Tor Books, 2001, 313–366.

_____. *The Children of the Sky*. New York: Tor Books, 2011.

_____. "Conquest by Default." 1968. *The Collected Stories of Vernor Vinge*, 159–186.

_____. *A Deepness in the Sky*. New York: Tor Books, 1999.

_____. *A Fire Upon the Deep*. New York: Tor Books, 1992.

_____. *Rainbows End*. New York: Tor Books, 2006.

Vinton, Arthur Dudley. *Looking Further Backward: Being a Series of Lectures Delivered to the Freshman Class at Shawmut College, by Professor Won Lung Li (Successor of Prof. Julian West)*. Albany, NY: Albany Book Co., 1890.

Voinovich, Vladimir. *Moscow 2042*. 1987. Translated from the Russian by Richard Lourie. San Diego: Harcourt Brace Jovanovich, 1990.

Walsh, William Thomas. *The Mirage of the Many*. New York: Holt, 1910.

Wandrei, Donald [as H.W. Guernsey]. "The Missing Ocean." *Unknown*, 1:3 (May 1939), 47–58.

_____ [as Howard D. Graham, Ph.D.]. "Time Haven." *Astounding Stories*, 14:1 (September 1934), 42–52.

Weir, Andy. *Artemis*. New York: Crown Publishers, 2017.

Welcome, S. Byron. *From Earth's Center: A Polar Gateway Message.* Chicago: Charles H. Kerr & Co., 1894.

Wells, H.G. *The Dream.* London: Jonathan Cape, 1924.

_____. *In the Days of the Comet.* London: Macmillan, 1906.

_____. *Men Like Gods.* London: Cassell, 1923.

_____. *A Modern Utopia.* 1905. Lincoln: University of Nebraska Press, 1967.

_____. "A Story of the Days to Come." 1899. *Three Prophetic Science Fiction Novels of H.G. Wells.* New York: Dover Publications, 1960, 189–262.

_____. *The War of the Worlds.* 1898. New York: Berkley, 1064.

_____. *When the Sleeper Wakes.* 1899. *Three Prophetic Science Fiction Novels of H.G. Wells,* 1–187.

West, Julian [pseudonym]. *My Afterdream: A Sequel to Edward Bellamy's "Looking Backward."* London: T. Fisher Unwin, 1900.

Wilbrandt, Conrad. *Mr. East's Experiences in Mr. Bellamy's World: Records of the Years 2001 and 2002.* Translated from the German by Mary J. Safford. Harper: New York, 1891.

Williams, F.P. *Hallie Williams: A True Daughter of the South.* New York: Abbey Press, 1900.

Williams, Michael. "The Mind Machine." *All-Story Weekly,* 95:3 (March 29, 1919), 377–392.

Williams, Ralph. "Business as Usual, During Alterations." 1958. *Prologue to Analog.* Edited by John W. Campbell, Jr. Garden City, NY: Doubleday, 1962, 230–258.

Wilson, Grosvenor. *The Monarch of Millions; Or, the Rise and Fall of the American Emperor.* New York: Neely Co., 1900.

Wollridge, C.W. *Perfecting the Earth: A Piece of Possible History.* Cleveland, OH: Utopia Publishing Co., 1902.

Zamiatin, Yegnevy. *We.* 1921. Translated from the Russian by Gregory Zilboorg. New York: Dutton, 1924.

II. Films and Television Programs

All That Glitters. Television series. Syndicated: Norman Lear/Tandem Productions, 1977.

Americathon. Lorimar, 1979.

Atlas Shrugged: Part I. Atlas Productions, 2011.

Automate. Hyper.bolic Films, 2017.

"Badda-Bing, Badda-Bang." *Star Trek: Deep Space Nine.* Los Angeles: KCOP, February 24, 1999.

"Bar Association." *Star Trek: Deep Space Nine.* Los Angeles: KCOP, February 19, 1996.

Batman Begins. Warner Brothers, 2005.

Black Panther. Marvel Studios/Walt Disney Pictures, 2018.

Blade Runner. Ladd Company, 1982.

Blade Runner 2049. Alcon Entertainment, 2017.

Born in Flames. the Jerome Foundation, 1983.

Branded. Mirumir, 2012.

Brazil. Embassy International Pictures, 1985.

"The Caves of Steel." *Story Parade.* London: BBC-TV, June 5, 1964.

Children of Dune. Television miniseries. New York: Sci Fi Channel, March 16, 17, and 18, 2003.

C.S.A.: The Confederate States of America. Hodcarrier Films, 2004.

The Dark Knight. Warner Brothers, 2008.

The Dark Knight Rises. Warner Brothers, 2012.

Downsizing. Paramount Pictures/Ad Hominem Enterprises, 2017.

Dune. Dino de Laurentiis Company, 1984.

Dune. Television miniseries. New York: Sci Fi Channel, December 3, 2000.

Earth 2011. ABC News Production Company, 2009.

Elysium. TriStar Pictures, 2013.

The Expanse. Television series. New York: Syfy Channel, 2015-present.

"False Prophets." *Star Trek: Voyager.* New York: UPN, October 2, 1996.

"Family Business." *Star Trek: Deep Space Nine.* Los Angeles: KCOP, May 15, 1995.

"Far Beyond the Stars." *Star Trek: Deep Space Nine.* Los Angeles: KCOP, February 11, 1998.

"Ferengi Love Songs." *Star Trek: Deep Space Nine.* Los Angeles: KCOP, April 21, 1997.

Firefly. Television series. New York: Fox Network, 2002–2003.

"Future's End." Two-part episode. *Star Trek: Voyager.* New York: UPN, November 6 and November 13, 1996.

Ghosts with Shit Jobs. No Media Kings, 2012.

The Girl from Monday. Possible Films, 2005.

"The Good, the Bad and the Wealthy." *Sliders.* New York: Fox Network, March 22, 1996.

"Greatfellas." *Sliders.* New York: Fox Network, May 31, 1996.

Gunpowder. Cinema and Theatre Seating Limited, 1988.

The Hunger Games. Lionsgate/Color Force, 2012.

The Hunger Games: Catching Fire. Lionsgate/Color Force, 2013.

The Hunger Games: Mockingjay—Part 1. Lionsgate/Color Force, 2014.

The Hunger Games: Mockingjay—Part 2. Lionsgate/Color Force, 2015.

"I, Mudd." *Star Trek.* New York: NBC-TV, November 3, 1967.

In Time. Regency Enterprises, 2011.

Interstellar. Paramount Pictures/Warner Brothers, 2014.

It Grows on Trees. Universal International, 1952.

The Jetsons. Hanna Barbera Productions, 1990.

Johnny Mnemonic. Tristar Pictures, 1995.

The Judas Project. Judas Project, 1990.

Killer Deal. Alliance Atlantis Corporation, 1999.

Limitless. Relatively Media, 2011.

"Live Fast and Prosper." *Star Trek: Voyager.* New York: UPN, April 19, 2000.

Looper. Endgame Entertainment, 2012.

"Luck of the Draw." *Sliders.* New York: Fox Network, May 17, 1995.

"The Magnificent Ferengi." *Star Trek: Deep Space Nine.* Los Angeles: KCOP, January 1, 1998.

"More Trouble, More Tribbles." *Star Trek.* Animated series. New York: NBC-TV, October 6, 1973.

"Mudd's Passion." *Star Trek.* Animated series. New York: NBC-TV, November 10, 1973.

"Mudd's Women." *Star Trek.* New York: NBC-TV, October 13, 1966.

"The Nagus." *Star Trek: Deep Space Nine.* Los Angeles: KCOP, March 27, 1993.

New Rose Hotel. Edward R. Pressman Film, 1998.

"Nineteen Eighty-Four." *BBC Sunday-Night Theatre.* London: BBC-TV, December 12, 1954.

1984. Columbia Pictures, 1956.

Nineteen Eighty-Four. Umbrella-Rosenblum Films, 1984.

1984. Royal Opera House, 2006.

"Of Late I Think of Cliffordville." *The Twilight Zone.* New York: CBS-TV, April 11, 1963.

"Once Upon a Time." *The Twilight Zone.* New York: CBS-TV, December 15, 1961.

"Past Tense." Two-part episode. *Star Trek: Deep Space Nine.* Los Angeles: KCOP, January 2, 1995, and January 9, 1995.

Paycheck. Paramount Pictures/Dreamworks, 2003.

"A Piece of the Action." *Star Trek.* New York: NBC-TV, January 13, 1968.

"Please Press One." *Sliders.* New York: Fox Network, July 23, 1999.

"Profit and Lace." *Star Trek: Deep Space Nine.* Los Angeles: KCOP, May 13, 1998.

"Prophet Motive." *Star Trek: Deep Space Nine.* Los Angeles: KCOP, February 20, 1995.

Ready Player One. Amblin Entertainment, 2018.

"The Rip Van Winkle Caper." *The Twilight Zone.* New York: CBS-TV, April 21, 1961.

"Rivals." *Star Trek: Deep Space Nine.* Los Angeles: KCOP, January 2, 1994.

"Rules of Acquisition." *Star Trek: Deep Space Nine.* Los Angeles: KCOP, November 11, 1993.

R.U.R. London: BBC-TV, March 4, 1948.

"R.U.R. (Rossum's Universal Robots)." *Broadway Television Theatre.* New York: WOR-TV, February 9, 1953.

Salvage 1. Television series. New York: ABC-TV, 1979.

A Scanner Darkly. Warner Brothers, 2006.

Serenity. Universal Pictures, 2005.

Snowpiercer. SnowPiercer/Moho Film, 2013.
Sorry to Bother You. Cinereach, 2018.
Space Truckers. Goldcrest Films International, 1996.
Star Trek VI: The Undiscovered Country. Paramount Pictures, 1991.
Target Audience 9.1. Emerald Rain Productions, 2007.
The Thirteenth Floor. Columbia Pictures, 1999.
THX 1138. American Zoetrope/Warner Brothers, 1971.
Time Lapse. Royal Pictures, 2014.
"Trials and Tribble-ations." *Star Trek: Deep Space Nine.* Los Angeles: KCOP, November 4, 1996.
"The Trouble with Tribbles." *Star Trek.* New York: NBC-TV, December 29, 1967.
Welt am Draht [World on a Wire]. Janus Films, 1973.
"Worlds Apart." *The Outer Limits.* New York: Showtime, March 22, 1996.
Xchange. Coolbrook Media, 2001.</BIB>

III. Nonfiction and Critical Studies

Alier, Juan M. "Ecological Economics and Concrete Utopias." *Utopian Studies,* 3:1 (1992), 31–52.
Ashley, Mike. *Gateways to Forever: The Story of the Science-Fiction Pulp Magazines from 1970 to 1980.* Liverpool: Liverpool University Press, 2007.
_____. *Science Fiction Rebels: The Story of the Science-Fiction Pulp Magazines from 1981 to 1990.* Liverpool: Liverpool University Press, 2016.
_____. *The Time Machines: The Story of the Science-Fiction Pulp Magazines from the Beginning to 1950.* Liverpool: Liverpool University Press, 2000.
_____. *Transformations: The Story of the Science-Fiction Pulp Magazines from 1950 to 1970.* Liverpool: Liverpool University Press, 2005.
Asimov, Isaac. "How Science Fiction Came to Be Big Business." 1980. *Asimov on Science Fiction.* 1981. New York: Avon Books, 1982, 99–108.
Asselin, Steve. "A Climate of Competition: Climate Change as Political Economy in Speculative Fiction, 1889–1915." *Science Fiction Studies,* 45:3 (November 2018), 440–453.
Baer, John W. "Edward Bellamy's Concept of Economic Equality—Practical or Utopian?" *Revisiting the Legacy of Edward Bellamy (1850–1898), American Author and Social Reformer.* Edited by Toby Widdicombe and Herman S. Preiser. Lewiston, ME: Edwin Mellen Press, 2002, 371–395.
Benford, Gregory. "Reactionary Utopias." *Storm Warnings: Science Fiction Confronts the Future.* Edited by George Slusser, Colin Greenland, and Eric S. Rabkin. Carbondale: Southern Illinois University Press, 1987, 73–83.
Bould, Mark. "Economics." *The Greenwood Encyclopedia of Science Fiction and Fantasy: Themes, Works, and Wonders.* Volume 1. Edited by Gary Westfahl. Westport, CT: Greenwood Press, 2005, 231–233.
Brande, David. "The Business of Cyberpunk: Symbolic Economy and Ideology in William Gibson." *Configurations,* 2:3 (1994), 509–536.
Brunner, John. "Economics of SF." *Vector,* 37 (January 1966), 2–7.
_____. "More SF Economics." *Vector,* 56 (Summer, 1970), 9–11.
Budrys, Algis. (as Algirdas Jonas Budrys) "Science Fiction in the Marketplace." *Nebula Winners Twelve.* Edited by Gordon R. Dickson. New York: Harper & Row, 1978, 101–115.
Byers, Thomas B. "Commodity Futures: Corporate State and Personal Style in Three Recent Science Fiction Movies." *Science-Fiction Studies,* 14:3 (November 1987), 326–339.
Cocroft, Horace E. "Economics in SF." *Galaxy's Edge,* No. 1 (March 2013), 105–112.
Coleman, Stephen. "Economics of Utopia: Morris and Bellamy Contrasted." *Journal of the William Morris Society,* 8:2 (Spring, 1989), 2–6.
Davies, William, editor. *Economic Science Fictions.* London: Goldsmiths Press, 2018.
Edwards, Malcolm. "SF Publishing: The Economics." *The Science Fiction Source Book.* Edited by David Wingrove. New York: Van Nostrand, 1984, 289–292.
Ekman, Stefan. "Money." *The Greenwood Encyclopedia of Science Fiction and Fantasy: Themes,*

Works, and Wonders. Volume 2. Edited by Gary Westfahl. Westport, CT: Greenwood Press, 2005, 530–533.

Ellison, Harlan. "How You Stupidly Blew $15 Million a Week, Avoided Having an Adenoid-Shaped Swimming Pool in Your Back Yard, Missed the Opportunity to Have a Mutually Destructive Love Affair with Clint Eastwood And/or Raquel Welch, and Otherwise Pissed Me Off." 1978. *Sleepless Nights in the Procrustean Bed: Essays by Harlan Ellison.* Edited by Marty Clark. San Bernardino, CA: Borgo Press, 1984, 87–98.

Forrest, Wolf. "'There Ain't No Such Thing as a Free Lunch': Supply Side Economics in *The Moon Is a Harsh Mistress.*" *Critical Insights: Robert A. Heinlein.* Edited by Rafeeq O. McGiveron. Amenia, NY: Grey House, 2015, 199–214.

Franklin, H. Bruce. "Foreword" to "The Subliminal Man." *The Mirror of Infinity: A Critics' Anthology of Science Fiction.* Edited by Robert Silverberg. 1970. New York: Perennial Library/Harper & Row, 1973, 222–225.

Freedman, Carl. "Capitalist Realism in Three Recent SF Films." *Paradoxa,* No. 26 (2014), 67–80.

Giannini, Erin. *Joss Whedon Versus the Corporation: Big Business Critiqued in the Films and Television Programs.* Jefferson, NC: McFarland, 2017.

Gillespie, Ryan. "Monstrous Capital: Frankenstein Derivatives, Financial Wizards, and the Spectral Economy." *Monster Culture in the 21st Century: A Reader.* Edited by Marina Levina and Diem-My T. Bui. London: Bloomsbury Publishing, 2013, 287–302.

Guerra, Stephanie. "Colonizing Bodies: Corporate Power and Biotechnology in Young Adult Science Fiction." *Children's Literature in Education,* 40:4 (December 2009), 275–295.

Hahnel, Robin. "The Influence of Edward Bellamy on the Future Evolution of Participatory Economics." *Revisiting the Legacy of Edward Bellamy (1850–1898), American Author and Social Reformer.* Edited by Toby Widdicombe and Herman S. Preiser. Lewiston, ME: Edwin Mellen Press, 2002, 396–416.

Harrison, Harry. "Footnote to the Economics of SF." *Australian Science Fiction Review,* No. 12 (October 1967), 13–15.

Hassler, Donald M. "Grace in the Marketplace: Tom Clancy and James Gunn." *The New York Review of Science Fiction,* 27:4 (December 2014), 26–29.

Heinlein, Robert A. "The Happy Days Ahead." *Expanded Universe: The New Worlds of Robert A. Heinlein.* New York: Grosset & Dunlap, 1980), 514–582.

Highfill, Jannett. "International Trade in *News from Nowhere.*" *Journal of the William Morris Society,* 12:2 (Spring, 1997), 31–35.

Hills, Matt. *Doctor Who: The Unfolding Event: Marketing, Merchandising and Mediatizing a Brand Anniversary.* Basingstoke, Hampshire: Palgrave Macmillan, 2015.

Howe, Ron. "Reconsidering Edward Bellamy in the Year 2000." *Revisiting the Legacy of Edward Bellamy (1850–1898), American Author and Social Reformer.* Edited by Toby Widdicombe and Herman S. Preiser. Lewiston, ME: Edwin Mellen Press, 2002, 417–432.

Hume, Kathryn. "The Hidden Dynamics of *The War of the Worlds.*" *Philological Quarterly,* 62:3 (Summer, 1983), 279–292.

Isaacson, Nathaniel. *Celestial Empire: The Emergence of Chinese Science Fiction.* Middletown, CT: Wesleyan University Press, 2017.

Jones, Jeremy L.C. "Neither the Billionaire Nor the Tramp: Economics in Speculative Fiction." *Clarkesworld,* No. 69 (June 2012). At http://clarkesworldmagazine.com/economics_interview/.

Jones, Robert Kenneth. "Battle at the Newsstands." *The Shudder Pulps: A History of the Weird Menace Magazines of the 1930s.* New York: New American Library, 1975, 112–120.

Kahm, Howard. "'They Couldn't Let Us Profit—It Wouldn't Be Civilized': Economic Modalities and Core-Periphery Relationships in the Political Economy of *Firefly-Serenity.*" *Firefly Revisited: Essays on Josh Whedon's Classic Series.* Edited by Michael Goodrum and Philip Smith. Lanham: Rowman and Littlefield, 2015, 155–170.

Killheffer, Robert K.J. "When Opportunity Knocks: SF & Fantasy Small Presses Find New Niches in a Changing Marketplace." *Science Fiction Chronicle,* No. 177 (October 1994), 33–37.

Konstantinou, Lee. "Only Science Fiction Can Save Us! What Sci-Fi Gets Wrong About

Income Inequality." *Slate* (September 2014). At http://www.slate.com/articles/technology/future_tense/2014/09/snowpiercer_elysium_what_sci_fi_gets_wrong_about_income_inequality.single.html.

Krugman, Paul. "Asimov's Foundation Novels Grounded My Economics." *The Guardian*, December 4, 2012. At https://www.theguardian.com/books/2012/dec/04/paul-krugman-asimov-economics.

Lake, Jay. "Advertising." *The Greenwood Encyclopedia of Science Fiction and Fantasy: Themes, Works, and Wonders.* Volume 1. Edited by Gary Westfahl. Westport, CT: Greenwood Press, 2005, 5–7.

Laver, Michael. "'Greed Can Be a Powerful Ally': The Trade Federation, the East India Companies, and Chaotic Worlds of Trade." *Star Wars and History.* Edited by Nancy R. Reagin and Janice Liedl. Hoboken, NJ: Wiley, 2013, 255 –282.

Leggatt, Judith. "Critiquing Economic and Environmental Colonization: Globalization and Science Fiction in *The Moons of Palmares.*" *Science Fiction, Imperialism and the Third World: Essays on Postcolonial Literature and Film.* Edited by Ericka Hoagland and Reema Sarwal. Jefferson, NC: McFarland, 2010, 127–140.

Lobdell, Jared C. "C.S. Lewis, Distributist, His Economics as Seen in *That Hideous Strength.*" *Orcrist*, No. 6 (Winter 1971/1972), 20–21.

Malzberg, Barry N. *The Bend at the End of the Road.* New York: Fantastic Books, 2018.

_____. *Breakfast in the Ruins: Science Fiction in the Last Millennium.* New York: Baen Books, 2007.

Markley, Robert. "Falling Into Theory: Simulation, Terraformation, and Eco-Economics in Kim Stanley Robinson's Martian Trilogy." *Modern Fiction Studies*, 43:3 (1997), 773–799.

McCarey-Laird, M. Martin. *Lester Dent: The Man, His Craft, and His Market.* West Des Moines, IA: Hidalgo Publishing Co., 1994.

McGuire, Patrick L. *Red Stars: Political Aspects of Soviet Science Fiction.* Ann Arbor, MI: UMI Research Press 1985.

Michaud, Thomas. "Science Fiction and Management." *Science Fiction and Innovation.* Paris: Marsisme, 2008, 63–87.

Nevala-Lee, Alec. *Astounding: John W. Campbell, Isaac Asimov, Robert A. Heinlein, L. Ron Hubbard, and the Golden Age of Science Fiction.* New York: William Morrow Dey Street, 2018.

Newitz, Annalee. "The Rise of Dismal Science Fiction: To Understand Our Economic System, We Need Speculative Stories." *Slate*, March 13, 2018. Emagazine. At https://slate.com/technology/2018/03/how-science-fiction-helps-us-understand-our-economic-system.html.

Olander, Joseph D., and Martin H. Greenberg. "Introduction." *Tomorrow, Inc.: SF Stories About Big Business.* New York: Taplinger, 1976, 11–16.

Platt, Charles. "The Rape of Science Fiction." *Science Fiction Eye*, No. 5 (July 1989), 44–49.

Pohl, Frederik. "The Publishing of Science Fiction." *Science Fiction, Today and Tomorrow.* Edited by Reginald Bretnor. Baltimore: Penguin Books, 1974, 17–44.

_____. *The Way the Future Was: A Memoir.* New York: Ballantine, 1978.

Potts, Stephen W. *The Second Marxian Invasion: The Fiction of the Strugatsky Brothers.* San Bernardino, CA: Borgo Press, 1991.

Preiser, Herman S. "Ethical Capitalism: Redirecting the Global Market Economy Toward Bellamy's Quest for a Just Society." *Revisiting the Legacy of Edward Bellamy (1850–1898), American Author and Social Reformer.* Edited by Toby Widdicombe and Herman S. Preiser. Lewiston, ME: Edwin Mellen Press, 2002, 433–486.

Price, E. Hoffmann. *Book of the Dead: Friends of Yesteryear: Fictioneers & Others (Memories of the Pulp Fiction Era).* Edited by Peter Ruber. Sauk City, WI: Arkham House, 2001.

Reinert, Sophus A. "The Economy of Fear: H.P. Lovecraft on Eugenics, Economics and the Great Depression." *Horror Studies*, 6:2 (October 2015), 255–282.

Resnick, Mike, and Barry N. Malzberg. *The Business of Science Fiction: Two Insiders Discuss Writing and Publishing.* Jefferson, NC: McFarland, 2010.

Reynolds, Mack. "Science Fiction and Socioeconomics." *Fantastic Lives: Autobiographical Essays by Notable Science Fiction Writers.* Edited by Martin H. Greenberg. Carbondale: Southern Illinois University Press, 1981, 118–143.

Robins, Tim. "Report from Farpoint: Heroes of the Marketplace." *Interzone,* No. 176 (February 2002), 60–63.

Roemer, Kenneth M. "What Future Readers Will See in Bellamy's *Looking Backward.*" *Revisiting the Legacy of Edward Bellamy (1850–1898), American Author and Social Reformer.* Edited by Toby Widdicombe and Herman S. Preiser. Lewiston, ME: Edwin Mellen Press, 2002, 487–497.

Sedgewick, Cristina. "The Fork in the Road: Can Science Fiction Survive in Postmodern, Megacorporate America?" *Science-Fiction Studies,* 18:1 (March 1991), 11–52.

Silverberg, Robert. *Reflections and Refractions: Thoughts on Science Fiction, Science, and Other Matters.* Revised and Expanded Edition. New York: Nonstop Press, 2016.

Smith, Curtis C. *Welcome to the Revolution: The Literary Legacy of Mack Reynolds.* Edited by Roger C. Schlobin. San Bernardino, CA: Borgo Press, 1996.

Song Mingwei. "After 1989: The New Wave of Chinese Science Fiction." *China Perspectives,* 1:101 (2015), 7–13.

Southard, Kate M. "*Beggars in Spain*: Economic Theory Explained in Science Fiction." *The New York Review of Science Fiction,* 14:12 (August 2002), 1, 4–7.

Soyka, David. "Business." *The Greenwood Encyclopedia of Science Fiction and Fantasy: Themes, Works, and Wonders.* Volume 1. Edited by Gary Westfahl. Westport, CT: Greenwood Press, 2005, 98–100.

Spinrad, Norman. *Science Fiction in the Real World.* Carbondale: Southern Illinois University Press, 1990.

Stableford, Brian M. "Adolf Hitler: His Part in Our Struggle—A Brief Economic History of British SF Magazines." *Interzone,* No. 57 (March 1992), 17–20.

_____. "Utopia—and Afterwards: Socioeconomic Speculation in the SF of Mack Reynolds." *Outside the Human Aquarium: Masters of Science Fiction.* San Bernardino, CA: Borgo Press, 1995, 49–75.

_____, and David Langford. "Economics." *The Encyclopedia of Science Fiction.* Third Edition. Edited by John Clute, Langford, Peter Nicholls and Graham Sleight. Gollancz, August 13, 2015. At http://www.sf-encyclopedia.com/entry/economics.

Stanley, O'Brien, Nicki L. Michalski, and Ruth J.H. Stanley. "Are There Tea Parties on Mars? Business and Politics in Science Fiction Films." *Journal of Literature and Art Studies,* 2:3 (March 2012), 382–396.

Stolyarov, Gennady. "Business as an Agent of Human Progress in *Time Will Run Back, Methuselah's Children,* and *The Transhumanist Wager.*" *Capitalism and Commerce in Imaginative Literature: Perspectives on Business from Novels and Plays.* Edited by Edward W. Younkins. Lanham, MD: Lexington, 2016, 331–358.

Warwick, Patricia S. "Mack Reynolds: The Future as Socio-Economic Possibility." *Voices for the Future: Essays on Major Science Fiction Writers.* Volume 2. Bowling Green, OH: Popular Press, 1979, 136–153.

Webster, Bud. *Anthropology 101: Reflections, Inspections and Dissections of SF Anthologies.* West Warwick, RI: Merry Blacksmith Press, 2010.

Westfahl, Gary. "Even Better Than the Real Thing: Advertising, Music Videos, Postmodernism, and (Eventually) Science Fiction." *Science Fiction, Children's Literature, and Popular Culture: Coming of Age in Fantasyland.* Westport, CT: Greenwood Press, 2000, 79–92.

_____. "'Factory in the Sky': Space Stations as Businesses." *Islands in the Sky: The Space Station Theme in Science Fiction Literature.* Second Edition. [Rockville, MD]: Borgo Press/Wildside Press, 2009, 56–79.

_____. "How to Make Big Money Writing Science Fiction, and Other Dangerous Delusions." *The Internet Review of Science Fiction,* July 10, 2006. At http://www.irosf.com/q/zine/article/10288.

_____. "In Search of Dismal Science Fiction." 2003. *An Alien Abroad: Science Fiction Columns from Interzone.* Holicong, PA: Wildside Press, 2016, 220–225.

_____. "The Marketplace." *The Oxford Handbook of Science Fiction.* Edited by Rob Latham. London: Oxford University Press, 2014, 81–92.

_____. "A New Campaign for Science Fiction." *Extrapolation,* 33:1 (Spring, 1992), 6–23.

_____. "Sturgeon's Fallacy." *Extrapolation,* 38 (Winter 1997), 255–277.

_____. "What Is a Science Fiction Magazine? (And Why on Earth Are They Still Around?)" *An Alien Abroad: Science Fiction Columns from Interzone.* Holicong, PA: Wildside Press, 2016, 108–113.

_____, George Slusser, and Eric S. Rabkin, editors. *Science Fiction and Market Realities.* Athens, GA: University of Georgia Press, 1996.

_____, and George Slusser, editors. *Science Fiction, Canonization, Marginalization, and the Academy.* Westport, CT: Greenwood Press, 2002.

Winter, Jerome. *Science Fiction, Space Opera and Neoliberal Globalism.* Cardiff: University of Wales Press, 2016.

About the Contributors

Jonathan **Alexander** is the Chancellor's Professor of English and Informatics at the University of California, Irvine. The author, co-author, or editor of fifteen books, he is committed to interdisciplinary troublemaking and works generally under the rubric of "writing studies" to explore the creation and uptake of "texts" as they perform different kinds of ideological work in specific contexts.

Gregory **Benford** is a Fellow of the American Physical Society and received the Lord Prize in science, Asimov Prize for fiction, and UN Medal in literature. His fiction and nonfiction have won many awards; he has published 32 novels, four volumes of nonfiction, and over 200 short stories and several hundred scientific papers in several fields.

Ari **Brin** obtained her BA in biological anthropology from NYU, and her MLitt in science fiction from the University of Dundee. She is pursuing her Ph.D. at the University of Dundee, studying nineteenth century science fiction and technological transformation at the turn of the century. Her podcast, *Novum*, is available on iTunes.

David **Brin** is an astrophysicist whose international best-selling novels include *The Postman* (1982, filmed in 1997), *Earth* (1990), *Existence* (2012), and the Uplift Series. He serves on advisory boards (e.g., NASA's Innovative and Advanced Concepts program [NIAC]) and speaks or consults on a wide range of topics. His nonfiction book about the information age, *The Transparent Society* (1998), won the Freedom of Speech Award of the American Library Association.

Joey **Eschrich** is the editor and program manager at the Center for Science and the Imagination at Arizona State University. He is also an assistant director for Future Tense, a partnership of ASU, *Slate*, and New America that explores emerging technologies and society. He is the coditor of *Overview* (2016), *Everything Change* (2016), and *Visions, Ventures, Escape Velocities* (2017), which was supported by a grant from NASA.

Robert L. **Heath** long served as a professor of plant physiology and biophysics at the University of California, Riverside before retiring as an emeritus. He received a Ph.D. from the University of California, Berkeley, and was a Post-Doctoral Fellow at Brookhaven National Laboratory. He was a founding member of the Biomedical

Sciences Program and associate dean of the College of Natural and Agricultural Sciences at the University of California, Riverside.

Howard V. **Hendrix**, California State University, Fresno, has taught at the college level for over thirty years. He holds a BS in biology from Xavier University and an MA and Ph.D. in English literature from the University of California, Riverside. He has authored, coauthored, or coedited three works of nonfiction and has written numerous articles, reviews, and editorials. He also served as Western Regional Director and two-term Vice President of the Science Fiction and Fantasy Writers of America (SFWA).

Bradford **Lyau** received a BA from the University of California, Berkeley and an MA and Ph.D. from the University of Chicago. He has taught history at colleges and universities in California and Europe and has published studies focusing on the ideologies underlying science fiction. His book *The Anticipation Novelists of 1950s French Science Fiction* (2011) has been cited as a basic reference work by the *Science Fiction Encyclopedia*.

Charles **Platt**, after dropping out of Cambridge University where he was studying economics, started selling stories to *New Worlds* magazine in the UK, became its designer, and was briefly its editor. He emigrated to the U.S. in 1970, wrote various novels, was science fiction editor at three New York publishers and became a senior writer at *Wired* magazine. He develops laboratory prototypes for rapid cooling of patients after cardiac arrest and lives in the Arizona wilderness.

Steven **Postrel** teaches business strategy at the Paul Merage School of Business at the University of California, Irvine. His research interests include the economics of competitive advantage, problems of organizational integration, knowledge specialization, and the uses and limitations of game theory in modeling business phenomena. He received his Ph.D. in economics from MIT and his AB in economics from Princeton University.

Stephen W. **Potts** retired from the University of California at San Diego, where he specialized in genre fiction and popular culture. Since the early 1980s, he has published multiple articles and books, fiction, editorials, and reviews. His publications include the science fiction anthology *Chasing Shadows* (2017), coedited with David Brin, and a collection of critical essays on *The Hobbit* (2016).

Lisa **Raphals** studies the cultures of early China and Classical Greece, with interests in comparative philosophy, history of science, and science fiction studies. She is a professor of Chinese, classics and comparative literature at the University of California, Riverside, and chair of the program in classical studies and program in comparative ancient civilizations. She is the author of *Divination and Prediction in Early China and Ancient Greece* (2013), among other books, and coeditor of *Old Society, New Belief* (2017).

Julia D. **Ree**, librarian, has been a fixture at the University of California, Riverside, Libraries and a strong supporter of the Eaton Collection of Science Fiction since the early 1980s. Her involvement has included participating in Eaton Conferences and attending science fiction conventions. In addition, she has acquired, cataloged and, for 12 years, acted as the subject specialist for science fiction, fantasy, horror, and utopian literature for the Eaton Collection, upon George Slusser's retirement.

George **Slusser**, the late professor emeritus of comparative literature at the University of California, Riverside, was renowned for coediting numerous volumes of essays about science fiction and fantasy, including 21 Eaton volumes. With wife Danièle Chatelain, he translated and edited works by Jules Verne, Honoré de Balzac, and J.-H. Rosny Aîné, and he wrote several author studies, including *Gregory Benford* (2014). In 1986, he received the SFRA's Pilgrim Award for lifetime contributions to science fiction and fantasy scholarship.

Gary **Westfahl**, professor emeritus at the University of La Verne, is the author, editor, or coeditor of 28 books, all but one about science fiction and fantasy, including the Hugo Award–nominated *Science Fiction Quotations* (2005) and *The Greenwood Encyclopedia of Science Fiction and Fantasy* (2005); he has also published hundreds of articles and reviews about science fiction. He received the SFRA's 2003 Pilgrim Award for lifetime contributions to science fiction and fantasy scholarship.

Gary K. **Wolfe** is an award-winning critic and scholar of science fiction, and emeritus professor of humanities at Roosevelt University. His books include *Soundings* (2005), *Bearings* (2010), *Sightings* (2011), *Evaporating Genres* (2011), *The Known and the Unknown* (1979), *Harlan Ellison* (2007, with Ellen Weil), and *American Science Fiction* (2012, editor). His lecture series *How Great Science Fiction Works* is available from The Great Courses, and his book reviews appear in *Locus* magazine and the *Chicago Tribune*.

Alvaro **Zinos-Amaro** is a Hugo and Locus Award finalist who has published some forty stories and over a hundred reviews, essays and interviews in venues like *Asimov's Science Fiction, Analog: Science Fiction/Science Fact, Clarkesworld*, and *The Los Angeles Review of Books*, among others, and anthologies such as *The Year's Best Science Fiction & Fantasy* (2016), *Cyber World* (2016), *Humanity 2.0* (2016), *This Way to the End Times* (2016), *18 Wheels of Science Fiction* (2018), and *Shades Within Us* (2018).

Index

273

www.ingramcontent.com/pod-product-compliance
Lightning Source LLC
Chambersburg PA
CBHW021411110726
47901CB00008B/2146

* 9 7 8 1 4 7 6 6 7 7 3 8 5 *